PENGUIN CLASSICS

THE BOOK OF THE COURTIER

BALDESAR CASTIGLIONE was born in 1478, a member of an ancient Italian aristocratic family. He received a thorough humanistic education, acquiring a refined appreciation of art. He was essentially a courtier, and his literary activities were spare-time occupations. In 1504, after an unhappy period in Mantuan employ, he entered the service of Guidobaldo of Montefeltro, Duke of Urbino. The ensuing years were the most satisfying of his life. He enjoyed the confidence of the Duke, who frequently entrusted him with important missions, and in his leisure moments he participated in the literary and intellectual activities of the court, then one of the most brilliant in Italy. After Guidobaldo's death in 1508, he remained in the service of the new Duke, Francesco Maria della Rovere, becoming, in 1513, resident ambassador in Rome. In 1515 the expulsion of Francesco Maria from Urbino deprived him of a job, and in the years 1516–19 he lived quietly on his estates near Mantua. His major work is *The Book of the Courtier*. He also wrote a small number of excellent poems both in Latin and Italian. In 1519 he returned to Rome, as Mantuan ambassador, and after further activities on behalf of his Mantuan masters entered Papal service in 1524. From that date until his death in 1592 he was Papal Nuncio in Spain.

GEORGE BULL is an author and journalist who has translated six volumes for the Penguin Classics: Benvenuto Cellini's *Autobiography*, *The Book of the Courtier* by Castiglione, Vasari's *Lives of the Artists* (two volumes), *The Prince* by Machiavelli and Pietro Aretino's *Selected Letters*. He was also Consultant Editor to the Penguin Business Library and abridged the Penguin edition of *Self-Help* by Samuel Smiles. After reading history at Brasenose College, Oxford, George Bull worked for the *Financial Times*,

McGraw-Hill *World News*, and for the *Director* magazine, of which he was Editor-in-Chief until 1984. His other books include *Vatican Politics*; *Bid for Power* (with Anthony Vice), a history of take-over bids; *Renaissance Italy*, a book for children; *Venice: The Most Triumphant City*; *Inside the Vatican*; and a translation from the Italian of *The Pilgrim: The Travels of Pietro della Valle*. George Bull was awarded an OBE in the 1990 New Year's Honours list.

THE BOOK OF
THE COURTIER

Baldesar Castiglione

TRANSLATED AND WITH
AN INTRODUCTION BY
GEORGE BULL

PENGUIN BOOKS

PENGUIN BOOKS

Published by the Penguin Group
Penguin Books Ltd, 27 Wrights Lane, London W8 5TZ, England
Penguin Books USA Inc., 375 Hudson Street, New York, New York 10014, USA
Penguin Books Australia Ltd, Ringwood, Victoria, Australia
Penguin Books Canada Ltd, 10 Alcorn Avenue, Toronto, Ontario, Canada M4V 3B2
Penguin Books (NZ) Ltd, 182–190 Wairau Road, Auckland 10, New Zealand

Penguin Books Ltd, Registered Offices: Harmondsworth, Middlesex, England

This translation published 1967
Reprinted with revisions 1976
15 17 19 20 18 16 14

Printed in England by Clays Ltd, St Ives plc
Set in Monotype Fournier

CONTENTS

FOR JULIAN AND SIMON

INTRODUCTION

BALDESAR CASTIGLIONE, courtier and diplomat, poet, scholar and soldier, is generally thought of as himself typifying the gentlemanly virtues expounded and extolled in *The Book of the Courtier*. The comment of the Emperor Charles V, when he heard of his death, has become famous: 'Yo vos digo que es muerto uno de los mejores caballeros del mundo' – 'I tell you, one of the finest gentlemen in the world is dead' (a tribute, ironically, in the language in which chivalry was to receive its literary death-blow from another well-rounded man, Miguel de Cervantes, about seventy years later). The portrait of Castiglione (now in the Louvre) by Raphael of Urbino confirms the Emperor's judgement. In the words of Castiglione's English biographer: 'The noble brow and broad forehead, the fine eyes, with their clear intense blue and vivid brightness, give the impression of intellectual power and refinement, tinged with a shade of habitual melancholy. All the spiritual charm and distinction of Castiglione's nature, all the truth and loyalty of his character, are reflected in this incomparable work, which is a living example of the ideal gentleman and perfect courtier.'*

Castiglione was sensitive, scrupulous and hard-working. It is refreshing to remember that the daunting paragon of refinement and courtesy was also indecisive, fussy, snobbish and ambitious; that his half-hearted approaches to marriage were inspired by his urgent need for money (his eventual marriage, none the less, was extremely happy); that he was not at all distinguished as a commander and indeed sickened by battle; that he was more than once suspected of treacherous conduct; and that he was excessively fond of fine clothes and horses. In short, he was very human.

He was born in 1478, on his father's estate at Casatico, in the Mantuan territory, and died, while serving as papal nuncio, at Toledo in 1529. This was a period of incomparable literary and

* Cartwright, Julia: *Baldassare Castiglione* (2 vols), John Murray, 1908.

artistic achievement in Italy, and also of grievous national shame, bounded on one side by the years when, in the words of Castiglione's near contemporary, Guicciardini, the calamities of Italy began (with invasion by the French), and on the other by the years when Rome was sacked and Italy finally fell under the domination of Spain.

Castiglione's life was intensely active and fruitful. He grew up in noble surroundings and company, with the Gonzaga princes of Mantua among his friends. He studied at Milan University (learning Latin and Greek, as well as jousting, fencing and wrestling), entered the service first of Lodovico Sforza and then of Francesco Gonzaga, ruler of Mantua. It was at this time that he first met Duke Guidobaldo and his wife, Elisabetta, after they had been driven out of the city-state of Urbino by Cesare Borgia. Their relationship prospered, and, after Guidobaldo had been restored to power, Castiglione entered his service – with a first command of a company of fifty men-at-arms – in 1504.

For twelve years, until 1516, he served the rulers of Urbino, first Guidobaldo, who died in 1508, and then (when Urbino became a papal fief) Francesco Maria della Rovere, the nephew of Pope Julius II, until he was driven from Urbino by the troops of Pope Leo X. Castiglione fled with him to Mantua, where, after years of busy service in war and diplomacy, he was able to marry, settle down to cultivate his own interests at home and enjoy social life at Court as one of the intimate circle of friends of the ruling family. On the death of Francesco Gonzaga in 1519, however, Castiglione was again employed on diplomatic missions, by the new marquis, Federico, who eventually appointed him as Mantuan ambassador to Rome. In 1524, impressed by Castiglione's charm and devotion to duty, Pope Clement VII offered him the post of papal nuncio to Spain, where he spent the remaining years of his life, harassed by the repercussions of the ceaseless diplomatic intrigues and squabbles of the rulers of Christendom.

The few years Castiglione spent in the service of Guidobaldo provided the inspiration for *The Courtier*. The Court had become famous through the achievements of the great soldier-scholar, Federico da Montefeltro, Guidobaldo's father, whose military talent Castiglione records in *The Courtier*, and who built Urbino's great palace, collected an impressive library and made the city a centre of patronage and learning. Guidobaldo, who succeeded him in 1482, was a melancholy and unfortunate ruler, impotent through illness, and hopeless at war. The life at Court, during Castiglione's years at Urbino, was shaped by the personality of Guidobaldo's wife, Elisabetta Gonzaga.

The idea of writing *The Courtier*, Castiglione records, came to him while he was still living at the Court of Urbino, in the service of Francesco Maria della Rovere (the 'Lord Prefect'). A first draft was roughed out quickly, added to when time was available during the years 1508–16 (especially in Rome, when he was there representing the interests of Francesco Maria and enjoying the company of many of his old friends from Urbino who were now papal officials), and then more or less finished during 1516–18, when Castiglione enjoyed leisure and home life in the company of his wife, Ippolita, and his mother (with whom his relations, throughout his life, were extremely fond), Albisa Gonzaga.

The manuscript was then shown to several of Castiglione's friends, including Pietro Bembo, because, Castiglione wrote to him in 1518, he was constantly being urged to publish it. Little more was done, however, till 1526, when the news of the death of Elisabetta reached Spain and Castiglione's memories of Urbino were intensely revived.

In a sense, Castiglione's whole life was lived for the sake of his book. He spent so many years polishing and pondering on what he had written that the work was very nearly never published at all. How this eventually came to pass he describes in the letter of dedication to Don Michel de Silva: he had entrusted some of the manuscript to the famous Renaissance blue-stocking, Vittoria Colonna, and some people in Naples were threatening to rush into print without his authorization. So in early 1527 he sent the manuscript, with his own careful corrections and instructions for printing, to the Aldine Press in Venice.

Immediately afterwards, in a letter to his steward, Cristoforo Tirabosco, Castiglione described his plans for the first edition. 'I am writing to Venice to say that one thousand and thirty copies are to be printed, and that I intend to pay half the expenses, because, of this thousand, five hundred are to be mine. The remaining thirty copies will all belong to me, and are to be printed on fine paper, as smooth and beautiful as possible – in fact, the best that can be found in Venice.'

In April 1528 *The Courtier* was published. Castiglione again wrote to Cristoforo to describe how the presentation copies were to be bound and distributed to friends and 'to the most important personages'. One copy for Castiglione himself was to be printed on vellum 'with the pages gilded and well pressed, and covered with leather of some rich colour purple or blue or yellow or green, according as to what you find . . . and adorned with ornaments of knots and foliage, or panels and compartments of some other description. . . .' *

In his letter to Don Michel (following his own rule that nonchalance is the mark of a gentleman) Castiglione modestly disclaimed any pretensions to literary achievement: the work is only too full of faults, he suggests, before resigning himself humbly to the judgement of Time. As the care he lavished on its composition and production testified, however, he was enormously proud of *The Courtier*. And Time 'accustomed to pronouncing always, on all writings a just sentence of life or death' has given him a favourable verdict. *The Courtier* has gone through scores of editions and translations; has exercised a profound influence on European sensibilities; and ranks today as the most representative book of the Renaissance.

The immediate and lasting success of *The Courtier* is certainly not attributable to its originality of thought. It is largely a series of echoes: of medieval ideals of chivalry, of classical virtues and of contemporary humanist aspirations. Its opening is in strict conformity with the humanist rules of imitation. Cicero, whom Castiglione studied hard as a boy and took for his model (and whose *De Officiis* was a Renaissance best-seller) supplies the very words for the beginning of the First Book. The *Orator* begins: 'For a long time I debated earnestly with myself, Brutus, as to which course would be more difficult or serious – to deny your oft repeated request, or to do what you ask.' † And *The Courtier*: 'I have spent a long time wondering, my dear Alfonso, which of two things was

* Cartwright: *Baldassare Castiglione*, pp. 374, 376.

† Cicero: *Brutus*, *Orator*, Loeb Classical Library.

the more difficult for me: either to refuse what you have asked me so often and so insistently, or to do it.' Hardly a page of *The Courtier* turns without a bold plagiarism from Plato, Plutarch, Cicero or Livy. Nor, where *The Courtier* is contemporary, does it add decisively to the commonplace subjects expounded by Castiglione's contemporaries: the responsibility of Italy's rulers for the country's shameful military weakness; the role of women in social and political life; the relative standing of the fine arts; the best type of government; the true nature of perfect love. Admittedly Castiglione did make major contributions to several lively issues of his day and time: to the long and vehement debate, for example, about the need in a divided country for a universal vernacular drawn from Italy's several regional languages. It is possible, too, to trace the influence of *The Courtier* on the aesthetic theory of the later Renaissance, and notably on the ideas of artistic grace, decorum and nonchalance expounded by the great art historian, Giorgio Vasari. None the less, even in these spheres, Castiglione's contributions were not of long-term significance. When *The Courtier* was finally published, indeed, the world of ideas and institutions which it idealized was, as far as Italy was concerned, and as Castiglione well knew, buried in the past.

But, outside Italy, *The Courtier* enjoyed for some generations at least a pervasive influence, and not least in Elizabethan England, where the first translation, by Sir Thomas Hoby, appeared (at a time of intense interest in Italian life and literature) in 1561. Even before then, it was influencing upper-class life and manners through books such as Sir Thomas Elyot's *Governor*, published three years after Castiglione's work went to press. In 1570, in *The Schoolmaster*, it was recommended by the influential educationist, Roger Ascham, as a book which, if read with diligence, would benefit a young man more than three years in Italy. The kind of behaviour recommended to the Italian courtiers became the accepted standard for English gentlemen. To Elizabethan literature it channelled Renaissance philosophy and conceits: Ben Jonson uses *The Courtier* for a scene in *Every Man out of his Humour*; a poem by Gabriel Harvey justly bases its praise of Sir Philip Sidney on his affinities with Castiglione's perfect courtier; the neo-Platonism expounded by Bembo in the Fourth Book provides a standard for the fresh endeavours to attain beauty and harmony in literature as well as life; even the witticisms in Shakespeare renew the jokes and puns recommended by Castiglione (and concerning which today's reader will probably form the same opinion as Lord Chesterfield apropos his own remark that Petrarch deserved his *Laura* better than his *Lauro* – 'and that wretched quibble would be reckoned an excellent piece of Italian wit').

The truth was that the self-interested endeavour of Castiglione's contempories at the small Courts of Italy to justify the profession of courtier – to synthesize the idea of the warrior and the scholar, the Christian believer and the classical hero, the self-contained man of *virtù* and the dutiful servant of the prince – provided an opportune answer, gracefully and fully expressed, to a need felt urgently in the north of Europe as medieval values dissolved. *The Courtier* was not only a book of courtesy which took an exalted place in the long line of such productions running from the Middle Ages to modern times. (These are discussed in an interesting appendix to R. Pine-Coffin's translation of the *Galateo* in Penguin Books.) It was also a political book, justifying the place in society of the courtier successor to the medieval knight, and aiming to establish his role and his status at the new kind of Court that came into being during the Renaissance. In this respect Professor Denys Hay sees Castiglione as an Italian theorist who was 'particularly adapted to instruct the northern world in the Renaissance attitude to politics'. And *The Courtier*, he adds, 'exactly expressed what was most easily assimilated by the northern world in the latter-day Renaissance in Italy. Its dignity and mannered elegance, its respect for both martial accomplishments and literary attainments, its placing of talent at the service of a prince, all expressed Italian civility in a way perfectly attuned to the aristocratic North.' *

During his life Castiglione enjoyed the friendship of men such as Raphael and the respect of rulers such as the Emperor Charles V. Throughout Renaissance Europe, his book became essential reading for the nobility. Both the man and the book have had their enthusiastic admirers ever since; but both have also proved capable of arousing intense suspicion and dislike.

* *The Italian Renaissance in its Historical Background*, Cambridge University Press, 1961, p. 197.

This reaction started very early. Emilia Pia – one of the most sharply drawn characters of *The Courtier* – caused a great scandal in counter-Reformation Rome, in 1528, when she died, it was whispered, without the sacraments of the Church and discussing passages from *The Courtier* with Count Lodovico instead of saying her prayers. For several reasons – its occasionally pagan attitudes to life, its anti-clerical sentiments, its suspect orthodoxy in this passage and that – though the book remained immensely popular in Italy during the sixteenth century, it incurred the censure of the ecclesiastical authorities. When Castiglione's son, Camillo, was preparing a new edition in 1576, he was warned that the work was already on the Index in Spain and that corrections would have to be made. This led to an expurgated edition of *The Courtier* (in which references to Fortune were removed and jokes about priests revised) in 1584, after a censored edition had already appeared in Spanish. In 1590, with an exception made for the expurgated edition, *The Courtier* found its way on to the Index. Early in the eighteenth century, the Inquisitors in Padua had to be consulted when a new edition was being prepared. And it was not until 1894, records Castiglione's English biographer, Julia Cartwright, that a correct version of Castiglione's work from the original manuscript was finally edited by Professor Cian.

Even then, in a good English version published in New York in 1903, the translator, Leonard Opdycke, felt compelled to bowdlerize, omitting one long passage and refraining from rendering the word *ignuda* in English.

Today the book still shocks, not of course because of its mild indelicacies but because of contemporary impatience with the fundamental values which it enshrines. It is hard, indeed, to think of any work more opposed to the spirit of the modern age. At an obvious level, its preoccupation with social distinction and outward forms of polite behaviour creates an intense atmosphere of artificiality and insincerity. (When James Joyce first read *The Courtier* his brother told him he had become more polite but less sincere.)

The great virtues it proposes for a gentleman are discretion and decorum, nonchalance and gracefulness.* As Luigi Barzini comments

* The concept of honour, as expressed in *The Courtier*, is a very complex one, alive throughout the world in the various honour codes that still

in his satirical book on the modern Italian, quoting Castiglione as the model, the 'show' is all.* The courtier must watch his dress, his speech, his gestures chiefly because of their effect on his reputation. If he fights well in battle, he must make sure his commander sees him do so. He has to consider earnestly whether it is correct behaviour to take part in sport with the common people or even to perform in front of them. In love, he must conquer where he can; whereas the women he most admires are those who regard dishonour as a fate worse than death. And then, even when the discussions in *The Courtier* take a more serious turn, and shallow values are repudiated, notably in the Fourth Book with Bembo's melding of Platonic love with Christian theology, the language and sentiments seem inflated and occasionally grotesque.

The combination of intense and selfish individualism with appalling snobbery naturally repels the modern reader, and also the modern historian, who is suspicious of the assumption that history consists in the exploits of the ruling class and the favoured few, and who is anxious to know less about the way gifted amateurs danced at Court and more about the mortality rate in the villages down the hill.

More seriously, *The Courtier* offends modern susceptibilities because it is a flight from the truth. Throughout the book, to be sure, there runs a vein of natural melancholy, partly attributable to Castiglione's constant awareness of the fickleness of Fortune and the inevitability of death. But by its very nature it is a book which turns aside from the realities of life to its idealization. War – which Castiglione experienced and disliked – is glorified; the criminal

persist. In this context, a key word is Castiglione's *vergogna*, mentioned in the Fourth Book as having been brought to earth by Mercury to make men civilized. *Vergogna* may be translated as either honour or shame; in Italian, as in other Romance languages, packed into it are fine shades of meaning, ranging from self-respect to an awareness of the regard in which one is held by others. It shows itself 'not only as chastity and modesty, as the blush which lewd speech or actions bring to the face, but also as respect for parents and elders, which prevents one from doing certain things in their presence, and as humility, reserve and respect for the laws and their representatives'. (Cf. *Honour and Shame: The Values of Mediterranean Society*, ed. J. G. Peristiany, Weidenfeld and Nicolson, 1965.)

* Barzini, Luigi: *The Italians*, Hamish Hamilton, 1964.

behaviour of some of the gay companions he knew at Urbino is glossed over or ignored; the crudeness of Court life in sixteenth century Italy – an earlier version of *The Courtier* was far nearer in this respect to the historical reality – is refined away. The political discussions – using the language and concepts of the ancient world with regard to the rule of the one, the best or the many – are totally unrealistic. When Machiavelli wrote *The Prince*, in all innocence he shocked the world for several hundred years because he set out to 'represent things as they are in real truth, rather than as they are imagined'. Machiavelli had the humanists very much in mind when he wrote this – 'Many have dreamed up republics and principalities which have never in truth been known to exist....' And the cap fits Castiglione, who purported to be teaching people how to behave and recording life as it was, and not writing a Utopia. Machiavelli, indeed, has come into his own in the modern world which understands and appreciates the unabashed language of power; whereas Castiglione's pretences – in the context of normal social behaviour or high politics – are remote.

As a handbook for gentlemen, *The Courtier* conceals the most shameless opportunism under the cloak of a tiresome refinement; as a memoir of life at the Court of Urbino, it touches up history to the point of distortion. None the less, even though many of Castiglione's values are questionable (though for their time they shone out in an uncouth world), *The Courtier* cannot be so easily dismissed. It is historically significant and instructive. It is, at the very least, an entertaining book. Most of all, it is a work of substantial literary achievement.

The historical value of *The Courtier*, apart from its influence outside Italy, is twofold. It is first and foremost a compendium of Renaissance thought. Not only does it provide the best illustration of the Renaissance preoccupation with the *uomo universale*, the many-sided man; it also touches, however briefly, on all the themes, great and trivial, pursued in contemporary Italian literature and thought, from the importance of study and imitation of the classical world to the role of Fortune in human affairs. Moreover, it sets before us the ideals of the Renaissance; and in this way it corrects and complements the picture of how Renaissance men did behave – as drawn, say, by Cellini – with an account of the moral and aesthetic standards to which many of them at least aspired.

As for its entertainment value, the reader fresh to *The Courtier* can judge for himself. The discussions concerning what constitutes the perfect courtier, taking place during four evenings in spring between an intimate circle of cultivated women, men of the world, scholars and buffoons, lead to the exploration of topics which in varying degrees still retain their interest and might even spark off conversation in a senior common room or a television studio: the importance of correct speech; the essential prerequisites for a gentleman, including good breeding and good looks; the superiority of the skilled amateur to the tedious professional; the kinds of witticism and practical joke that are really funny; the qualities men look for in their women; the duties of a good government; and, finally, the true nature of love.

The style, very Latin and sonorous, skilfully catches the tone of the conversations and the mood of the speakers: simple and direct in argumentative dialogue, sometimes like comedians' cross-talk; matter of fact, cutting and even coarse in the interjections, involved and elevated in the occasional rhetorical flights. The pace is generally brisk and confident (though now and then Castiglione rides a hobby-horse of his own too long) and the transitions from one subject or mood to another are smooth and natural. When the talk grows too pompous, Castiglione hurriedly dispels the gloom with a dramatic interruption or a joke. One of his most attractive aspects, indeed, is his obvious fear of boring anyone or seeming too serious. Gaiety keeps breaking in – and sometimes with disconcerting bathos, as at the very end of *The Courtier* when, after Bembo's invocation to Love has struck the whole company dumb, Emilia Pia brings them abruptly back to earth with a matter of fact remark about the next day's debate. This, incidentally, throws fresh light on her character which, like those of the others taking part in the conversations, is portrayed with notable economy and effect. Gaspare Pallavicino, Count Lodovico da Canossa, Pietro Bembo, Elisabetta Gonzaga, Emilia Pia are clearly revealed through their words as misogynist, nobleman, scholar, duchess and mordant feminine wit, respectively, but also as living persons, with whose complex attitudes and temperament the reader becomes increasingly familiar and whom he even learns to like.

Castiglione's sensitivity to character and atmosphere and his ability to recreate them convincingly, his delicate psychological perception and his powers of narrative and description betray, in fact, the novelist and the poet. *The Courtier* may be approached as a romance rather than as an historical record. The story is in the past, almost in the golden days of Italy before the full force of the foreign invasions made themselves felt. Castiglione over the years changed what had been a memoir into a fiction. The first shrewd device was to pretend that he himself had been away in England when the conversations were held: 'as our Castiglione writes from England', remarks Ottaviano in the Fourth Book, 'promising to tell us much more on his return . . .'. The Palace of Urbino is transformed from the local habitation of a petty Italian ruler into a model for all time. First, it is described, with a touch of realism, as being in a city 'surrounded by hills which are perhaps not as agreeable as those found in many other places'; when the conversations end, the abstract beauty described by Bembo is complemented by a final look at the beauty of Urbino itself, where dawn has just come to the east, a delicate breeze is blowing, and the birds are breaking into song. It was beyond his power, Castiglione protested, to do a portrait of Urbino as ambitiously as Raphael or Michelangelo, since he knew only how to draw the outlines and could not adorn the truth with pretty colours or use perspective to deceive the eye. And yet there are passages in *The Courtier* which do nothing so much as suggest a scene by a great painter of the High Renaissance, as when, on the first evening, as Cesare Gonzaga begins to speak there was heard 'the noise of a great tramping of feet, and, as everyone turned to see what was happening, there appeared at the door a blaze of torches preceding the arrival of the Prefect, with a large and noble escort . . .'

By the time *The Courtier* was finished it had become, too, a work of piety towards not only Duke Guidobaldo but also all the other 'outstanding men and women who used to frequent the Court of Urbino'. For, as Castiglione sighed, as he read his manuscript, 'I recalled that most of those introduced in the conversations were already dead. . . .' And so they too were idealized in this glowing account of the last days of Italian chivalry: Castiglione's remembrance of things past.

G.B.

Sutton, Surrey

TRANSLATOR'S NOTE

THE best-known version of *The Courtier* in English is still the vigorous Elizabethan translation by Hoby, who recommended him to mature men as 'a pathway to the beholding and musing of the mind . . . To young Gentlemen, an encouraging to garnish their minds with morall vertues, and their bodies with comely exercises . . . To Ladies and Gentlewomen, a mirrour to decke and trimme themselves with vertuous conditions, comely behaviours and honest entertainment toward all men: And to the all in generall, a storehouse of most necessarie implements for the conversation, use, and trayning up of mans life with Courtly demeaners.' A new translation, by Robert Samber, appeared in 1724. Modern translations have included Leonard Opdycke's (referred to in this Introduction), in a usefully illustrated edition, and Charles S. Singleton's (New York, 1959).

I lack, therefore, the excuse for translating *The Courtier* given by Hoby, namely, that he had waited in vain for this to be done by someone 'of a more perfect understanding in the tongue, and better practised in the matter of the booke . . .'. And whether an attempt to put *The Courtier* into fairly informal but decorous modern English, aiming above all at readability, is justified, is for the reader to decide. The Italian edition I have used is that of Vittorio Cian (Florence, 1947) which is also the basis for many of my brief notes on the text and the characters. I have also consulted the text of *The Courtier* in Volume 27 of *La Letteratura Italiana* (ed. Carlo Cordié, Ricciadi; Milan, Naples). A stimulating 'reassessment' of *The Courtier* has been written by J. R. Woodhouse (Edinburgh University Press, 1978).

I must record my thanks to Sir Michael Quinlan and David Richardson for their helpful suggestions, and to Professor Sir John Hale for his encouragement and help. Acknowledgement is due also to John Murray for permission to quote from

Baldassare Castiglione by Julia Cartwright, and to Weidenfeld & Nicolson for permission to quote from *Honour and Shame: The Values of Mediterranean Society*, edited by J. G. Peristiany.

In revising the translation for the 1976 reprint, I consulted the late Bruce Penman on several points, and must acknowledge gratefully the benefit of his sensitive and scholarly advice.

CHARACTERS IN *THE COURTIER*

THE conversations take place on four successive evenings during March 1507 in the Palace of Urbino. The previous autumn, the warrior Pope, Julius II, had visited the city on his way to attack Bologna in his campaign to reassert his authority over the papal dominions. On this expedition he was accompanied by Guidobaldo, who, however, was bedridden most of the time and played no part in the conquest. On his way back to Rome the Pope again stayed at Urbino, leaving on 5 March. As Castiglione records, several members of the papal entourage remained at Urbino for a while longer; and this was the occasion he chose for the conversations, when most of the people mentioned in *The Courtier* were, in fact, guests at the Palace.

ACCOLTI, BERNARDO (1458–1535), better known by his nickname or *nom de guerre* of Unico Aretino, was the son of a well-known lawyer and historian, Benedetto Accolti. He grew up in Florence and then embarked on the fashionable career of poet and extemporizer, visiting the Courts of Milan, Urbino, Mantua, Naples, Ferrara and notably Rome, where he was patronized by both Julius II and Leo X. His reputation in these noble circles was considerable, and he came to suppose himself, wrongly, as being on the same level as Petrarch and Dante.

ARIOSTO, ALFONSO (1475–1525), a close friend of Castiglione and Bembo, and the man to whom *The Courtier* was originally dedicated. The son of a Bonifacio d'Aldobrandini, and a distant relation of the great poet, Ludovico Ariosto, he entered the service of the Este family at Ferrara early in life, and he may first have met Castiglione in Milan. He read the manuscript of *The Courtier* for Castiglione, and their friendship survived his pro-French proclivities.

BARLETTA is mentioned twice in *The Courtier*, where he is described as a fine musician and dancer. In a letter written by

Castiglione in 1507 (to Cardinal Ippolito d'Este) Barletta was said to be the Duchess Elisabetta's favourite musician.

BEMBO, PIETRO (1470–1547) came from an upper-class Venetian family, lived as a child in Florence, and acquired great facility in Latin, Greek and Tuscan. From 1506 for six years he was a member of the Court circle at Urbino, where he spent his time on linguistic studies and the enjoyment of a varied social life. In 1512 he moved to Rome, where Pope Leo X made him a papal secretary. Subsequently he retired to Padua. During these years he became famous as a literary pundit – insisting on Florentine as the norm and Petrarch and Boccaccio as the models of good writing – a poet, and a courtier, his most notable works being the *Asolani* (1505) and the *Prose della Volgar Lingua* (1525). Bembo was made a cardinal in 1539, and then spent most of his remaining years in Rome.

CALMETA (1460–1508) was the Court or pen-name of Vincenzo Collo, an indifferent poet with an ingratiating manner who found favour at the Courts of Milan, Mantua and, sometime after 1490, Urbino.

CANOSSA, LODOVICO (1476–1532) came of a noble Veronese family, and was a friend and relation of Castiglione. He grew up in Mantua, spent some time – from 1496 – at the Court of Urbino, and served as a diplomat in the service of the papacy and then of King Francis I, through whose influence he was made Bishop of Bayeux in 1516. He was a man of great culture and ability, a friend of Erasmus and Raphael.

CEVA (FEBUS AND GHIRARDINO) were two brothers of a noble Piedmontese family who during the early years of the sixteenth century served as mercenaries indiscriminately for either the French or the Emperor. They were notorious for their violence and brutality.

DOVIZI, BERNARDO (1470–1520) was better known as Bibbiena. He was in the service of the Medici family and in particular attached himself to Giovanni de' Medici who, after his election as

Pope Leo X, made him Cardinal of S. Maria in Portico. His influence on Leo was so considerable that he became known as 'the other Pope'. He was a close friend of Castiglione and a patron of Raphael. His comedy *La Calandria* was first presented at Urbino, before the Duchess Elisabetta, with a prologue written by Castiglione.

ETTORE, ROMANO, was (probably) the Giovenale Ettore who distinguished himself as one of the Italian champions in the famous combat between thirteen Italians and thirteen Frenchmen at Barletta in 1503, when the French were routed. He appears in *The Courtier* in the service of Francesco Maria della Rovere, Prefect of Rome and future Duke of Urbino.

FLORIDO, ORAZIO came from Fano, served as chancellor to Duke Guidobaldo and stayed on in the service of Francesco Maria, to whom he remained commendably loyal after he had been driven from Urbino.

FREGOSO, COSTANZA was received at Urbino after her family had been exiled from Genoa, since her mother, Gentile, was the natural daughter of Duke Federico. She married Count Marcantonio Landi of Piacenza.

FREGOSO, FEDERICO, a distinguished courtier and diplomat, the brother of Costanza and Ottaviano, was an intimate friend of many contemporary men of letters, such as Bembo and Castiglione himself, a student of philology, and an expert in oriental languages. He was an active politician (helping and then opposing his brother, Ottaviano, when the latter ruled Genoa) and a soldier. He was given the red hat by Pope Paul III in 1539, partly through the recommendation of Bembo.

FREGOSO, OTTAVIANO (1470–1524) was politically the most outstanding member of his family. After being exiled from Genoa in 1497 he returned to Urbino, where he had spent several years in his youth. Francesco Maria della Rovere appointed him ambassador to France. Subsequently, after two abortive attempts to seize power in

Genoa, he was elected Doge in 1513. He had to rely, however, on French protection, and when this failed, in 1522, he was taken prisoner (after the sack of Genoa by Imperial troops) by the Marquis of Pescara and died in exile.

FRISIO, OR FRIGIO, NICCOLÒ was a German who spent most of his life in Italy, where he became friendly with Castiglione and Bembo and acquired a reputation as a skilled diplomat and man of culture. In 1510 he retired to a monastery in Naples.

GIOVAN CRISTOFORO ROMANO (*c.* 1465–1512) was a sculptor and medallist, given the task in *The Courtier* of expounding one of the favourite subjects of the Renaissance: the superiority of one kind of art over another (and in this case, of sculpture over painting). He was also an accomplished musician, who probably first met Castiglione in Mantua in 1497 and is known to have visited Urbino in August 1506 and March 1507.

GONZAGA, CESARE (1475–1512) was a cousin of Castiglione and like him studied in Milan and served the Marquis of Mantua before entering the service of the rulers of Urbino as a soldier and diplomat. His relations with Bembo and Castiglione were very close and affectionate.

GONZAGA, ELISABETTA (1471–1526), the second daughter of the Marquess Federico Gonzaga of Mantua, married Duke Guidobaldo in 1488 and earned great admiration during twenty years of childless married life for her fortitude and virtue. In his edition of *The Courtier* Cian cites as an instance of the process of idealization by her admirers some verse by Castiglione describing her great beauty – in rather exaggerated terms to judge from her portrait in the Uffizi. After her widowhood and exile, she returned to Urbino in 1522 and there spent the remaining years of her life.

GONZAGA, MARGHERITA was Elisabetta's niece, and the natural daughter of the Marquess Francesco. She was reputed to be vivacious, gay and, according to Bembo, extremely witty. A marriage was planned for her in 1511 with Agostino Chigi, who cried off when he discovered that she was threatening to go into a decline at the prospect of being tied to such an old man.

MARIANO, FRA (1460–1531): a Florentine, Mariano Fetti entered the Medici service as a young man (he was Lorenzo's barber), and in 1495 became a Dominican friar. The Medici Pope, Leo X, enjoyed his jolly company at Rome, and he was a talented buffoon and versifier.

MEDICI, GIULIANO DE' (1479–1516) was the youngest of the children of the great Lorenzo de' Medici and Clarice Orsini. He spent a good deal of time at Urbino after the exile of the Medici from Florence in 1494. When they were restored to power, he became governor of Florence for a time before being called to Rome by his brother, Pope Leo X, and made a General of the Church. More of a courtier than a warrior, he sorely disappointed the Pope as a commander, lived a dissolute life, but was spoken well of by Castiglione, had his portrait painted by Raphael, was immortalized in sculpture by Michelangelo, and but for his death would have had Machiavelli's *The Prince* dedicated in his honour.

MONTE, PIETRO, a Court official, was probably the Pietro del Monte mentioned by the Venetian, Luigi da Porto, in his Letters as 'squint-eyed but extremely brave' and 'an experienced soldier as well as a man of the world'. For a time he was in the service of Duke Guidobaldo at Urbino, where he was Master of the Horse in charge of the tournaments.

MONTEFELTRO, GUIDOBALDO DA (1472–1508), the Duke of Urbino to whom the references in *The Courtier* are few and rather snide. He succeeded his father, the renowned Federico, in 1482, soldiered as a *condottiere* for the Church, but failed to live up to his father's reputation. His marriage to Elisabetta being childless, in 1504 he adopted his nephew, Francesco Maria della Rovere, as his heir. This was after the death of Alexander VI during whose reign Cesare Borgia had twice driven him out of Urbino not, it appears, altogether to the displeasure of the citizens.

MORELLA DA ORTONA was probably a member of the Abruzzese family of Ricciardi. He served Guidobaldo vigorously as a soldier and, when past fighting, as a trusted retainer at Court, being a witness, for example, to the Instrument of Adoption of Francesco Maria della Rovere. He is the only *old* courtier portrayed by Castiglione, with a rather endearing tetchiness.

PALLAVICINO GASPARE (1486–1511) was one of the youngest (namely, twenty-one) of those taking part in the conversations. He was a Lombard, a descendant of the Marchesi of Cortemaggiore, near Piacenza. He died young after a life of constant illness.

PIETRO DA NAPOLI makes only a brief appearance in *The Courtier* in order to tell a joke. He is mentioned elsewhere as one of the six men to accompany Pope Julius to Viterbo on his return from the Bologna expedition.

PIA, EMILIA (*d.* 1528) was the daughter of Marco Pio of Carpi and Benedetto del Carretto, and the faithful companion of the Duchess of Urbino. She remained in Urbino with her children, Veronica and Lodovico, after the death in 1500 of her husband, Antonio da Montefeltro (a natural brother of Guidobaldo). Like the Duchess, on a less lofty plane, she was extolled as a model of virtue and gaiety.

PIO, LODOVICO (*d.* 1512) was distantly related to Emilia. He probably first made friends with Castiglione at the Court of Milan where he married one of Lodovico Il Moro's maids of honour. He served as a papal captain with Castiglione, and in the end died of wounds received in battle.

ROBERTO DA BARI (*d.* 1512), another of Castiglione's wide circle of devoted friends, belonged to the noble Massimi family of Bari. He was a clever mimic, a keen dancer and an extremely elegant courtier.

ROVERE, FRANCESCO MARIA DELLA (1490–1538) spent his early youth in France. In 1504 Pope Julius II made him Prefect of Rome, as which he appears in *The Courtier*, aged seventeen. Papal pressure won him the succession to Urbino and he served as a commander of the papal forces against Venice and subsequently against the French. During this period he stabbed to death Cardinal Francesco Alidosi, in revenge for the loss of Bologna (where Alidosi was Legate) for which Francesco Maria was blamed. After trial he was acquitted and restored to favour. In 1516, he was ignominiously driven from Urbino by Pope Leo X, who bestowed the Duchy on his own nephew, Lorenzo de' Medici. After Leo's death, Francesco Maria reconquered Urbino (the papal governor being thrown out of the palace windows as he stormed in) in 1522. He was an incapable Captain-General of the armies of the Church at the time of the sack of Rome. After his death, Urbino remained in the hands of the Rovere family until 1631, when it passed under the direct rule of the Papacy.

SERAFINO, FRA was probably born at Mantua and at any rate resided most of the time at the Gonzaga Court. He was a great traveller and correspondent and a frequent visitor to Urbino. His rather crude humour got him into trouble in Rome, in 1507, when he was assaulted because of his lack of respect for the Pope.

SILVA, MICHEL DE (*c.* 1480–1556), to whom *The Courtier* is dedicated, was Dom Miguel da Silva, son of the Count of Portalegre, a province of central Portugal. Castiglione knew him in Rome, at the Court of Leo X, and met him again in Seville. For some years, he represented the Portuguese king at the papal Court. In 1541 he was publicly created a cardinal by Pope Paul III.

TERPANDRO was called Anton Maria and was probably a Roman who acquired his nickname in reference to the Greek poet and musician, Terpander of Lesbos. He was a good musician and singer, and a frequent visitor to Urbino during the reign of Julius II.

To the Reverend and Illustrious

SIGNOR DON MICHEL DE SILVA

Bishop of Viseu

AFTER the death of Guidobaldo da Montefeltro, Duke of Urbino, I, along with some other gentlemen who had served him, remained in the service of Duke Francesco Maria della Rovere, who was Guidobaldo's heir and successor; and since my recollection of Duke Guido's great qualities and of the happiness I had known in the friendly company of those outstanding men and women who used to frequent the Court of Urbino was still fresh and vivid, I was encouraged to write these books on Courtly life and behaviour. I spent but a short time on them, intending to correct later on the errors caused by anxiety to discharge my debt as soon as possible. Unfortunately, for many years I have been so continuously harassed and burdened that I have never been able to bring the work to the state that would satisfy even my poor judgement. As a result, I was naturally more than a little aggrieved, when in Spain, to receive from Italy the news that the Marchioness of Pescara, Vittoria Colonna, to whom I had once entrusted the work, had, contrary to her promise, had a large part of it written out. I was worried to think of the kind of mishaps that are likely in such circumstances. Nevertheless, I felt confident that the good sense and discretion of that lady (whose qualities I have always respected and admired beyond words) would prevent any misfortune resulting from my having obeyed her in writing what I did. Eventually I discovered that the part of the book concerned had found its way into the hands of many people in Naples; and since men are always eager for something new, it appeared that they would try to have it printed. I was so alarmed by this threat that I at once made up my mind to revise what little I could in the time available with the intention of publishing it myself, in the belief that it would do less harm to let the work be seen only slightly corrected by my own hand rather than badly mangled by others. So with this resolve I began to re-read it; and the moment I looked at it, my memories being stirred by the heading itself, I experienced no little sorrow, which intensified as I read farther and as I recalled that most of those introduced in the conversations were already dead. Thus, apart from those who are mentioned at the beginning of the last book, death has taken the one to whom it is dedicated, Alfonso Ariosto himself, an affable and discreet young man, who was of perfect behaviour and proficient in everything required of someone living at Court. Duke Giuliano de' Medici, whose goodness, nobility and courtesy the world deserved to enjoy longer, is also dead. And Bernardo Dovizi, Cardinal of Santa Maria in Portico, whose keen and ready wit charmed and delighted all who knew him, is also dead. So is signor Ottaviano Fregoso, one of the exceptional men of our time, magnanimous, devout, full of goodness, talent, prudence and courtesy, a true friend of honour and virtue, and so deserving of praise that even his enemies could never withhold it from him. (The misfortunes which Ottaviano endured so bravely, I may say, were enough to prove that Fortune hasn't changed her ways: she still hates virtue as much as she ever did.) Many of the others named in the book, who seemed destined to live for a very long time, are also dead. But what should not be recounted without tears is that the Duchess herself is dead; and if I am so distraught through the loss of all the noble friends I have mentioned that I seem to be living in a desert of solitude and misery, it is no wonder that my grief over her death is more bitter still, seeing that she was of even greater worth than the others and that I was even closer to her than to them. Therefore in order not to delay in paying what I owe to the memory of so great a lady and of those others who are no longer living, and in view of the threat I mentioned, I have had the book printed and published in such form as was possible in the short time available. And since, except for Duke Giuliano and the Cardinal of Santa Maria in Portico, you knew neither the Duchess nor the others while they were living, in order, as far as I can, to make you acquainted with them after their death I am sending you this book as a portrait of the Court of Urbino, not indeed by the hand of Raphael or Michelangelo but by a worthless painter who knows only how to draw the outlines and cannot adorn the truth with pretty colours or use perspective to deceive the eye. Moreover, although I determined to indicate in these conversations the character and qualities of those who are named, I have to admit that I have not even suggested, let alone done justice to, the virtues of the Duchess, because not only is my style incapable of expressing them but my mind of conceiving them. And if I am censured for this or the other fault in this book (and I know there are only too many) I shall not deny the truth.

All the same, people sometimes get so much pleasure out of passing censure that they find fault even with what does not deserve it. So to those who blame me for not having imitated Boccaccio or followed current Tuscan usage I shall not hesitate to answer that although Boccaccio was a man of noble discernment by the standards of his time, and although to some extent he wrote with discrimination and ability, nevertheless he wrote far better when he let himself be guided solely by his natural genius and instinct, without care or concern to polish his writings, than when he went to great pains to correct and refine his work. For this reason his own partisans declare that he greatly deceived himself when he judged his work himself, and that he put little value on what has done him honour and a great deal on what is worthless. So if I had imitated the style of writing for which he is censured by those who praise him otherwise, I certainly could not have escaped the same accusations as are levelled against him in this regard; in fact, I would have deserved them all the more in that he committed his error in the belief that he was doing right, whereas I would have done so knowing I was wrong. And if I had imitated him in the style which many people hold to be good, but which he himself thought little of, then in doing so I would have proved that I disagreed with the opinion of the author I was following, and this, in my judgement, would have been quite wrong. Even if I had not been influenced by this consideration, I could not imitate Boccaccio in subject matter, since he never wrote anything on the lines of these books on the courtier; and I thought it wrong to do so in the matter of language, since the power and correct rules of good speech consist more in usage than in anything else and it is always wrong to employ words which are not current. So it was inappropriate for me to employ many of those used by Boccaccio, which were current when he was alive but which have now fallen into disuse among the Tuscans themselves. At the same time, I was unwilling to commit myself to using contemporary Tuscan. After all, intercourse between different peoples has always carried new words from one place to another, just like articles of trade, after which they either take root or disappear, depending on whether they are admitted or rejected by usage. And not only is this proved by what happened in the ancient world but it can also be clearly seen in the case of Boccaccio, in whom there are so many French, Spanish and Provençal words, as well as some that are probably meaningless to Tuscans today, that it would greatly reduce the size of his book if they were all cut out. Moreover, in my opinion we should not simply reject the language in use in the other noble cities of Italy, where one finds men who are talented, wise and eloquent, and who are concerned with important political subjects as well as with literature, warfare and business affairs. I think that of the words current in such centres I have been justified in employing those which are graceful, euphonious and generally accepted as valid and expressive, even though they are not Tuscan and may even have originated outside Italy itself. Moreover, in Tuscany they use many words which are quite obviously corruptions of the Latin but which in Lombardy and other parts of Italy have remained unchanged in their original form, in which everyone uses them, so that they are acceptable in upper-class speech and yet understood without any trouble by ordinary people. So I do not think I have done wrong in using some of these words in my writing, preferring to take from my own country what is intact and genuine rather than from another's what is corrupt and mutilated. Neither do I agree that it is a sensible rule (as many people claim) that the further away ordinary speech is from the Latin the more attractive it is. Nor, again, do I understand why one idiom should be granted so much more authority than another that, whereas corrupt and defective Latin words are held to be ennobled and enhanced by being used in Tuscan, and therefore, quite rightly, universally acceptable, yet the same Latin words in their proper form, pure, intact and unaltered, are rejected when found in Lombard or any other tongue. Indeed, just as to try to coin completely new words or to preserve old ones, regardless of usage, is silly and presumptuous, so also, as well as being difficult, it is surely almost impious, equally regardless of usage to try to destroy and, as it were, bury alive, those which have already survived many centuries and under the protection of usage have defended themselves against the envy of time and maintained their dignity and splendour despite all the changes, caused by war and upheaval in Italy, of language, buildings, dress and customs. Therefore if in my writing I have refused to use words found in Boccaccio which are no longer current in Tuscan, or to accept the rules imposed by those who believe that it is impermissible to use words not found in modern Tuscan, I believe I have every excuse. So both in the subject matter of my book and in its linguistic style, insofar as one style can help another, I think I have followed writers who are at least as praiseworthy as Boccaccio. Nor do I think I should be held at fault for having chosen to make myself known as a Lombard speaking the language of Lombardy rather than as someone who is not a Tuscan speaking Tuscan, and so having avoided the mistake of Theophrastus[1] who was easily recognized as not being Athenian by a simple old woman, because he spoke Attic too much. However, since this is discussed enough in the first Book I shall say nothing more now, save that, to forestall all debate, I confess to my critics that I do not know this terribly difficult and recondite Tuscan language of theirs; and I admit that I have written in my own, just as I speak, and for those who speak in the same way. So I don't think I have done anyone any harm; for, in my view, nobody in the world is forbidden to write and speak in his own language, and still less is anyone forced to read or listen to what he does not like. Therefore if they do not want to read my *Courtier*, I shall not consider myself the slightest bit offended.

There are others who claim that, as it is so difficult and almost impossible to find a man as perfect as I wish the courtier to be, what I have written is a waste of time, because it is pointless to teach what cannot be learned. My answer to them is that I shall be quite content to have erred in the company of Plato, Xenophon and Cicero. For (leaving aside any dispute about the Intelligible World and the Ideas) just as, according to them, there exists the Idea of the perfect Republic, of the perfect King and the perfect

Orator, so there exists that of the perfect Courtier. And if my language falls short of the ideal, then it will be all the easier for courtiers to approach in real life the end and goals set before them. On the other hand, if, despite that, they cannot achieve the perfection, such as it is, that I have endeavoured to convey, the one who comes nearest to it will be the most perfect, in the same way as when a number of archers shoot at a target, though no one hits the bull's eye, the one who gets closest is certainly better than the rest. There are others who even allege that I had it in mind to offer myself as a model, being persuaded that all the qualities which I attribute to the courtier are my own. To these critics I shall not deny that I have tried to write down all that I should want the courtier to know; and I think that anyone who did not have some knowledge of the things expounded in the book, however erudite he might be otherwise, would scarcely have been able to write about them. But I am not so lacking in judgement and self-knowledge as to presume to know all I could wish to know.

So the defence against these, and doubtless many other, accusations I shall leave for the time being to the tribunal of public opinion, because more often than not, although the many may not understand everything, they can tell by natural instinct what seems good or bad, and, without being able to give any reason for it, they enjoy and love the one and reject and despise the other. Therefore if the book meets with general approval, I shall take it that it is good and believe that it will survive; and if, on the other hand, it fails to please, I shall take it that it is bad and shall at once accept that it must sink into obscurity. Then if my accusers are not satisfied with the verdict of public opinion, let them at least be content with the verdict of time, which eventually reveals the hidden defects in all things and, as the father of truth and a dispassionate judge, is accustomed to pronouncing always, on all writings, a just sentence of life or death.

BALD. CASTIGLIONE

THE FIRST BOOK OF THE COURTIER

TO MESSER ALFONSO ARIOSTO

I HAVE spent a long time wondering, my dear Alfonso, which of two things was the more difficult for me: either to refuse what you have asked me so often and so insistently, or to do it. On the one hand, it seemed to me to be very hard to refuse anything, and especially something praiseworthy, to one whom I love dearly and by whom I feel I am very dearly loved; yet on the other hand, to embark on a project which I was uncertain of being able to finish seemed wrong to one who respects adverse criticism as much as it ought to be respected. Eventually, after a great deal of thought, I have made up my mind to find out how diligent I can be when helped by affection and the anxiety to please, which usually act as a sharp spur to all kinds of activity.

Now your request is that I should describe what, in my view, is the form of courtiership most appropriate for a gentleman living at the Courts of princes, by which he will have the knowledge and the ability to serve them in every reasonable thing, winning their favour and the praise of others. In short, you want to know what kind of man must be one who deserves the name of a perfect courtier and has no shortcomings whatsoever. Considering this request, I must say that, if I did not think it a greater fault to be judged wanting in love by you than wanting in prudence by others, I would have rejected the task, for fear of being accused of rashness by all those who know how difficult an undertaking it is to select from all the many and various customs followed at the Courts of Christendom the most perfect model and, as it were, the very flower of courtiership. For familiarity often causes the same things to be liked and disliked: and thus it sometimes happens that the customs, behaviour, ceremonies and ways of life approved of at one period of time grow to be looked down on, and those which were once looked down on come to be approved. So we can see clearly enough that usage is more effective than reason in introducing new things among us and in wiping out the old. And anyone who tries to judge what is perfect in these matters often deceives himself. Being well aware of this, therefore, and of the many other problems connected with the subject proposed to me, I am compelled to say something by way of excuse and to testify that what I am doing wrong (if it can be called so) you are responsible for as well, and that if I am to be blamed for it you must share the blame. After all, you must be judged to be as much at fault in imposing on me a task greater than my resources as I am in having accepted it.

But let us now begin to discuss the subject we have chosen and, if it is possible, create a courtier so perfect that the prince who is worthy of his service, even though his dominion is small, can count himself a truly great ruler. In these books we shall not follow any strict order or list a series of precepts, as is the normal practice in teaching. Instead, following many writers of the ancient world, and reviving a pleasant memory, we shall recount some discussions which once took place among men who were singularly qualified in these matters. Even though I did not take part in them in person (being in England when they were held), they were faithfully reported to me soon after my return by someone who was present, and I shall endeavour to reproduce them as accurately as my memory allows so that you may discover what was held and thought on the subject by eminent men whose judgement can always be trusted completely. Nor will it be beside the purpose, in order to continue the story in logical order, to describe the occasion of the discussions that took place.

On the slopes of the Apennines, almost in the centre of Italy towards the Adriatic, is situated, as everyone knows, the little city of Urbino. Although it is surrounded by hills which are perhaps not as agreeable as those found in many other places, none the less it has been favoured by Nature with a very rich and fertile countryside, so that as well as a salubrious atmosphere it enjoys an abundance of all the necessities of life. Among the blessings and advantages that can be claimed for it, I believe the greatest is that for a long time now it has been governed by outstanding rulers, even though in the turmoils into which Italy was plunged by war it was for a time deprived of them. Without looking any further, we can find a splendid example in Duke Federico of glorious memory, who in his day was the light of Italy. Nor are there lacking today any number of reliable witnesses to his prudence, humanity, justice, generosity and unconquerable spirit, and to his military skill, which was brilliantly attested by his many victories, his ability to capture impregnable places, his swift and decisive expeditions, his having routed many times with few troops great and formidable armies, and his never having lost a single battle. So we can fairly compare him with many famous men of the ancient world. Among his other commendable enterprises, Duke Federico built on the rugged site of Urbino a palace which many believe to be the most beautiful in all Italy; and he furnished it so well and appropriately that it seemed more like a city than a mere palace. For he adorned it not only with the usual objects, such as silver vases, wall-hangings of the richest cloth of gold, silk and other similar material, but also with countless antique statues of marble and bronze, with rare pictures, and with every kind of musical instrument; nor would he tolerate anything that was not most rare and outstanding. Then, at great cost, he collected a large number of the finest and rarest books, in Greek, Latin and Hebrew, all of which he adorned with gold and silver, believing that they were the crowning glory of his great palace.

Following, therefore, the course of Nature, and being already sixty-five years old, Duke Federico died as gloriously as he had lived, leaving as his heir his only son, a little, motherless boy of ten named Guidobaldo. And Guidobaldo seemed to inherit not only his father's state but all his virtues as well, immediately showing in his marvellous disposition the promise of more than can be expected from a mortal man. In consequence, it was widely said that of all the wonderful things that Duke Federico had done, the greatest was to have fathered such a son. But envious of his great qualities, Fortune set herself with all her might to frustrate what had begun so nobly, with the result that before he was yet twenty years old Duke Guido fell sick with the gout which, inflicting terrible pain, grew steadily worse and within a short space of time crippled him so badly that he could neither stand nor walk. Thus one of the best and most handsome men in the whole world was deformed and ruined while still of tender age. Not satisfied even with this, Fortune so opposed him in all his projects that he rarely succeeded in what he undertook;

and although he was a man of mature deliberation and unconquerable spirit, everything he set his hand to, whether in arms or anything else, great or small, always ended unhappily, as we can see from the many diverse calamities which befell him, and which he always bore with such fortitude that his will was never crushed by fate. On the contrary, with great resilience and spirit, he despised the blows of Fortune, living the life of a healthy and happy man, despite sickness and adversity, and achieving true dignity and universal renown. Thus even though he was infirm, he campaigned with a most honourable rank in the service of their Serene Highnesses Kings Alfonso and Ferdinand the Younger of Naples, and subsequently with Pope Alexander VI as well as the Signories of Venice and Florence. Then, after the accession of Pope Julius II, he was made Captain of the Church; and during this time, following his customary style of life, he saw to it that his household was filled with very noble and worthy gentlemen, with whom he lived on the most familiar terms, delighting in their company. In this the pleasure he caused others was no less than what he received, for he was very well versed in both Latin and Greek, and possessed as well as an affable and charming nature, an infinite range of knowledge. Moreover, his indomitable spirit so spurred him on that, even though he himself was unable to take part in chivalrous activities, as he once used to, he loved to see them pursued by others, and he would show his fine judgement when commenting on what they did, correcting or praising each one according to his merits. So in jousts and tournaments, in riding, in handling every kind of weapon, as well as in the festivities, games and musical performances, in short, in all the activities appropriate to a well-born gentleman, everyone at his Court strove to behave in such a way as to deserve to be judged worthy of the Duke's noble company.

So all day and every day at the Court of Urbino was spent on honourable and pleasing activities both of the body and the mind. But since the Duke always retired to his bedroom soon after supper, because of his infirmity, as a rule at that hour everyone went to join the Duchess, Elisabetta Gonzaga, with whom was always to be found signora Emilia Pia, a lady gifted with such a lively wit and judgement, as you know, that she seemed to be in command of all and to endow everyone else with her own discernment and goodness. In their company polite conversations and innocent pleasantries were heard, and everyone's face was so full of laughter and gaiety that the house could truly be called the very inn of happiness. And I am sure that the delight and enjoyment to be had from loving and devoted companionship were never experienced elsewhere as they once were in Urbino. For, apart from the honour it was for each of us to be in the service of a ruler such as I described above, we all felt supremely happy whenever we came into the presence of the Duchess; and this sense of contentment formed between us a bond of affection so strong that even between brothers there could never have been such harmonious agreement and heartfelt love as there was among us all. It was the same with the ladies, whose company we all enjoyed very freely and innocently, since everyone was allowed to talk and sit, make jokes and laugh with whom he pleased, though such was the respect we had for the wishes of the Duchess that the liberty we enjoyed was accompanied by the most careful restraint. And without exception everyone considered that the most pleasurable thing possible was to please her and the most displeasing thing in the world was to earn her displeasure. So for these reasons in her company the most decorous behaviour proved compatible with the greatest freedom, and in her presence our games and laughter were seasoned both with the sharpest witticisms and with a gracious and sober dignity. For the modesty and nobility which informed every act, word and gesture of the Duchess, in jest and laughter, caused even those seeing her for the first time to recognize that she was a very great lady. It seemed, from the way in which she influenced those around her, that she tempered us all to her own character and quality, so that everyone endeavoured to imitate her personal way of behaviour, deriving as it were a model of fine manners from the presence of so great and talented a woman, whose high qualities I do not intend to describe now, since this is not to my purpose and they are well known to all the world, apart from being beyond the reach of whatever I could say or write. But I must add that those qualities in the Duchess which might have remained somewhat hidden, Fortune, as if admiring such rare virtues, chose to reveal through many adversities and harsh blows, in order to demonstrate that in the tender soul of a woman, and accompanied by singular beauty, there may also dwell prudence and a courageous spirit and all those virtues very rarely found even in the staunchest of men.

To continue, let me say that it was the custom for all the gentlemen of the house to go, immediately after supper, to the rooms of the Duchess; and there, along with pleasant recreations and enjoyments of various kinds, including constant music and dancing, sometimes intriguing questions were asked, and sometimes ingenious games played (now on the suggestion of one person and now of another) in which, using various ways of concealment, those present revealed their thoughts in allegories to this person or that. And occasionally, there would be discussions on various subjects, or there would be a sharp exchange of spontaneous witticisms; and often 'emblems',[2] as we call them nowadays, were devised for the occasion. And everyone enjoyed these exchanges immensely, since, as I have said, the house was full of very noble and talented persons, among whom, as you know, the most famous was signor Ottaviano Fregoso, his brother Federico, the Magnifico Giuliano de' Medici, Pietro Bembo, Cesare Gonzaga, Count Lodovico da Canossa, Gaspare Pallavicino, signor Lodovico Pio, signor Morello da Ortona, Pietro da Napoli, Roberto da Bari and countless other high-born gentlemen. There were also many who, although they did not as a rule stay permanently, yet spent most of their time there: they included Bernardo Bibbiena, the Unico Aretino, Giovan Cristoforo Romano, Pietro Monte, Terpandro and Nicolò Frisio. So gathered together at the Court of Urbino there were always to be found poets, musicians, buffoons of all kinds, and the finest talent of every description anywhere in Italy.

Now after Julius II had by his presence and with the help of the French brought Bologna under the rule of the Apostolic See, in the year 1506, he passed through Urbino on his way back to Rome. There he was received with the greatest honour and welcomed with as magnificent and splendid a reception as could have been offered in any of Italy's great cities. So besides the Pope, all the cardinals and other courtiers were extremely gratified. And there were some who were so drawn by the charm of the company they found at Urbino that, when the Pope and his Court went their way, they stayed on for many days. During this time, not only were the customary amusements and entertainments continued in the usual style but everyone did his best to contribute something more, and especially in the games that were played nearly every evening. As far as these were concerned, the rule was that as soon as anyone came into the presence of the Duchess he would take his place in a circle, sitting down wherever he wished or wherever he happened to find himself; the group was arranged alternately one man and one woman, as long as there were women, for invariably they were outnumbered by the men. Then the company was governed according to the wishes of the Duchess, who usually left this task to signora Emilia. So the day after the Pope's departure, they all assembled in the customary place at the usual time, and after many pleasant discussions, the Duchess decided that signora Emilia should begin the games; and she, after resisting the suggestion for a little while, spoke as follows:

'Madam, since it is your wish that I should be the one to begin the games this evening, as I cannot rightly refuse to obey you, I want to suggest a game which I think will cause me little criticism and even less trouble. And this is that each one of us should suggest some game he likes that has not been played before; and then the choice will be made of the one that seems worthiest of us.'

Saying this, she turned to signor Gaspare Pallavicino and told him to say what his proposal would be; and he immediately replied:

'It is for you, madam, to tell yours first.'

'But I've already done so,' she answered, 'so now,' (turning to the Duchess) 'you, my lady, order him to do what he is told.'

At this the Duchess laughed and said: 'So that everyone will obey you, I make you my deputy and give you all my authority.'

'It really is remarkable,' said signor Pallavicino, 'that women are always allowed this exemption from work, and it would only be reasonable to insist on knowing just why. However, as I don't want to be the first to disobey, I shall leave this matter for another time and do what I am supposed to.'

And then he began as follows:

'It seems to me that in love, just as in everything else, we all judge differently. Therefore it often happens that what one person finds adorable another finds most detestable. Despite this, we are all alike in cherishing the one we love, and quite often the blind devotion of the lover makes him think the person he loves is the only one in the world possessing every virtue and completely without defect. Yet since human nature does not allow such complete perfection, and since there is no one who is wholly without defect, it cannot be said that such people do not deceive themselves, or that love is not blind. So the game I would like played this evening is that each of us should say what quality he would most like the person he loves to possess; and then, since everyone must have some defect, what fault he would choose as well. This is so that we can see who will think of the most commendable and useful qualities and of the faults that are the most excusable and the least harmful to either the lover or the one he loves.'

After signor Gaspare had spoken, signora Emilia made a sign to the lady Costanza Fregoso, as it was her turn, to speak next; and madam Costanza was about to do so when the Duchess suddenly remarked:

'Since signora Emilia is unwilling to give herself the trouble of thinking of a game, it is only right for the other ladies to enjoy the same privilege and also be exempt from making any effort this evening, especially as we have so many men with us that there is no danger of running out of games.'

'Very well, then,' said signora Emilia. And imposing silence on madam Costanza, she turned to Cesare Gonzaga, who sat by her side, and told him to speak next. So he began in this way:

'Anyone who studies our actions carefully, always finds in them various shortcomings. And this is because Nature, being fond of variety in this as in other matters, has made one man sensible in regard to one thing and another in regard to something else. So, since one person knows what another does not, and is ignorant of what another understands, we find that everyone all too easily perceives his neighbour's error and not his own, and we all think we are very wise, perhaps most of all in regard to things about which we are most foolish. For example, we have seen in this household how many who, to begin with, were reputed to be extremely shrewd, as time has passed have been recognized as being very stupid, and this discovery has been made only because of our diligence. Thus they say that in Apulia when someone is bitten by a tarantula many musical instruments are played and various tunes are tried until the humour which is causing the sickness all of a sudden responds to the sound with which it has a certain affinity and so agitates the sick man that he is shaken back into good health. In the same way, whenever we have suspected some hidden strain of folly, we have stimulated it so cunningly and with so many different inducements and in so many various ways that eventually we have discovered its nature; then, having recognized the humour for what it was, we have agitated it so thoroughly that it has always been brought to the culmination of open madness. In that way, one man turned out to be foolish in verse, another in music, another in dancing, another in ballet, another in riding and another in fencing: each according to his own innermost vibrations. And in this, as you know, we have enjoyed some marvellous entertainment. Therefore I hold this for certain: that in each one of us there is some seed of folly which, once it is stirred, can grow indefinitely. So I suggest that our game this evening should be to discuss this subject and that each one of us should answer the question: "If I had to be openly mad, what kind of folly would I be thought likely to display, and in what connexion, going by the sparks of folly which I give out every day?"; and let the same be said of all the others, following the usual order of our games, and let each of us seek to base his decision on some genuine signs and evidence. Thus each of us shall benefit from this game in finding out his faults and being able to guard against them all the better; and if the vein of folly we disclose proves so abundant that it is beyond remedy, let us encourage it and, according to Fra Mariano's[3] teaching, we shall have saved a soul, which is no little achievement.'

The idea for this kind of game provoked a great deal of laughter, and for a while no one could stop talking. One person said that he would be foolish 'when it came to thinking'; another 'in looking'; yet another, 'I'm already a fool in love' and so forth.

Then Fra Serafino, laughing as usual, said: 'This suggestion would take too long, but if you want a really fine game get everyone to give his opinion why it is that almost all women hate rats and love snakes; and you'll discover that no one will hit upon the truth except myself, for I have discovered this secret in a strange way.'

And he had already launched into his usual nonsense when signora Emilia ordered him to keep quiet and, passing over the lady who sat next in line, made a sign to the Unico Aretino, whose turn it now was. And without waiting for anything more, he said:

'I would like to be a judge with the authority to employ any kind of torture in order to extract the truth from criminals. This is so that I could reveal the deceits of a certain ungrateful woman who, with the eyes of an angel and the heart of a serpent, never says what she is thinking in her mind and who, with a feigned and deceitful compassion, does nothing but cut open human hearts. And I tell you, there is no venomous serpent in all the sands of Libya as avid of human blood as this deceiver, who is a veritable Siren not only in the sweetness of her voice and her honeyed words but also in her eyes, her smiles, her looks and in all her ways. However, since I am not allowed, as I would wish, to make use of chains, rope or fire to learn the truth about a certain thing, I would like to find it out through a game, which is as follows: namely, that each one of us should say what he believes is the meaning of the letter 'S' that the Duchess is wearing on her forehead.[4] Although this is certainly only another cunning subterfuge, someone may chance to give an explanation for it which she has not perhaps been expecting, and it will be found that Fortune, who looks at men's sufferings with such compassion, has led her unwittingly to reveal by this little sign her secret plan to smother with calamities and kill whoever gazes at her or serves her.'

The Duchess burst out laughing; and then Aretino, seeing that she wished to protest her innocence, went on: 'No, madam, it is not your turn to speak now.'

So then signora Emilia turned to him and said:

'Sir, there is no one among us who does not yield to you in

everything, and especially in your knowledge of what is in the Duchess's mind. And just as you know her mind better than the rest of us, because of your inspired understanding, so you love it more than we, who are like those weak-sighted birds which cannot look at the sun and therefore cannot know how perfect it is. So, apart from what you yourself decided, every effort we made to resolve this problem would be useless. Therefore you must undertake the task on your own, as the only one who can carry it through successfully.'

Aretino stayed silent for a little while, and then, when he was again asked to speak, he eventually recited a sonnet on the subject he had raised, describing what was the meaning of the letter 'S', which many of those present thought he had made up on the spot but which others decided must have been composed beforehand since it was more ingenious and polished than seemed possible in the time.

So then, everyone having applauded happily and praised Aretino's sonnet, after a moment's conversation signor Ottaviano Fregoso, whose turn it was to speak, began laughingly as follows:

'Gentlemen, if I were to claim that I had never experienced the passion of love, I am sure that the Duchess and signora Emilia, even though they did not believe it, would pretend to do so, and they would argue that it was because I had always doubted whether I could ever persuade any women to love me. But to tell the truth, up to now I have never tested this so thoroughly as to have reason to despair of being able to succeed some time or other. Nor indeed have I refrained because I have such a high opinion of myself, or so little regard for women, that I doubt whether there are many among them worthy of my love and service. Rather, I have been frightened off by the endless laments of certain lovers, who are pale and sad and taciturn and who always seem to carry their unhappiness in their eyes. And when they do speak they accompany every word with repeated sighs and talk of nothing else save tears, torments, despair and their longing for death. In consequence, even if at times some amorous spark has been kindled in my heart, I have at once forced myself to do everything possible to extinguish it, not through any hatred of women, as these ladies may suppose, but for my own safety. I have also known others go to the opposite extreme from these groaners, and not only derive joy and satisfaction from the kind looks and tender words and gracious beauty of their ladies but also flavour all their unpleasant experiences with sweetness, positively relishing all their lovers' wars and quarrels and fits of temper. Now these men seem to me to be happy beyond words: for if they derive such sweet satisfaction from the amorous outbursts that the others think worse than death, surely in the manifestations of love they should experience that supreme beatitude which we cannot find in this world. So this evening I would like as our game that each one of us should say what, if the one he loves has to be angry with him, he would want the cause of her anger to be. For if there are any here who have experienced these sweet outbursts of anger, I am sure that out of kindness they would choose one of the causes that make them so sweet. And then perhaps I shall pluck up the courage to venture further in love, in the hope of finding this sweetness for myself, where some find only bitterness. In this way, these ladies would no longer be able to slander me with the accusation that I love no one.'

This idea was very well received, and already everyone was ready to say something on the subject. But as signora Emilia made no comment at all, Pietro Bembo, who was next in turn, spoke as follows:

'Gentlemen, the game proposed by signor Ottaviano has raised no few doubts in my mind, for he speaks of the slights of love which, even though they are of various kinds, I have always found a bitter experience. And I do not think that one could learn from me anything capable of making them sweet. But perhaps they are more or less bitter according to what provokes them. For I remember once having seen the lady I was serving furious with me either through some unjustified suspicion she had concerning my loyalty or because of some other false notion given her by what someone said to spite me; and in consequence I believed that no suffering could be worse than mine, and it seemed to me that the greatest pain I felt was in suffering without deserving it and in having this affliction not through any fault of mine but through her lack of love. On other occasions I saw her angry because of some mistake I had made, and I recognized that this was my fault; and then I decided that my former misery had been nothing to what I felt now, and it seemed to me that the greatest torment possible was to have displeased through my own fault the lady I was so anxious to serve and who was the only one I loved. So I would like our game to be that each of us should say whether, if the one he loves has to be angry with him, he would want the reason for her anger to be found in her or in himself. In this way we shall establish whether it is more painful to give displeasure to the person one loves or to receive it from her.'

Everyone was waiting for signora Emilia to answer, when without saying a word to Bembo she turned to Federico Fregoso and indicated that he should say what game he would suggest; and he immediately began as follows:

'Madam, I would like to be allowed, as sometimes happens, to defer to someone else's judgement, because for my part I would gladly approve any of the games proposed by these gentlemen, since I feel sure that they would all prove agreeable. However, so as not to evade my turn, let me say that if anyone should wish to praise our Court – leaving aside the merits of the Duchess which, together with her divine virtue, are capable of transporting the meanest spirits from earth to heaven – he would be fully justified in observing, without the slightest trace of flattery, that one would be hard put to it to find anywhere in Italy an equal number of knights as outstanding and as skilled in so many different things, apart from their main profession of chivalry, as are found here. Therefore if men are to be found anywhere who deserve to be called good courtiers and who are capable of judging what constitutes perfect courtiership, one must reasonably accept that they are with us now. So to teach a lesson to the many fools who in their presumption and absurdity think they are entitled to be called good courtiers, I would like our game this evening to be this: that one of us should be chosen and given the task of depicting in words a perfect courtier, explaining the character and the particular qualities needed by anyone who deserves such a title. And, just as in philosophical disputations, if anything is said which does not seem appropriate, each of us may be allowed to contradict.'

Federico was continuing to speak, when signora Emilia interrupted him to say: 'If the Duchess wishes, this will be our game for this evening.'

And the Duchess answered: 'Yes, that is my wish.'

Then almost without exception all those who were present began to say among themselves and to the Duchess that this was the best game of all; and hardly waiting to hear each other talk, they all urged signora Emilia to decide who should make a start. So, turning to the Duchess, she said:

'Decide, madam, who it is you wish to undertake this task; for I don't want in choosing one rather than another to appear to be judging whom I think the most capable, and so give offence.'

The Duchess answered: 'No, you must make the choice yourself; and take care lest by disobeying me you set a bad example to the others to do the same.'

Then, with a smile, signora Emilia said to Count Lodovico da Canossa:

'Well, then, so that we won't lose any more time, you will be the one to undertake the task as described by Federico. Not, let me say, that we believe you are such a fine courtier that you know what befits one, but because if you say everything contrariwise, as we hope you will, then the game will be still better since everyone will have a reason for challenging you, whereas if the task were given to someone knowing more than you do, no one could contradict anything he said, since it would be the truth, and so the game would prove very dull.'

The Count immediately retorted:

'But, madam, since you are present we need have no fear that the truth would go unchallenged.'

After everyone had laughed at this for a while, he continued:

'All the same, I would willingly be excused the labour involved, because it seems to me to be too difficult and also because I know that what you have said about me for a joke is indeed only too true, namely, that I do not know what befits a good courtier. Nor do I need to provide any proof for this other than the fact that since I do not act like a good courtier it can be judged that I do not have the knowledge. However, I think I am therefore less blameworthy, seeing that it is surely worse not to want to perform well than not to know how to do so. Still, since you want me to undertake the task, I cannot and will not refuse it, so as not to contravene either our rules or your judgement, which I value far more than my own.'

Then Cesare Gonzaga remarked:

'As it is already quite late and there are many other ways in which we can entertain ourselves, perhaps it would be as well to defer this discussion until tomorrow and give the Count time to think about what he has to say. For it is certainly very difficult to have to speak unprepared on such a subject.'

The Count replied: 'I don't want to be like the man who stripped down to his shirt and then jumped a shorter distance than he had in his greatcoat. So as far as I am concerned it is very fortunate that the hour is late, because as there is little time I shall have to say far less, and not having given the matter any thought I will be held excusable and allowed to say without being censured all the things that come to my mind. And now in order not to have to carry the burden any longer, let me start by saying that to recognize true perfection in anything is so difficult as to be scarcely possible; and this because of the way opinions vary. Thus there are many who like to hear someone talking a great deal and who will call him an agreeable companion. Some will prefer reticence; others an active and restless man; others one who always acts with calmness and deliberation; and so everyone praises or condemns according to his own opinion, always camouflaging a vice under the name of the corresponding virtue, or a virtue under the name of the corresponding vice. For example, a presumptuous man will be called frank, a modest man, dull; a simple-minded man, good; a rascal, shrewd; and so on and so forth. Still, I do think there is a perfection for everything, even though it may be concealed, and I also think that this perfection can be determined through informed and reasoned argument. And since, as I have said, the truth is often concealed and I do not claim to be informed, I can only praise courtiers of the kind I esteem myself and approve what seems to my limited judgement to be nearest to what is correct; and you can follow my judgement if it seems good, or keep to your own if it differs. Nor shall I argue that mine is better than yours, for not only can you think one thing and I another but I myself can think one thing at one time and something else another time.'

The Count then continued: 'So, for myself, I would have our courtier of noble birth and good family, since it matters far less to a common man if he fails to perform virtuously and well than to a nobleman. For if a gentleman strays from the path of his forbears, he dishonours his family name and not only fails to achieve anything but loses what has already been achieved. Noble birth is like a bright lamp that makes clear and visible both good deeds and bad, and inspires and incites to high performance as much as fear of dishonour or hope of praise; and since their deeds do not possess such noble brilliance, ordinary people lack both this stimulus and the fear of dishonour; nor do they believe that they are bound to surpass what was achieved by their forbears. Whereas to people of noble birth it seems reprehensible not to attain at least the standard set them by their ancestors. Thus as a general rule, both in arms and in other worthy activities, those who are most distinguished are of noble birth, because Nature has implanted in everything a hidden seed which has a certain way of influencing and passing on its own essential characteristics to all that grows from it, making it similar to itself. We see this not only in breeds of horses and other animals but also in trees, whose offshoots nearly always resemble the trunk; and if they sometimes degenerate, the fault lies with the man who tends them. So it happens with men, who, if they are well tended and properly brought up, nearly always resemble those from whom they spring, and are often even better; but if they have no one to give them proper attention, they grow wild and never reach maturity. It is true that, through the favour of the stars or of Nature, certain people come into the world endowed with such gifts that they seem not to have been born but to have been formed by some god with his own hands and blessed with every possible advantage of mind and body. Similarly, there are many to be found so uncouth and absurd that it can be believed simply that Nature was motivated by spite or mockery in bringing them into the world at all. Just as even with unceasing diligence and careful training the latter cannot usually be made to bear fruit, so with only the slightest effort the former reach the summit of excellence. And to give you an example, look at Don Ippolito d'Este, Cardinal of Ferrara, whose fortunate birth has influenced his person, his appearance, his words and all his actions. Because of this favour, despite his youth, even among the most venerable cardinals he carries such weighty authority that he seems more suited to teach than to be taught. Similarly, when conversing with men and women of every sort, when playing or laughing or joking, he has such charming ways and such a gracious manner that anyone who speaks to, or merely sets eyes on the Cardinal feels a lasting affection for him. However, to return to the subject, I say that between such supreme grace and such absurd folly can be found a middle way, and that those who are not perfectly endowed by Nature can, through care and effort, polish and to a great extent correct their natural defects. So in addition to noble birth, I would have the courtier favoured in this respect, too, and receive from Nature not only talent and beauty of countenance and person but also that certain air and grace that makes him immediately pleasing and attractive to all who meet him; and this grace should be an adornment informing and accompanying all his actions, so that he appears clearly worthy of the companionship and favour of the great.'

Then, refusing to wait any longer, signor Gaspare Pallavicino remarked:

'So that our game may proceed as it is meant to, and to show that we are not forgetting our privilege of contradicting, let me say that I do not believe that nobility of birth is necessary for the courtier. And if I thought I was saying something new to us, I would cite many people who, though of the most noble blood, have been wicked in the extreme, and, on the other hand, many of humble birth who, through their virtues, have won glory for their descendants. And if what you have just said is true, namely, that concealed in everything is the influence of its first seed, we should all be of the same character, since we all had the same beginning; nor would anyone be more noble than another. In fact, I hold that the various gradations of elevation and lowliness that exist among us have many other causes. The first and foremost is Fortune, who rules everything that happens in this world, and often appears to amuse herself by exalting whomever she pleases, regardless of merit, or hurling down those worthiest of being raised up. I fully concur with what you said about the happiness of those endowed at birth with all the perfections of mind and body; but this is seen among those of humble origins as well as those of noble birth, since Nature has no regard for these fine distinctions. On the contrary, as I have said, the finest gifts of Nature are often found in persons of very humble family. Therefore, since this nobility of birth is acquired neither through talent nor through force or skill, and is a matter for congratulating one's ancestors rather than oneself, it seems very odd to insist that, if the courtier's parents are of low birth, all his good qualities are spoilt and the other qualities you have mentioned are insufficient to bring him to the height of perfection: these being talent, good looks and disposition, and the grace which makes a person always pleasing at first sight.'

Count Lodovico answered: 'I do not deny that the same virtues can exist in men of low birth as in those of noble family. However, not to repeat what we have said already, let me give one more reason among many for praising nobility of birth, which, since it stands to reason that good should beget good, everyone always respects; and it is that (since we are to create a courtier without any defects, and endowed with every kind of merit) he must be a nobleman if only because of the immediate impression this makes on all concerned. For given two gentlemen of the Court, neither of whom as yet has shown what he is like by his actions, either good or bad, as soon as it is discovered that one of them was well born and the other not, the latter will be respected far less than the former, and only after a great deal of time and effort will he win the good opinion that the other acquires instantly, merely because of his nobility. It is well understood how important these impressions are, for, speaking of ourselves, we have seen men coming to this house who, although very stupid and dull, have been regarded throughout Italy as very great courtiers; and even though they were eventually found out, they still fooled us for a long time and sustained in our minds the opinion of themselves already formed before they arrived, despite the fact that their behaviour was in keeping with their lack of merit. We have seen others, who were regarded with very little favour to begin with, eventually meet with great success. Now there are various reasons for these mistakes, including the obstinacy of princes who, in the hope of achieving a miraculous transformation, sometimes deliberately favour someone who they know does not deserve it. Then again, sometimes they are themselves deceived; but, since princes always have countless imitators, their favour confers considerable fame which in turn influences the rest of us. And if people discover something that seems to contradict the prevailing opinion, they accept that they are mistaken and they always wait for some revelation. This is because it seems that what is universally believed must be based on true and reasonable grounds. Moreover, we are always most anxious to take sides either passionately for or against, as can be seen in public combats or games or any kind of contest, where the onlookers often for no clear reason favour one or other of the participants, desperately anxious that he should win and his opponent lose. Then as regards men's characters, their good or bad reputation, as soon as we hear of it, arouses in us either love or hatred, so that for the most part we judge on the basis of one of these emotions. So you see how important are first impressions, and how hard a man must strive to give a good impression at the beginning if he is ambitious to win the rank and name of a good courtier.

'But to come to specific details, I judge that the first and true profession of the courtier must be that of arms; and this above everything else I wish him to pursue vigorously. Let him also stand out from the rest as enterprising, bold, and loyal to whomever he serves. And he will win a good reputation by demonstrating these qualities whenever and wherever possible, since failure to do so always incurs the gravest censure. Just as once a woman's reputation for purity has been sullied it can never be restored, so once the reputation of a gentleman-at-arms has been stained through cowardice or some other reproachful behaviour, even if only once, it always remains defiled in the eyes of the world and covered with ignominy. The more our courtier excels in this art, therefore, the more praise he will deserve, although I do not think he needs to have the professional knowledge of such things and the other qualities appropriate to a military commander. However, since the subject of what constitutes a great captain takes us into very deep waters, we shall be content, as we said, for the courtier to show complete loyalty and an undaunted spirit, and for these to be always in evidence. For men demonstrate their courage far more often in little things than in great. Very often in the face of appalling danger but where there are numerous witnesses one will find those who, though ready to drop dead with fear, driven on by shame or the presence of others, will press forward, with their eyes closed, and do their duty; and only God knows how. But in things of trifling importance, when they believe they can avoid danger without its being noticed, they are only too willing to play for safety. As for those who, even when they are sure they are not being observed or seen or recognized by anyone, are full of ardour and avoid doing anything, no matter how trivial, for which they would incur reproach, they possess the temper and quality we are looking for in our courtier. All the same, we do not wish the courtier to make a show of being so fierce that he is always blustering and bragging, declaring that he is married to his cuirass, and glowering with the haughty looks that we know only too well in Berto.[5] To these may very fairly be said what a worthy lady once remarked jokingly, in polite company, to a certain man (I don't want just now to mention him by name) whom she had honoured by asking him to dance and who not only refused but would not listen to music or take part in the many other entertainments offered, protesting all the while that such frivolities were not his business. And when at length the lady asked what his business was, he answered with a scowl: "Fighting ..."

' "Well then," the lady retorted, "I should think that since you aren't at war at the moment and you are not engaged in fighting, it would be a good thing if you were to have yourself well greased and stowed away in a cupboard with all your fighting equipment, so that you avoid getting rustier than you are already."

'And of course everyone burst out laughing at the way she showed her contempt for his stupid presumption.

'Therefore,' Count Lodovico went on, 'the man we are seeking should be fierce, rough and always to the fore, in the presence of the enemy; but anywhere else he should be kind, modest, reticent and anxious above all to avoid ostentation or the kind of outrageous self-glorification by which a man always arouses loathing and disgust among those who have to listen to him.'

'As for me,' signor Gaspare replied, 'I have very seldom known men who are any good at anything who do not praise themselves. It seems to me that it is only right to allow them to do so, since, when a man who knows he is of some worth sees what he does being ignored, he grows angry at the way his qualities are hidden from sight and is forced to reveal them in some way lest he be cheated of the honour which is the rightful prize for virtuous endeavour. Thus, among the writers of the ancient world, rarely does anyone of any worth refrain from praising himself. Those who praise themselves even though they lack merit are certainly intolerable; but then we assume that our courtier will not be one of them.'

At this, the Count said:

'If you were listening, what I did was to censure those who praise themselves extravagantly and brashly. But I certainly agree that it would be wrong to take exception when a worthy man indulges in some modest self-praise; indeed it is then more convincing than if it comes from someone else. What I am saying is that a man who praises himself in the right way, and does not cause envy or annoyance in doing so, is well within the bounds of discretion; and he deserves the praise of others as well as what he allows himself, because he is achieving something very difficult.'

'You must teach us how to do it,' remarked signor Gaspare.

'Well,' the Count replied, 'there are those who taught this among the writers of the ancient world. However, in my opinion it all depends on saying things in such a way that they do not seem to be spoken with that end in view, but are so very much to the purpose that one cannot refrain from saying them; and also on giving the impression of avoiding self-praise, while indulging in it: but not in the style of those braggarts who open their mouths and let the words pour out heedlessly. As one of our own did the other day, who, after he had had his thigh run through by a spear at Pisa, said he thought a fly had stung him; and another who said he didn't keep a looking-glass in his room because when he lost his temper his expression was so terrible that if he saw it he would frighten himself to death.'

Everyone laughed at this, but Cesare Gonzaga added:

'What are you laughing at? Don't you know that after Alexander the Great had heard that in the opinion of a certain philosopher there were countless other worlds, he began to weep, and when asked why he did so, he replied: "Because I haven't yet conquered a single one" – as if he had it in him to conquer them all? Doesn't this seem to you to be more boastful than that remark about the fly?'

Then the Count remarked:

'And Alexander was a greater man than the one who mentioned the fly. But surely we must forgive outstanding men when they presume too much of themselves? After all, a man who has to achieve great things must have the courage to do them and must have confidence in himself. He should not be cowardly or abject, though he should be modest in his words, presuming less of himself than he achieves and being careful, too, that his presumption does not turn to rashness.'

After the Count had fallen silent for a moment, Bernardo Bibbiena said, with a smile:

'I remember your saying earlier that this courtier of ours should be naturally endowed with beauty of countenance and person and with an attractive grace. Well, I feel sure that I possess both grace and beauty of countenance, and that's why so many women, as you know, are madly in love with me. But when it comes to the beauty of my person, I am rather doubtful, and especially as regards these legs of mine which do not seem to me to be as good as I would wish; still, as to my chest and so on, I am quite satisfied. So please explain in more detail about what shape of body one should have, so that I can extricate myself from doubt and put my mind at rest.'

After everyone had laughed at this for a moment, the Count said:

'Certainly it's no lie to say that you possess the grace of countenance that I mentioned, and I have no need of any other example to illustrate it; for undoubtedly we can see that your appearance is very agreeable and pleasing to all, even if your features are not very delicate, though then again you manage to appear both manly and graceful. This is a quality found in many different kinds of faces. And I would like our courtier to have the same aspect. I don't want him to appear soft and feminine as so many try to do, when they not only curl their hair and pluck their eyebrows but also preen themselves like the most wanton and dissolute creatures imaginable. Indeed, they appear so effeminate and languid in the way they walk, or stand, or do anything at all, that their limbs look as if they are about to fall apart; and they pronounce their words in such a drawling way that it seems as if they are about to expire on the spot. And the more they find themselves in the company of men of rank, the more they carry on like that. Since Nature has not in fact made them the ladies they want to seem and be, they should be treated not as honest women but as common whores and be driven out from all gentlemanly society, let alone the Courts of great lords.

'Then, as for the physical appearance of the courtier, I would say that all that is necessary is that he should be neither too small nor too big, since either of these two conditions causes a certain contemptuous wonder and men built in this way are stared at as if they were monsters. However, if one is forced to choose between the two evils, then it is better to be on the small side than unduly large; for men who are so huge are often found to be rather thick-headed, and moreover, they are also unsuited for sport and recreation, which I think most important for the courtier. So I wish our courtier to be well built, with finely proportioned members, and I would have him demonstrate strength and lightness and suppleness and be good at all the physical exercises befitting a warrior. Here, I believe, his first duty is to know how to handle expertly every kind of weapon, either on foot or mounted, to understand all their finer points, and to be especially well informed about all those weapons commonly used among gentlemen. For apart from their use in war, when perhaps the finer points may be neglected, often differences arise between one gentleman and another and lead to duels, and very often the weapons used are those that come immediately to hand. So, for safety's sake, it is important to know about them. And I am not one of those who assert that all skill is forgotten in a fight; because anyone who loses his skill at such a time shows that he has allowed his fear to rob him of his courage and his wits.

'I also believe that it is of the highest importance to know how to wrestle, since this often accompanies combat on foot. Next, both for his own sake and for his friends, the courtier should understand about seeking restitution and the conduct of disputes, and he should be skilled in seizing the advantage, and in all this he must show both courage and prudence. Nor should he be too anxious for these engagements, save when his honour demands it; for, as well as the considerable danger that an uncertain outcome brings with it, whoever rushes into these things precipitately and without urgent cause deserves to be gravely censured, even if he is successful. However, when a man has committed himself so far that he cannot withdraw without reproach then both in the preliminaries and in the duel itself he should be very deliberate. He should always show readiness and courage; and he should not behave like those who are always quibbling and arguing over points of honour, and when they have the choice of weapons, select those which can neither cut nor prick, arm themselves as if they had to face a cannonade, and, thinking it enough if they are not defeated, retreat all the time and keep on the defensive, giving proof of utter cowardice, and in this way making themselves the sport of children, like those two men from Ancona who fought at Perugia a little while ago, and made everyone who saw them burst out laughing.'

'And who were they?' asked Gaspare Pallavicino.

'Two cousins,' answered Cesare.

'And in their fighting, more like two dear brothers,' said the Count. Then he continued:

'Weapons are also often used in various sports during peacetime, and gentlemen often perform in public spectacles before the people and before ladies and great lords. So I wish our courtier to be an accomplished and versatile horseman and, as well as having a knowledge of horses and all the matters to do with riding, he should put every effort and diligence into surpassing the rest just a little in everything, so that he may always be recognized as superior. And as we read of Alcibiades, that he surpassed all those peoples among whom he lived, and each time in regard to what they claimed to be best at, so this courtier of ours should outstrip all others, and in regard to the things they know well. Thus it is the peculiar excellence of the Italians to ride well with the rein, to handle spirited horses very skilfully, and to tilt and joust; so in all this the courtier should compare with the best of them. In tourneys, in holding his ground, in forcing his way forward, he should compare with the best of the French; in volleying, in running bulls, in casting spears and darts, he should be outstanding among the Spaniards. But, above all, he should accompany his every act with a certain grace and fine judgement if he wishes to earn that universal regard which everyone covets.

'There are also many other sports which, although they do not directly require the use of weapons, are closely related to arms and demand a great deal of manly exertion. Among these it seems to me that hunting is the most important, since in many ways it resembles warfare; moreover, it is the true pastime of great lords, it is a suitable pursuit for a courtier, and we know that it was very popular in the ancient world. It is also fitting that the courtier should know how to swim, jump, run and cast the stone for, apart from the usefulness of these accomplishments in war, one is often required to display one's skill and such sports can help to build up a good reputation, especially with the crowd which the courtier always has to humour. Another noble sport which is very suitable for the courtier to play is tennis, for this shows how well he is built physically, how quick and agile he is in every member, and whether he has all the qualities demonstrated in most other games. I think no less highly of performing on horseback, which is certainly very exhausting and difficult but more than anything else serves to make a man wonderfully agile and dextrous; and apart from its usefulness, if agility on horseback is accompanied by gracefulness, in my opinion it makes a finer spectacle than any other sport. Then if our courtier possesses more than average skill in all these sports, I think he should ignore the others, such as turning cartwheels, tight-rope walking and that kind of thing, since these are more like acrobatics and hardly suitable for a gentleman. Then again, since one cannot always be taking part in such strenuous exercises (besides which constant repetition causes satiety and destroys the regard we have for rare things) one must always be sure to give variety to the way one lives by doing different things. So I would like the courtier sometimes to descend to calmer and more restful games, and to escape envy and enter pleasantly into the company of all the others by doing everything they do; although he should never fail to behave in a commendable manner and should rule all his actions with that good judgement which will not allow him to take part in any foolishness. Let him laugh, jest, banter, romp and dance, though in a fashion that always reflects good sense and discretion, and let him say and do everything with grace.'

Then Cesare Gonzaga said: 'It is certainly too soon to interrupt this discussion, but if I stay silent I shall not be taking advantage of my privilege of speaking and I shall fail to learn something more. And I hope I may be forgiven if I ask a question instead of contradicting. I believe this may be allowed me, following the example set by our Bernardo who, through his excessive desire to be thought handsome, has already violated the laws of our game by doing the same.'

'You see,' the Duchess commented, 'how a single transgression leads to any number of others. So the one who sins and gives a bad example, as Bernardo has done, deserves to be punished not only for his wrongdoing but also for that of the others.'

Then Cesare remarked: 'In that case, madam, I will be exempt from any penalty, since Bernardo is to be punished both for his own transgression and for mine.'

'On the contrary,' said the Duchess, 'you must both of you be punished twice: he for his own wrongdoing and for having persuaded you to err, and you for your own mistake and for having imitated the criminal.'

'Madam,' answered Cesare, 'I've done nothing criminal so far; so in order to let Bernardo have all the punishment to himself I'll keep quiet.'

He had already stopped talking when signora Emilia said with a laugh:

'Say whatever you please, because, if the Duchess allows, I shall forgive both the one who has transgressed and the one who is going to do something nearly as bad.'

Said the Duchess: 'Very well, then. But take care you do not deceive yourself and perhaps think that you deserve more praise for being clement than for being just. For if one is too forgiving with a transgressor, one injures the innocent. However, I don't want my sternness in reproaching your indulgence to mean that we fail to hear what Cesare has to ask.'

So then, at a sign from the Duchess and from signora Emilia, he at once began:

'If I remember rightly, my dear Count, it seems to me that you have repeated several times this evening that the courtier has to imbue with grace his movements, his gestures, his way of doing things and in short, his every action. And it appears to me that you require this in everything as the seasoning without which all other attributes and good qualities would be almost worthless. Now I admit that everyone should easily be persuaded of this, seeing that, by the very meaning of the word, it can be said that a man who behaves with grace finds it with others. You have said that this is very often a natural, God-given gift, and that even if it is not quite perfect it can be greatly enhanced by application and effort. It seems to me that those who are born as fortunate and as rich in such treasures as some we know have little need of any further instruction, since the gracious favour they have received from heaven raises them, almost despite themselves, higher than they might have desired, and makes everyone both like and admire them. I do not argue about this, since it is not in our power to acquire it of ourselves. But regarding those who receive from Nature only so much as to make it possible for them to acquire grace through enterprise, application and effort, I should like to know by what art, teaching and method they can gain this grace, both in sport and recreation which you believe are so important, and in everything else they say or do. Now since by praising this quality so highly you have, I believe, aroused in all of us a strong desire to obtain it, because of the task given you by signora Emilia, you are also obliged to satisfy us by teaching the way to do so.'

'I am not obliged,' said the Count, 'to teach you how to acquire grace, or indeed anything else, but only to show you what a perfect courtier should be. And I would not undertake the task of teaching you how to acquire this quality, especially as a little while ago I said that the courtier ought to know how to wrestle, and vault and so many other things which, never having learned them myself, I'm sure you know full well how I could teach them. Let it be enough that just as a good soldier knows how to tell the smith what style and shape and quality his armour should be, and yet cannot teach him how to hammer or temper it, so perhaps I shall know how to tell you what a perfect courtier should be, but not be able to teach you what you have to do to become one. However, although it is almost proverbial that grace cannot be learned, to satisfy your request as far as I can, I say that if anyone is to acquire grace as a sportsman or athlete (first assuming that he is not disqualified by Nature) he should start young and learn the principles from the best teachers. How important this seemed to King Philip of Macedon, for instance, can be seen from the fact that he wanted it to be Aristotle, the eminent philosopher, and perhaps the greatest ever, who should teach the elements of letters to his son Alexander. Then, coming to our own contemporaries, consider the physical grace and agility of Signor Galleazzo Sanseverino,[6] Grand Equerry of France, who performs so well in this respect because in addition to his natural aptitude he has made every endeavour to learn from good teachers and to keep company with outstanding men, taking from each of them the best he can give. Thus just as for wrestling, vaulting and the handling of various kinds of weapons he has taken as his guide our Pietro Monte, who as you know is the sole and unchallenged master in regard to every kind of trained strength and agility, so for riding, jousting and so forth he has always taken as his models those who have won recognition for such skills.

'Therefore anyone who wants to be a good pupil must not only do things well but must also make a constant effort to imitate and, if possible, exactly reproduce his master. And when he feels he has made some progress it is very profitable for him to observe different kinds of courtiers and, ruled by the good judgement that must always be his guide, take various qualities now from one man and now from another. Just as in the summer fields the bees wing their way among the plants from one flower to the next, so the courtier must acquire this grace from those who appear to possess it and take from each one the quality that seems most commendable. And he should certainly not act like a friend of ours, whom you all know, who thought that he greatly resembled King Ferdinand the Younger of Aragon, but had not tried to imitate him except in the way he raised his head and twisted a corner of his mouth, a habit which the King had acquired through illness. There are many like this, who think they are marvellous if they can simply resemble a great man in some one thing; and often they seize on the only defect he has. However, having already thought a great deal about how this grace is acquired, and leaving aside those who are endowed with it by their stars, I have discovered a universal rule which seems to apply more than any other in all human actions or words: namely, to steer away from affectation at all costs, as if it were a rough and dangerous reef, and (to use perhaps a novel word for it) to practise in all things a certain nonchalance which conceals all artistry and makes whatever one says or does seem uncontrived and effortless. I am sure that grace springs especially from this, since everyone knows how difficult it is to accomplish some unusual feat perfectly, and so facility in such things excites the greatest wonder; whereas, in contrast, to labour at what one is doing and, as we say, to make bones over it, shows an extreme lack of grace and causes everything, whatever its worth, to be discounted. So we can truthfully say that true art is what does not seem to be art; and the most important thing is to conceal it, because if it is revealed this discredits a man completely and ruins his reputation. I remember once having read of certain outstanding orators of the ancient world who, among the other things they did, tried hard to make everyone believe that they were ignorant of letters; and, dissembling their knowledge, they made their speeches appear to have been composed very simply and according to the promptings of Nature and truth rather than effort and artifice. For if the people had known of their skills, they would have been frightened of being deceived. So you see that to reveal intense application and skill robs everything of grace. Who is there among you who doesn't laugh when our Pierpaolo dances in that way of his, with those little jumps and with his legs stretched on tiptoe, keeping his head motionless, as if he were made of wood, and all so laboured that he seems to be counting every step? Who is so blind that he doesn't see in this the clumsiness of affectation? And in contrast we see in many of the men and women who are with us now, that graceful and nonchalant spontaneity (as it is often called) because of which they seem to be paying little, if any, attention to the way they speak or laugh or hold themselves, so that those who are watching them imagine that they couldn't and wouldn't ever know how to make a mistake.'

Then, without waiting, Bernardo Bibbiena said:

'Well, it seems that our Roberto has now found someone who will praise his style of dancing, which you all despise. For if the excellence we are discussing consists in being nonchalant, and displaying indifference, and thinking of anything except what one is actually doing, then when it comes to dancing Roberto is without equal, because to demonstrate that he isn't thinking of what he is doing he lets his clothes fall from his back and his slippers from his feet, and he dances away without bothering to pick them up.'

The Count went on: 'Since you wish me to continue with the discussion, I shall now say something about our faults. Do you not realize that what you are calling nonchalance in Roberto is in fact affectation, since he evidently goes to great pains to show that he is not thinking about what he is doing? He is really taking too much thought, and by passing the bounds of moderation his nonchalance is affected and inappropriate, and it has exactly the opposite effect of what is intended, namely, the concealment of art. So although nonchalance is praiseworthy as such, when it leads to someone letting the clothes fall off his back it degenerates as easily into affectation as does a meticulous regard for one's personal appearance (also praiseworthy as such) when it means holding one's head rigid for fear of spoiling one's coiffure, or carrying a mirror in the fold of one's cap and a comb in one's sleeve, and walking through the streets always followed by a page with a brush and sponge. For this kind of self-regard and nonchalance goes too much to extremes, which is always a fault and the opposite of the pure and agreeable simplicity which appeals to everyone. Notice how ungraceful a rider is when he forces himself to sit bolt upright in the saddle, as is said, in the Venetian way, in comparison with another who sits on his horse as free and relaxed as if he were on the ground. How much more agreeable and admired is a warrior when he is modest, saying little and boasting hardly ever, than one who is forever singing his own praises and threatening all and sundry with his swearing and bragging! And this is simply the affectation of wanting to appear a bold fellow. The same applies whatever one's profession; indeed, it holds good for every single thing we do or say.'

At this, the Magnifico Giuliano remarked: 'It certainly holds true in music, in which it is very wrong to have two perfect consonances one after the other; for our sense of hearing abhors this, whereas it often likes a second or a seventh, which in itself is a harsh and unbearable discord. This is because to continue in perfect consonances produces satiety and offers a harmony which is too affected; but this disappears when imperfect consonances are introduced to establish the contrast which keeps the listener in a state of expectancy, waiting for and enjoying the perfect consonances more eagerly and delighting in the discord of the second or seventh, as in a display of nonchalance.'

'So you see,' answered the Count, 'that affectation is as dangerous in music as in other things. Moreover, it is said to have been proverbial among certain great painters of the ancient world that excessive diligence is harmful; and Protogenes is said to have been censured by Apelles[7] for not knowing when to take his hands from the board.'

Then Cesare added: 'It seems to me that our Fra Serafino shares this same fault of not being able to take his hands from the board, at least not before all the food has been taken away as well.'*

The Count laughed and continued: 'What Apelles meant was that when painting Protogenes did not know when he had done enough; in other words, he was blaming him for finishing his work too thoroughly. So this quality which is the opposite of affectation,

* The pun, untranslatable into English, relies on the use of the same word *tavola* for both table and board or panel.

and which we are now calling nonchalance, apart from being the real source of grace, brings with it another advantage; for whatever action it accompanies, no matter how trivial it is, it not only reveals the skill of the person doing it but also very often causes it to be considered far greater than it really is. This is because it makes the onlookers believe that a man who performs well with so much facility must possess even greater skill than he does, and that if he took great pains and effort he would perform even better. To give other examples, consider a man using weapons, and about to throw a dart or handle a sword or some other weapon. If, without thinking about it, he casually takes up a position at the ready, so naturally that it seems as if his whole body assumes the right posture without any strain, then even if he does nothing more he demonstrates that he is in complete command of what he is doing. Similarly in dancing, a single step, a single unforced and graceful movement of the body, at once demonstrates the skill of the dancer. When a musician is singing and utters a single word ending in a group of notes with a sweet cadence, and with such ease that it seems effortless, that touch alone proves that he is capable of far more than he is doing. Then again, in painting, a single line which is not laboured, a single brush stroke made with ease, in such a way that it seems that the hand is completing the line by itself without any effort or guidance, clearly reveals the excellence of the artist, about whose competence everyone will then make his own judgement. The same happens in almost every other thing. Our courtier, therefore, will be judged to be perfect and will show grace in everything, and especially in his speech, if he shuns affectation. However, affectation is a vice of which only too many people are guilty, and sometimes our Lombards more than others, who, if they have been away from home for a year, on their return immediately start speaking Roman or Spanish or French, and God knows what. And all this springs from their over-anxiety to show how much they know; so that they put care and effort into acquiring a detestable vice. Certainly it would require a great deal of effort on my part if in these discussions of ours I wished to use those old Tuscan words which the Tuscans of today have discarded; and what's more I'm sure you would all laugh at me.'

At this, Federico remarked: 'It is true that in talking among ourselves as we are doing now it would perhaps be wrong to use those old Tuscan words; because, as you say, they would prove tedious both for the speaker and his listeners, and many of us would have difficulty in understanding them. But for myself I believe that it would be wrong not to make use of them in writing, because they impart considerable grace and authority to what is written, and they produce a style which is more dignified and sonorous than can be achieved with modern words.'

To this, the Count replied: 'I can hardly think how grace and authority may be conferred by words which should be eschewed not only (as you yourself admit) in the kind of conversation we are enjoying at the moment but also in any conceivable circumstance. For if any man of good judgement had to make a speech on a serious subject before the very senate of Florence, which is the capital of Tuscany, or had to discuss important business in private with a high-ranking Florentine, or even amusing things with a close friend, or romantic affairs with ladies or gentlemen, or had to join in the jesting and joking at feasts, games or anywhere else, whatever the time, place or subject, I am certain that he would go out of his way to avoid using those old Tuscan words. And if he did use them, as well as making a fool of himself he would give no little annoyance to anyone listening. So it seems to me very curious to accept as good in writing those very words which are shunned as wrong in all kinds of conversation, and to insist that what is never appropriate in speech should be highly appropriate when it comes to writing. For it is my belief that writing is nothing other than a kind of speech which remains in being after it has been uttered, the representation, as it were, or rather the very life of our words. And so in speech, which ceases to exist as soon as it is uttered, some things are perhaps tolerable which are not so in writing; because writing preserves the words and submits them to the judgement of the reader, who has the time to give them his considered attention. Therefore it is right that greater pains should be taken to make what is written more polished and correct; not, however, that the written words should be different from those which are spoken, but they should be chosen from the most beautiful of those employed in speech. If we were to allow in writing what is not allowed in speech, in my opinion there would be one very unfortunate result: namely, more liberties could be taken in an area demanding the strictest discipline, and all the endeavour that goes into writing would be harmful instead of beneficial. So surely the rule is that what is proper in writing is also proper in speaking; and the finest speech resembles the finest writing. Moreover, I believe that it is more important to make one's meaning clear in writing than in speaking; because unlike someone listening, the reader is not always present when the author is writing. However, I would praise any man who, as well as shunning the use of many old Tuscan words, also makes certain, whether he is writing or speaking, that he employs words in current usage in Tuscany or elsewhere in Italy which possess a certain grace when they are pronounced. It seems to me that anyone who follows some other practice runs the risk of that affectation which attracts so much censure and about which we were talking a moment ago.'

Then Federico said: 'I cannot deny, Count, that writing is a kind of speech. I would say, however, that if the spoken word is at all obscure what is said will fail to penetrate the mind of the listener and, since it will not be understood, will be useless. And this is not the case with writing, for if the words used by the writer carry with them a certain, I will not say difficulty but veiled subtlety, and so are not as familiar as those commonly used in speech, they give what is written greater authority and cause the reader to be more attentive and aware, and so reflect more deeply and enjoy the skill and message of the author; and by judiciously exerting himself a little he experiences the pleasure that is to be had from accomplishing difficult tasks. If the reader is so ignorant that he cannot overcome these difficulties, that is not the fault of the writer and his language should not, on this account, be judged to lack beauty. Therefore in writing I believe that it is right to use Tuscan words, and only those employed by the ancient Tuscans, because that is a convincing proof, tested by time, that they are sound and effective in conveying what they mean. Furthermore, they possess the grace and dignity which great age imparts not only to words but also to buildings, statues, pictures and to everything that is able to endure.

And often simply by such splendour and dignity they beautify one's diction, through whose force and eloquence everything, no matter how mean, can be so embellished that it deserves the highest praise. But this matter of contemporary usage, on which you put so much stress, seems to me highly dangerous and very often wrong. If some solecism or other is adopted by many ignorant people, this, in my opinion, hardly means that it should be accepted as a rule and followed by others. What is more, current practice varies a great deal, and there's not a city in Italy where the mode of speech is not different from everywhere else. However, since you have not felt obliged to declare which of them is the best, a man might just as well take up Bergamasque as Florentine and, according to you, this would be perfectly correct. It seems to me, therefore, that if one wants to avoid all misgivings and be absolutely certain, one has to decide to imitate someone who by common consent is accepted as sound, and to employ him continuously as a guide and protection against hostile critics. And this model (I mean in the vernacular) should be none other, I think, than Petrarch or Boccaccio;[8] and whoever strays from these two has to grope his way, like a man walking through the darkness without a light, and will frequently take the wrong path. But nowadays we are so headstrong that we are contemptuous of doing what the best men did in the ancient world, namely, of practising imitation. But unless we do I believe it is impossible to write well. It seems to me that there is convincing proof of this in Virgil who, although his inspired judgement and genius were such that he made it impossible for anyone afterwards to hope to imitate him successfully, yet himself wished to imitate Homer.'

At this, signor Pallavicino remarked: 'This discussion about writing is certainly worth hearing. Nevertheless it would be more to our purpose if you would teach us the manner in which the courtier should speak, for it seems to me that he has more need of that, seeing that he has to make use of speech more often than of writing.'

The Magnifico answered: 'Rather, there is no doubt that so excellent and perfect a courtier must know both how to write and how to speak well, and without these two abilities surely all the rest would scarcely deserve praise. So if the Count wishes to fulfil his duty, he will teach the courtier not only to speak but also to write.'

At this, the Count said: 'Signor Magnifico, I will not accept this task, for it would certainly be the height of folly for me to wish to teach others what I do not know myself; and, even if I did know it, to think that in so few words I could do what very learned men have scarcely been able to do for all their diligence and effort. Indeed, if I still had to teach our courtier to write and speak I should refer him to their writings.'

Then Cesare said: 'The Magnifico means speaking and writing in the vernacular and not in Latin. So those writings by learned men which you mention are not to our purpose. But what you must do is tell us all that you know about this, and for the rest we shall hold you excused.'

'I've already said all I know,' answered the Count. 'But if we are concerned with the Tuscan language, no doubt it is the Magnifico more than anyone else who ought to express his opinion.'

The Magnifico said: 'I cannot and in all reason I should not contradict anyone who contends that the Tuscan language is more beautiful than the others. It is certainly the case that many words to be found in Petrarch and Boccaccio have been left behind by contemporary usage; and for myself, I would never use these, either in speaking or writing, and I believe that they, too, had they lived till now, would no longer employ them.'

Federico remarked:

'On the contrary, they would employ them; and you Tuscan gentlemen ought to renew your own language and not allow it to die, as you are doing. For it can be said nowadays that there is less knowledge of Tuscan in Florence than in many other parts of Italy.'

Bernardo commented:

'Those words that are no longer heard in Florence are still in use among the peasants, but are rejected by the well-born because they have been corrupted and spoiled by age.'

At this point, the Duchess said: 'Rather than stray from our original purpose, let us have Count Lodovico teach the courtier how to speak and write well, either Tuscan or something else.'

'Madam,' answered the Count, 'I have already told you what I know on this score, and I maintain that the rules that apply to speaking are the same as those for writing. But since you command me, I will say what comes to mind in answer to Federico, who differs from my opinion. Perhaps I will have to speak at somewhat greater length than is suitable, but it will be all I am able to say. First of all, then, in my opinion, this language of ours which we call the vulgar tongue is still fresh and new, although it has already been in use for some while. For, since Italy has not only been despoiled and ravaged but also, for a long period of time, occupied by the barbarians, through contact with these nations the Latin language has been corrupted and spoiled, and other languages have emerged from that corruption. These, like the rivers that divide at the crest of the Apennines and flow into the sea on either side, have also divided. Some that were tinged with elements of Latin have flowed through various channels to various regions of the world; one of them, tinged with barbarism, remained in Italy. And this language, since there was no one to take care of it or use it for writing or endeavour to give it any grace or splendour, was for a long time in a state of disorder and flux. Subsequently, however, it came to be cultivated more in Tuscany than anywhere else in Italy; and because of this it appears to have flourished there from those early times, because more than any others the Tuscans preserved a cultured pronunciation and the correct grammatical order, and moreover have had three noble writers* who expressed their ideas ingeniously, using contemporary words and terms. (And, in my opinion, in this the most successful, when it came to the subject of love, was Petrarch.) Then, from time to time, not only in Tuscany but throughout Italy, among well-born men, experienced in courtly behaviour, arms and letters, there arose the ambition to speak and write more elegantly than in those early rude and uncultivated years, when the flames from the disasters caused by the barbarians were still flickering. So, many words were discarded, in the city of Florence itself and throughout Tuscany, as in the rest of Italy, and others were adopted in their place, causing the change that occurs in all human affairs, and this has always been the experience of other languages. For if the earliest Latin writings had

* Namely, Petrarch, Boccaccio and Dante (1265–1321).

survived until now, we should discover that Evander and Turnus and the other Latins of those times spoke otherwise than the last kings of Rome or the first consuls. For example, the verses the Salian priests sang were scarcely understood by later generations, but since they were composed in that way by those who first formally set them down, out of religious reverence they were left unaltered. And then one after the other the orators and poets gradually abandoned many of the words employed by their predecessors: for Antonius, Crassus, Hortensius and Cicero rejected many of Cato's words, and Virgil many of those used by Ennius; and others followed suit. Even though they revered antiquity, they did not regard it so highly as to wish to be limited by it in the way you want us to be today. On the contrary, whenever they saw fit to do so they criticized it, as did Horace, for example, who says that his forbears had been foolish in their praise of Plautus, and asserts his right to acquire new words. Then again, in many places Cicero reprehends many of his predecessors, and in criticizing Sergius Galba he asserts that his orations tend too much towards the antique; and he also says that Ennius himself spurned his predecessors in certain things.[9] So by insisting on imitating the ancients we fail to imitate them. And as for Virgil, who you say imitated Homer, he did not imitate his language.

'So for myself I would always shun the use of these antique words, except on certain occasions and even then very rarely; and it seems to me that the man who does otherwise is making as big a mistake as someone who, in order to imitate the ancients, would choose to make a meal of acorns even though there was plenty of flour. And to your claim that antique words, simply because of their ancient splendour, enhance every subject so greatly that, no matter how trivial it is, they make it praiseworthy, I reply that I do not judge even good let alone antique words so uncritically as to believe that they should be valued even if they lack the substance of good sense. Because to divorce sense from words is like divorcing the soul from the body: in neither case can this be done without causing destruction. What the courtier especially requires in order to speak and write well, therefore, is knowledge, because the man who lacks knowledge and has nothing in his mind worth hearing has nothing worth writing or speaking. Then, it is necessary to arrange what is to be said or written in its logical order, and after that to express it well in words that, if I am not mistaken, should be appropriate, carefully chosen, clear and well formed, but above all that are still in popular use. For it is the words themselves which give an oration its greatness and magnificence, provided the orator employs good judgement and care, knows how to choose those which best express what he means, and how to enhance them, shaping them to his purpose like wax and arranging them in relation to one another so well that their clarity and worth are immediately evident, as if they were paintings hung in a good and natural light. I intend this to hold good both for writing and for speaking, although the orator needs some additional qualities, such as a good voice, not too thin and soft like a woman's nor so hard and rough as to sound boorish, but sonorous, resonant and well articulated, with distinct enunciation and accompanied by a suitable manner and gestures. These, in my opinion, should consist in certain movements of the entire body, not affected or violent but tempered by an agreeable expression of the face and movement of the eyes giving grace and emphasis to what is said, together with gestures to make as plain as possible the meaning and sentiments of the orator. But all this would be futile and of little consequence if the ideas conveyed by the words being used were not beautiful, witty, shrewd, elegant or solemn, according to the need.'

'I'm afraid,' said signor Morello, 'that if this courtier of ours spoke with such elegance and gravity some of us would not understand him.'

'On the contrary,' answered the Count, 'he would be understood by all, since lucidity can go hand in hand with elegance. But I would have him speak not always of serious subjects but also of amusing things, such as games and jests and jokes, according to the occasion. He should always, of course, speak out fully and frankly, and avoid talking nonsense or displaying any kind of vanity or childish silliness. And when he comes to discuss obscure or difficult matters, I want both his ideas and words to be so precisely formulated that he makes his meaning absolutely plain, taking pains to clarify every ambiguity, without being pedantic. Similarly, when the circumstances are opportune, he should be capable of speaking with dignity and emphasis, and of arousing our deepest emotions, kindling and stirring them as the need arises. And at other times he should know how to speak with such simple candour that it seems like Nature herself softening and, as it were, drugging our emotions with sweetness, and doing all this with such easy competence that the listener is given to believe that with very little effort he would be able to achieve the same standard of excellence, though when he makes the attempt he falls a long way short. This is the manner in which I would have our courtier speak and write; he should choose clear and beautiful words from the speech current in all parts of Italy, though I would also praise him for sometimes employing terms, whether French or Spanish, that are now accepted here. Thus, if the need arose, I would not be upset if he were to say *primor*, *accertare*, *avventurare*, or were to make use of the phrase *ripassare una persona con ragionamento*, meaning to observe and keep company with someone so as to know him perfectly. He may also say *un cavalier senza rimprocio*, or *attillato*, or *creato d'un principe*, and other such terms, provided he hopes to be understood.* Sometimes, too, I would like him to use certain words in a metaphorical sense, whenever it is appropriate, putting them to novel use like a gardener grafting a branch on to a healthier trunk, and so increasing their attractiveness and beauty, so that what is said or written makes us seem to experience things at first hand and greatly increases our enjoyment. Then again, he should not hesitate to coin new words altogether, and to make use of novel figures of speech, taking these over elegantly from the Latin as the Romans once took them from the Greeks.

'Therefore if among educated men, living today, of good intellect and judgement, some were to take the trouble to write in Italian, in the way I described, things which were worth reading, we should soon find our language adorned and enriched with fine

* The meaning of these words or phrases, some of which became fully accepted in Italian, was: *primor*, excellence or goodness; *accertare*, to hit the mark, to turn out well; *avventurare*, to venture; *un cavalier senza rimprocio*, a man of honour; *attillato*, attired; *creato*, a servant or dependent. *Ripassare* now has the meaning of 'to rebuff'.

phrases and figures of speech, and as good a medium for literature as any other. And if it did not then have the purity of old Tuscan, it would yet be Italian, universal, rich and varied, like a delightful garden full of all kinds of flowers and fruits. This phenomenon would be nothing new, since from each of the four languages on which they could draw, the Greeks selected whatever words, expressions and figures of speech they wished, and constructed a new so-called common language; and subsequently all five of these dialects were known collectively as the Greek language. Certainly, Attic was more elegant, pure and rich than the rest, but good writers who were not Athenians did not adopt it so slavishly as to destroy the distinctiveness of their own style and, as it were, the accent and savour of their natural dialect. But they were not despised because of this; on the contrary, writers were censured when they tried to appear too Athenian. Among Latin writers also there were many from outside Rome who in their day were highly regarded, even though they were seen not to possess that purity of Latin which those speaking another language are rarely able to acquire. Thus Titus Livius was not rejected, even though one critic said he found traces of Paduan in his work; nor was Virgil, on the grounds that he did not speak the Latin of Rome; and, as you know, in Rome many writers of barbarian origins, even, were read and esteemed. But we, being far more strict than the ancients, impose on ourselves certain outrageous new laws, and although the beaten track is there for us to see, we wander away from it. For although the function of our own language, as of all the others, is to express clearly and well what is in our minds, we take delight in being obscure; and although we call it the common tongue we want to employ in it words that are not understood even by noble and educated men, let alone the common people, and are everywhere obsolete, regardless of the fact that all the educated men of the ancient world spurn words that have fallen out of use. Indeed, in my opinion you simply do not understand this question of usage, since if there is some solecism current among uneducated people you say that therefore it should not be called common usage or accepted as proper speech. And from what I have heard you say on other occasions you would have us use *Campidoglio* in place of *Capitolio*, *Girolamo* instead of *Jeronimo*, *aldace* instead of *audace*, *padrone* instead of *patrone* and so forth, because these words were written in that way by some ignorant Tuscan long ago and are current in the same form today among Tuscan peasants. Thus good usage in speech, so I believe, is established by men of discernment, who through learning and experience have acquired sound judgement, which enables them to agree among themselves and consent to accept those words which commend themselves to them; and these they recognize by means of a certain instinctive judgement and not by any formula or rule. Do you not realize that these figures of speech which give such grace and clarity to what we say are all abuses of grammatical rules but are accepted and established by usage because (and this is the only possible reason) they are pleasing and insinuate their charm through our sense of hearing? To my mind, this is the essence of good usage, of which the Romans, the Neapolitans, the Lombards and the rest are as capable as the Tuscans.

'To be sure, some qualities are always good in any language: for example, fluency, correct sequences, richness, well-constructed periods and harmonious clauses. On the other hand, affectation, like everything else that contradicts what I have just said, is deplorable. Admittedly, there are certain words that remain good for some time, and then grow stale and lose their charm, as there are others that acquire new force and come into favour. Just as the seasons of the year divest the earth of its flowers and fruits, and then adorn it again with others, so time causes those first words to decline and then usage gives life to others, endowing them with grace and dignity until, gradually worn away by the envious depredations of time, they also go to their death; for, at the last, we and all our possessions are mortal. For example, we no longer have any knowledge of the Oscan language. And Provençal, which we may say only a short while ago was honoured by the most eminent writers, is now unknown by the people of that region. I think therefore that as the Magnifico so rightly said, if Petrarch and Boccaccio were living now they would discard many of the words to be found in their writings; and so it does not seem right to me to copy the words they use. I certainly yield to no one in praising those who know how to imitate what should be imitated; nevertheless, I think it is possible to write perfectly well even without imitation, and especially in our own language in which we can be guided by usage, which I would not venture to say of Latin.'

Then Federico asked: 'Why, would you have usage more highly regarded in the vernacular than in Latin?'

'No,' replied the Count, 'I maintain that usage rules both. But since those to whom Latin was as natural as the vernacular is to us are no longer living we must go to what they wrote to learn what they learned from usage. And when we refer to the language of the ancient world all we mean is the usage of the ancient world in its language. It would be foolish to love the language of the classical world for no other reason than to want to speak as was the custom then rather than as we do now.'

'Then you mean,' asked Federico, 'that the men of that time did not practise imitation?'

'I believe,' the Count replied, 'that there were many who did so, but not in everything. For if Virgil had slavishly imitated Hesiod[10] he would not have surpassed him; neither would Cicero have surpassed Crassus, nor Ennius those who preceded him. Remember that Homer lived so long ago that he is believed by many to have been the first heroic poet in point of time as well as excellence of style; and whom do you think he can have imitated?'

'Someone else,' said Federico, 'still earlier than he, of whom we lack knowledge since it was so long ago.'

'Who was it, then,' the Count went on, 'that provided a model for Petrarch and Boccaccio who, we may say, wrote only the day before yesterday?'

'I have no idea,' Federico answered. 'But we can be sure that they were also intent on imitating someone, although we do not know who it was.'

Then the Count said: 'We can also rest assured that those who were copied were superior to their imitators; and it would be too astonishing for words if their names and reputations, if they were good, had been utterly forgotten so soon. For myself, I believe that their true teacher was their own instinctive judgement and genius; and no one should be surprised by this, since in every sphere one can almost always reach the height of perfection in various ways. Nor is there anything which does not contain various elements which are related but dissimilar, and all of which merit equal praise. In music, for example, the strains are now solemn and slow, now very fast and different in mood and manner. Yet the performance is always agreeable, though for varying reasons. For example, Bidon's style of singing is so skilful, quick, vehement and passionate, and of such melodious variety, that the spirits of those listening are excited and aroused, and feel so exalted that they seem to be drawn up to heaven. Then the singing of our own Marchetto Cara is just as moving, but its harmonies are softer; his voice is so serene and so full of plaintive sweetness that he gently touches and penetrates our souls, and they respond with great delight and emotion.[11] Similarly, our eyes are equally delighted by spectacles of various kinds, so that it is difficult to decide what pleases them best. In painting, for example, Leonardo da Vinci, Mantegna, Raphael, Michelangelo and Giorgio da Castelfranco are all outstanding; nevertheless, they are all unlike each other in their work. So considered separately, none of them seems to lack anything, since each is perfect in his own personal style. The same holds good for many Greek and Latin poets, all writing in different ways, yet all of equal merit. Orators, too, have always been so different the one from the other that almost every age has produced and revered those whose talents were peculiar to their time and who could be distinguished not only from their predecessors but also from each other, as we find it written of Isocrates, Lysias, Aeschines and many others among the Greeks, who were all outstanding and each of whom resembled only himself. Again, among the Romans, Carbo, Laelius, Scipio Africanus, Galba, Sulpicius, Cotta, Gracchus, Marcus Antonius, Crassus and so many others that it would take too long to name them, were all good yet all very dissimilar.[12] In consequence, if we were to be able to study all those that have ever lived we would find as many different styles of oratory as there have been orators. Moreover, I seem to remember that somewhere Cicero has Marcus Antonius say to Sulpicius that there are many who imitate no one and yet reach the highest pitch of excellence; and he speaks of certain orators who had introduced a new form and fashion of speech-making, which was beautiful but unusual for its time, in which they followed no one but themselves.

And he also affirms that teachers should study the disposition of their pupils and, guided by that, direct and assist them along the path to which they are inclined by their own instincts and genius. Therefore, my dear Federico, I believe that it is wrong to force an author to imitate someone for whom he feels no natural affinity; for his creative vigour will be weakened and frustrated by being turned from the path which it might otherwise have followed to advantage. Therefore I do not understand how it can be right, instead of enriching our language and giving it its own genius, grandeur and insight, to make it impoverished, meagre, abject and obscure, and to try to cramp it by insisting that everyone should imitate only Boccaccio and Petrarch and refuse to place any confidence in Politian, Lorenzo de' Medici, Francesco Diacceto[13] and several others who are also Tuscan and no doubt just as learned and judicious as Boccaccio and Petrarch. Surely it would be a great shame to stop and refuse to go beyond that which the very earliest of our writers may have achieved, and to despair of the possibility of so many highly talented men finding more than one beautiful way of expressing themselves in their own natural language. Yet today there are certain pedants who make such an ineffable mystery and cult of this Tuscan language of theirs that they frighten those who hear them and thereby make even many noble and learned men nervous of opening their mouths and ready to confess that they do not understand the language they learned from their nursemaids when they were still in swaddling clothes. But now I think we have said more than enough on this subject; so let us continue with our discussion of the courtier.'

However, Federico replied: 'I should like to add just a little more, namely, that I certainly don't deny that men possess varying opinions and talents; nor do I believe that a man who has an emotional and assertive nature should set himself to write about restful subjects or still less a serious and grave man write in a frivolous way. For as far as this is concerned it seems to me reasonable that everyone should follow his own inclination. And this, I think, was what Cicero meant when he said that teachers should pay regard to the nature of their pupils and not act like stupid farmers who would sometimes sow grain in ground fit only for vines. But I cannot for the life of me understand why, when it is a matter of a particular language which is not common to all men (as are speaking and thinking and many other functions), but an invention with rules and limit, it should not be more reasonable to imitate those who speak it well than to speak at random; or why, just as in Latin one should strive to emulate the language of Virgil and Cicero rather than that of Silius or Cornelius Tacitus, it should not be better in the vernacular to emulate that of Petrarch and Boccaccio rather than anyone else. Certainly, one should express one's own thoughts and in so doing follow one's natural inclinations, as Cicero teaches. In this way it will be found that the difference which you say exists among good orators consists in the sense of what they say and not the language they use.'

In response to this, the Count said: 'I'm afraid we are now entering a very wide field of discussion and losing sight of our original theme. Still, let me ask you: what does the genius of language consist in?'

'In carefully observing its proprieties,' answered Federico, 'in adopting the same meanings, and using the same style and rhythms, as all the best writers.'

'I should like to know,' asked the Count, 'if that style and those rhythms belong to the thoughts expressed or to the words themselves.'

'To the words,' replied Federico.

'Then,' the Count went on, 'do you not think that the words in Silius and Cornelius Tacitus are the same as those used by Virgil and Cicero, and carry the same meaning?'

'Indeed yes,' said Federico, 'they are the same, but some of them have been corrupted and are used in a different sense.'

The Count replied: 'So if one removed from books by Tacitus and Silius those very few words used in a different sense from what they have in Virgil and Cicero, would you not then agree that as a writer Tacitus was the equal of Cicero and Silius of Virgil, and that it would be right to imitate their style?'

At this point, signora Emilia interrupted: 'It seems to me that this argument of yours has grown too protracted and tedious. So it would be as well to postpone it to another time.'

Federico started to answer all the same, but signora Emilia refused to let him; and eventually the Count remarked:

'There are many who want to judge style and discuss the rhythms of language and the question of imitation, yet cannot explain to me what style and rhythm are, or how to define imitation, or why things taken from Homer or someone else read so well in Virgil that they seem improved rather than plagiarized. Perhaps the reason for this is that I am not capable of understanding them. But since it is a convincing proof of whether a man understands something that he has the ability to teach it, I fear that they understand it very little themselves, and that they praise both Virgil and Cicero because they are aware that many others praise them and not because they recognize the difference between them and the rest. For certainly the difference does not consist in their preserving a few words or so in a usage different from that of the others. In Sallust, in Caesar, in Varro and in other good writers we find several terms used differently from the way Cicero employs them; yet both ways are perfectly acceptable, since the strength and genius of a language does not consist in such trifles: as Demosthenes rightly said to Aeschines, who asked him sarcastically whether some of the words he had used, which were not Attic, were monsters or portents; and Demosthenes simply laughed at this and replied that the fortunes of Greece hardly depended on that.[14] So what cause should I have to worry if some Tuscan or other reproved me for saying *satisfatto* rather than *sodisfatto*, *onorevole* rather than *orrevole*, *causa* rather than *cagione*, *populo* rather than *popolo* and so forth?'*

At this Federico stood up and exclaimed: 'Now I beg you, listen to me for a moment.'

But signora Emilia said with a laugh: 'No, I shall be most displeased with any one of you who continues with this subject at the moment, for I wish the discussion to be postponed until another evening. But you, my dear Count, please continue with your discussion of the courtier, and show us what a good memory you have, because I think that if you can begin where you left off it will be quite a feat.'

* The Italian words cited by Count Lodovico mean: satisfied, honourable cause and people.

'I fear,' answered the Count, 'that I have lost the thread. However, unless I am mistaken, we were saying that the taint of affectation always robs everything of grace and that the highest degree of grace is conferred by simplicity and nonchalance, in praise of which, and in condemnation of affectation, much more could be said. However, I want to add just one more thing and that is all. Now, every woman is extremely anxious to be beautiful or at least, failing that, to appear so. So when Nature has fallen short in some way, she endeavours to remedy the failure by artificial means. That is why we have women beautifying their faces so carefully and sometimes painfully, plucking their eyebrows and forehead, and using all those tricks and suffering all those little agonies which you ladies imagine men know nothing about but which they know only too well.'

Here, madonna Costanza Fregoso laughed and said: 'It would be far more courteous of you to continue with your discussion and to say what is the source of grace and speak of courtiership, rather than seek to expose the faults of women to no purpose.'

'On the contrary, it is very much to the purpose,' answered the Count, 'because these faults of yours that I mention rob you of grace, seeing that they spring only from affectation, through which you make it clear to everyone that you are excessively anxious to be beautiful. Surely you realize how much more graceful a woman is who, if indeed she wishes to do so, paints herself so sparingly and so little that whoever looks at her is unsure whether she is made-up or not, in comparison with one whose face is so encrusted that she seems to be wearing a mask and who dare not laugh for fear of causing it to crack, and who changes colour only when she dresses in the morning, after which she stays stock-still all the rest of the day, like a wooden statue, letting herself be seen only by torchlight, in the way a wily merchant shows his cloth in a dark corner. How much more attractive than all the others is a pretty woman who is quite clearly wearing no make-up on her face, which is neither too pallid nor too red, and whose own colouring is natural and somewhat pale (but who occasionally blushes openly from embarrassment or for some other reason), who lets her unadorned hair fall casually and unarranged, and whose gestures are simple and natural, betraying no effort or anxiety to be beautiful. Such is the uncontrived simplicity which is most attractive to the eyes and minds of men, who are always afraid of being tricked by art. In a woman, lovely teeth are always very pleasing, for since they are hidden from view most of the time, unlike the rest of the face, it can be believed that less effort has been spent on making them look beautiful; and yet those who laugh to no purpose and merely to display their teeth, betray their artificiality, and however good-looking they may be would seem to everyone most ungraceful, like Catullus' Egnatius.[15] The same is true of the hands which, if they are delicate and fine, and are uncovered at the right time, when there is need to use and not just to display their beauty, leave one with a great desire to see more of them, especially after they have been covered again with gloves. For it appears that the person who covers them hardly cares or worries whether they are seen or not, and has beautiful hands more by Nature than through any effort or design. Surely, too, you have sometimes noticed when a woman, passing along the street on her way perhaps to church, happens, in play or for some other reason, to raise just enough of her skirts to reveal her foot and often a little of her leg as well. Does it not strike you as a truly graceful sight if she is seen just at that moment, delightfully feminine, showing her velvet ribbons and pretty stockings? Certainly I find it very agreeable, as I'm sure you all do, because everyone assumes that elegance in a place where it is generally hidden from view must be uncontrived and natural rather than carefully calculated, and that it cannot be intended to win admiration.

'In this way affectation is avoided or hidden; and now you can see how incompatible it is with gracefulness and how it robs of charm every movement of the body or of the soul, about which, admittedly, we have so far said very little. However, we should not neglect it; for, as the soul is far more worthy than the body, it deserves to be all the more cultivated and adorned. As for what our courtier ought to do in this respect, we shall leave aside the precepts of all the many wise philosophers who have written on the subject, defining the virtues of the soul and discussing their worth with such subtlety; instead, keeping to our purpose, we shall state very simply that it is enough if he is, as we say, a man of honour and integrity. For this includes prudence, goodness, fortitude and temperance of soul, and all the other qualities proper to so honourable a name. And I believe that he alone is a true moral philosopher who wishes to be good; and for this he needs few precepts other than the ambition itself. Therefore Socrates was perfectly right in affirming that in his opinion his teaching bore good fruit when it encouraged someone to strive to know and understand virtue; for those who have reached the stage where they desire nothing more eagerly than to be good have no trouble in learning all that is necessary. So I shall say no more about this.

'However, in addition to goodness, I believe that for all of us the true and principal adornment of the mind is letters; although the French, I know, recognize only the nobility of arms and think nothing of all the rest; and so they not only do not appreciate learning but detest it, regarding men of letters as basely inferior and thinking it a great insult to call anyone a scholar.'

Then the Magnifico Giuliano remarked:

'You are right in saying that this error has prevailed among the French for a long time now; but if good fortune has it that Monseigneur d'Angoulême,[16] as it is hoped, succeeds to the throne, then I believe that just as the glory of arms flourishes and shines in France, so also with the greatest brilliance must that of letters. For, when I was at that Court not so long ago, I set eyes on this prince, and it seemed to me that, besides his handsome looks, there was such an air of greatness about him, accompanied, however, by a certain gracious humanity, that the kingdom of France on its own must always seem too limited for him. And subsequently from many gentlemen, both French and Italian, I heard a great deal in praise of his noble courtesy, his magnanimity, his valour and his generous spirit; and among other things I was told that he greatly loved and esteemed learning and respected all men of letters, and that he condemned the French themselves for being so hostile to this profession, especially as they have in their midst as magnificent a university as Paris, where people flock from all over the world.'

Then the Count added: 'It is a marvellous thing that at such a tender age, guided solely by his natural instincts and departing from the usual attitudes of his countrymen, he should of himself have chosen so commendable a path. And since subjects always imitate the behaviour of their rulers, it could well be, as you say, that the French may yet come to value learning at its true worth. They could easily be persuaded to if they would listen to reason, since nothing is more naturally desired by men or more proper to them than knowledge, and it is the height of folly to say or believe that it is not always a good thing.

'If I could speak with them or with others whose opinion does not agree with mine I would endeavour to show them how useful and necessary letters are to human dignity and life. For they were surely given by God as his supreme gift to mankind. And I should not lack examples from among those many great commanders of the ancient world, in all of whom prowess at arms was accompanied by the glory of learning. For, as you know, Alexander revered Homer so highly that he always kept the *Iliad* at his bedside. And he gave the greatest attention not only to these studies but also to philosophical speculations, under the guidance of Aristotle. Taught by Socrates, Alcibiades used letters to increase and enhance his good qualities. The attention which Caesar gave to study is attested by his own inspired writings. It is said that Scipio Africanus constantly had by him the works of Xenophon, in which, under the name of Cyrus, is drawn the portrait of a perfect king. I could cite Lucullus, Sulla, Pompey, Brutus and many other Romans and Greeks; but I shall just remind you that so excellent a commander as Hannibal, though naturally fierce and a stranger to humanity, treacherous and contemptuous both of men and the gods, none the less was something of a scholar and understood the Greek language. And if I am not mistaken I once read that he even left a book written by himself in Greek.[17] But there is no call to tell you this, since I well know that you all realize how wrong the French are in thinking that letters are detrimental to arms. You know that in war what really spurs men on to bold deeds is the desire for glory, whereas anyone who acts for gain or from any other motive not only fails to accomplish anything worth while but deserves to be called a miserable merchant rather than a gentleman. And it is true glory that is entrusted to the sacred treasury of letters, as everyone knows except those who are so unfortunate as not to have made their acquaintance. When he reads about the great deeds of Caesar, Alexander, Scipio, Hannibal and all the others, who is so cringing, timorous and abject that he does not burn with the ambition to emulate them and is not ready to relinquish his all too brief natural life in favour of an almost eternal fame, which makes him live on more splendidly after death? But those who do not appreciate the pleasures of learning cannot realize how great is the glory that they preserve for so long, and measure it only by the life of one or two men, since their own memories are limited. The kind of glory of which they have experience is nothing in comparison with the almost everlasting glory about which, unfortunately, they know nothing; and since, therefore, glory means so little to them, we may reasonably believe that, unlike those who understand its nature, they will run few risks in pursuing it. Now someone may object to what I am saying and attempt to disprove it by various examples: citing, for instance, the knowledge of letters shown by the Italians compared with their lack of valour on the battlefield during recent years. This is only too true; but surely it may be said that here the weakness of a few has inflicted grave misfortune along with lasting infamy on the many, and they are responsible for our ruin and the way our spirit has been weakened if not crushed. Yet it would be more shameful for us to make this known to the world than it is for the French to be ignorant of letters; so it is better to pass over in silence what we cannot recall without sorrow, and leaving this subject (which I took up unwillingly) to return to our courtier.

'I should like our courtier to be a more than average scholar, at least in those studies which we call the humanities; and he should have a knowledge of Greek as well as Latin, because of the many different things that are so beautifully written in that language. He should be very well acquainted with the poets, and no less with the orators and historians, and also skilled at writing both verse and prose, especially in our own language; for in addition to the satisfaction this will give him personally, it will enable him to provide constant entertainment for the ladies, who are usually very fond of such things. But if because of his other activities or through lack of study he fails to achieve a commendable standard in his writing, then he should take pains to suppress his work, to avoid ridicule, and he should show it only to a friend he can trust. And the exercise of writing will be profitable for him at least to the extent that it will teach him how to judge the work of others. For it is very unusual for someone who is not a practised writer, however erudite he may be, to understand completely the demanding work done by writers, or appreciate their stylistic accomplishments and triumphs and those subtle details characteristic of the writers of the ancient world. Moreover, these studies will make our courtier well informed and eloquent and (as Aristippus said to the tyrant) self-confident and assured no matter whom he is talking to.[18] However, I should like our courtier to keep one precept firmly in mind: namely, that in what I have just discussed and in everything else he should always be diffident and reserved rather than forward, and he should be on his guard against assuming that he knows what he does not know. For we are instinctively all too greedy for praise, and there is no sound or song that comes sweeter to our ears; praise, like Sirens' voices, is the kind of music that causes shipwreck to the man who does not stop his ears to its deceptive harmony. Recognizing this danger, some of the philosophers of the ancient world wrote books giving advice on how a man can tell the difference between a true friend and a flatterer. Even so, we may well ask what use is this, seeing that there are so many who realize perfectly well that they are listening to flattery, and yet love the flatterer and detest the one who tells them the truth. Indeed, very often, deciding that the one who praises them is not being fulsome enough, they lend him a hand themselves and say such things that even the most outrageous flatterer feels ashamed. Let us leave these blind fools to their errors and decide that our courtier should possess such good judgement that he will not be told that black is white or presume anything of himself unless he is certain that it is true, and especially in regard to those flaws which, if you remember, when he was suggesting his game for the evening Cesare recalled we had often used to demonstrate the particular folly of this person or another. To make no mistake at all, the courtier should, on the contrary, when he knows the praises he receives are deserved, not assent to them too openly nor let them pass without some protest. Rather he should tend to disclaim them modestly, always giving the impression that arms are, as indeed they should be, his chief profession, and that all his other fine accomplishments serve merely as adornments; and this should especially be his attitude when he is in the company of soldiers, lest he behave like those who in the world of scholarship want to be taken for warriors and among warriors want to seem men of letters. In this way, as we have said, he will avoid affectation, and even his modest achievements will appear great.'

At this point, Pietro Bembo interrupted: 'I cannot see, my dear Count, why you wish this courtier, who is so literate and so well endowed with other worthy qualities, to regard everything as serving to adorn the profession of arms, and not arms and the rest as serving to adorn the profession of letters, which, taken by themselves, are as superior in dignity to arms as is the soul to the body, since letters are a function of the soul, just as arms are of the body.'

Then the Count answered: 'On the contrary, the profession of arms pertains both to the soul and to the body. But I should not want you to be the judge of this, Pietro, because by one of the parties concerned it would be assumed that you were prejudiced. And as this is a controversy that the wisest men have already thrashed out, there is no call to re-open it. As it is, I consider that it has been settled in favour of arms; and since I may form our courtier as I wish, I want him to be of the same opinion. If you think the contrary, wait until you hear of a contest in which the man who defends the cause of arms is allowed to use them, just as those who defend the cause of letters make use of letters in their defence; for if each one uses his own weapons, you will see that the men of letters will lose.'

'Ah,' said Pietro Bembo, 'you were only too ready earlier on to damn the French for their scant appreciation of letters, and you mentioned the glory that they bring to men and the way they make a man immortal. And now you seem to have changed your mind. Do you not remember that:

Giunto Alessandro alla famosa tomba
del fero Achille, sospirando disse:
O fortunato, che sì chiara tromba
*trovasti, e chi di te sì alto scrisse!**

* The first quatrain of a sonnet by Petrarch, literally: 'When Alexander reached the famous tomb of fierce Achilles, he sighed and said: O happy man, who found so illustrious a trumpet, and one to write of you so nobly!'

And if Alexander was envious of Achilles not because of what he had done himself but because of the way he was blessed by fortune in having his deeds celebrated by Homer, we must conclude that he put a higher value on the writings of Homer than on the arms of Achilles. What other judge do you want, or what other verdict on the relative worth of arms and letters than the one delivered by one of the greatest commanders that has ever lived?'

The Count replied: 'I blame the French for believing that letters are harmful to the profession of arms, and I maintain myself that it is more fitting for a warrior to be educated than for anyone else; and I would have these two accomplishments, the one helping the other, as is most fitting, joined together in our courtier. I do not think that this means I have changed my opinion. But, as I said, I do not wish to argue which of them is more praiseworthy. Let it be enough that men of letters hardly ever choose to praise other than great men and glorious deeds, which deserve praise both on their own account and because, in addition, they provide writers with a truly noble theme. And this subject-matter embellishes what is written and, no doubt, is the reason why such writings endure, for otherwise, if they dealt not with noble deeds but with vain and trivial subjects, they would surely be read and appreciated less. And if Alexander was envious of Achilles because he was praised by Homer, it still does not necessarily follow that he thought more of letters than of arms; and if he had thought that he was as inferior to Achilles as a soldier as he believed that all those who would write about him were inferior to Homer as writers, he would, I am sure, have far preferred brave exploits on his own part to brave talk from others. Therefore I believe that when he said what he did, Alexander was tacitly praising himself, and expressing a desire for what he thought he lacked, namely supreme ability as a writer, rather than for what he took for granted he already had, namely prowess as a warrior, in which he was far from acknowledging Achilles as his superior. So when he called Achilles fortunate he meant that if so far his own fame did not rival that of Achilles (which had been made bright and illustrious through so inspired a poem) this was not because his valour and merits were less notable or less deserving of the highest praise but because of the way fortune had granted Achilles a born genius to be his herald and to trumpet his deeds to the world. Moreover, perhaps Alexander wanted to encourage some gifted person to write about him, showing that his pleasure in this would be as great as his love and respect for the sacred monuments of literature. And now we have said enough about this subject.'

'Indeed, far too much,' remarked signor Lodovico, 'for I don't think that one could discover anywhere in the world a vessel big enough to hold all the things you want to put into our courtier.'

'Just wait a moment,' replied the Count, 'because there are still many more things to come.'

Then Pietro da Napoli added: 'In that case, Grasso de' Medici[19] will have a great advantage over Pietro Bembo.'

After everyone had laughed at this, the Count continued as follows:

'Gentlemen, I must tell you that I am not satisfied with our courtier unless he is also a musician and unless as well as understanding and being able to read music he can play several instruments. For, when we think of it, during our leisure time we can find nothing more worthy or commendable to help our bodies relax and our spirits recuperate, especially at Court where, besides the way in which music helps everyone to forget his troubles, many things are done to please the ladies, whose tender and gentle souls are very susceptible to harmony and sweetness. So it is no wonder that both in ancient times and today they have always been extremely fond of musicians and have welcomed music as true refreshment for the spirit.'

Signor Gaspare commented: 'I think that music, like so many other vanities, is most certainly very suited to women, and perhaps also to some of those who have the appearance of men, but not to real men who should not indulge in pleasures which render their minds effeminate and so cause them to fear death.'

'Do not say that,' retorted the Count, 'or I shall launch into oceans of praise for music and remind you how greatly it was honoured in the ancient world, and held to be sacred, and that the wisest of philosophers held the opinion that the universe was made up of music, that the heavens make harmony as they move, and that as our own souls are formed on the same principle they are awakened and have their faculties, as it were, brought to life through music. And because of this it is recorded that Alexander was sometimes so stirred by music that almost against his will under its influence he was constrained to rise from the banquet table and rush to arms; then the musician would play something different, and growing calmer he would return from arms to the banquet. And, let me also tell you, grave Socrates, when he was already very old, learned to play the cithara. Moreover, I remember having heard that Plato and Aristotle insist that a well-educated man should also be a musician; and with innumerable arguments they show that music exerts a powerful influence on us, and, for many reasons that would take too long to explain, they say that it has to be learned in childhood, not so much for the sake of its audible melodies but because of its capacity to breed good new habits and a virtuous disposition and make the soul more receptive to happiness, just as exercise makes the body more robust; and they add that music far from being harmful to the pursuits of peace or war is greatly to their benefit. Then again, in the stern laws which he made, Lycurgus gave his approval to music. And we read that in battle the bellicose Spartans and Cretans used citharas and other sweet-sounding instruments; and that many outstanding commanders of the ancient world, such as Epaminondas, practised music, and those who were ignorant of music, such as Themistocles, were far less respected. Have you not heard, as well, that among the first subjects which the good Chiron taught to the young Achilles was music, and that this wise and venerable teacher wished the hands that were to shed so much Trojan blood often to be employed in playing the cithara?[20] What kind of warrior, then, would be ashamed to follow the example of Achilles, let alone all the other famous commanders whom I could cite? So you must not wish to deprive our courtier of music, which not only soothes the souls of men but often tames wild beasts. Indeed, the man who does not enjoy music can be sure that there is no harmony in his soul. And remember that it has such powers that once it caused a fish to let itself be ridden by a man over the tempestuous sea. We see it used in sacred places to render praise and thanks to God; and we may well believe that it is agreeable to God, and that He has given it to us as a soothing balm for our toils and tribulations. Thus common labourers in the field working under the burning sun will often relieve their tedium with simple country songs. And the ordinary peasant girl, rising before dawn to spin or weave, uses music to ward off sleep and make her work agreeable; distressed mariners, after the rains and the winds and the storms, love to relax with the help of music; weary pilgrims find solace in music on their long and exhausting journey, as so often do chained and fettered prisoners in their misery. As even stronger evidence that even the most unsophisticated melodies lighten the burden of all our toils and tribulations in this world, we find that Nature herself has taught it to the nurse as the sure way to still the persistent crying of young babies, who are lulled to quiet rest and sleep by the sound of her singing, forgetting the tears which at that age are right and proper as a presage of our later life.'

After the Count had been silent for a moment, the Magnifico Giuliano said:

'I am not at all of the same opinion as signor Gaspare; on the contrary, for the reasons you have given and for many others besides, I believe that music is not only an ornament but a necessity for the courtier. However, I should like you to explain how he is to practise this and the other accomplishments that you assign to him, and on what occasions and in what manner; for there are many things which in themselves are commendable but which are most unseemly when practised at the wrong time; and on the other hand, there are many things that seem inconsequential but which are greatly esteemed when performed on the appropriate occasion.'

'Before we launch into this subject,' the Count replied, 'I should like us to discuss something else again which, since I consider it highly important, I think our courtier should certainly not neglect: and this is the question of drawing and of the art of painting itself. And do not be surprised that I demand this ability, even if nowadays it may appear mechanical and hardly suited to a gentleman. For I recall having read that in the ancient world, and in Greece especially, children of gentle birth were required to learn painting at school, as a worthy and necessary accomplishment, and it was ranked among the foremost of the liberal arts; subsequently, a public law was passed forbidding it to be taught to slaves. It was also held in great honour among the Romans, and from it the very noble family of the Fabii took its name, for the first Fabius was called *Pictor*. He was, indeed, an outstanding painter, and so devoted to the art that when he painted the walls of the Temple of Salus he signed his name: this was because (despite his having been born into an illustrious family, honoured by so many consular titles, triumphs and other dignities, and despite the fact that he himself was a man of letters, learned in law and numbered among the orators) Fabius believed that he could enhance his name and reputation by leaving a memorial pointing out that he had also been a painter. And there was no lack of other celebrated painters belonging to other illustrious families. In fact, from painting, which is in itself a most worthy and noble art, many useful skills can be derived, and not least for military purposes: thus a knowledge of the art gives one the facility to sketch towns, rivers, bridges, citadels, fortresses and similar things, which otherwise cannot be shown to others even if, with a great deal of effort, the details are memorized. To be sure, anyone who does not esteem the art of painting seems to me to be quite wrong-headed. For when all is said and done, the very fabric of the universe, which we can contemplate in the vast spaces of heaven, so resplendent with their shining stars, in the earth at its centre, girdled by the seas, varied with mountains, rivers and valleys, and adorned with so many different varieties of trees, lovely flowers and grasses, can be said to be a great and noble painting, composed by Nature and the hand of God. And, in my opinion, whoever can imitate it deserves the highest praise. Nor is such imitation achieved without the knowledge of many things, as anyone who attempts the task well knows. Therefore in the ancient world both painting and painters were held in the greatest respect, and the art itself was brought to the highest pitch of excellence. Of this, a sure proof is to be found in the ancient marble and bronze statues which still survive; for although painting differs from sculpture, both the one and the other derive from the same source, namely from good design. So if the statues which have come down to us are inspired works of art we may readily believe that so, too, were the paintings of the ancient world;

indeed, they must have been still more so, because they required greater artistry.'

Then signora Emilia, turning to Giovan Cristoforo Romano, who was seated with the others, asked him:

'What do you think of this opinion? Would you agree that painting allows for greater artistry than sculpture?'

'Madam,' replied Giovan Cristoforo, 'I maintain that sculpture requires more effort and more skill than painting, and possesses greater dignity.'

The Count then remarked:

'Certainly statues are more durable, so perhaps they may be said to prove more dignified; for since they are intended for monuments, they serve the purpose for which they are made better than paintings. But, leaving aside the question of commemoration, both painting and sculpture also serve a decorative purpose, and in this regard painting is far superior. And if it is not, so to say, as enduring as sculpture, all the same it survives a long time, and for as long as it does so it is far more beautiful.'

Then Giovan Cristoforo replied:

'I truly believe that you are not saying what you really think, and this solely for the sake of your Raphael; and perhaps, as well, you feel that the excellence you perceive in his work as a painter is so supreme that it cannot be rivalled by any sculpture in marble. But remember that this is praise for the artist and not for his art.'

Then he continued:

'Indeed, I willingly accept that both painting and sculpture are skilful imitations of Nature; yet I still do not understand how you can maintain that what is real and is Nature's own creation cannot be more faithfully copied in a bronze or marble figure, in which all the members are rounded, fashioned and proportioned just as Nature makes them, than in a picture, consisting of a flat surface and colours that deceive the eye. And don't tell me that being is not nearer the truth than merely seeming to be. Moreover, I maintain that working in stone is far more difficult, because if a mistake is made it cannot be remedied, seeing that repairs are impossible with marble, and the figure must be started again; whereas this is not the case with painting, which can be gone over a thousand times, being improved all the time as parts of the picture are added to or removed.'

Then, with a smile, the Count replied:

'I am not arguing for the sake of Raphael, nor should you think me so ignorant as not to recognize the excellence shown by Michelangelo and yourself and other sculptors. But I am speaking of the art and not the artists. You say truly enough that both painting and sculpture are imitations of Nature; but it is not the case that the one seems to be what it portrays and the other really is so. For although statues are made in the round, like objects in real life, and painting is seen only on the surface, sculpture lacks many things to be found in painting, and especially light and shade: for example, the natural colouring of the flesh, which appears altogether changed in marble, the painter copies faithfully, using more or less light and shade according to need, which the sculptor cannot do. And even though the painter does not fashion his figures in the round, he does depict the muscles and members of the body rounded and merging into the unseen parts of his figures in such a way as to demonstrate his knowledge and understanding of these as well. The painter requires still greater skill in depicting members that are foreshortened and taper gradually away from the point of vision, on the principles of perspective. This, by means of proportioned lines, colours, light and shade, simulates foreground and distance on an upright surface, to the degree that the painter wishes. Does it, then, seem of little importance to you that Nature's colours can be reproduced in flesh-tints, in clothing and in all the other objects that are coloured in life? This is something the sculptor cannot do. Still less can he depict the love-light in a person's eyes, with their black or blue colouring; the colour of blond hair; the gleam of weapons; the darkness of night; a tempest at sea; thunder and lightning; a city in conflagration; or the break of rosy dawn with its rays of gold and red. In short, it is beyond his powers to depict sky, sea, land, mountains, woods, meadows, gardens, rivers, cities or houses; but not beyond the powers of the painter.

'So it seems to me that painting is nobler and allows of greater artistry than sculpture, and I believe that in the ancient world it reached the same perfection as other things; and this we can see from a few surviving works, especially in the catacombs in Rome, but far more clearly from the evidence of classical literature, which contains so many admiring references to both painting and painters, and informs us of the high esteem in which they were held by governments and rulers. For example, we read that Alexander was so fond of Apelles of Ephesus that once, after he had had him portray one of his favourite mistresses, and then heard that the worthy painter had fallen desperately in love with her marvellous beauty, without a second thought he gave the woman to him: this was an act of generosity truly worthy of Alexander, to give away not only treasures and states but his own affections and desires; and it showed, too, how deeply fond he was of Apelles, to please whom he cared nothing about the displeasure of the lady whom he loved so much himself, and who, we may well believe, was more than grieved to lose so great a king in exchange for a painter. Many instances are recorded of Alexander's kindness towards Apelles; but the clearest evidence of his esteem for him is seen in the decree he issued that no other painter should dare to do his portrait. Here I could tell you of the contests of so many noble painters, who were the admiration and wonder of the world; I could tell you of the magnificence with which the ancient emperors adorned their triumphs with pictures, dedicated them in public places, and acquired them as cherished possessions; I could tell you how some painters have been known to give their pictures away, believing that they could not be adequately paid for with gold or silver; and how a painting by Protogenes was so highly regarded that when Demetrius was laying siege to Rhodes and could have entered the city by setting fire to the quarter where he knew the painting was, rather than cause it to be burned he called off the attack, and so failed to take the place; and how Metrodorus, an outstanding painter and philosopher, was sent by the Athenians to Lucius Paulus to teach his children and to decorate the triumph that he had to make.[21] Moreover, many great authors have written about painting, and this is convincing evidence for the high regard in which it was held. But I would not have us carry this discussion any further. So let it be enough simply to state that it is fitting that our courtier should also have a knowledge of painting, since it is a worthy and beneficial art, and was greatly valued in the times when men were greater than now. And even if it had no other useful or pleasurable aspects, painting helps us to judge the merits of ancient and modern statues, of vases, buildings, medallions, cameos, intaglios and similar works, and it reveals the beauty of living bodies, with regard to both the delicacy of the countenance and the proportion of the other parts, in man as in all other creatures. So you see that a knowledge of painting is the source of very profound pleasure. And let those reflect on this who are so carried away when they see a beautiful woman that they think they are in paradise, and yet who cannot paint; for if they did know how to paint they would be all the more content, since they would then more perfectly discern the beauty that they find so agreeable.'

Cesare Gonzaga laughed at what had been said, and then commented:

'Of course, I am no painter myself, but I certainly derive far more pleasure from looking at a certain lady than would that most worthy Apelles whom you mentioned a moment ago, were he to come back to life.'

The Count replied: 'But this pleasure of yours is caused not entirely by her beauty but also by the affection you surely feel towards her. And, if you were truthful, you would confess that the first time you looked at that lady you did not feel the thousandth part of the pleasure you experienced later on, although her beauty was no less. So you can see that the pleasure was caused far more by your affection than by her beauty.'

'I would not deny that,' answered Cesare. 'But just as pleasure arises from affection, so affection is prompted by beauty. So we may still argue that the lady's beauty is the source of my pleasure.'

'Besides beauty, the heart is stirred by many other qualities, such as attractive manners, wisdom, speech, gestures and a hundred and one other things, all of which might be called forms of beauty; but, above all, by the feeling that one is loved oneself,' replied the Count.

'So even if that beauty you talk about were lacking, it would still be possible to love most ardently. But surely the love that is generated merely by physical beauty will give far more pleasure to the one who understands it more than to the one who understands it less. Therefore, to return to our subject, I think that when Apelles contemplated the beauty of Campaspe he must have enjoyed himself far more than did Alexander, since we may readily believe that both men's love for her was prompted solely by her beauty, and that this was why Alexander decided to give her to someone who, he believed, would understand it more perfectly. Have you not read that those five girls of Crotone, whom the painter Zeuxis chose from among all the others of that city for the purpose of forming from all five a single figure of consummate beauty, were celebrated by many poets because their beauty had won the approbation of one who must have been the most perfect judge?'[22]

Cesare was evidently not at all satisfied with this and was totally unwilling to grant that others besides himself could share the pleasure he felt in contemplating the beauty of the woman he mentioned, so he began to say more. Then, however, was heard the noise of a great tramping of feet and of raised voices, and, as everyone turned to see what was happening, there appeared at the door a blaze of torches preceding the arrival of the Prefect, with a large and noble escort. He was just coming back from accompanying the Pope on part of his journey; and immediately on entering the palace, having asked what the Duchess was doing, he had been told about the game for that evening and about the task given to Count Lodovico to discuss the nature of courtiership. So he was hurrying as fast as possible to join the gathering in time to hear something of what was being said. After he had paid his respects to the Duchess, therefore, and asked the others to sit down (since they had all risen to their feet on his arrival) he too sat down in the circle along with some of his gentlemen, among whom were the Marquess Febus da Ceva and his brother Ghirardino, Ettore Romano, Vincenzo Calmeta, Orazio Florido and many more. Then, as everyone remained silent, the Prefect said:

'Gentlemen, my arrival would have been most unfortunate if it meant interrupting the course of the splendid discussions which I believe have been taking place among you. But do not treat me badly by depriving me, and you yourselves, of such pleasure.'

Count Lodovico answered: 'On the contrary, sir, I think that everyone would find it more agreeable to keep silent than to speak; for as the task has fallen to me more than to the others this evening, I am tired of talking, and, I imagine, all the others are tired of listening, since my remarks were not worthy of this gathering nor equal to the importance of the subject that was chosen, concerning which, having given myself little satisfaction, I think I have given the others still less. So, sir, you were very fortunate to arrive at the end. And the best course now would be to hand over what remains to someone taking my place, because whoever he may be he will, I know, perform far better than I would if I were to carry on, being as tired as I am.'

'I absolutely refuse,' said the Magnifico Giuliano, 'to be cheated of the promise you made me; and I am sure that the Prefect will not be displeased to hear this part of the discussion.'

'And what was the promise?' asked the Count.

'To explain how the courtier should make use of the good qualities you said were fitting for him to have,' answered the Magnifico.

Now the Prefect, although still very young, was more wise and discreet than seemed possible for such tender years, and in all he did he displayed both magnanimity and a lively intelligence which was a true presage of his high qualities in later life. So, without hesitating, he said:

'If all this is still to be explained, it seems that I have arrived in very good time. For in hearing how the courtier should make use of his good qualities I shall also hear what they are, and so I shall come to learn everything that has been said so far. So do not refuse, Count, now that you have settled part of the debt, to pay the rest.'

'I would not have such a heavy debt to pay,' said the Count, 'if the work were divided more fairly. The mistake was made of giving the authority of command to too partial a lady.' And at this, laughing, he turned to signora Emilia, who at once retorted:

'It is not for you to complain of my partiality. However, since you do so for no reason, we shall give a share in the honour, or as you call it, the work, to someone else.'

Then, turning to Federico Fregoso, she said:

'It is you who proposed this game of the courtier, so it is only right that it should fall to you to continue with part of it: and this will be to meet the Magnifico's request, explaining how and in what manner and when the courtier should put his good qualities into use and practise those things which the Count said it was right for him to know.'

Then Federico answered: 'Madam, in wanting to distinguish the way and manner and timing of the good qualities practised by the courtier you want to separate what are inseparable; for these are the very things that decide whether his qualities and the way he employs them are good. Therefore, seeing that the Count has spoken at such length and so well, and has also touched on these aspects, and has prepared in his mind the rest of what he has to say, it was only right that he should carry on to the end.'

Signora Emilia replied:

'Well, now, just you count yourself to be the Count, and say what you think he would say, and in that way you will give complete satisfaction.'

Then Calmeta said: 'Gentlemen, since the hour is late, so that Federico should have no excuse for not saying what he knows, I think it would be well to defer the rest of the discussion until tomorrow. And let the short time that is left be spent on some less ambitious entertainment.'

As everyone agreed with this, the Duchess called on madonna Margherita and madonna Costanza Fregosa to dance. And then immediately Barletta, a delightful musician and an excellent dancer, who always kept the Court agreeably entertained, began to play, and the two ladies, taking each other by the hand, danced first a *bassa* and then a *roegarze*, extremely gracefully, and to everyone's satisfaction.[23] Finally, since the night was now far gone, the Duchess rose to her feet, at which everyone reverently took his leave and retired to sleep.

THE SECOND BOOK OF THE COURTIER

TO ALFONSO ARIOSTO

I HAVE many times asked myself, not without wonder, the source of a certain error which, since it is committed by all the old without exception, can be believed to be proper and natural to man: namely, that they nearly all praise the past and blame the present, revile our actions and behaviour and everything which they themselves did not do when they were young, and affirm, too, that every good custom and way of life, every virtue and, in short, all things imaginable are always going from bad to worse. And truly it seems against all reason and a cause for astonishment that maturity of age, which, with its long experience, in all other respects usually perfects a man's judgement, in this matter corrupts it so much that he does not realize that, if the world were always growing worse and if fathers were generally better than their sons, we would long since have become so rotten that no further deterioration would be possible. However, we see that not only in our own times but also in the past this fault was always peculiar to old age; this can be clearly understood from the writings of many of the earliest authors, and especially the writers of comedy who, more than the others, reflect the nature of human life. For myself, I think that the reason for this faulty judgement in the old is that the passing years rob them of many of the favourable conditions of life, among other things depriving the blood of a great part of its vitality; and in consequence the physical constitution changes and the organs through which the soul exercises its power grow feeble. Thus in old age the gay flowers of contentment fall from our hearts, just as in autumn the leaves fall from the trees; and in place of bright and clear thoughts the soul is possessed by a dark and confused melancholy attended by endless distress. Thus the mind as well as the body grows weak; it retains only a faint impression of past pleasures, and only the image of those precious hours of youth, when, so long as they last, heaven and earth and the whole of creation seem to be rejoicing and smiling as we look, and a gay springtime of happiness seems to flower in our thoughts as in a delightful and lovely garden.

So when cold winter comes to our lives and the sun starts to go down in the west it would be well, as our pleasures fade, if we always lost the memory of them, and discovered, as Themistocles said, the secret of forgetfulness.[1] For our bodily senses are so untrustworthy that they often confuse our judgement as well. Because of this, it seems to me that the old resemble those who, as they sail from harbour, keep their eyes on the land and imagine that their ship is motionless whereas the shore is receding, though the contrary is true. For, like the harbour, time and the pleasures of life stay the same while we, sailing away in the ship of mortality, cross the stormy sea which engulfs and swallows us up one by one; nor are we ever permitted to regain the land but, constantly assailed by hostile winds, eventually we come to grief upon a rock. Since, therefore, the senile spirit is an unsuitable vessel for many of the pleasures of life, it cannot enjoy them; and just as even rare and delicate wines taste sour to those whose palates are spoilt through sickness, so to old people because of their incapacity (which does not, however, lack desire) pleasures seem cold and insipid and very different from those they recall having once enjoyed, although the pleasures themselves are the same. In consequence, feeling themselves deprived, they grumble and condemn the present as evil, not appreciating that the change is in themselves and not in the times; and on the other hand, when they remember the pleasures of the past they also recall the time when they enjoyed them, and they praise it as good because it seems to carry with it the savour of what they felt when it was present. For the truth is that our minds detest all the things that have accompanied our sorrows and love all those that have accompanied our joys. So we find that a lover sometimes rejoices to look at a window, even though it is shuttered, because it was there that he once was favoured by the sight of his lady; and similarly he rejoices to see a ring or a letter, a garden or some other place, or anything whatever that may seem to him to have been a conscious witness of his pleasures. On the other hand, often the most ornate and beautiful room will be obnoxious to one who has been held a prisoner or suffered some other unhappiness there. And I have known people to refuse ever to drink again from a cup used for their medicine when they were ill. To one man, a window or a ring or a letter provides the joyful memory that gives him so much pleasure and seems therefore to have been part of his enjoyment; to another, in the same way, the room or the cup seems to bring back the memory of his captivity or his sickness. And these are the reasons, I think, why old people praise the past and blame the present.

So old people talk about Courts in the same way as they talk about everything else and affirm that those which they remember from the past were far more excellent and full of outstanding men than those we know today; and as soon as the subject is being discussed, they begin to praise to the skies the courtiers of Duke Filippo or Duke Borso; they repeat the sayings of Niccolò Piccinino;[2] they remind us that in those days there were no murders (or only very rarely), there were no fights or plots or treacheries, but only a certain loyal and loving goodwill among all men, and complete truth; and they recall that in the Courts in those days so many good customs prevailed along with such worthiness that courtiers were all like monks, and woe betide anyone who spoke a bad word to another or acted less than honourably towards a woman. Then, on the other hand, they say that nowadays everything is the opposite; and that not only have brotherly affection and good customs disappeared among courtiers but in the Courts nothing prevails except envy and ill-will, wicked customs, dissolute living and every kind of vice: the women lascivious and shameless and the men effeminate. They also condemn modern dress as indecent and luxurious. In short, they condemn all and everything, including, to be sure, many things which deserve censure, for it cannot be denied that there are many evil and wicked men among us or that our age is far more degenerate than the times they praise. However, I am quite sure that they fail to discern the cause of the difference and that they are being very foolish, for they would have the world contain only good things and nothing evil, and this is impossible. For (since evil is the opposite of good and good of evil) the one must always sustain and reinforce the other, and if the one diminishes or increases, the other, as its necessary counter-force, must do the same. We all know that there would be no justice in the world if there were no wrongs; no magnanimity if no one were pusillanimous; no continence without incontinence; no health without sickness; no truth without falsehood; and no happiness without misfortune. Thus Socrates is very right when he wonders, as Plato describes, why Aesop did not write a fable pretending that, since He had never been able to unite them, God had joined pain and pleasure end to end, so that the beginning of one should be the end of the other. For we find that we are never allowed pleasure without pain beforehand. And who can enjoy his rest unless he has felt the burden of fatigue? Who enjoys eating, drinking and sleeping unless he has first known hunger, thirst and sleeplessness? I believe, therefore, that sickness and suffering were given to man by Nature, not chiefly to make him subject to them, since the source of every good would hardly inflict so many miseries on us deliberately, but because the health, happiness and other blessings of Nature were necessarily followed by sickness, suffering and other misfortunes. Thus when the world was favoured by Nature with the gift of all the virtues, these were inevitably accompanied, because of the linking of opposites, by all the vices, and in consequence as the former grow or diminish so must the latter.

Therefore when our old men praise the Courts of the past, on the grounds that they did not have in them men as vicious as some we have now, they do not realize that neither did they have men as virtuous as some we have today. And this is not surprising, since there is no evil so bad as that which grows from the corrupted seed of good; and so as Nature nowadays produces men far more capable than in the past, those who turn to good do far better than they did in the past just as those who turn to evil do far worse. Hence we must not say that those who refrained from doing evil because they did not know how deserve any praise for it; because, granted that they did very little evil, they still did the worst they could. And that the men of those times were, generally speaking, far less capable than those of today is fully apparent from the work they have left for us to see, in letters as well as in pictures, statues, buildings and everything else. These old men also blame us for many things, in themselves neither good nor bad, simply because they did not do them; and they complain that it is not right for young men to ride about the city on horseback, and especially wearing pumps, or to wear fur coats or long robes in winter, or to wear a hat before the age of eighteen at least, and other such things. But to be sure they are deceiving themselves in saying all this, because these fashions, besides being useful and convenient, have been established by usage and are universally acceptable, just as it was once perfectly acceptable to go about in sumptuous dress with uncovered breeches and polished shoes and, in order to cut a figure, always to carry a sparrow hawk on the wrist to no purpose; to dance without touching the lady's hand; and to adopt many other customs as highly regarded then as they would be thought ludicrous today. So let us also be allowed to follow the customs of our day and age without being slandered by these old men who, wanting to praise themselves, will often say:

'When I was twenty years old, I was still sleeping with my mother and sisters, and it was a long time after that before I even knew what women were, but now young people have scarcely been christened before they know more wickedness than grown men did in those days.'

In saying this, they don't realize that they are confirming that young people nowadays are far brighter and more capable than their old men used to be. So they should stop condemning the present as being full of vices, since if they removed the vices they would have to let the virtues go with them; and they should also remember that there were many rascals to be found among the fine men of the ancient world, at a time when the world was full of virtuous and exalted spirits and men of exceptional genius. And if these were still alive today, they would outdo our evil men in wickedness just as the good men of that age would excel those of today. And all history is a witness to this.

But I think enough has now been said to refute these old men. So we shall end this argument, which has surely gone on too long but was not, I hope, altogether beside the point. And since it is enough to have shown that the Courts of our own time are no less praiseworthy than those the old men praise so much, we shall now go back to the discussion concerning the courtier, from which can readily be understood the standing of the Court of Urbino among other Courts, what manner of prince and lady they were who were served by such noble spirits, and how fortunate those could be called who lived in such a society.

The following day, therefore, many and various discussions were held among the ladies and gentlemen of the Court concerning what had been debated the previous evening; and this was chiefly because the Prefect, eager to discover what had been said, questioned almost everyone only to receive, as usually happens, the most diverse replies. For some praised one thing and others another, and many also disagreed as to what the Count's opinion had really been, since no one fully remembered all that had been said. Almost the whole day was taken up with this discussion; and then when night began to fall the Prefect decided that they should eat, and led all the gentlemen into supper. As soon as this was over, he went to the rooms of the Duchess; and when she saw the arrival of so many people, earlier than was customary, she said:

'Federico, it seems to me that a very heavy burden has been placed on your shoulders, and that you have to live up to some very high expectations.'

At this, not waiting for Federico to answer, the Unico Aretino remarked:

'But what is this great burden? Who is so foolish, when he knows how to do something, as not to do it in his own good time?'

So, talking of this, everyone sat down in his usual place and order, eagerly awaiting the proposed discussion.

Federico then turned to the Unico Aretino and said:

'So, signor Unico, you do not believe that I have been given a challenging task and a heavy burden this evening, in having to show how, and in what way, and when the courtier ought to use his good qualities and practise the things that have been declared appropriate to him?'

'It seems no great thing to me,' replied the Unico. 'And all that need be said, I think, is that the courtier should possess good judgement, the need for which was rightly mentioned by the Count yesterday evening. If he does have it, then he needs no other instructions about how to practise what he knows at the right time and in the proper manner. To attempt to provide him with more precise rules would be too difficult and surely superfluous. For I do not know who would be so inept as to want to take up arms when others are attending to music; or to do a morris-dance in the streets, no matter how good he is at it; or comfort a mother for the loss of her son by laughing and joking. I'm sure no gentleman would do such things, unless he were completely out of his wits.'

'It seems to me, signor Unico,' replied Federico, 'that you are taking things to the extreme. For sometimes people are inept in ways that are not quite so obvious, and the mistakes they make are not all of the same kind. And it can happen that a man will refrain from some only too obvious, public folly, such as dancing around the square in the way you mention, and yet will not know how to refrain from singing his own praises at quite the wrong time, from indulging in tiresome arrogance, or from sometimes saying something meant to raise a laugh which is so out of place that it falls completely flat. Often these mistakes are veiled in such a way that the one who makes them, unless he watches out very carefully, fails to perceive what is happening. And although there are many reasons why our vision is limited, it is clouded chiefly by over-ambition. For everyone shows off in regard to what, rightly or wrongly, he has persuaded himself he knows. So it seems to me that in this matter the correct rule of behaviour is to observe a certain prudence and wise discrimination, and to understand the exact emphasis to give to various actions so that they may always be done seasonably. The courtier may be so judicious that he can discern these distinctions; but it will surely be easier for him to achieve the end he seeks if his mind is broadened by some precept, and if he is shown the way forward and, so to speak, the foundations on which to build, than if he relies solely on general principles.

'Yesterday evening, the Count spoke about courtiership so eloquently and agreeably as to arouse in me no little fear and doubt whether I should be able to satisfy this noble gathering with what I have to say, as well as he did with his contribution. However, in order to share as much as possible in the praise he won, and to be sure of making no mistakes regarding this aspect of the subject at least, I shall not contradict anything he has said. So, agreeing with the Count's opinions, including those he gave concerning the courtier's noble birth, talents, physical constitution and graceful appearance, I say that to be praiseworthy and highly thought of by everyone, and to secure the goodwill of the rulers whom he serves, the courtier should know how to order his whole life and to exploit his good qualities generally, no matter with whom he associates, without exciting envy. And just how difficult this is may be seen from the few who are successful; for indeed we are all instinctively more prone to condemn mistakes than to praise what is well done, and it seems that, out of some kind of innate malice, many men, even when they see what is clearly good, strive with all their might and main to find fault or at least what looks like a fault. Thus in everything he does our courtier must be cautious, and he must always act and speak with prudence; and he should not only strive to perfect his various attributes and qualities but also make sure that the tenor of his life is such that it corresponds with those qualities, is always and everywhere consistent in itself, and is perfectly of a piece with all his fine attributes. In consequence, in everything he does he should, as the Stoics maintain is the duty or purpose of the wise man, be inspired by and express all the virtues; and though each act is always dominated by a particular virtue, yet all the virtues are so linked that they tend to the same end and they can all contribute to and assist every purpose. Therefore the courtier must know how to avail himself of the virtues, and sometimes set one in contrast or opposition to another in order to draw more attention to it. This is what a good painter does when by the use of shadow he distinguishes clearly the lights on his reliefs, and similarly by the use of light deepens the shadows of plane surfaces and brings different colours together in such a way that each one is brought out more sharply through the contrast; and the placing of figures in opposition to each other assists the painter in his purpose. In the same way, gentleness is most impressive in a man who is a capable and courageous warrior; and just as his boldness is magnified by his modesty, so his modesty is enhanced and more apparent on account of his boldness. Hence to talk little and to do much, and not to praise oneself for praiseworthy deeds but to dissimulate them politely, serve to enhance both these virtues in anyone who knows how to employ this method discreetly; and the same holds true for all the other good qualities. Then in everything he does or says I should like our courtier to follow certain general rules which, I think, contain the essence of all I have to tell you. And first and most important, he should (as the Count so rightly advised yesterday evening) above all avoid affectation. Next let him consider well whatever he does or says, the place where he does it, in whose presence, its timing, why he is doing it, his own age, his profession, the end he is aiming at, and the means that are suitable; and so, bearing all these points in mind, let him prepare himself discreetly for all he wishes to do or say.'

After having spoken in this way, Federico appeared to pause for a moment. But then signor Morello da Ortona said abruptly:

'It seems to me that these rules of yours teach us very little; and for myself I'm no wiser than I was before you explained them, although I do remember having heard them some time or other from the friars at confession, and I believe they called them "the circumstances".'

Federico laughed when he heard this and then he went on:

'If you remember, yesterday evening the Count said he wished the courtier's chief profession to be that of arms, and he spoke at length about the way he should pursue it. So we shall not repeat this. All the same, it should also be understood from the rule I gave that when the courtier finds himself involved in a skirmish or pitched battle, or something of that nature, he should arrange to withdraw discreetly from the main body and accomplish the bold and notable exploits he has to perform in as small a company as possible and in view of all the noblest and most eminent men of the army, and, above all, in the presence, or if possible under the very eyes, of the prince he is serving. For it is certainly right to exploit the things one does well. And I believe that just as it is wrong to seek false glory or what is not deserved, so also it is wrong to cheat oneself of due honour and not to seek that praise which is the only true reward of prowess. And I recall in the past having known men who, though very able, were extremely stupid in this regard and would as soon risk their lives to capture a flock of sheep as in being the first to scale the walls of a besieged town; but this is not how our courtier will behave if he bears in mind the motive that leads him to war, which ought to be honour pure and simple. But, then, if he happens to engage in arms in some public spectacle, such as jousting, tourneying or volleying, or other kind of physical recreation, mindful of where and in whose presence he is, he will make sure that he is as elegant and attractive in the exercise of arms as he is competent, and that he feeds the eyes of those who are looking on with everything that can give him added grace. He will ensure that the horse he has is beautifully caparisoned, that he himself is suitably attired, with appropriate mottoes and ingenious devices to attract the eyes of the onlookers in his direction as surely as the loadstone attracts iron. He will never be one of the last to show himself, knowing that the crowd, and especially the women, scrutinize the first far more than the last. For at the beginning our eyes and our minds are avid for this kind of novelty, take note of every least thing and are impressed by it; whereas by and by they are not only sated but wearied by what they see. Thus there was a great actor of the ancient world who, for this reason, always insisted on being the first on stage to say his part. Then again, to continue speaking of arms, our courtier will pay attention to the occupation of those with whom he is speaking and will behave accordingly; and he will speak one way with men and another way with women; and if he should want to suggest something to his own credit, he will do it with dissimulation, as if purely by chance, and in passing, and with the discretion and caution that Count Lodovico explained to us yesterday.

'Now don't you think, signor Morello, that our rules are able to teach something? Do you not agree that that friend of ours, of whom I spoke to you the other day, had completely forgotten whom he was talking to and why, when, to entertain a lady whom he had never seen before, he began their conversation by announcing that he had slaughtered so many men, how fierce he was, and that he knew how to wield a sword with both hands? And before he left her he was wanting to teach her how certain blows of the battle-axe should be parried, both when one was armed and when one was unarmed, and the various ways of brandishing a sword, until the poor girl was suffering agonies and every moment seemed like an eternity till she could make her escape before being cut down like the others. These are the kind of mistakes made by those who have no regard for those "circumstances" you say the friars told you about.

'So now as far as sports are concerned, there are some which are hardly ever performed except in public, including jousting, tourneying and dart throwing, and all the rest in which weapons are used. When, therefore, our courtier has to take part in these, first he must arrange to be so well equipped as to horses, weapons and dress that nothing is lacking; and if he does not feel assured that everything is just as it should be he must on no account take part, for if he fails to perform well he cannot excuse himself by saying that this is not his profession. Next he should give full consideration to the kind of audience present and to who his companions are; for it would be unbecoming for a gentleman to honour by his personal appearance some country show, where the spectators and participants were common people.'

At this, signor Pallavicino said: 'In Lombardy we are not so fussy. On the contrary, many of our young gentlemen are to be found, on holidays, dancing all day in the open air with the peasants, and taking part with them in sports such as throwing the bar, wrestling, running and jumping. And I'm sure there is no harm in this, for the contest is not one of nobility but of strength and agility, regarding which ordinary villagers are often just as good as nobles; and I think this kind of familiar behaviour has a certain charming open-mindedness about it.'

'Well, to me,' replied Federico, 'this dancing in the open air is most displeasing, and I can see no advantages in it at all. But if anyone is anxious to wrestle, to run or to jump with peasants, then he ought, in my opinion, to do it casually, out of *noblesse oblige*, so to say, and certainly not in competition with them; and he should be almost certain of winning, or else not take part at all, for it is too sad and shocking, and quite undignified, when a gentleman is seen to be beaten by a peasant, especially in a wrestling-match. Hence I think it would be as well to abstain, at least when there are many onlookers, because the advantage in winning is very negligible and the disadvantages in being beaten very serious. The game of tennis is also nearly always played before an audience, and it is one of those spectacles which gains considerably from the presence of a crowd. So I would like our courtier to take part in this game and in all the others, apart from those involving the use of arms, as an amateur, making it clear that he neither seeks nor expects any applause. Nor, even though his performance is outstanding, should he let it be thought that he has spent on it much time or trouble. Neither should he behave like those people who are fond of music and, whenever they are speaking with someone, if there is a lull in the conversation always start to sing *sotto voce*; or like others who, walking through the streets or in church, are for ever dancing; or like others who, when they meet a friend in the square or wherever it happens to be, immediately act as if about to fence or to wrestle, depending on their favourite sport.'

Here Cesare Gonzaga said: 'One of the young cardinals we have in Rome does even better. Because he fancies himself as an athlete, when people come to see him, even if he has never met them before, he leads them into his garden, and insists against all protests that they should strip down and try to beat him at jumping.'

Federico laughed at this, and then he went on:

'There are various other kinds of recreation, such as dancing, that can be enjoyed in public and in private. And I consider that the courtier should take great care over this; for when he is dancing in front of a crowd and along with many others it is fitting, or so I think, that he should maintain a certain dignity, though tempered by the lightness and delicate grace of his movements. He may feel himself to be very light on his feet and a master of time and movement, but even so he should not attempt those quick movements of the feet and double steps which we approve of in our Barletta but which, to be sure, are unsuitable for a gentleman. On the other hand, when he is performing in a private room, of the kind we are in now, then I think he should be allowed to try them, and to dance the morris and the *brando*[3] as well, but not in public unless he is at a masked ball, when it does no harm even if he is recognized. Indeed, there is no better way of demonstrating one's skill in such things at public spectacles, whether armed or not; because masquerading carries with it a certain licence and liberty, and this, among other things, enables the courtier to choose the role at which he feels himself best, to bring out its most important elements with diligence and elegance, while showing a certain nonchalance with regard to what is not essential. All of this greatly enhances the attractiveness of what he is doing, as when a youth dresses up as an old man yet wears loose attire so as to be able to show his agility; or when a knight dresses up as a country shepherd, but rides a beautiful horse and wears a handsome and appropriate costume. For the spectators assume they are seeing what they are meant to imagine, and then when shown far more than what is promised by the costume being worn they are highly amused and delighted.

'Then again, in games and festivities like these, when people are masked, it would not be right for the prince to choose to play the part of the prince himself, since the pleasure which the spectators derive from the novelty of the proceedings would be almost entirely lost, seeing that everyone already knows quite well who he is. Moreover, when he wishes to play as well as to be the prince, he sacrifices the freedom to do all those things that are below his dignity; and, besides, if there is any competitive element in the games, especially in arms, he would also make people think that he wanted to maintain his identity so as not to be beaten by others but indulged. In addition, by acting in a game in the same way as he must act in real life, he would undermine his lawful authority and make it seem that real life, too, was a game. But if on these occasions the prince puts off his royal identity and mixes with his inferiors as an equal (though in such a way that he is still recognizable) in putting aside his own he achieves an even higher stature, by striving to surpass others by prowess and not by authority and showing that it is not being a prince that accounts for his worth.

'It follows that in my opinion the courtier when taking part in military displays must observe the same kind of discretion appropriate to his rank. Then in saddle vaulting, in wrestling, in running and jumping, I should certainly like him to refrain from mixing with the common people, or at least to appear among them only on the rarest occasions. For there is nothing so perfect in the world that the ignorant do not tire of it and despise it when they see it often. My judgement is the same with regard to music. Thus I should not like our courtier to behave as do so many others who as soon as they put in an appearance, even in the presence of gentlemen who are strangers to them, immediately, hardly waiting to be asked, start showing off what they know, and often what they don't know, in such a way that it seems they have come along just for this purpose and that it is their main pursuit in life. So the courtier should turn to music as if it were merely a pastime of his and he is yielding to persuasion, and not in the presence of common people or a large crowd. And although he may know and understand what he is doing, in this also I wish him to dissimulate the care and effort that are necessary for any competent performance; and he should let it seem as if he himself thinks nothing of his accomplishment which, because of its excellence, he makes others think very highly of.'

Then signor Gaspare Pallavicino remarked:

'There exist many different kinds of music, both vocal and instrumental. So I would be gratified to hear which is the best of all and on what occasion the courtier should perform.'

'Truly beautiful music,' answered Federico, 'consists, in my opinion, in fine singing, in reading accurately from the score and in an attractive personal style, and still more in singing to the accompaniment of the viola. I say this because the solo voice contains all the purity of music, and style and melody are studied and appreciated more carefully when our ears are not distracted by more than one voice, and every little fault, too, is more clearly apparent, something which does not happen when a group is singing, because then one singer covers up for the other. But above all, singing poetry accompanied by the viola seems especially pleasurable, for the instrument gives the words a really marvellous charm and effectiveness. All keyboard instruments, indeed, are harmonious, because their consonances are perfect and they make possible many effects which fill the soul with sweetness and melody. And no less delightful is the playing of a quartet, with the viols producing music of great skill and suavity. The human voice adds ornament and grace to all these instruments, with which I think it is good enough if our courtier has some acquaintance (though the more proficient he is the better) without concerning himself greatly with those which both Minerva and Alcibiades rejected, because it seems they have something repulsive about them.[4] Then as to the occasions when these various kinds of music should be performed, I would instance when a man finds himself in the company of dear and familiar friends, and there is no pressing business on hand. But above all, the time is appropriate when there are ladies present; for the sight of them softens the hearts of those who are listening, makes them more susceptible to the sweetness of the music, and also quickens the spirit of the musicians themselves. As I have already said, one should avoid playing in the presence of a large number, especially of the common people. But in any case, everything should be tempered by discretion; for it is just not possible to imagine all the circumstances possible, and if the courtier is a good judge of himself he will adapt himself to the occasion and will know when his audience is in the mood to listen and when not; and he will act his own age, for it is certainly most unbecoming and unsightly when an old grey-haired gentleman, who is toothless and wrinkled, takes up the viola and plays and sings in front of a gathering of ladies, even if his performance is quite good. This is because the words of songs are nearly always amorous, and in old men love is altogether ridiculous; although it sometimes seems that Cupid along with the other miracles he works delights in melting even the icy hearts of the old.'

Then the Magnifico replied: 'Do not rob such poor old men of this pleasure, Federico; for I have known men of advanced years who possess the most perfect voices and are accomplished musicians, and far more so than some young men.'

'It is not my wish,' answered Federico, 'to rob them of this pleasure, but it certainly is my wish to rob you and these ladies of the chance to laugh at their absurdity; and if old men have the desire to sing to the viola, then let them do so in private with the object of shedding from their minds the disturbing thoughts and bitter vexations of which life is full, and of tasting the divinity which, I believe, Pythagoras and Socrates attributed to music. And even if they do not practise it themselves, if they have cultivated a taste for music they will enjoy it far more than those who know nothing about it. After all, very often, because he exercises them a great deal, a blacksmith whose body is otherwise puny will have stronger arms than someone who is more robust; likewise, someone whose ears have been trained to listen to harmony will understand it better and more readily and appreciate it more intelligently than others whose hearing may be very sharp and sound but whose ears are untrained in the varieties of musical consonances; for the modulations of music have no significance for ears that are unaccustomed to them, though admittedly music can tame even a wild animal. This, then, is the pleasure that old men may suitably take in music. And I am of the same opinion as regards dancing; because, to be sure, such pleasures ought to be given freely before we are forced to abandon them because of our years.'

'Well then,' broke in signor Morello, as if he were angry, 'you mean it is better to exclude all the old men and to reserve the name of courtier just for the young?'

Federico replied with a laugh: 'Consider, signor Morello, that those who are fond of these things even if they are not young are anxious to appear so; and so they dye their hair and trim their beard twice a week for the simple reason that Nature is tacitly telling them that such things are only fitting for the young.'

At this, all the ladies burst out laughing, because they realized that these words were aimed at signor Morello himself; and as for him, he seemed quite disconcerted.

'But of course,' Federico added quickly, 'there are other kinds of recreation to be enjoyed with the ladies that are suitable for old men.'

'And what are they?' asked signor Morello. 'Telling stories?'

'That as well,' said Federico. 'But, as you know, every age brings its own cares with it, and has its own characteristic vices and virtues. For example, old men, just as they are usually more prudent than young men, and wiser and more continent, so they are more loquacious, meaner, more difficult and more timid; and then again, about the house they are for ever scolding, they are harsh to their children, and they always want their own way. In contrast, young men are spirited, generous and frank, but also quick to start a quarrel, volatile, loving and hating the same instant, wrapped up in their own pleasures, resentful of good advice. However, of all possible ages, the age of manhood is the most composed, since it has shed the unpleasant attributes of youth and not yet attained those of old age. The old and the young, being at the two extremes as it were, must learn how to behave reasonably and correct the faults planted in them by Nature. Thus old men should be on their guard against praising themselves too much and against the other faults we have noted as characteristic, and they must make use of the prudence and knowledge they will have acquired through their long experience, act like oracles to whom everyone will turn for advice, talk good sense with grace and dignity, and accompany the gravity of their years with a certain amusing and measured humour. In this way they will be good courtiers, they will be good company whether with men or women, and they will always be welcome, without needing to sing or dance; and when the need arises, they will prove their worth in matters of importance.

'Young men should be just as careful and judicious, not of course after the fashion of the old (since what is suitable for the one would hardly be so for the other, and it is usual to say that too much wisdom is a bad sign in a young man) but in correcting their natural faults. Thus it pleases me greatly to see a young man, especially when he is engaging in arms, be somewhat grave and taciturn, and I like to see him self-possessed, without those restless ways that are so common at that age; for then he appears to possess a certain something that the others lack. Moreover, a relaxed attitude of this kind suggests a kind of impressive strength, since it appears to arise not from anger but from deliberation, and to be ruled by reason rather than by emotion. This quality is nearly always to be found in men of real courage, and we also see it in those wild beasts which are nobler and more powerful than the rest, such as the lion and the eagle. Nor is this strange, since a sudden and impetuous movement which, without words or any show of anger, erupts in a concentrated burst, like the explosion of a cannon, following the quietness which is its opposite, is far more violent and furious than one which mounts in intensity little by little, getting hotter only by degrees. Thus those who, when they are about to embark on some enterprise, talk such a lot and hop from one foot to another without ceasing, seem to exhaust themselves before they start; and, as our Pietro Monte rightly says, they act like children in the dark singing to themselves to pluck up courage, as if they were driving away their fears with song. So just as in a young man a measured and sober youthfulness is most praiseworthy, since it tempers and corrects the levity which is the characteristic vice of that time of life, so in an old man we must esteem a fresh and spirited old age, because then the vigour of his soul seems so robust that it warms and strengthens a time of life that is weak and cold, maintaining it in that middle condition which is the best time of our life.

'But when all is said and done even all these qualities will not be enough to enable our courtier to win universal favour with lords, knights and ladies unless he also has a gentle and agreeable manner in his day-to-day relationships. However, as far as this is concerned, I truly think that it is difficult to give any rule, because of the infinite variety of things that must be taken into account, seeing that there are no two people in the whole world who are of identical mind. Therefore whoever has to accommodate his behaviour to dealings with a considerable number of people must be guided by his own judgement and, recognizing the differences between one man and another, must change his style and method from day to day, according to the nature of those with whom he wants to converse. And for my part I know no other rules to give on this subject, except perhaps the one we have already heard from signor Morello, which he learned at confession as a child.'

Here signora Emilia laughed and said: 'You are too anxious to shirk your duty, Federico; but you will not be successful, for you must go on talking until it is time to go to bed.'

'And if, madam, I have nothing more to say?' asked Federico.

'Then we shall be able to see how ingenious you can be,'

answered signora Emilia. 'After all, I once heard of a man so ingenious and eloquent that he did not want for material in writing a whole book in praise of a fly, others in praise of the ague and another in praise of baldness; and if that is true, then haven't you got it in you to find enough to talk about courtiership for the space of an evening?'

'Already,' replied Federico, 'we have said so much about it that we have enough material for two books. But since excuses do not help me, I shall continue talking until you decide that I have fulfilled if not my duty, then all I am capable of.

'I consider that the dealings the courtier has with his prince are those which he should chiefly endeavour to make agreeable. I know that to talk of a courtier being conversant with his prince in this way implies a certain equality that can hardly exist between a ruler and his servant; but for the time being we shall let this go. Well then, I want the courtier not only to make it clear on all occasions and to all persons that he is of the quality we have already described but also to devote all his thought and strength to loving and almost adoring the prince he serves above all else, devoting all his ambitions, actions and behaviour to pleasing him.'

At this, without waiting further, Pietro da Napoli said:

'We would find plenty of courtiers like this nowadays, for it seems to me that in a few words you have sketched for us a first-class flatterer.'

'You are very much mistaken,' replied Federico. 'For flatterers love neither their prince nor their friends, and I am saying that this is, above all, what I want our courtier to do; and he can obey and further the wishes of the one he serves without adulation, since I am referring to those wishes that are reasonable and right, or that in themselves are neither good nor bad, as, for example, in sport, to devote oneself to one kind of recreation rather than another. And I would have our courtier try to act in this manner, even if it is against his nature, in such a way that whenever his prince sees him he believes that the courtier will have something agreeable to say. And this will be the case if he has the discretion to discern what pleases his prince, and the wit and judgement to know how to act accordingly, and the considered resolve to make himself like what he may instinctively dislike. Prepared in this way, he will never appear before his prince in a bad humour, or in a melancholy mood; nor will he be as taciturn as are so many who seem to bear a grudge against their masters, which is truly odious. He will not speak evil, and least of all of his lords: something that often happens, for in Courts there seems to be a tempest that drives those who are most favoured by their lords and are raised from the humblest condition to the most exalted always to complain and speak ill of them; and this is unseemly not only in their kind but also in those who may be treated badly. Our courtier will avoid foolish arrogance; he will not be the bearer of bad news; he will not be careless in sometimes saying things that may give offence, instead of striving to please; he will not be obstinate and contentious, as are some who seem to enjoy nothing more than being irritating and obnoxious like flies and make a habit of contradicting everyone spitefully without any misgivings; he will not be an idle or lying babbler, nor a stupid flatterer or boaster, but will be modest and reserved, observing always, and especially in public, the reverence and respect which should mark the attitude of a servant towards his master. And he will not behave in the way that so many do, who when they cross the path of a great prince, even if they have spoken to him only once before, go up to him with a certain smiling and friendly countenance, just as if they were going to embrace an equal or do a favour to someone of lower rank. Very rarely, or hardly ever, will he ask his master anything for himself, lest his prince, being reluctant to refuse, concedes it grudgingly, which is far worse. And when he asks for something on behalf of others he will take careful note of the time and place, and will request only what is right and reasonable; and he will present the request in such a way, leaving out the items he knows could be displeasing and cleverly smoothing over the difficulties, that his lord will always grant it or, if he wishes not to, will be able to refuse without worrying about giving offence to the petitioner. For very often when lords have refused to grant a favour to someone who has been seeking it importunately they imagine that the person who has been so insistent must be very anxious to get what he wants and therefore, when he is baulked, must be ill-disposed towards the one who has denied him; and this belief breeds in them a hatred of the person concerned, whom subsequently they can never see without distaste.

'The courtier will never attempt to make his way into the chamber or private quarters of his master uninvited, even though he possesses considerable authority himself; for often, when princes are by themselves, they enjoy the liberty of saying and doing just what they please, and so they do not want to be seen or overheard by anyone in a position to criticize, and this is quite proper. So it seems to me that those people are in error who condemn a ruler for keeping in his rooms persons of little worth except in the matter of knowing how to give good personal service, for I do not see why princes should not be free to relax just as we like to do. But if a courtier who is accustomed to dealing with important matters should find himself privately with his lord, he should then become another person, defer serious things for another time and place, and engage in conversation which will be pleasing and agreeable to his master, in order not to disturb his peace and quiet. However, in this as in everything else he will take care not to annoy his lord; and he should wait for favours to be offered freely rather than seek them, as do only too many who are so grasping that it seems they will die if they are refused, and who, if they happen to fall out of favour or if others are preferred instead, suffer such agonies that they find it impossible to conceal their envy. In this way, they win nothing but ridicule, and often they tempt their lord to bestow his favours indiscriminately, just to spite them. Then if they happen to be favoured out of the ordinary, they are so swept away that they seem almost drunk with joy, hardly know what to do with their hands or their feet, and can scarcely restrain themselves from calling the whole world to come and congratulate them, as if for something they have never experienced before. No, I do not wish our courtier to be like this. I wish him, on the contrary, to enjoy favours, but not to value them so highly as to appear unable to exist without them. And when they are granted to him, he should not let himself appear unaccustomed or alien to the experience, or amazed that such things should happen; nor should he decline them in the way some do, who out of pure ignorance refuse to accept and thereby show the bystanders that they are convinced of their own unworthiness.

A man should, moreover, always be a little more humble than his rank requires, not accepting too easily the favours and honours offered him, but declining them modestly while showing that he values them highly, and yet in such a way that he inspires the person offering them to do so with still greater insistence. For the more resistance that is shown in accepting favours, the more the prince who is giving them will think that he is esteemed; and the favour he is granting will seem greater, the more the recipient shows his thanks and appreciation for the honour being done to him. These are the true and tangible favours which enhance the reputation of the one who is seen to be receiving them; for, since they are granted without being asked for, everyone realizes that they are the reward of true merit; and the more so if they are accepted modestly.'

Then Cesare Gonzaga remarked: 'It seems to me that you have plagiarized that passage in the Gospel where it says: "When you are invited to a wedding, go and sit down in the lowliest place, so that, when the one who has invited you comes, he may say: My friend, go higher; and thus you will be honoured in the presence of the other guests."'[5]

Federico laughed and said: 'It would be too great a sacrilege to plagiarize the Gospel; but you are more learned in Holy Scripture than I thought.'

And then he continued: 'You see what great dangers those men sometimes run who rashly begin a conversation in the presence of a great prince without being asked. Often, in order to shame them, the lord will refuse to answer and look the other way; and if he does reply, everyone sees that he does so resentfully. So to receive a favour from one's lord, the best way is to deserve it. Nor when his prince is pleased with someone else, for whatever reason, must a man expect to achieve the same result simply by copying what the other person does; for the same things do not suit everybody alike. Sometimes one finds a man who is by nature so spontaneously witty that whatever he says provokes laughter, and he seems to have been born just for that; and then if someone who is more dignified tries to do the same, even if he is very clever, the result will be so flat and awkward that it will cause embarrassment; and he will be exactly like the ass that wanted to imitate the dog and play with its master. So it is necessary for everyone to know himself and his capabilities, and to accommodate himself accordingly, and decide what things he must imitate and what not.'

'Before you go on any further,' interrupted Vincenzo Calmeta, 'if I heard aright it seems to me that you said earlier that the best way to win favours is by deserving them, and that the courtier should rather wait for them to be offered than seek them presumptuously himself. But I fear that this precept is of little use, and I think that experience clearly teaches us the contrary. For nowadays very few people are favoured by lords, save only the arrogant; and I know that you yourself can testify that some who have found themselves little in favour with their princes have made themselves agreeable to them only through presumption. For myself, I know none who have risen through modesty; and I will even give you time to think about this, because I am confident that you will find very few of them yourself. Thus if you will consider the Court of France, which today is among the noblest of all Christendom, you will find that all those who there enjoy universal favour tend to be arrogant, not only among themselves but even towards the King.'

'Do not say so,' replied Federico. 'On the contrary, the gentlemen of France are very courteous and modest. It is true that they allow themselves a certain liberty as well as an unceremonious familiarity which is peculiar and natural to them and should not, therefore, be called presumption. For in the way they conduct themselves, whereas they laugh at and mock the arrogant, they greatly esteem those they believe to be worthy and modest.'

Calmeta replied: 'Look at the Spaniards, who appear to be the leaders in courtiership, and consider how many are to be found who are not extremely arrogant both with ladies and gentlemen. And they are worse than the French in so far as they first make a show of great modesty; and in this they are very shrewd because, as I said, the rulers of our day all keep their favours for those who behave in that way.'

Then Federico answered: 'I will certainly not allow you, Vincenzo, to slander our present-day rulers in this manner. For there are also many who love modesty, although I do not claim that this in itself is enough to make a man agreeable. However, I maintain that when it is accompanied by genuine valour, then it does great credit to the one who possesses it. And although modesty is silent, praiseworthy deeds speak for themselves and are far more admirable than if they were accompanied by arrogance and rashness. I will not deny that there are to be found many arrogant Spaniards; but I maintain that those who are highly esteemed are, for the most part, extremely modest. Then there are certain others who are so frigid that they go to absurd lengths to avoid the company of others and so unbalanced that they are judged to be either excessively timid or excessively proud. For these I have no praise at all, nor do I wish modesty to be so dry and arid as to degenerate into boorishness. So let the courtier be eloquent when it suits his purpose, and when discussing affairs of state, prudent and wise; and let him be judicious enough to know how to adapt himself to the customs of the people he may be living among. Then in lesser matters let him be entertaining, and in everything sensible. But above all else he should always hold to what is good; he should be neither envious nor slanderous, and he should never seek to gain grace or favour through wicked methods or by dishonest means.'

Calmeta then commented: 'I assure you that all other methods are far more uncertain and protracted than those you condemn. For nowadays, to repeat what I have already said, our rulers love only those who follow such paths.'

'Do not say so,' replied Federico, 'for that would be too plainly to argue that the rulers of our time are all wicked and evil; and this is not so, since we find some good princes among them. But if our courtier happens to find himself in the service of a lord who is wicked and malignant, he should leave as soon as he is aware of this, to avoid experiencing the bitter anguish of all those good men who serve bad masters.'

'We must pray God,' Calmeta replied, 'to grant us good ones, for once we have them we have to put up with them as they are. This is because there are countless considerations that prevent a gentleman from leaving his master once he has entered his service. The misfortune is in his ever having begun to do so, and in this matter courtiers are like caged birds.'

'It seems to me,' said Federico, 'that duty should come before all other considerations. Certainly, the courtier must not abandon his master when he is at war or in serious trouble, for then it could be believed that he did so to promote his own fortunes or because he thought that his chances of gainful advantage had disappeared. But at any other time he has the right and the duty to quit a service which is sure to bring him disgrace among honourable men. For everyone assumes that those who serve good masters are good and those who serve bad masters are bad.'

Then signor Lodovico Pio remarked: 'I should like you to clear up a doubt that exists in my mind: namely, whether a gentleman is obliged to obey the prince he is serving in everything that may be commanded, even if it is dishonourable or shameful.'

'In dishonourable things we are not bound to obey anyone,' answered Federico.

'But then,' went on signor Lodovico, 'if I were to be in the service of a prince who treated me well and was confident that I would do everything possible for him, and he were to command me to go and kill a certain person, or something of the sort, should I refuse?'

'What you must do,' answered Federico, 'is to obey your lord in everything that redounds to his profit and honour, but not as regards things that bring him loss and shame. Therefore, if he were to order you to commit some treacherous deed not only are you not obliged to do it but you are obliged not to do it, both for your own sake and to avoid ministering to your master's shame. It is true that many things which seem good at first sight are evil, and many things which seem evil are good. Thus it is sometimes allowable, in the service of one's masters, to kill not just one man but ten thousand, and to do many other things which on a superficial view would appear evil although they are not.'

Then signor Gaspare Pallavicino replied: 'Well, I beg you then, explain about this a little more, and teach us how to distinguish what is really good from what merely appears to be.'

'Allow me to refuse that,' answered Federico, 'for there would be too much to say. But let everything be decided by your discretion.'

'At least resolve another of my doubts,' said signor Gaspare.

'What is that?' asked Federico.

'It is as follows,' signor Gaspare continued. 'If I have been told precisely what I am to do in some project or affair of importance, what should I decide if during the course of it I become convinced that by departing more or less from his detailed instructions I can achieve a better or more profitable result for the master who gave me my orders? Should I obey his first command to the letter, or should I do what seems to me best?'

'Concerning this,' said Federico, 'I would base my opinion on the example of Manlius Torquatus, who in such circumstances killed his son because he was too dutiful, if I considered him at all praiseworthy which indeed I do not; none the less I would not venture to blame him, against the judgement of so many centuries, for without doubt it is highly dangerous to transgress the commands of one's superiors, and to trust one's own judgement more than that of those whom it is legitimate to obey.[6] For if by chance one then fails in one's purpose, and the enterprise collapses, one is guilty of disobedience as well as failure, and no excuse or pardon is at all possible. On the other hand, if one achieves one's purpose, then one must give the credit to Fortune, and be satisfied with that. Then again, this kind of behaviour encourages people to slight the commands of their superiors; and following the example of one individual (who may have been successful but was perhaps a prudent man, making a considered departure and helped by Fortune) a thousand other ignorant and shallow men will trust themselves to follow their own inclinations in highly important matters and, to demonstrate their wisdom and powers of authority, will deviate from their lords' commands. This is a very heinous offence and often leads to countless other blunders. But in my opinion the person concerned should consider at length and, so to say, weigh in the balance the benefits and advantages accruing to him should he disobey, given that his purpose is achieved. On the other side, he should weigh the losses and the disadvantages that would ensue should it happen that, after he had disobeyed, his plan misfired. And if he realizes that, if he fails, the evil consequences will be greater and more serious than the advantages if he succeeds, he should check himself and obey meticulously the orders he has been given. On the other hand, if the advantages, in the case of success, would be greater than the harm resulting from failure, he can, I believe, reasonably set out to do what his judgement and common sense suggest, and depart a little from the letter of command, following the example of a merchant who will risk a little to gain a great deal, but not risk a great deal merely to gain a little. I would, above all, commend him for studying the nature of the lord whom he serves, and governing his own actions accordingly; for if his master were to be as strict as many rulers are, then if he were a friend of mine I would never advise him to modify his orders in the slightest. Then he would escape what is recorded to have happened to a military engineer of the Athenians to whom Publius Crassus Mucianus, when he was in Asia and intending to besiege a town, sent a request for one of two ships' masts that he had seen in Athens, in order to make a battering-ram, stipulating that he send the larger one. The engineer, being a highly skilled expert, knew that the larger mast was hardly suited for the purpose, and since the smaller was both easier to transport and more fitted for the machine that was to be constructed this was the one he sent to Mucianus. Hearing what had transpired, Mucianus sent for the wretched engineer and, after he had asked why he had disobeyed him, refusing to accept any of his explanations, he had him stripped naked and flogged and scourged with rods until he died; for he considered that rather than obey him the fellow had wanted to give him advice.[7] When dealing with masters as strict as this, one should be on one's guard.

'But now let us leave the question of how to deal with princes and come to the matter of relations with one's equals, or those who are nearly so. For we must study this as well, seeing that it is the more common experience and a man finds himself more often dealing with his peers than with princes. Of course, there are some fools who if they were enjoying the company of the best friend they had in the world and were then to meet someone better dressed, would immediately attach themselves to him; and then if someone better dressed still came along, they would move on once more. And if the prince should pass by in some public place, they elbow their way through the crowd until they are by his side, and even though they have nothing to say to him they insist on speaking and launch into a long discourse, laughing and clapping their hands and slapping their heads, to let it be understood that they have important business with him so that everyone imagines they are in his good books. However, since men like this deign to speak only with lords, we shall not deign to speak of them.'

At this, the Magnifico Giuliano remarked: 'Federico, since you have mentioned those who are so eager to be seen with the best-dressed people, I should like you to explain to us how the courtier should be dressed, and what clothes are most fitting for him to wear, and also what rules he should follow regarding his physical appearance in general. For in this matter we see endless variations: some dress after the French style, others like the Spaniards and others again like the Germans; and there are also those who dress in the manner of Turks. Some wear beards whereas others do not. It would, therefore, be rewarding to know, given all this confusion, what way is best.'

Federico replied: 'To be sure, I would not know how to lay down any hard and fast rules about dress, save that one should adapt oneself to the custom of the majority; and since, as you say, customs are so varied and the Italians are so eager to adopt the styles of others, I believe that everyone may be allowed to follow his own inclinations. But I do not know by what fate it happens that Italy does not have, as it used to, a distinctively Italian costume: for although the new fashions in use may make earlier ways of dressing appear uncouth, still these were perhaps a sign of our freedom, as the former have proved to be an augury of servitude, in my opinion now clearly fulfilled. It is recorded that when Darius, the year before he fought with Alexander, changed the style of the sword he wore at his side from Persian to Macedonian, the soothsayers interpreted this as meaning that those into whose style Darius had changed his Persian sword would come to be the rulers of Persia; and in the same way it seems to me that our having exchanged our Italian style of dress for that of foreigners means that all those whose fashions we have adopted in place of our own must come to subjugate us. And this has proved only too true, since there is no nation in the world that has not preyed upon us, to the extent that little is left to prey upon, although the depredations go on.

'However, I do not want to embark on a tale of woe and so we would do better to discuss the clothes our courtier ought to wear. And I consider that provided these are not outlandish or inappropriate to his calling they will for the rest be perfectly acceptable if they please the one who wears them. Admittedly, for my part, I should prefer them not to be in any way exaggerated, as the French tend to be in the way they are overdressed and the Germans in the way their clothes are skimped, but as the one and the other style can be when corrected and given a better appearance by the Italians. I am also always pleased when clothes tend to be sober and restrained rather than foppish; so it seems to me that the most agreeable colour is black, and if not black, then at least something fairly dark. I am talking of ordinary attire, for there is no doubt that light and gay colours are more suitable for wearing on top of armour, and it is also more fitting for holiday clothes to have trimmings, and to be ornate and gay. The same applies when it comes to public occasions, such as festivals, games and masquerades, because if they are designed in this way they suggest a certain liveliness and exuberance, very appropriate for arms and sport. But for the rest, I should like the clothes our courtier wears to reflect the sobriety characteristic of the Spaniards, since external appearances often bear witness to what is within.'

Then Cesare Gonzaga remarked: 'I am quite happy about this, because if a gentleman is worthy in other things, what he wears will neither enhance nor diminish his reputation.'

'You are right,' answered Federico, 'although who of us when he sees a gentleman passing by wearing a gown quartered in various colours, or covered with strings and ribbons and bows, and cross-lacings, does not take him for a fool or a clown?'

'Anyone who may have lived for some while in Lombardy,' said Pietro Bembo, 'would take him neither for a fool nor a clown, since everyone there goes about like that.'

'In that case,' added the Duchess with a laugh, 'if everyone goes about like that they cannot be blamed for it, since that kind of attire is as fitting and proper for them as it is for the Venetians to wear puffed sleeves or the Florentines to wear hoods.'

'I am not speaking of Lombardy more than of other places,' said Federico, 'because every nation has its share of those who are foolish and those who are sensible. But, to let you know what I think is important when it comes to the way one should dress, let me add that I would like our courtier always to appear neat and refined and to observe a certain modest elegance, though he should avoid being effeminate or foppish in his attire and not exaggerate one feature more than another, as do some who attend so much to their hair that they forget the rest, others who concentrate on their beard, others on their boots, their bonnets or their coifs. For then they seem to have borrowed the things that are rather carefully looked after, whereas the rest, which are completely tasteless, are recognized as being their own. So my advice to our courtier is to shun this kind of dress; and I would add that he should decide for himself what appearance he wants to have and what sort of man he wants to seem, and then dress accordingly, so that his clothes help him to be taken for such, even by those who do not hear him speak or see him perform anything at all.'

'It does not seem to me,' said signor Gaspare Pallavicino, 'that it is either right or indeed usual for people of quality to judge a man's character by his dress rather than by his words or actions, for in that case there would be many mistakes; and there is good reason for the proverb which says that the habit does not make the monk.'

'I am not saying,' replied Federico, 'that clothes provide the basis for making hard and fast judgements about a man's character, or that we cannot discover far more from someone's words and actions than from his attire. But I do maintain that a man's attire is also no small evidence for what kind of personality he has, allowing that it can sometimes prove misleading. Moreover, habits and manners, as well as actions and words, provide clues to the quality of the man.'

'And on what kind of things, other than words or actions, do you suggest we can base our judgement?' asked signor Gaspare.

Federico replied: 'I think you are splitting hairs. But to explain what I mean; there are some activities which still endure after they have been completed, such as building and writing, and there are others which do not endure, and those are what I am thinking of now. Thus in this sense I do not call walking, laughing, looking and so forth, activities, and yet all these external things often provide information about what is within. Tell me, didn't you decide that that friend of ours of whom we were speaking only this morning was a conceited and frivolous man, as soon as you saw him walking with that head-tossing and wriggling about, and smiling invitations to all and sundry to doff their caps to him? So too, whenever you see someone staring too intently, with blank eyes like an idiot, or laughing stupidly like those goitred mutes of the mountains of Bergamo, even though he doesn't say or do anything else, don't you take him for a great oaf? Do you not see, therefore, that these habits and manners, which for the moment I do not think of as acts, are in great part what men are known by?

'But there is another thing which seems to me greatly to damage or enhance a man's reputation, and this is his choice of really intimate friends. For to be sure it stands to reason that persons who are joined together in close amity and indissoluble companionship should also conform in their wishes, thoughts, opinions and aptitudes. So a man who associates with the ignorant or wicked is taken to be ignorant or wicked; and, on the other hand, a man who associates with those who are good, wise and discreet, is taken for such himself. For it seems natural for like to attract like. Hence I think it is right to take great care in forming these friendships, for of two close friends whoever knows one immediately assumes the other to be of the same character.'

To this, Pietro Bembo answered: 'In contracting such intimate friendships as you describe it certainly seems to me that one ought to be extremely careful, not only because of the question of enhancing or damaging one's reputation but also because nowadays there are very few true friends to be found. Indeed, I doubt whether there exist in the world any more a Pylades and Orestes, a Theseus and Pirithous,[8] or a Scipio and Laelius. Rather, I wonder by what fate it happens every day that two friends, after years of heartfelt and mutual affection, will end by deceiving one another in some way or other, either from malice or envy or inconstancy or some other evil motive. And they heap on each other the blame both doubtless deserve. Thus for my own part I have more than once been deceived by the person I loved most and of whose love, above everyone else's, I have been most confident; and because of this I have sometimes thought to myself that it may be as well never to trust anyone in this world nor to give oneself as a hostage to a friend, however dear and cherished he may be, to the extent of telling him all one's thoughts without reserve as if he were one's very self. For there are so many concealed places and recesses in our minds that it is humanly impossible to discover and judge the pretences hidden there. So I believe that it may be right to love and serve one person above all others, according to merit and worth, but never to trust so much in this tempting trap of friendship as to have cause to repent of it later on.'

Then Federico remarked: 'But certainly the loss would be far greater than the gain if from human intercourse should be removed that supreme degree of friendship which, I maintain, contains the best of life. Therefore I can in no way allow that what you say is reasonable; on the contrary, I would go so far as to maintain, for the most cogent reasons, that without this perfect friendship men would be the unhappiest of all creatures; and because some profane persons sully the sacred name of friendship, this does not mean that we should uproot it from our souls and because of the faults of the wicked deprive the good of so much happiness. And it is my opinion that here in our midst may be found more than one pair of friends, whose love is constant and without deceit, and bound to endure in all its intimacy until death, no less than if they were those of the ancient world whom you named earlier on. This is what happens when one chooses for a friend someone of similar ways, apart from the influence of the stars; and all that I have said I mean as regards good and virtuous persons, since the friendship of wicked men is not friendship at all. I also believe that the bond of friendship should not involve more than two people, for otherwise it could perhaps be dangerous. The reason for this is that, as you know, harmony is more difficult to achieve with several instruments than with two. I wish our courtier, therefore, to have a sincere and intimate friend of his own, if possible, of the kind we have described; and then that he should love, honour and respect all his other friends, according to their worth and merits, and also endeavour to associate more with those who are highly esteemed and noble and recognized as virtuous than with the ignoble and those of little worth, so that he in turn may be loved and honoured by them. And he will succeed in this if he is courteous, compassionate, generous, affable and charming as a companion, lively and diligent in serving and forwarding the advantage and honour of his friends, whether they are absent or present, tolerating their natural and excusable defects, without breaking with them for trifling reasons, and correcting in himself the defects that are amicably pointed out to him. He will succeed by never pushing in front of others to secure the first and most honoured place and by never doing as some do, who affect to despise the world and wish to lay down the law to everyone with a certain tiresome severity, and who, as well as being contentious over every little thing at all the wrong times, seek to censure what they do not do themselves and always find cause to complain of their friends, which is a detestable habit.'

After Federico had fallen silent, signor Gaspare Pallavicino began as follows:

'I should like you to go into rather more detail than you have done on the subject of behaviour between friends, for truly you talk very much in generalities and seem to discuss everything, as it were, merely in passing.'

'What do you mean, "in passing"?' replied Federico. 'Do you perhaps want me to tell you as well the very words you ought to use? Do you not agree that we have said enough on the subject?'

'Enough, I think,' answered signor Gaspare. 'But I should like to hear some more particulars concerning the manner in which men and women ought to converse among themselves. For in my opinion this is of considerable importance, seeing that at Court this is the chief occupation for most of the time, and if it never varied it would soon become tiresome.'

'It seems to me,' replied Federico, 'that we have given the

courtier a knowledge of so many subjects that he can readily vary his conversation a great deal and adapt himself to the qualities of those with whom he has dealings, assuming that he possesses good judgement and allows himself to be ruled by that, and, depending on the circumstances, attends sometimes to grave matters and sometimes to festivities and games.'

'And which games?' asked signor Gaspare.

Federico answered with a laugh: 'For this, let us go for advice to Fra Serafino, who invents new ones every day.'

'Joking apart,' answered signor Gaspare, 'does it seem to you that it is wrong for the courtier to play at cards and dice?'

'To me, no,' said Federico, 'unless he does so too assiduously, and in consequence neglects things of greater importance, or indeed for no other reason than to win money and cheat his partner, and then, when he loses, is so dismayed and angry as to prove his avarice.'

Signor Gaspare replied: 'And what do you say about the game of chess?'

'That is certainly a refined and ingenious recreation,' said Federico, 'but it seems to me to possess one defect; namely, that it is possible for it to demand too much knowledge, so that anyone who wishes to become an outstanding player must, I think, give to it as much time and study as he would to learning some noble science or performing well something or other of importance; and yet for all his pains when all is said and done all he knows is a game. Therefore as far as chess is concerned we reach what is a very rare conclusion: that mediocrity is more to be praised than excellence.'

Signor Gaspare replied: 'But there are to be found many Spaniards who excel at chess and at a number of other games, and yet do not study them too exhaustively or neglect other things.'

'You may take it for granted,' said Federico, 'that they put in a great deal of study, but they conceal it. However, the other games you mention, apart from chess, are doubtless like many I have seen played which are of little moment and serve only to make the common people marvel; so I do not consider they deserve any praise or reward other than what Alexander the Great gave to the man who at some distance was so good at impaling chickpeas on a pin.

'But because it seems that Fortune, in this as in so many other things, has great influence on men's opinions, we sometimes see that a gentleman, however finely endowed and gifted he may be, proves disagreeable to his lord and always, as we say, raises his gall; and this is for no discernible reason. Thus when he comes into his lord's presence, and before he has been recognized by the others, though his conversation may be fluent and ready and though his behaviour, gestures and words and everything else may be all that can be desired, his lord will show that he has no high regard for him and, indeed, will display his contempt. And as an immediate result of this, the others will at once fall in line with the wishes of the prince and to each one of them it will seem that the man is worthless; nor will there be found any to value or respect him, or laugh at his witticisms or regard him as being of any account; on the contrary, they will all immediately start to mock him and hound him down. Nor will it do the wretch any good to answer agreeably and well or take what is being said in good part, since they will all, down to the page-boys themselves, set about him so that even if he were the worthiest man in the world he would still be hounded down and frustrated. In contrast to this, if the prince should show that he favours some ignorant fellow, who knows neither how to speak or behave, often his manners and ways, however foolish and uncouth they may be, will be praised to the skies by everyone and the whole Court will seem to admire and respect him, and everyone will laugh at his jokes and at certain flat and boorish sayings calculated to make people feel sick rather than entertained. This is the extent to which men obstinately adhere to opinions engendered by the favour or disfavour of princes. Therefore I should wish our courtier to bolster up his inherent worth with skill and cunning, and ensure that whenever he has to go where he is a stranger and unknown he is preceded by a good reputation and that it becomes known that elsewhere, among other lords, ladies and knights, he is very highly regarded. For the fame which appears to rest on the opinions of many fosters a certain unshakeable belief in a man's worth which is then easily maintained and strengthened in minds already thus disposed and prepared. Moreover, by taking these steps the courtier avoids the annoyance I always feel when I am asked who I am and what my name is.'

'I fail to see how this helps,' commented Bernardo Bibbiena, 'for it has several times been my experience (and, I believe, that of others) to have decided, in the light of what was said by those able to judge, that something was of outstanding quality before I saw it; but then, when I have come to see it I have been greatly disappointed, and it has fallen a long way short of what I expected. This has been the result simply of relying too much on hearsay and having formed such an exaggerated notion in my mind of what to expect that when I have had to compare what I anticipated with the real thing, for all its possible excellence and grandeur, the latter has seemed of little or no account. And the same kind of fate can, I fear, befall our courtier. So I do not see that it is right to raise such expectations and rely on advance reports of what we are like. For our minds often imagine things that cannot be lived up to, and in that way more is lost than gained.'

Here Federico said: 'The things that you and others discover to be far less impressive than their reputation are usually of the kind that can be summed up at a glance, as if, for example, you had never visited Naples or Rome but had heard a great deal about them and were to imagine them as being far more impressive than perhaps proved to be the case. But this does not happen when it is a question of a man's character, because the outward appearances are the least important. For instance, if you were to hear someone speak for the first time, not finding in him the qualities you had been anticipating, you would not change your opinion as swiftly as you would regarding matters of which the eye can judge immediately; rather, you would expect to discover from day to day some hidden virtue, and you would hold firm to the impression created in your mind by what so many others had said; and then if the gentleman concerned were to be as well endowed as our courtier is supposed to be, the good reports received about him would be confirmed with every hour that passed, since he would bring this about by his actions and you would always give him credit for even more than was apparent.

'To be sure, it cannot be denied that these first impressions carry great force and that we should pay considerable attention to them. And to make you realize just how important they are, let me tell you about a gentleman I once knew who, although he was of pleasing appearance and modest behaviour, and also a very capable warrior, was not so outstanding as regards any of these qualities that there were not to be found many who were his equal and even better. However, as luck would have it, a certain lady fell very deeply in love with him. She saw that he felt the same way, and as her love grew day by day, there not being any way for them to speak to each other, she revealed her sentiments to another lady, who she hoped would be of service to her in this affair. Now this lady neither in rank nor beauty was a whit inferior to the first; and it came about that when she heard the young man (whom she had never seen) spoken of so affectionately, and came to realize that the other woman, whom she knew was extremely discreet and intelligent, loved him beyond words, she straight away began to imagine that he must be the most handsome, the wisest, the most discreet of men, and, in short, the man most worthy of her love in all the world. So, never having set eyes on him, she fell in love with him so passionately that she set out to win him not for her friend but for herself. And in this she succeeded with little effort, for indeed she was a woman more to be wooed than to do the wooing. And now listen to the splendid sequel: not long afterwards it happened that a letter which she had written to her lover fell into the hands of another woman of comparable rank, charm and beauty; and since she, like most women, was curious and eager to learn secrets, she opened the letter and read it. Realizing that it was written from the depths of passion, in the most loving and ardent terms, she was at first moved with compassion, for she knew very well from whom the letter came and to whom it was addressed; then, however, such was the power of the words she read, turning them over in her mind and considering what kind of man it must be who had been able to arouse such great love, she at once began to fall in love with him herself; and the letter was without doubt far more effective than if the young man had himself written it to her. And just as it sometimes happens that the poison prepared for a prince kills the one who tastes his food, so that poor woman, in her greediness, drank the love potion prepared for another. What more is there to say? The affair was no secret, and things so developed that many other women besides, partly to spite the others and partly to follow their example, put every care and effort into winning this man's love, squabbling over it for a while as boys do for cherries. And all this was the consequence of the first impression formed by the lady who saw how much he was loved by another.'

Here signor Gaspare Pallavicino said with a laugh:

'But to find reasons for your opinion you are citing what is done by women, who are quite unreasonable. And if you were to tell us the whole truth, this fellow who won the favours of so many women must have been a fool and a good-for-nothing, because it is the practice of women always to favour the worst and to follow their leader like sheep, whether for good or ill. Moreover, they are so jealous of each other that even if he had been a monster they would still have wished to steal him away from one another.'

At this, almost everyone tried to say something in contradiction to signor Gaspare, but the Duchess made them all keep quiet, and then she said:

'I would allow someone to answer you were it not that the wicked things you are saying about women are so far from the truth that they reflect shame and discredit on the one who is saying them rather than on women. However, I have no intention of letting you be cured of your bad habits by hearing all the conclusive arguments against what you are saying, lest you escape the severe punishment that you deserve for your sin, namely, the poor opinion which everyone who hears the way you talk will have of you.'

Then Federico added: 'You must not say that women are completely irrational, signor Gaspare, even if sometimes they fall in love more by someone else's judgement than by their own. For there are very often noble and wise men who do the same, and, if the truth were told, you yourself and all of us frequently, and at this very moment, rely more on the opinions of others than on our own. And to prove this, consider that not so long ago, when certain verses were presented here as being by Sannazaro, everyone thought they were extremely fine and praised them to the skies;

then when it was established that they were by someone else their reputation sank immediately and they seemed quite mediocre. Then again, when a motet was sung in the presence of the Duchess, it pleased no one and was considered worthless, until it became known that it had been composed by Josquin des Près.[9] What clearer proof do you want of the force of opinion? Do you not remember that once when drinking a certain wine one moment you were saying that it was absolutely perfect and the next that it was really insipid? And this was because you were persuaded that you were drinking two different kinds of wine, one from the Riviera of Genoa and the other from this locality? And even when the mistake was discovered you simply refused to believe it, so firmly entrenched in your mind was the false opinion which, of course, arose from what others had said.

'Therefore the courtier should at the outset take great care to give a good impression of himself, and bear in mind how harmful and fatal it is to do the opposite. Men who expose themselves to this danger more than others are those who make it their profession to be very amusing and think by these pleasantries of theirs to be allowed a certain licence which makes it proper and permissible for them to do and say whatever they wish, without thinking. Thus people like this very often embark on certain things without knowing how to finish, and they then try to extricate themselves by raising a laugh. But they do this so awkwardly that it does not succeed, and instead their efforts fall flat and they inspire the greatest distaste in whoever sees or hears them. On other occasions, convinced they are being terribly witty and amusing, they use filthy and indecent language in the presence of noble ladies, and often to their face. And the more they make the ladies blush, the more they are convinced that they are being good courtiers; they never stop laughing and they pride themselves on the fine talents they think they possess. But the only reason they behave in such a beastly fashion is because they believe it makes them the life and soul of the party: this is what they think really praiseworthy and what they pride themselves on most. And to acquire this reputation they indulge in the most shameful and shocking discourtesies in the world. Sometimes they push one another downstairs, belabour each other with sticks and bricks, throw handfuls of dust in each other's eyes, cause their horses to collapse on one another in ditches or downhill; then at table they hurl the soup, or the sauce or jelly, in one another's face, and they burst out laughing; and the one who knows how to do most things of this kind prides himself on being the better courtier and the more gallant, and thinks he has covered himself in glory. Then sometimes they ask a gentleman to join in their amusements, and if he does not wish to take part in their horseplay they immediately allege that he thinks himself a cut above them and too important, and has no party spirit. But there is worse to come. There are even some who compete among themselves and wager as to who can eat and drink the most revolting and filthy things, and they hit upon things so abhorrent to our senses that it is impossible to mention them without a shudder.'

'And what things can these be?' asked signor Lodovico Pio.

'Ask Marquess Febus to tell you,' answered Federico, 'for he has often seen them done in France, and perhaps taken part himself.'

Marquess Febus remarked: 'Well, I have seen nothing of this kind done in France that is not also done in Italy; indeed, all that is good among the Italians in their dress and recreations, their banquets and feats of arms, and everything that befits a courtier, they have had from the French.'

'I do not say,' replied Federico, 'that there are not to be found the most cultivated and well-mannered gentlemen in France, and I for one have known very many worthy of the highest praise. But there are also some to be found who are very careless; and, broadly speaking, it seems to me that the customs of the Spaniards are more suited to the Italians than those of the French, because the calm dignity characteristic of the Spaniards seems to me more appropriate to us than the ready vivacity we see in almost everything the French people do. In them, this is not unbecoming; in fact, it is full of charm since it is natural and proper and so carries no suggestion of affectation. And admittedly there are many Italians who do their best to imitate the way the French behave; but all they understand is wagging their heads as they speak and bowing clumsily to one side and walking so fast when they are out on the streets that their attendants can't keep pace with them. Acting like this, they imagine they are being good Frenchmen and have their ease of manner. But this is rarely possible except for those who have been brought up in France and been taught these things from childhood. The same is true of knowing many languages, which is a gift I like to see in the courtier, especially as regards French and Spanish, since in Italy we have very frequent dealings with both countries and their ways conform more with ours than any others, and their rulers (who are powerful in war and splendid in peace) keep their courts full of fine gentlemen who then travel the world; and we are obliged to converse with them.

'Now I do not want to go into great detail as regards matters that are already very familiar, such as that your courtier should not profess to be a great eater or drinker, or indulge in bad habits, or be disgusting and dissolute in his manner of life, and act like a peasant who stinks of the soil a mile off. For a man of this sort can never hope to become a good courtier and indeed can be given no occupation other than looking after the farm animals. So, to conclude, I maintain that the courtier would do well to understand everything we have said is appropriate to him, so that he can do everything possible and that everyone marvels at him and he at no one. But this is on the understanding that he does not display a certain proud and inhuman impassivity, as do some who will never seem astonished at what others accomplish because they assume they can do far better themselves, and by their silence scorn those things as undeserving of mention; and they do this as if to suggest that there is no one their equal let alone capable of appreciating the profundity of their knowledge. Our courtier must avoid this hateful kind of behaviour and praise the achievements of others with great kindness and goodwill; and although he may think himself a man to be admired and by a long chalk superior to everyone else, he should not reveal this. However, since perfection of this kind is hardly ever if at all to be found in human nature, the man who feels he is wanting in some particular ought not to become diffident or give up hope of achieving an excellent standard, even though he cannot reach the supreme perfection to which he aspires. For in every accomplishment there are many commendable grades besides the highest, and if a man aims at the top, he is nearly always certain of reaching at least half-way. Therefore if our courtier finds he is skilled in something other than arms I should wish him to derive profit and honour from it in a suitable way; and he should know how to use his discretion and good judgement in bringing people skilfully and opportunely to see and hear what he considers he is good at, always seeming to do so without ostentation, but casually and as if at the request of others rather than of his own will. And, if at all possible, he should always be well briefed and prepared for everything he has to do or say, though giving the impression that it is off the cuff. As regards matters in which he is unsure of himself, he should treat them merely in passing, without going too deeply into them, but in such a way as to make people credit him with far more knowledge than he displays, as sometimes happens with poets who hint at subtle matters of philosophy or other branches of knowledge, and doubtless understand very little about them. And then as regards things about which he knows he is totally ignorant, I should wish our courtier to keep completely silent and not to seek to acquire any reputation for understanding them; rather, when necessary, he ought to confess his ignorance.'

Then Calmeta said: 'That is not what Nicoletto[10] would have done. He was a very good philosopher, but he knew no more about law than about how to fly, and when the mayor of Padua decided to give him a lectureship in law, despite the urgings of many scholars, he would never disabuse him and confess that he knew nothing about it. He was always protesting that in this instance he disagreed with the opinion of Socrates, and that it was never for a philosopher to admit his ignorance.'

'I do not say,' replied Federico, 'that a courtier should volunteer a confession of his ignorance, without its being required. For I also dislike the silly habit of accusing or denigrating oneself. Thus sometimes I laugh to myself at certain men who quite needlessly tell things that reflect rather poorly on themselves, even though they may not involve them in any fault, as did a certain gentleman you all know who whenever he heard mention of the encounter with King Charles in the Parmesan would at once begin to describe how he had fled from the field, giving the impression that he had seen and heard nothing of the battle. Then when a certain famous tournament was spoken of, he always told the story of how he had fallen; and in his conversation he always appeared to be wanting to find the opportunity to be able to recount how one night, when he had paid a visit to a certain lady, he had received a thrashing. I do not want our courtier to indulge in this kind of folly; but I certainly believe that when the opportunity arises for him to display his ignorance over something, then he should let it pass by, and if compelled to do so he should plainly admit that he is ignorant rather than run any risks; and in this way he will escape the censure nowadays justly deserved by many who, I do not know through what perverse instinct or irrational motive, always strive to do what they cannot and avoid things they understand. In proof of this, I know an outstanding musician who has given up music and devotes himself completely to composing verse, in doing which he imagines he is a great genius, and he makes everyone laugh at him and has now lost even his music. Another, one of the world's finest painters, despises the art for which he has so rare a talent and has set himself to study philosophy; and in this he has strange notions and fanciful revelations that, if he tried to paint them, for all his skill he couldn't.[11] There are countless people who act like this. Then again there are those who knowing they are outstanding in one field, devote most of their energies to another that they happen to know something about. Then whenever they are called upon to show what they can do as regards the subject in which they know they have talent, they give a redoubtable performance; and it often happens that when they are seen by all and sundry to be so competent with regard to something they do not profess, it is believed that they must be even more competent in what is their main activity. This stratagem, provided it is used judiciously, does not displease me in the slightest.'

Then signor Gaspare Pallavicino replied: 'What you are describing seems to me more like crude deception than art. Nor do I believe such deceit is ever fitting for one who wishes to be a man of honour.'

'It is not a question of deceit,' answered Federico, 'but of an embellishment for whatever one does; and even if it is deception, it is not to be censured. In the case of two men who are fencing, would you not say that the one who defeats the other is deceiving him when he does so because he has more skill than his partner? And if you have a lovely jewel without a setting, and it passes into the hands of a good goldsmith who greatly enhances its beauty by setting it well, would you not say that he is deceiving the eye? And yet he deserves praise for the deception, since with good judgement and skill his cunning hands often add grace and adornment to ivory or silver or to a lovely stone by setting it in fine gold. So we must not say that art (or this kind of deceit, if you want to call it so) deserves censure. Nor is it wrong for a man who believes he is competent in some matter to seek cleverly for the occasion when he can demonstrate his abilities and, in the same way, to conceal the things that he believes merit little praise, though everything should be done with circumspection and reserve. Do you not recall that, without appearing to seek them out, King Ferdinand was always ready to seize the opportunity from time to time to go about in his doublet? And this he did because he was proud of his physique. And also, since he did not have attractive hands, that he rarely if ever took off his gloves? I also seem to remember having read that Julius Caesar very readily took to wearing a laurel wreath, in order to hide his baldness. But in all these matters one must be very prudent and judicious so as not to exaggerate in any way; for very often in avoiding one error a man falls into another, and in seeking to win praise, wins blame.

'Therefore in our way of life and our dealings with others the safest thing is to observe the golden mean, and this, to be sure, provides a strong and reliable protection against envy, which is always to be avoided as much as possible. I also wish our courtier to be careful not to acquire the name of a liar or a boaster, which can sometimes happen even to those who do not deserve it. So in his conversation he should always be on his guard against departing from the truth or telling too often those truths that have the appearance of falsehoods, unlike those who never speak of anything except miracles and yet want to be held in such authority that every incredible thing they say must be believed. There are others who at the beginning of a friendship, to win favour with their new friend, swear, on the very first day they speak to him, that there is no one in the world they love more than him, and that they would willingly die to serve him, and so on, out of all reason. And when they part from him they make a show of weeping and of being speechless with grief. So in wanting to be thought extremely loving, they acquire a reputation for being liars and stupid flatterers. However, it would take too long and be too tedious to discuss all the vices possible in our dealings with others; so, as far as my wishes for the courtier are concerned, let it suffice to add to what I have already said that he should be so constituted that he never lacks for eloquence adapted to those with whom he is talking, and that he should know how to refresh and charm the minds of his listeners, and move them to merriment and laughter with his agreeable pleasantries and witticisms, in such a way that, without ever being tedious or boring, he is always a source of pleasure.

'I think that by now signora Emilia will be ready to allow me to stay silent. If she denies me this, then on the strength of my own words I shall be convinced that I am not the good courtier whom I have been discussing. For not only is eloquence (which you have not been hearing, and perhaps never have heard from me) beginning to fail me completely but also such things, for what they are worth, as I am capable of saying.'

Here, the Prefect said with a smile: 'I do not want anyone here to be under the illusion that you are not an excellent courtier; for your desire to be silent is caused by your wanting to avoid work rather than from lack of something to say. Therefore, to avoid giving the impression that in a gathering as worthy as this and in such an excellent discussion anything is being neglected, be good enough to teach us how we are to make use of those pleasantries you have mentioned, and explain the skill that goes with all this kind of amusing talk, intended to arouse laughter and merriment in a polite and appropriate way, for it seems to me that this is very important and most fitting for the courtier.'

'My lord,' replied Federico, 'pleasantries and witticisms are the gift and favour of Nature rather than of art; but in this certain people are quicker than the others, and notably the Tuscans who are truly very sharp. It also seems that the Spaniards are instinctively witty. But there are many among them, and of other races too, who let their loquacity run away with them and become insipid and inept, because they pay no regard to the kind of people with whom they are talking, to the place where they happen to be, or to the rules of sobriety and modesty that they ought to observe.'

Then the Prefect answered: 'You deny that there is any art in pleasantries, and yet it seems to me that when you condemn those who do not observe the rules of sobriety and modesty and have no respect for the circumstances or for the persons with whom they are talking you prove that this is also a subject that can be taught and has some method in it.'

'These rules, my lord,' replied Federico, 'are so universal that they fit and apply to everything. But I said there was no skill in light conversation, since it seems to be that there are only two kinds to be found. The first is sustained through a long narrative, as we see in the case of some men who very charmingly and agreeably recount and describe something that has happened to them or that they have seen or heard, and by their words and gestures bring it before our very eyes, as if we could reach out and touch it; and this, for want of another name, we can perhaps call "polished" or "urbane discourse". The other kind of pleasantry is extremely brief and consists merely in sayings, such as are often heard among us, that are sharp and spontaneous or caustic; and unless they are rather cutting they seem to lack elegance. In the ancient world these used to be called *dicta*, and now some call them quips. Now as for the first kind of light conversation, in urbane story-telling, there is no need for any art, since Nature herself creates and fashions men with a talent for agreeable story-telling, and she gives them the countenance, the gestures, the voice and the words all suited to imitating what they want. As for quips, what place is there for art? For in this case, a pungent remark must be uttered and must hit the target before the speaker seems to have had time to think. Therefore I consider that this springs entirely from genius and Nature.'

At this point, Pietro Bembo joined in and said:

'The Prefect is not denying what you say, namely, that Nature and genius play the chief role, and especially as regards invention. But surely however brilliant he is a man receives good and bad ideas, of lesser and greater worth; and then these are corrected and refined by judgement and art, which reject the bad and select the good. Therefore, leaving aside what springs from genius, explain to us the part played by art, namely, concerning the pleasantries and witticisms that provoke laughter, which befit the courtier and which not, and on what occasions and in what manner they should be employed; for this is what the Prefect is asking of you.'

Then with a smile Federico said: 'There is no one here to whom I do not yield in everything, and especially in the matter of being facetious; unless perhaps sheer silliness (which often makes people laugh more than clever sayings) is also accepted as wit.'

And then, turning to Count Lodovico and Bernardo Bibbiena, he added: 'Here are the masters in this matter, from whom, if I am to speak of amusing talk, I must first learn what to say.'

Count Lodovico replied: 'It seems to me that you are already practising what you say you know nothing about, namely, by trying to make us all laugh by making fun of Bernardo and me; because everyone here knows that you are far better at what you are praising us for. Therefore if you are weary, it would be better to ask the Duchess to consent to postpone the rest of the discussion until tomorrow rather than shift the burden off your shoulders by deceitful means.'

Federico started to answer, but signora Emilia at once interrupted him to say:

'It is not in the rules that the discussion should now be devoted to praising you; for we know you all very well. But since I recall that you, my dear Count, alleged yesterday evening that I did not share the work fairly, it would be right for Federico to rest for a moment, and the task of speaking of pleasantries we shall give to Bernardo Bibbiena, because not only do we know that he is most amusing when he talks at length but we remember that he has several times promised that he would write on the subject, and so we may well believe that he has given it a lot of thought and so should be able to satisfy us completely. Then, after we have finished speaking about pleasantries, Federico shall continue with what he still has to tell us about the courtier.'

Then Federico remarked: 'Madam, I do not know what I have yet to say about the courtier. However, like a traveller weary from his long journey when the sun is high, I shall find repose listening to the discourse of Bernardo and the sound of his voice as if I were resting under some lovely, shady tree and hearing the gentle murmuring of a flowing spring. Then, refreshed a little, perhaps I will have something more to say.'

Bernardo answered with a smile: 'If I showed you the top of my head you would soon realize what kind of shade could be expected from its leaves. As for listening to the murmur of a flowing spring, perhaps you will be lucky, because I was once turned into a spring not by any of the ancient deities but by our own Fra Mariano, and since then I have never lacked water.'

Then everyone burst out laughing, for the joke to which Bernardo alluded and which occurred in Rome in the presence of Cardinal Galeotto of San Pietro in Vincoli,[12] was well known to all.

After the laughter had died down, signora Emilia said:

'Now stop making us laugh with your pleasantries and teach us how we are to use them, and how they are devised, and all that you know on the subject. And so as not to waste any more time, please begin immediately.'

'I fear,' said Bernardo, 'that the hour is late; and lest my speaking of pleasantries should prove rather unwelcome and wearisome, perhaps it would be as well to postpone it until tomorrow.'

At this, everyone at once started to protest that the time at which it was customary to end the discussion was still a long way off. So then, turning to the Duchess and to signora Emilia, Bernardo said:

'I do not want to shirk my task; but just as I always marvel at the boldness of those who dare to sing to the viol in the presence of our Giacomo Sansecondo, so I wonder whether I should talk about jokes in the presence of an audience which understands what I should say far better than I do. However, to avoid providing an excuse for any of these gentlemen to decline what they may be ordered to do, I shall say, as briefly as I can, whatever occurs to me on the subject of the causes of laughter, which is so natural to mankind that to define a man it is customary to say that he is an animal capable of laughing. For laughter is seen only in men, and it is nearly always the sign of a certain inward hilarity of the spirit, which is naturally attracted to pleasure and desirous of rest and recreation. So we see many things devised by men for this purpose, such as festivals and various kinds of spectacle. And because we like those who are responsible for providing us with our recreations, the kings of the ancient world, the Roman, the Athenian and many others, in order to secure the goodwill of the populace and to feed the eyes and mind of the multitude, used to build great theatres and other public edifices, and there they would show new kinds of sport, horse and chariot races, combats, strange beasts, comedies, tragedies and mime. Nor were grave philosophers averse to such displays, and they would often, both at spectacles of that kind or at banquets, relax their minds which were weary from their exalted discourses and inspired thoughts; and this is something all kinds and conditions of men willingly do, for not only labourers in the fields, sailors and all those who do hard and rough work with their hands but also holy men of religion and prisoners waiting in hourly expectation of death, all seek solace in light recreation. Therefore everything which provokes laughter exalts a man's spirit and gives him pleasure, and for a while enables him to forget the trials and tribulations of which life is full. So you can see that laughter is most agreeable to everyone and the one who inspires it at the right time and place deserves every praise. But what laughter is, and where it is to be found, and how it sometimes takes possession of our veins, our eyes, our mouth and sides, and sometimes seems about to make us burst, being uncontrollable no matter how hard we try, I shall leave to Democritus[13] to explain; who, even if he should promise to find the words, would not be able to.

'Now the location and, as it were, the source of the ridiculous is to be found in a kind of deformity; for we laugh only at things that contain some elements of incongruity and seem disagreeable though they are not really so. I know no way of explaining it otherwise; but if you think about it, you will realize that invariably what causes laughter is something that is incongruous and yet not really unpleasing. Now, as for the ways in which the courtier should try to cause laughter and the limits he should observe in doing so, I shall endeavour to explain as far as my judgement allows. For to cause laughter is not always fitting for the courtier, nor should he do so after the manner of fools and drunkards, or stupid clowns and buffoons. And though it appears that people like this are in demand at the Courts, they do not merit the name of courtier but each should be called by his proper name and judged for what he is. It is also necessary to consider with great care the reservations and limits to be acknowledged when causing laughter by means of sarcasm, and also who it is who is being stung; for there is nothing to laugh at in deriding some unfortunate creature or some rascal or known criminal, since the last deserve a worse punishment than mockery, and normal people are not disposed to make sport of the unfortunate, unless they boast of their misfortune and are proud and presumptuous. The courtier should also guard against mocking those who are universally favoured and loved by all and who are powerful, because by doing so he can sometimes stir up dangerous enmities. But it is allowable to hold up to derision and laugh at the vices of those who are neither so wretched as to excite compassion nor so wicked as to seem to deserve capital punishment, nor again of such exalted rank that their slightest anger can do one great harm.

'You must also understand that what can be phrased as an amusing witticism can also be interpreted as a serious comment intended for praise or censure, sometimes with the use of exactly the same words. Thus in praise of a generous man who puts his belongings at the disposal of his friends, it is frequently said that what he has is not his own; and the same words may be used to accuse someone who has obtained his belongings through theft or some other evil means. One also hears it said: "She is a much-loved lady," meaning to praise a woman for her prudence and virtue; but the same words might be used to censure her for bestowing her favours widely. More often, however, it is a question of exploiting the same situations rather than the same words. For example, just the other day when a lady was hearing mass in church with three gentlemen, one of whom was her gallant, a poor beggar approached and standing in front of the lady asked her for alms; although he begged her insistently, whining and demanding, she not only gave him nothing but did not even dismiss him, and instead stood with a distracted expression as if she were thinking of something else. Her lover said to his two companions: "You see what I can expect from my lady, who is so cruel that not only does she refuse to give alms to that naked wretch who is dying of hunger and who is pleading all this time so pitiably but she refuses even to send him away, she so much enjoys the sight of someone languishing in misery and imploring her favour in vain."

'One of his friends answered: "This is not cruelty, but a tacit way of teaching you to understand that she is never pleased with someone who is too importunate."

'Said the other: "No, it is a sign that although she does not grant what is asked, she likes to be begged for it."

'So there you see,' continued Bernardo, 'that the refusal of that lady to dismiss the beggar prompted words of severe censure, of modest praise, and of biting sarcasm.

'Now, to go back to the kind of pleasantries that pertain to our subject, I maintain that, in my opinion, there are three varieties, although Federico mentioned only two: namely, a long and amusing narrative, in a polished style, that tells us how some incident was resolved; and the spontaneous thrust of a single cutting remark. But we shall add the third kind, called practical jokes, which include story-telling, brief comments, and also a certain amount of action. The first kind of pleasantries, which consist in a flow of narrative, are, as it happens, just like short stories. And, to give you an example: the time when Pope Alexander VI died and Pius III was made pope, your fellow Mantuan, my lady, Antonio Agnello being at Rome and in the Vatican Palace, was discussing the death of the one and the creation as pope of the other; and while giving his opinion on these occurrences to certain of his friends he remarked: "Gentlemen, in the time of Catullus doors began to speak without tongues and to hear without ears, and thus to disclose the adulteries that had been committed. And now, even if men are not as worthy as they were in those days, it may be that doors, many of which, at least here in Rome, are made of ancient marble, have the same powers as they had then. And for myself, I believe that these two in front of us would know how to resolve all our doubts if we wished to learn from them."

'At this, the gentlemen with him waited in suspense, wondering what the outcome would be. Antonio continued to walk to and fro, and then all of a sudden he lifted his eyes to look at one of the doors in the hall in which they were strolling, and, after pausing a moment, he pointed out to his companions the inscription that it bore. This showed the name of Pope Alexander, followed by the letters V and I, signifying, as you know, the Sixth. Then Antonio said: "See that this door says 'Pope Alexander VI', meaning to tell us that he became pope by means of the violence he has employed, and that he has made use more of violence than of reason.* And now let us see whether we can learn something about the new pontiff from the other door." Then, turning casually to the other door, Antonio pointed out the inscription which contained the letters N, PP and V, standing for Nicolaus Papa Quintus; and straight away he cried: "Oh dear, this is bad news. The door is telling us: Nihil Papa Valet."†

'Now you see that this kind of joke is both elegant and agreeable, and befits a courtier whether the story is true or fictitious. For in this case one may invent as much as one pleases without being blamed for it; and in telling the truth one may embroider it with a little falsehood, more or less, according to need. But perfect grace and true merit in this consist in using both gestures and words effortlessly to express exactly what one wants, so that those who are listening seem to see what is being described before their very eyes. When this is achieved, it is so effective that sometimes it enhances and makes very amusing something which would not, of itself, be

* VI is either 'the Sixth' or the ablative of the Latin *vis*, meaning 'by force'.

† Meaning 'the Pope is worthless'. Rather inappropriate as a comment on either Pope Nicholas V – a saintly man and a notable theologian and patron – or indeed on the worthy Pope Pius III, who admittedly reigned for only two months.

very witty or ingenious. And although stories like this require both gestures and the power of the spoken word, yet sometimes they can achieve their purpose effectively when written down. Who does not laugh when, in the Eighth Day of his *Decameron*, Giovanni Boccaccio tells how much trouble the priest of Varlungo would take in singing a *Kyrie* or a *Sanctus* when he was aware that Belcolore was in church?* What he writes about Calandrino† also counts as an amusing discourse, as do many other of his stories. And under the same heading may be considered causing laughter by mimicry or imitation, in which I have never seen anyone more outstanding than our Roberto da Bari.'

'That would be no small praise,' said Roberto, 'if it happened to be true, because I would certainly endeavour to imitate the good rather than the bad, and if I could resemble some men I know I would count myself very fortunate indeed. But I'm afraid I know how to imitate only those things which cause laughter and which, you said earlier, are defective.'

Bernardo replied: 'Defective, yes, but not disagreeable. And it must be said that this imitation of which we are speaking is not possible without talent. For as well as choosing appropriate words and gestures, and setting before the very eyes of those who are listening the face and manners of the person being talked about, we must be prudent and pay considerable attention to the place and timing and the kind of people to whom we speak, and not descend to buffoonery or go beyond bounds; and as you observe all these things admirably, I imagine that you know all about them. For to be sure it would not be right for a gentleman to pull faces, to weep and laugh, mimic voices and wrestle with himself, as Berto does, or dress up in peasants' clothes, in front of everyone, like Strascino, and things of that kind, which are suitable for them,

* The story (the second of the Eighth Day of the *Decameron*) is about the affair between the priest of Varlungo and Belcolore, the wife of a farmer, and the trick played by the priest to get back the cloak he left her in lieu of payment for her favours.

† The painter Calandrino (Giovannozzo di Perino) occurs in four of Boccaccio's stories as a simple-minded soul brilliantly exploited by practical jokers.

since that is their profession. But what we must do is to make use of this kind of imitation casually and subtly, remembering always our dignity as gentlemen, eschewing vile words and indecorous acts, not contorting the face or person grotesquely but making our movements in such a way that whoever hears and sees us imagines from our words and gestures far more than he can hear and see and is therefore moved to laughter. In this kind of imitation one must eschew satire that is too cruel, especially as regards facial or physical deformities; for physical defects often provide splendid material for laughter if one exploits them discreetly, but to be too savage in doing this is the work not only of a clown but of an enemy. Thus it is necessary, though difficult, to follow in this the style of our Roberto, who mimics everyone and touches them on their raw spots, even in their presence; and yet no one is upset, nor does it seem that anyone can take it ill. And I shall not provide any examples of this, since every day he provides us with plenty.

'It also causes great mirth (in this matter of story-telling) to list elegantly all the defects of certain persons, provided they are minor faults and not deserving of any greater punishment: such as foolish remarks which may be sometimes straightforward and sometimes tinged with a little quick and compelling extravagance; or again, certain extreme examples of affection; or sometimes a fine, big lie. For example, a few days ago our Cesare described a splendid piece of folly, namely, something he witnessed when, being in the presence of the local mayor, he saw a peasant come in to complain that he had had his donkey stolen; and when he was describing his poverty and the way he had been tricked by that thief, to make his loss seem all the more serious, he said: "Sir, if you had seen my donkey you would realize even more that I have good reason to complain; for when he had his pack on he looked just like Cicero."

'And then again, a friend of ours encountering a herd of goats led by a huge billy-goat stopped and said with a look of astonishment: "Look at that fine billy-goat! He is a veritable St Paul!"

'And signor Gaspare tells of having known a man who, being an old retainer of Duke Ercole of Ferrara, had offered the Duke his two sons as pages; but before the boys could enter his service they both died. When the Duke heard of this, he condoled with the father very affectionately, saying that he grieved very much, because the one time he had seen them they had appeared to be very handsome and sensible boys. To this the father had replied: "My lord, you have seen nothing, for these last few days they had grown far more handsome and able than I could ever have believed, and they were already singing together like two hawks."

'Then only the other day one of our doctors was watching a man who had been condemned to be whipped round the square and feeling sorry for him, when he saw that although his shoulders were bleeding profusely the poor wretch was ambling along as if he were merely out for a walk; so he said to him: "Hurry along, my poor fellow, and get your punishment over soon." At this the man turned and stared at him as if in wonder, and then after a pause he said: "When you are whipped, you have it done your way; and now let me have it done mine."

'You must still remember the foolishness of that abbot, about which the Duke was talking to us a little while ago. He was present one day when Duke Federico was discussing what should be done with a great load of earth that had been excavated for the foundations of this palace, which he was then building, and he remarked: "My lord, I have the perfect answer for where it should go. Order a great pit to be dug, and then it can be put there without any further ado." And to this Duke Federico replied, not without laughing: "And where will we put the earth that comes out of the pit?" Responded the abbot: "Have it dug so large that it will take both loads." And even though the Duke kept insisting that the larger the pit was made, the more earth there would be to dispose of, the man could never get it into his head that it could not be made big enough to take the two loads; and all he would say was: "Well, make it bigger still." So you see what fine brains he had.'

Then Pietro Bembo asked: 'Why do you not tell the story about your Florentine commissary? This was the man who was being besieged in Castellina by the Duke of Calabria when one day he found a number of poisoned bolts that had been fired from the camp; and so he wrote to the Duke to say that if the war had to be waged so barbarously he would have the same medicine put on his cannon balls, and then heaven help those who had the worst of it!'

Bernardo burst out laughing and said:

'Pietro, unless you keep quiet I will tell all the things (and there are plenty of them) that I have seen and heard of your Venetians, and especially when they try to ride on horseback.'

'Please do not,' replied Pietro, 'and I promise to keep quiet about two splendid stories I know concerning Florentines.'

'They must surely have been Sienese,' replied Bernardo, 'who often slip up in this way, such as the one who just recently, on hearing certain letters read in Council, in which to avoid repeating the name of the person concerned use was made of the term "the aforesaid", said to the one who was reading: "Wait a moment, please, and tell me, this 'aforesaid', is he a friend of our city?"

Pietro laughed and added: 'I am talking about the Florentines, not the Sienese.'

'Well speak freely then,' said signora Emilia, 'and do not be so cautious.'

So Pietro continued: 'When the rulers of Florence were waging war against the Pisans, the expenses were so high that they sometimes found their funds exhausted. And one day when it was being discussed in Council how to raise money for their immediate needs, after various suggestions had been made one of the oldest of the citizens said: "I have thought of two ways in which we can find a large sum of money without too much bother. The first is as follows: seeing that we have no more profitable source of revenue than the customs levied at the gates of Florence, and we have eleven gates altogether, let us immediately have built another eleven, and then we shall double the revenue. The other way is this: let orders be given for the immediate opening of mints at Pistoia and Prato, in the same way as at Florence, and day and night let them do nothing except mint money, which should be all gold ducats. And now in my opinion the latter course would be quicker, and far less costly."'

Everyone laughed a great deal at the clever ingenuity of this citizen; and then after the laughter had died away, signora Emilia said:

'Bernardo, will you allow Pietro to make fun of the Florentines without having your revenge?'

Bernardo, who was still laughing, replied: 'I forgive him his offence, for if he had displeased me in making fun of the Florentines, he has pleased me in obeying you, which I myself would always do.'

Then Cesare said: 'I heard a splendid piece of oafishness from a Brescian who earlier this year had gone to Venice for the feast of the Ascension and who in my presence was telling some of his friends the fine things he had seen there: how much merchandise there was, and how much silverware, spices, cloth and fabrics. Then he described how the Signory went forth very ceremoniously to wed the sea in the *Bucentaur*,[14] on which there were so many finely dressed gentlemen and so much music and singing that it seemed just like heaven. Then after one of those friends of his had asked him what kind of music of all he had heard had pleased him most, he said: "It was all good. But I especially noticed someone playing on a strange sort of trumpet which with every move he thrust down his throat more than two palms' length, and then straight away would draw it out, only to thrust it down again; and you never saw the like!"'

At this, everyone began to laugh, realizing the silly notion the man had had in imagining that the musician was thrusting down his throat that part of the trumpet which disappears when it slides in.

Bernardo then added: 'Affectation is simply tiresome when it is only moderate; but when it is highly exaggerated it can be extremely laughable, as with what we hear some persons say on the subject of greatness, the nature of courage or noble birth; or sometimes, in the case of women, on beauty or refinement. Thus just recently a lady who was present at a great festival seemed to be extremely aggrieved and abstracted, and when she was asked what she was thinking about to make her so unhappy she replied: "I was thinking of something that always makes me shudder when it comes to mind and always oppresses my heart. And this is that on the Day of Judgement all our bodies must rise and appear naked before the tribunal of Christ and I cannot tell you the distress I feel at the thought that my body will have to appear naked as well."

'Affectation of this kind, being so exaggerated, is more laughable than annoying. Then you are all acquainted with those lies that are so big and splendid that they make us laugh. And that friend of ours, who never lets us go without them, told me a marvellous one only the other day.'

Then the Magnifico Giuliano said: 'That may be so, but it could not have been finer or more subtle than what one of our Tuscans, a merchant from Lucca in fact, swore was true the other day.'

'Let us hear it,' prompted the Duchess.

The Magnifico Giuliano replied with a laugh:

'Well, this merchant, so I was told, finding himself in Poland decided to buy a large number of sables, with the idea of importing them into Italy and securing a fat profit. After many negotiations, since he could not enter Muscovy himself, in view of the war being waged between the King of Poland and the Duke of Muscovy, using the services of some of the inhabitants of the country he arranged that on the appointed day certain Muscovite merchants should come with their sables to the Polish border, where he promised he would be himself, ready for business. So the merchant made his way with his companions towards Muscovy, and when he came to the Dnieper he found it frozen over like marble and saw that the Muscovites were already on the other bank, but, being in turn fearful of the Poles because of the war, would approach no nearer than the width of the river. Both parties having recognized each other, after signs had been made the Muscovites began to shout the price they wanted for their sables. But it was so bitterly cold that they could not be heard; and the reason for this was that before they could reach the other bank where the merchant stood with his interpreters their words froze in the air and hung there frozen and suspended in such a way that the Poles, who knew the thing to do, chose as their course of action to build a great fire right in the middle of the river. This was because they judged that that was as far as the warmth of the voice carried the words before they had been intercepted by the ice; and the river was, moreover, so solid that it could easily bear the weight of the fire. After the fire had been prepared, the words, which had been frozen for the space of an hour, began to melt and to descend with a murmur like snow falling from the mountains in May; and so they were immediately heard very clearly, even though the Muscovites had already gone their way. All the same, since the merchant considered that the words he heard were asking too high a price for the sables he refused to close the deal, and so he returned home without them.'

After everyone had laughed, Bernardo said: 'What I wish to tell you is certainly not as ingenious as that; all the same it is very fine, and it goes as follows. A few days ago the friend I have told you of was speaking about the country or world just discovered by the Portuguese mariners, and of the various animals and other things they bring back from there to Portugal; and he claimed that he had set eyes on a monkey, of a very different kind from those we are used to seeing, which could play chess extremely well. And on one occasion, when the gentleman who had brought it was in the presence of the King of Portugal and was playing it at chess, the monkey made some moves that were so clever as to press him hard, and eventually checkmated him. As a result the gentleman flew into a rage (as people who lose at chess invariably do), took up the King (which, being of Portuguese make, was very big) and gave the monkey a great blow on the head. At once the monkey skipped aside and began to complain loudly, seeming to be demanding justice from the King himself for the wrong done to it. The gentleman thereupon invited it to play another game, and the monkey, after a few signs of refusal, began to do so and, just as before, once again it got him into trouble. At length the monkey saw that it was in a position to give the gentleman checkmate again, and so it applied itself with fresh cunning to avoiding being struck once more. Unobtrusively, without revealing what it intended, it put its right paw under the gentleman's left elbow, which he was resting rather fastidiously on a taffeta cushion, and using its left hand to checkmate him with a pawn, having suddenly snatched the cushion away, at one and the same time it placed the cushion on its head as a shield against his blows. Then it jumped for joy in front of the King, as it celebrated its triumph. So you see how wise, wary and discreet that monkey proved to be.'

Then Cesare Gonzaga remarked: 'It goes without saying that that monkey must have been a very learned member of its tribe, with great authority; and I think that the Republic of Indian Monkeys must have sent it to Portugal to win fame in a foreign land.'

At this everyone laughed both at the lie that had been told and the way in which Cesare Gonzaga had added to it.

The discussion continuing, Bernardo said:

'You have now heard all I have to say about those jokes which rely on a continuous narration; so now we should talk of those which consist in a single remark, and whose sharp wit is concentrated in a brief sentence or word. And just as with the first kind of amusing anecdote one must, when telling the story or indulging in mimicry, avoid resembling clowns and parasites and those who make others laugh by their own foolishness, so in these terse comments the courtier should guard against appearing malicious or spiteful, or repeating witticisms and quips merely to tease and wound. Because such men often have their whole body deservedly chastised for the sins of their tongue.

'Now, of the spontaneous jokes that consist in a brief remark, those which arise from some ambiguity are the most effective, although they do not always arouse mirth, since they are more usually praised for their ingenuity than for their humour. For example, a few days ago our Annibale Paleotto was talking to someone who was recommending him a tutor to teach his sons grammar and who, after commending the teacher for his learning, when he came to the question of his salary said that as well as money he wanted to have a room furnished for living and sleeping, because he lacked a bed. Annibale immediately retorted: "Then how can he be learned, if he hasn't read?"* You see how well he exploited the ambiguous meaning of *non aver letto*. But since these puns are very subtle, in that someone employs words in a sense quite different from what is given them by everyone else, it appears that, as I have said, they inspire wonder more often than laughter, except when they are accompanied by something more. The kind

* The pun is on *letto*, which means either 'bed' or 'read'.

of witticism that customarily arouses laughter occurs when we expect to hear one thing and the one who is talking says something different, and this is called the "unexpected retort"; and if there is also some double meaning, then the witticism becomes extremely rich, as happened the other day when there was a discussion about making a fine brick floor for the Duchess's room, and after a lot had been said you, Gian Cristoforo, remarked: "If we could get the Bishop of Potenza and lay him flat it would suit the purpose well, since he is the biggest born fool I ever saw." Everyone laughed out loud, for you made a pun by splitting the word *mattonato* into two; and then in addition your saying that a bishop should be laid flat and used for the floor of a room was a totally unexpected notion, and so the joke was very pointed and very funny.*

'However, there are many different kinds of pun; and so one must be cautious in their use, hunting carefully for the right words, and avoiding those that cause the joke to fall flat and seem too laboured, or, as we have said, that are too wounding. For example, once when several companions met at the house of one of their friends, who happened to be blind, after the host had asked them to stay for dinner, they all left except one, who remarked: "Well, I'll stay, since I see you've got an empty place." And he pointed his finger at the man's empty socket. This of course is too cruel and discourteous, for it wounded the blind man's feelings to no purpose and without provocation; moreover, the jibe could have been at the expense of all those who are blind, and sweeping insults of this kind give no pleasure, because they appear to be premeditated. Of this sort was the remark made to a man who had lost his nose, namely: "Where, then, do you rest your spectacles?" or "How do you smell the roses every year?"

'Among other witticisms, however, those are very elegant which depend on turning someone's own sarcastic remarks against him, using the very same words as he does, and hoisting him with his own petard. For example, there was the litigant who, in the presence of the judge, was asked by his adversary: "What are you barking for?" And he retorted: "Because I see a thief." The same

* *matto nato* means a 'born fool' and *mattonato* a 'brick floor'.

kind of joke was when Galeotto Marzi was on his way through Siena and stopped in the street to ask the way to the inn; and when a Sienese noticed how corpulent he was, he laughed and said: "Others bring their baggage along behind but this fellow carries his in front." And Galeotto retorted: "That's what you have to do in a land of robbers."

'There is another kind still, which we call playing on words, and this relies on changing a word by adding or taking away a letter or a syllable; as when someone said: "You must be more experienced in the literature of the *latrines* [Latins] than of the Greeks." And to you, madam, a letter was addressed: "To signora Emilia impia."

'It is also amusing to quote a verse or two, putting it to a use other than what the author intended, or some other common saying, perhaps to the same purpose, but with a word altered. Thus a gentleman who had an ugly and shrewish wife, being asked how he was, replied: "Just you imagine, seeing that *Furiarum maxima iuxta me cubat*."*

'And Girolamo Donato,[15] when in company with many other gentlemen he was making the Stations in Rome during Lent, encountered a group of beautiful Roman ladies; and when one of the gentlemen said: "*Quot coelum stellas, tot habet tua Roma puellas*," he immediately added: "*Pascua quotque haedos, tot habet tua Roma cinaedos*,"† pointing out a group of young men who were coming from the other direction.

'Then there is the way in which Marc'Antonio dalla Torre spoke to the Bishop of Padua. For there was a nunnery in Padua in charge of a cleric who was thought to be extremely devout and learned, and who used to go the familiar rounds of the convent, often hearing the nuns' confessions. And then five of the mothers, and there were no more than as many again, became pregnant, and

* This is a play on Virgil's '*Furiarum maxima iuxta accubat*' (Aeneid VI, 605–6), meaning 'Lying nearby the greatest of the Furies . . .', to give the sense 'The greatest of the Furies sleeps with me.'

† The line from Ovid's *Ars Amatoria* (*Art of Love*) running 'Your Rome has as many girls as the sky has stars' is answered by: 'Your Rome has as many homosexuals as the meadows have kids.'

the father was seized by the Bishop after he had tried unsuccessfully to run away. He immediately confessed that because of the temptation of the devil he had got those five nuns pregnant, and consequently my Lord Bishop was resolved to chastise him very severely. However, the culprit was a very learned man and so he had very many friends, all of whom made efforts to help him; and along with the others Marc'Antonio also went to the Bishop to plead with him to be lenient. After they had been very insistent, recommending the culprit and pleading in extenuation the easy opportunities he had been given, the frailty of human nature and various other factors, the Bishop said at length: "I will do nothing for him, because I have to render my account to God." They still insisted, however; and then the Bishop added: "What shall I answer when on the Day of Judgement the Almighty says to me: '*Redde rationem villicationis tuae?*'" To which Marc'Antonio swiftly replied: "My Lord, in the words of the Evangelist: Domine, quinque talenta tradidisti mihi; ecce alia quinque superlucratus sum."* At this the Bishop could not stop from laughing and he greatly mitigated both his anger and the punishment he had designed for the wrongdoer.

'It is also amusing to guess the meaning of names and to invent explanation for why someone is called what he is, or why some particular thing is done. Thus a few days ago when Proto da Lucca, who as you know is very entertaining, asked for the bishopric of Cagli, the Pope replied: "Don't you know that in Spanish *caglio* means, I keep quiet? Well, you are a chatterbox, and it would never do for a bishop never to be able to mention his title without telling a lie. So now, all I can say to you is: *cagli* . . . be quiet." Then Proto made a reply which, though not of the same kind, was just as beautifully to the purpose; for having repeated his request several times, and seeing that it was no use, at length he said: "Holy Father, if your Holiness gives me this bishopric, it will not be for nothing. For I shall bequeath you two offices." The Pope asked: "And what offices do you have to

* Namely, God will say: 'Give an account of your stewardship' (Luke xvi, 2) and the bishop should answer: 'Lord, you delivered five talents to me: see, I have gained over and above them five more.' (Matthew xxv 20.)

bequeath?" Proto retorted: "I shall bequeath the full office, and the Office of the Madonna." And the Pope, though a very stern man, could not help laughing.

'Another man, also at Padua, once said that Calfurnio was so named because he used to stoke ovens.* And one day when I asked Fedra why it was that although on Good Friday the Church prayed not only for Christians but also for pagans and Jews there was no mention of cardinals, or of bishops and other prelates, he answered that the cardinals were included in that prayer which goes: *Oremus pro haereticis et scismaticis.*† And once our Count Lodovico alleged that I reproached a lady for using a cosmetic that was very shiny because when her face was made up I could see myself as in the mirror, and, being very ugly, I would rather not. Camillo Palleotto made the same kind of joke to Antonio Porcaro who, when speaking of a friend of his who told the priest at confession that he fasted very readily, went to mass and all the holy offices, and did all the good in the world, commented: "Instead of accusing himself, he praises himself." And then Camillo replied: "No, he confesses these things because he thinks it's a great shame to do them."‡ And do you not recall how cleverly the Prefect spoke the other day? Giovantomaso Galeotto was astonished that someone was asking two hundred ducats for a horse; and when he remarked that the beast wasn't worth a penny and among its other defects so fled the sound of weapons that it couldn't be brought near them, the Prefect, meaning to reproach him for cowardice, commented: "If that horse has the habit of fleeing from weapons, I'm astonished he doesn't ask a thousand ducats."

'Sometimes, as well, the same word is used, but in an unusual sense. Thus when the Duke was about to cross a very rapid river

* Giovanni Calfurnio was a humanist who held the chair of rhetoric at the University of Padua in 1486. The allegation of a rival that he was the son of a charcoal-burner and used to stoke ovens relies on the Latin meaning of *calescit furnos*.

† 'Let us pray for heretics and schismatics.'

‡ Camillo's answer is '*Sia gran peccato*' meaning either 'a great shame' or 'a great sin'.

he said to a trumpeter: "Cross now." And the trumpeter turned with his hat in his hand and answered very respectfully: "After your Lordship."* It is also entertaining when someone accepts what is said literally and not for what is meant, as when earlier this year in Rome a certain German one day ran into our Filippo Beroaldo, whose pupil he was, and said: "*Domine magister, Deus det vobis bonum sero,*" and Beroaldo at once replied: "*Tibi malum cito.*"† Similarly, when Diego de Quiñones was once at table with the Great Captain, another Spaniard who was present, meaning to ask for drink, called out: "*Vino.*"‡ And Diego replied: "*Y no lo conocistes,*" attacking him as an unbeliever. Then Iacopo Sadoleto[16] once said to Beroaldo, who was insisting on going to Bologna: "What makes you want to leave Rome, where it is so enjoyable, to go to Bologna where everything is in turmoil?" Beroalda replied: "I've got to go there on three counts. . . ." And he had already raised three fingers of his left hand to list the three reasons for his going, when Iacopo suddenly interrupted him by saying: "These three counts making you go to Bologna are, first, Count Ludovico da San Bonfacio, next Count Ercole Rangone and third the Count of Pepoli." Then everyone laughed, since these Counts had been pupils of Beroaldo, and were very handsome youths who were then studying at Bologna. This kind of witticism makes us laugh a good deal because it involves the unexpected answer that strikes us as very funny when we see how we have been taken in.

'As well as this, attractive figures and modes of speech belonging to grave and serious discussions can nearly always be used in games and pleasantries as well. When words are set off against each other, with one sentence in antithesis to another, the result is extremely agreeable; and this way of speaking can be very witty.

* More puns. The Duke says '*Passa*', meaning 'Cross now' and the trumpeter answers '*Passì la Signoria Vostra*' or 'After you . . .'

† The German muddles up his Latin and says 'God give you good late' instead of 'good morning' getting the reply: 'And evil quickly to you.'

‡ *Vino* in Spanish means either 'wine' or 'he came' and receives the New Testament answer: 'And you knew him not.'

For example, a Genoese, who was a great spendthrift, was being reproached by a very miserly moneylender, who said to him: "And when will you ever stop throwing your wealth away?" And he retorted: "When you stop stealing other people's." And then, since, as we have already said, the same situations which give rise to sharp witticisms can also inspire serious words of praise, in either case it is very diverting and sophisticated to confirm or agree to what someone else is saying, but to take it in a sense other than what is meant. For example, not so long ago, when a village priest was saying mass for his parishioners, after he had given out the feast days for the week, he started the general confession in the people's name, saying: "I have sinned in doing evil, in speaking evil, in thinking evil . . .", and continuing with the rest he mentioned all the mortal sins. Then one of his cronies, for a joke, said to the by-standers: "Now all of you bear witness to what he has confessed with his own lips; for I intend to inform the bishop." The same trick was used by Sallaza dalla Pedrada to pay a tribute to a lady with whom he was conversing when, after he had praised her for her beauty as well as her virtuous character, she had replied that she did not merit such praise, seeing how old she was. To this, he answered: "Madam, your age serves merely to make you like the angels, who are the first and oldest of all the creatures God ever made."

'Well-turned metaphors are also very useful for humorous sarcasm as they are for serious praise, and especially if employed in repartee and if the one who replies carries on with the same metaphor used by the other. Of this kind was the answer given to Palla Strozzi, who being banished from Florence sent one of his sons back on some business and said to him, with a threatening expression: "Tell Cosimo de' Medici from me that the hen is broody." The messenger did the errand as he had been ordered, and completely off-the-cuff Cosimo retorted: "And you tell Palla from me that hens can't brood outside the nest."* Camillo Porcaro also used a metaphor very gracefully to praise signor Marc'Antonio Colonna[17] on the occasion when, having heard that Camillo in

* The implication was that Palla Strozzi (a wealthy Florentine aristocrat, exiled by Cosimo de' Medici in 1434) was plotting revenge.

one of his orations had celebrated various Italian gentlemen who were famous in war and had given him an honourable mention among the rest, Marc'Antonio thanked him and said: "You, Camillo, have dealt with your friends as merchants sometimes do with their money, who when they discover a bad coin in order to pass it off put it in with the good ones when it goes unnoticed; so to do me honour, despite my inadequacies, you have put me in the company of men who are so able and outstanding that their merits cover up for my defects." And then Camillo replied: "Those who counterfeit ducats are in the habit of gilding them so well that they seem to the eye far more beautiful than the good ones. So if there were counterfeit men as there are counterfeit ducats, one might rightly suspect that you were one of them, seeing that you are made of finer and brighter metal than any of the others." You see that both kinds of witticism shared the same basis, as do many others of which any number of examples could be given, especially as regards remarks that are meant very seriously. For example, there was the occasion when the Great Captain[18] was seated at table, and all the other places were taken, and he noticed that some Italian gentlemen who had done good service in the war remained on their feet; so immediately he got up himself, making all the others stand as well, to find them a place, and he said: "Let these two gentlemen sit down and eat, for were it not for them none of us would have anything to eat." On another occasion he said to Diego Garcia, who was urging him to retire from a danger spot which was under bombardment: "Since God has not put any fear into your soul, do not put any in mine." Then there was the time when King Louis, now King of France, was told soon after he came to the throne that he should now punish his enemies, who had done him so much wrong when he was Duke of Orleans; and he replied that it was not the concern of the King of France to avenge the injuries done to the Duke of Orleans.

'One can also often be facetious rather than funny in making cutting remarks in a serious tone, as when Djem Othman, the brother of the Grand Turk, being a prisoner in Rome, gave it as his opinion that jousting, as we practise it in Italy, was too much if done in play and too little if done in earnest. And he added, on being told that King Ferdinand the Younger was very skilled and agile in running, jumping, vaulting and the like, that in his country the slaves indulged in such sport but gentlemen from their childhood were taught how to behave nobly, and it was for that they were praised. Almost the same kind of witticism, but somewhat more amusing, was what the Archbishop of Florence said to the Cardinal of Alexandria, namely, that all that men possess is their property, their body and their soul, and that their property is fought over by lawyers, their body by doctors and their soul by theologians.'

Then the Magnifico Giuliano remarked: 'We could add to this what Nicoletto used to say, namely, that rarely do we find a lawyer indulging in litigation, a doctor taking medicine or a theologian being a good Christian.'

Bernardo laughed at this, and then he added: 'There are countless examples of this kind of witticism, attributable to great lords and very grave men. But we also laugh at comparisons, such as the one our Pistoia wrote to Serafino: "Send back the big portmanteau that looks like you," for, if you remember, Serafino did very much resemble a portmanteau. And then there are some who like to compare men and women to horses, dogs, birds and even chests, chairs, wagons and chandeliers; and the result is sometimes very felicitous, though occasionally the joke falls flat. In this regard one must pay attention to place, time and persons and all the other circumstances we have so often mentioned.'

Then signor Gaspare Pallavicino added: 'It was an agreeable comparison that our signor Giovanni Gonzaga[19] made between Alexander the Great and his own son, signor Alessandro.'

'I do not know that one,' replied Bernardo.

'Well,' said signor Gaspare, 'Giovanni was playing at three dice and, as was usual for him, had lost many ducats and was still losing, and his son, signor Alessandro, who though still a child plays no less eagerly than his father, stood watching him very attentively, and seemed very downcast. Then the Count of Pianella, who was there with many other gentlemen, remarked: "Look, sir, how disconsolate signor Alessandro is because of your losing, and how he is fretting for you to win so that he can have something from the winnings. So let him out of his misery and before you lose the rest of your money give him at least a ducat so that he, too, can go and play with his friends." Then signor Giovanni replied: "You are deceiving yourself, for Alessandro is not thinking of anything so trifling. On the contrary, just as we read that when Alexander the Great heard, as a child, that his father, Philip, had won a great battle and taken a certain kingdom, he started to cry because, he explained, he feared his father would conquer so many countries that there would be none left for him, so now my son, Alessandro, is sad and tearful at seeing his father losing, because he fears I may lose so much that there will be nothing left for him to lose."'

After everyone had laughed at this for a moment, Bernardo resumed:

'We should also avoid irreligious jokes, for these can turn an attempt at wit into blasphemy, and then we find ourselves growing more and more ingenious in the way we blaspheme; and thereby a man seems to be seeking glory from something for which he deserves not merely condemnation but also severe punishment. This is an abominable thing; and therefore those who wish to appear amusing by showing little reverence for the Almighty ought to be driven out of good society. The same holds for those whose speech is obscene and foul, who show no respect for the presence of ladies, and who are constantly searching for witticisms and quips merely for the pleasure of making them blush for shame. For example, earlier this year in Ferrara, in the presence of many ladies at a banquet, there happened to be a Florentine and a Sienese who, as you know, are usually at odds with each other; and in order to taunt the Florentine, the Sienese said: "We have married Siena to the Emperor, and we have given him Florence as the dowry." And he said this because at the time it was reported that the Sienese had given a certain amount of money to the Emperor and he had taken Siena under his protection. Then, without hesitating, the Florentine retorted: "Siena will first be ridden" (meaning this in the French sense, though he used the Italian word) "then the dowry will be settled at leisure." As you see, the joke was very clever, but as ladies were present it was also indecent and unseemly."

Then signor Gaspare Pallavicino remarked: 'Women take pleasure in hearing nothing else, and yet you want to deprive them of it. And as for me, I have found myself blushing for shame far more because of words said by women than by men.'

'I am not speaking of women of that sort,' replied Bernardo, 'but of virtuous women whom every gentleman should honour and respect.'

Answered Gaspare: 'You would need to discover a very subtle way of recognizing them, seeing that most times those who appear the best are in fact the worst.'

Then Bernardo, with a laugh, said: 'If it were not for the presence of our signor Magnifico, who is universally recognized to be the protector of women, I should undertake the task of refuting you; but I do not want to usurp his place.'

And then signora Emilia, laughing as well, added:

'Women have no need of a defender against a critic of so little authority. So leave signor Gaspare to his perverse opinion, which is caused more by the fact that he has never found a woman to look at him than by any frailty that exists in women themselves, and continue with your discussion of pleasantries.'

Then Bernardo went on: 'Indeed, madam, it seems to me that I have now spoken of the many possible sources of clever witticisms, all of which are enhanced by being part of an entertaining story. But there are many others I could mention: as when, for example, by overstatement or understatement, things are said that are miles away from the truth. Of this kind was what Mario da Volterra said of a certain prelate, that he was so conscious of his great stature, that when he entered St Peter's he would stoop so as not to knock his head on the beam of the door. And our Magnifico here once said that his servant Volpino was so lean and thin that one morning, when he was blowing on his fire to make it go, he was wafted up the chimney by the smoke; but he had been fortunate enough to be forced crosswise against one of the little openings and so escape disappearing altogether. Then again, Agostino Bevazzano told the story of the miser who in desperation after he had refused to sell his grain for a good price, and then seen the price tumble, hanged himself from a rafter in his bedroom; however, a servant of his heard the noise, ran in to see his master hanging there and quickly cut the rope, saving him from death. Subsequently, after the miser had recovered, he insisted that the servant pay him for the rope. The same kind of joke was what Lorenzo de' Medici said to a very tedious clown: "You couldn't make me laugh if you tickled me." And in the same vein he replied to another buffoon who, one morning, had found him in bed late and reproached him for sleeping so long in these words: "I've already been to the New Market and the Old, and outside the San Gallo Gate and around the walls for exercise, and I've done a thousand other things besides, and here you are still asleep!" Lorenzo retorted: "What I have dreamed in an hour is worth more than what you've done in four."

'It is also entertaining when, without seeming to mean to, we rebuke someone in the way we answer him. For example, the Marquess Federico of Mantua, the father of our Duchess, was once at table with a number of gentlemen when one of them, having eaten a whole bowl of thick soup, said: "Marquess, pardon me," and then started to guzzle what was left of the broth. Immediately, the Marquess retorted: "Ask pardon of the pigs, for you certainly do me no harm." Then Niccolò Leonico,[20] in order to condemn a tyrant who enjoyed a false reputation for liberality, once remarked: "Consider how liberal he is, to give away not only his own property, but also that of others."

'A very sophisticated kind of joke relies on a certain amount of dissimulation, when one says one thing and means another. I do not mean saying the exact opposite, such as calling a dwarf a giant, or a Negro, white, or a very ugly man, extremely handsome; for these are contraries that are only too obvious, even though they, too, may sometimes raise a laugh. I mean when speaking gravely and seriously, one says in an amusing way what is not really meant. For example, when a certain gentleman was telling an outright lie to Agostino Foglietta, and was affirming it vehemently, since it seemed that he was having difficulty in believing it, at length

Agostino said: "Sir, if I may ever hope for a favour from you, do me the goodness to allow me not to believe what you are saying." But when the man kept repeating and swearing that he was speaking the truth, finally Agostino said: "Since you wish it, I shall believe it for your sake, for to be sure I would do even more for you." Something similar was said by don Giovanni di Cardona concerning a person who wanted to leave Rome: "In my opinion, he is taking the wrong decision, because he's such a rascal that if he stayed in Rome, given time he'd become a cardinal." Alfonso Santa Croce made a joke of the same kind, shortly after he had been subjected to various outrages at the hands of the Cardinal of Pavia, when he was strolling with certain gentlemen outside Bologna near the place of public execution and noticed a man who had recently been hanged; for he turned towards the corpse with a reflective expression and remarked in a voice loud enough for all to hear: "Happy you, who do not have to deal with the Cardinal of Pavia!"

'This sort of joke, with an element of irony, is very suitable on the lips of men of some importance, for it is both grave and pungent, and can be used whether talking of amusing or serious matters. For this reason it was popular among those of the ancient world, including very distinguished figures such as Cato and Scipio Africanus the Younger; but the philosopher Socrates is said to have been the most witty in this regard, and also, in our own time, King Alfonso I of Aragon. For example, one morning when the King was about to dine he took off the many precious rings he wore on his fingers in order not to wet them when washing his hand, and he handed them to the nearest person, without seeming to look who it was. The servant concerned supposed that the King had paid no attention to whom he had given the rings and that, distracted by matters of greater importance, he might easily forget all about it; and his thoughts were confirmed when the King neglected to ask for them again. So after days and weeks and months had passed without a word being said, he grew certain that he was safe. And then, nearly a year later, he approached when the King was about to dine and held out his hand for the rings; but the King, bending close to his ear, said to him: "Let those you had before be enough for you, since these will do very well for someone else." You see how this witticism was ingenious, pungent and serious, and truly worthy of the magnanimity of an Alexander.

'Similar to this ironic style of humour is another which relies on the use of innocent words to describe something unworthy. Thus after the battle of Cerignola when the engagement was already over successfully, one of the gentlemen of the Great Captain approached him wearing the richest armour imaginable, as if prepared for battle; and at this the Great Captain, turning to don Ugo di Cardona, remarked: "Have no more fear of the tempest, for here is St Elmo." So with those innocent and inoffensive words he stung the man badly; for you know that St Elmo always appears to sailors after a storm and gives them a sign of calm weather, and so the Great Captain meant to say that the arrival of this gentleman was a sign that the danger was already a thing of the past. Again, when signor Ottaviano Ubaldino was at Florence in the company of some very influential citizens, as they were talking of soldiers one of them asked him if he knew Antonello da Forlì, who had just fled from Florence; and signor Ottaviano replied: "I do not know him, except that I have heard him spoken of as an expeditious soldier." And then another of the citizens remarked: "You see how expeditious he is, since he runs off before he asks leave."

'Those witticisms are also very telling which rely on our giving to someone's words an interpretation other than what was intended. I understand that this was the way in which the Duke replied to that Castellan who lost San Leo when the state of Urbino was seized by Pope Alexander and handed over to Duke Valentino. For when this happened the Duke was in Venice, where he was continuously visited by many of his subjects bringing secret information about how the affairs of the state were going, and among others to arrive was this same Castellan, who, having excused himself as best he knew how, and blaming everything on his own bad luck, added: "My lord, have no fear, for I have it in me to make sure that San Leo can be recovered." Then the Duke replied: "Do not exert yourself over this any more, for by losing it you have already made sure that it can be recovered."[21] There are various other quips, as when a person known for his wit says something that seems to spring from foolishness, as when the other day Camillo Palleotto remarked of someone: "He was an idiot to die just as he was starting to get rich." Similar to this is the kind of rich and keen dissimulation shown when a man, of good sense, as I said, pretends not to understand what he does understand. Thus recently the Marquess Federico of Mantua was being tormented by a tiresome pest who was complaining that certain of his neighbours were snaring the doves from his dovecot and who stood there all the while holding one of the doves hanging dead in the snare by its foot just as he had found it, and the Marquess said that he would look into matters. However, the pest repeated what he had lost, not only once but many times, still standing with the dove hanging down and saying: "Sir, what is to be done about this?" And at length the Marquess remarked: "In my opinion, on no account should that dove be buried in church, for since it hanged itself we must believe it was guilty of suicide." Much the same kind of answer was that given by Scipio Nasica to Ennius. For after Scipio had gone to where Ennius lived in order to speak to him, when he called up from the street one of the maids replied that he was not at home. Scipio clearly heard Ennius himself telling the maid she was to say that he wasn't home; and so he decided to leave. Not long afterwards Ennius visited Scipio's house, and he too called to him from below; whereupon Scipio himself replied in a loud voice that he wasn't at home. At this Ennius answered: "What, don't I recognize your voice?" And to this Scipio retorted: "You are too discourteous for words. The other day I believed your maid when she said you were not at home, and now you won't believe even me!"

'It is also splendid when a person is stung regarding the same thing in which he has previously scored over his companion. Thus when at the Court of Spain Alonso Carrillo was guilty of some youthful misdemeanours on the orders of the King he was thrown into prison for the night; the following day he was released, and that morning he made his way to the palace where, as he entered the hall, and encountered many lords and ladies laughing at his imprisonment, signora Bobadilla said: "Signor Alonso, I am very grieved by this misadventure of yours, for all those who know you thought the King should have had you hanged." Then straight away Alonso retorted: "Madam, I was also very afraid of that, but then I formed the hope that you would ask to marry me."[22] You see how sharp and witty this answer was, since in Spain, as in many places elsewhere, it is the custom that when a man is on his way to the gallows, his life is spared if a common whore asks to marry him. This was also the kind of answer given by Raphael, the painter, to two cardinals with whom he was friendly and who, in his presence, in order to get him to talk, found fault with a painting of his which contained SS. Peter and Paul, by commenting that the two figures were too red in the face. Immediately, Raphael retorted: "My lords, you should not be surprised, for I did this very deliberately, as we may well believe that St Peter and St Paul are as red in heaven as you see them here, for shame that the Church should be governed by such as you."

'Those witticisms are also very telling where the humour is subtly disguised, as when a man came up to someone grieving for his wife who had hanged herself from a fig tree and, tugging at his coat, inquired: "Friend, as a great favour, could you let me have a little branch from your fig tree to graft on to one in my own garden?" Then there are witticisms of a forbearing kind, said slowly and with a certain gravity, as when a peasant jostled Cato with a box he was carrying on his shoulders and then cried out. "Watch out!" And Cato answered: "Don't you carry anything on your shoulders besides that box?" It is also laughable when, having made a blunder, someone tries to retrieve the situation by adding something uttered with great deliberation which sounds silly but which meets his need and thereby helps to save him embarrassment. Thus not so long ago in the Council at Florence there were two enemies, as often happens in these republics; and one of them, belonging to the Altoviti family, fell asleep. Then, although his adversary, who belonged to the Alamanni family, was not speaking and had said nothing, the person sitting next to him nudged him with his elbow, woke him up and said, for a laugh: "Don't you hear what he is saying? Give your answer, because the Signori are asking for your opinion." Then Altoviti, very sleepy and not thinking what he was saying, got to his feet and remarked: "My lords, I say completely the opposite to what Alamanni has just said." Alamanni replied: "But I haven't said anything." And at once Altoviti retorted: "Then to what you are going to say." The same kind of remark was made by master Serafino, your physician here in Urbino, to a peasant who had decided to come to him for treatment after having had his eye forced out by a blow. When he saw him, although he knew there was no cure, Serafino swore that he would make him better, in order to squeeze some money from him, just as the blow had squeezed the eye from his head; and so he continued to ask him for payment every day, claiming that within five or six days he would begin to recover his sight. The wretched peasant gave him the little he had, but then seeing how long it was taking he started to complain to the doctor and to say that he felt no improvement and that he could see no more with that eye than if he had never had it in his head. At length, realizing that there was little more he could squeeze out of him, Serafino said: "My friend, you must be patient. You have lost that eye and there is no remedy; and God grant that you don't lose the other one, too." On hearing this, the peasant started to weep and complain loudly, saying: "But, doctor, you've ruined me and robbed me of my money. I shall protest to the Lord Duke." And then he started to make the most shattering din. At this, Serafino, lost his temper and cried out to justify himself: "Ah, you miserable peasant! So you would like to have two eyes just like townsfolk and respectable people. Off with you, and be damned!" And he uttered these words with such fury that the poor peasant was terrified into silence and, oh so quietly, went his way.

'It is also splendid when something is explained or interpreted in a humorous way. For example, one morning when there appeared at the Court of Spain a knight, who was very ugly, accompanied by his wife, who was most beautiful, both being dressed in white damask, the Queen asked Alonso Carrillo: "What do you think of these two, Alonso?" To which Alonso replied: "I think, madam, that she is the *dama* and he is the *asca*"* (namely, a repulsive-

* *Dama* meaning lady, *asca* repulsive.

looking person). Then there was the occasion when Rafaello de' Pazzi saw a letter which the Prior of Messina had written to a lady-friend, with the following superscription: *Esta carta s'ha de dar a quien causa mi penar.** And he commented: "I think the letter is meant for Paolo Tolosa."[23] You may imagine how the bystanders laughed, for everyone knew that Paolo Tolosa had lent the Prior ten thousand ducats, and he, being a great spendthrift, had found it impossible to repay him. Similar to this kind of wit is when a friendly admonition is subtly conveyed in the form of advice: as was done by Cosimo de' Medici to a friend of his who was very rich but not very knowledgeable and who, through Cosimo, had obtained a mission away from Florence; for when he was leaving he asked Cosimo how he thought he should behave and conduct himself to perform his duties properly, and Cosimo answered: "Dress like a lord and keep your mouth shut." Very similar was the reply given by Count Lodovico to someone who wanted to travel incognito through a certain dangerous place and did not know how best to disguise himself. For when the Count was asked he said: "Dress up as a professor or some other kind of learned man. . . ." Then again, Giannotto de' Pazzi said to someone who wanted to make a military cloak of as many different colours as possible: "Copy the way the Cardinal of Pavia painted his life."[24]

'We also laugh at incongruities, as when the other day someone said to Antonio Rizzo about a certain man from Forlì: "Think how mad he is, with the name Bartolomeo."† And another: "You are looking for a certain Stalla,‡ yet you have no horses." And: "He lacks nothing at all except money and brains." Other kinds of apparent inconsistency are amusing, too. For example, recently it was suspected that a friend of ours had had the renunciation of a benefice forged, and then, when another priest fell sick, Antonio Torello said to the first: "Why all this delay in not sending for that lawyer of yours and grabbing this benefice as well?" Then we

* This letter is to be delivered to the one who causes my suffering.

† A name associated with fairly formidable personalities, such as the great *condottiere*, Bartolomeo Colleoni.

‡ *Stalla* means stable.

laugh at things that do not accord with each other, as when the other day, after the Pope had sent for Giovan Luca da Pontremolo and Domenico della Porta (both hunchbacks, as you know) to make them auditors, saying that he wanted to set the Rota to rights, Latino Giovenale remarked: "His Holiness is deceiving himself if he thinks to put the Rota straight with crooked men."

'It is also a frequent cause of laughter when someone concedes all that is said to him, and more, and yet pretends to take it in a different sense. Thus, when Captain Peralta was conducted to the field for his duel with Aldana, Captain Molart, who was Aldana's second, asked Peralta to swear on oath that he was not wearing any pentacles or charms to protect him from harm, and Peralta swore that he was not wearing any pentacles, charms, relics or any other holy objects in which he had faith. Then, taunting him for being an infidel, Molart retorted: "Don't trouble yourself any further, even without your protestation I can well believe you have no faith even in Christ."[25] It is also splendid on such occasions to make use of a timely metaphor. For instance, our Marc'Antonio once remarked to Botton da Cesena, who had been teasing him by what he said: "Botton, Botton, one day you'll be the button and your button-hole will be the noose." And another time, when Marc'-Antonio had composed a very long comedy in several acts, this same Botton said to him: "To stage your play we would need all the timber in Slavonia." To which Marc'Antonio answered: "And to stage your tragedy we'll need only three planks."

'Often, too, we use a word in which there is a hidden meaning quite remote from the one we seem to intend. There was the time, for example, when our Prefect here happened to be discussing a certain captain who, as a matter of fact, usually lost his battles but now chanced to be the victor; and the person who was talking was saying that when the captain made his entry into the city he had worn a very fine cloak of crimson velvet, as he always did following a victory. So the Prefect remarked: "Then it must be quite new." It also makes us laugh when the question answered is not what was asked, or when we pretend to believe that someone has done what he should have but hasn't. For instance, when Andrea Coscia visited a gentleman who very discourteously let him remain standing while he was sitting down, he said: "Since your Lordship commands, I shall sit down to obey you." And thereupon he did so.

'We laugh, too, when a man cheerfully accuses himself of some fault, as when the other day, after I had told the Duke's chaplain that Monsignor[26] had a chaplain who said mass faster than he did, he replied: "It's not possible." And coming close he said in my ear: "Let me tell you that I say under a third of the Secret."* Again, there was the time when, after a certain priest had died in Milan, Biagio Crivelli asked the Duke for his benefice, but the Duke remained determined to give it to someone else. So at length, seeing that his other arguments were achieving nothing, Biagio said: "What's this? If I've had the priest killed, why won't you give me his benefice?" It is also pleasing when one shows a desire for things that cannot be, as when the other day one of our friends on seeing all these gentlemen jousting, while he was still stretched out in bed, remarked: "Oh, how agreeable it would be if this too were the right kind of exercise for a fine man and a good soldier." And then again, it is very entertaining and piquant, especially on the part of serious and important people, to say the opposite of what the person being spoken to would wish, but to do so slowly, and with a certain doubtful and hesitant deliberation. Thus King Alfonso I of Aragon once gave one of his servants some weapons, horses and clothes, because the fellow told him that the night before he had dreamt that his Majesty did so; and then not long afterwards when the same servant reported that he had now had another dream, in which the King gave him a large number of gold florins, his Majesty remarked: "Don't believe in dreams from now on; for they don't tell the truth." In this manner, too, the Pope replied to the Bishop of Cervia when, to sound out his intentions, the Bishop told him: "Holy Father, they say in Rome and in the Palace that your Holiness will make me governor." For the Pope replied: "Let them talk, for they are only rascals. And you need have no fear, since it is quite untrue."

* The Secret, or Secrets, is the name given to prayers said inaudibly by the priest during mass immediately after the Offertory and before the Preface.

'Now, gentlemen, I could perhaps cite all the many other sources of wit and humour: such as remarks uttered with timidity, with amazement, with threats, as well as remarks that are beside the point or said with too much anger; and in addition, certain other strange instances that cause laughter when they occur, as when taciturnity is accompanied by a certain amazement, or laughter itself is quite pointless. However, it seems to me that I have now said enough, since I think we have discussed all possible kinds of jests. Then, of course, there are jokes that depend on action of some sort and which, though they are very various, can be summarized under a few heads. But as regards both kinds the main thing is to cheat expectation and to respond in a way that is unexpected. And, if the joke is to be really elegant, it must be flavoured with deceit, or dissimulation, or ridicule, or censure or comparison, or whatever other quality is desired. Moreover, although all jokes are meant to provoke laughter, yet in this respect they produce varying effects. For there are some which are characterized by a certain modest humour and grace, others which have a hidden or obvious sting, others slightly indecent, some which provoke laughter as soon as they are heard, and others which do so the more they are thought about, others which cause blushes as well as laughter, and still others which arouse a show of anger. But at all times attention should be paid to the disposition of those who are listening, for jokes can often make those who are suffering suffer still more, and there are some illnesses that only grow worse the more they are treated. So if the courtier, in his witticisms and pleasantries, has regard for time and person and his own rank, and does not indulge in them too frequently (since it can be very tedious to be joking day in and day out, and in all one says to no purpose) then he may be called an amusing man. But he should also take care not to be so sharp and biting that he earns a reputation for malice; he should never attack without cause or with manifest hatred those who are extremely powerful, which would be imprudent, or those who are defenceless, which would be cruel, or those who are really wicked, which would be a waste of time; nor should he say things that offend those he would rather not offend, which simply displays ignorance. For there are some who think they are under an obligation to have their say and attack others regardlessly whenever they have the chance and whatever the consequences. Included among them are those who, for the sake of scoring a point, do not hesitate to impugn a lady's honour, which is a very evil thing to do and which deserves severe punishment, since in this respect women are to be counted among the defenceless and so do not deserve such treatment, having no weapons with which to protect themselves. In addition to all this, if a courtier is to be amusing and witty, he must be endowed with a certain natural aptitude for pleasantries of all kinds and must be able to adapt his behaviour, gestures and expressions as required; and the more grave, severe and unmoved he appears, the more pungent and sharp will his words seem to be.

'But as for you, Federico, who thought to find repose under this leafless tree and in my arid discourse, I'm sure you have regretted it by now and must have gained the impression that you had wandered into the Montefiore inn.* So you would do well, like an experienced courier, to escape from a poor inn by getting up rather earlier than usual and resuming your journey.'

'On the contrary,' answered Federico, 'I have come to such a good inn that I am thinking of staying longer than I first intended. So I shall continue to rest here until you have exhausted everything that was proposed for our discussion, of which you have left out a part you mentioned at the start, namely, the question of practical jokes. And it would be wrong for you to cheat us all on this score. However, just as in the matter of jests and anecdotes you have taught us many splendid things and have emboldened us to use them, following the example of so many marvellous wits and distinguished men, princes, kings and popes, so far as practical jokes are concerned I think you will make us so daring that we shall feel confident enough to try them ourselves, and even play them on you.'

'You would not be the first,' replied Bernardo with a laugh. 'But perhaps you would not be successful, for I have had so many played on me that I am on my guard against everything, like the dogs who are afraid even of cold water, once they've been scalded

* Montefiore, a little village to the north-east of Urbino, was notorious at this time and earlier for an infamous inn. Most country inns were bad, but this, being on a busy route, was singled out for abuse.

with hot. However, since you want me to speak on this subject, I think I can cover it in just a few words.

'Now it seems to me that a practical joke consists simply in an amicable deception regarding things that give little or no offence. And just as in jests laughter is caused by our saying something contrary to what is expected, so in practical jokes it is caused by our doing something contrary to what is expected. And they are more agreeable and appreciated, the shrewder and more discreet they are; for a person who wishes to play practical jokes unthinkingly frequently gives offence and provokes retribution and serious enmities. However, practical jokes arise from almost the same situations as do the jests we were discussing; so to avoid repeating them, I will say simply that there are two kinds of practical joke, each of which can then be divided into several varieties. The first kind is when someone or other is cleverly tricked, in an adroit and amusing fashion; and the other is when, as it were, a net is spread and a little bait is offered, so that the victim causes his own downfall. We have an example of the first kind of practical joke in the way in which, just recently, two ladies whom I do not wish to name were taken in by a Spaniard called Castillo.'

'And why,' interrupted the Duchess, 'are you unwilling to name them?'

'Because I do not want them to take offence,' replied Bernardo.

'And yet,' the Duchess answered with a smile, 'it is not improper sometimes to play practical jokes even on great lords; indeed, I have heard that many were played on Duke Federico, on King Alfonso of Aragon, on Queen Isabella of Spain and on many other great rulers, and that not only did they not take offence but that they even rewarded the jokers.'

Bernardo replied: 'Even the hope of that will not persuade me to name them.'

'Well, go on as you please,' answered the Duchess.

So Bernardo continued: 'Well, a few days ago there arrived at the Court I have in mind a peasant from Bergamo, in the service of a noble courtier. He was so well attired in his livery and so elegantly decked out that, though he was only accustomed to looking after cattle and knew no other profession, by anyone not hearing him speak he would have been taken for a very fine gentleman indeed. Now, the two ladies I mentioned were told that a Spanish retainer of Cardinal Borgia had arrived, by the name of Castillo, and that he was an extremely clever man as well as being a musician, a dancer, a ballerino and the most accomplished courtier of all Spain; consequently in their extreme anxiety to speak to him they sent for him at once, and after a gracious welcome they asked him to be seated and began to talk to him with great deference in the presence of everyone. And there were few present who did not know that he was a cowherd from Bergamo, and who did not laugh uproariously when they saw how deferentially the ladies were entertaining him and paying him honour, all the more since the good fellow said everything in his guttural Bergamasque dialect. As it happened, the gentlemen responsible for the joke had beforehand told those ladies that among other things the visitor was himself a great practical joker, and that he spoke all languages extremely well, and especially the country dialect of Lombardy; and in consequence they thought all the while that he was putting on an act, and every so often they would turn in amazement to one another and say: "Just imagine! How well he mimics the language!" Well, to finish, their conversation lasted so long that everyone's sides were aching from laughter, and the fellow himself aped the gentleman in such a way that at length, though not without difficulty, those ladies were themselves convinced that he was what he was.

'This kind of joke is played very often; but more amusing still are jokes that are frightening to begin with but have a happy ending, for then the victim too laughs at himself and realizes that there was nothing to be afraid of. For example, one night I was staying in Paglia and in the same inn there happened to be three other guests, two from Pistoia and the third from Prato, who, as often happens, sat down after supper to gamble. Before very long one of the Pistoians had lost all he had and was left penniless, and he began to swear and curse and grumble with all his might; and then he went off to bed, blaspheming wickedly. After the other two had been playing a little longer, they decided to play a practical joke on the one who had left. So, when they knew that he had fallen asleep, they put out all the lights and covered the fire; and then they began to talk loudly and make a tremendous din, pretending that they had fallen out over their game, with one of them saying: "You dealt a card from underneath," and the other retorting: "You bet on a flush; the game goes to the bank." They carried on in this way, making such an uproar that they woke their colleague up; and, hearing that they were still playing and were talking as if they could see the cards, when he failed to see anything himself, he said: "And what the devil are you up to, shouting all night?" Then he immediately settled down again. All his two companions did, however, was to continue as before, until, being now wide awake, he started to wonder and then, when he was quite sure that he could see neither the fire nor any other light, even though the other two were still playing and quarrelling, he said: "But how can you see your cards in the dark?" One of them remarked: "You must have lost your sight as well as your money. Can't you see by these two candles over there?" At this, the man in bed raised himself on his elbows and said angrily: "Either I'm blind or drunk or you're telling lies." Then the other two got up and groped their way to their beds, laughing and pretending to believe that he was making fun of them, whereas for his part he kept repeating: "I tell you, I can't see you." At length the two of them pretended to be very astonished, and one said to the other: "Oh dear, I really think he's telling the truth. Give me that candle and let's see if perhaps his sight is clouding over." At this the poor wretch thought for sure that he had become blind, and weeping copiously he said: "Dear brothers, I've lost my sight. . . ." And then he started to call on Our Lady of Loreto and beseech her to pardon the blasphemies and curses he had hurled at her after having lost his money. His two friends meanwhile were comforting him and saying: "It's impossible that you don't see us. This must be some kind of fantasy you've taken into your head." But he only answered: "Oh dear me, it's no fantasy and I can no more see you than if I never had eyes in my head." They answered: "But your sight is quite clear"; and then the one said to the other: "See how well he opens his eyes! And how bright they are! And who could believe that he cannot see?" All the while the poor fellow wept the more loudly and asked God for mercy. At length they said to him: "Make a vow to visit Our

Lady of Loreto for a penance, barefoot and naked, for this is the best remedy to be found. And in the meantime we'll go to Acquapendente and the other towns near by and see if we can find some doctor, and we promise not to fail you in anything." Straight away the unfortunate fellow knelt down by his bed, and crying all the time and showing the most bitter penitence for his blasphemies, he made a solemn vow to go naked to the shrine of Our Lady of Loreto and to offer her a pair of silver eyes, not to eat meat on Wednesdays or eggs on Fridays, and to fast on bread and water in her honour every Saturday, if Our Lady would only favour him with the recovery of his sight. Then his two friends, having gone into another room, came back with a lighted candle, laughing uproariously. The poor wretch, though relieved from such great anguish as you can imagine, was still so stunned by the fright he had received that he couldn't even speak a word, let alone laugh. But his two friends never left off teasing him, saying that he was bound to fulfil all the vows he had made, since he had won the favour he asked.

'Concerning the other kind of practical joke, where a man tricks himself, I shall merely give the example of what happened to me not so long ago. For during the recent carnival, my Monsignor, Cardinal San Pietro in Vincoli, who knows how much I enjoy playing jokes on the friars, when I am in masquerade, and had earlier arranged all he meant to do, came along one day with Monsignor of Aragon and several other cardinals to certain windows in the Banchi, as though he intended to stay there to see the maskers pass by, as is the custom in Rome. Then I appeared on the scene in my mask and, seeing a friar standing to one side and looking rather hesitant, I decided this was a good opportunity and at once swooped on him like a falcon on its prey. After I had first asked him who he was, and he had replied, I pretended to know him and talking fast I began to persuade him that the chief of police was looking for him because of some damning information that had been lodged against him; and I also urged him to come with me to the Chancery where I would make him safe. Frightened and trembling all over, the friar seemed unsure what to do next, and said that he feared that if he went far from San Celso he would be taken. But I kept encouraging him, and at last managed to persuade him to mount behind me; and then, judging that my plan had already succeeded, I immediately spurred my horse, which was bucking and kicking wildly, towards the Banchi. Now just think what a fine spectacle it was to see a friar riding behind a masker, with his robe flying and his head jerking backwards and forwards and always seeming on the verge of tumbling off! At the sight, those gentlemen began to throw eggs at us from the windows, as did the people who lived in the Banchi and all the others who were there, until there were eggs falling from the windows with greater force than ever hail fell from the sky; but since I was masked I wasn't worried, and I imagined that all the laughter was at the friar's expense and not mine. So several times I rode up and down the Banchi through that barrage of eggs, although very tearfully the friar kept begging me to let him dismount and not to make him disgrace his cloth. Then, without my knowing, the rascal got certain lackeys, who had been stationed there for that purpose, to pass him some eggs, and, pretending to hold me tight so as not to fall, he crushed some of them on my chest, more on my head and several on my very face until I was streaming with them. At length, when everyone was tired of laughing and throwing eggs, he jumped down, threw back his scapular to show his long hair and said: "Bernardo, sir, I'm one of the grooms of San Pietro in Vincoli, the one who looks after your little mule!" Well, I hardly know what was greatest, my grief, or anger, or shame. However, as the lesser evil I made my way home in a great hurry, and hadn't the courage to appear even the next day. All the same, the laughter caused by this practical joke reverberated not only all the following day but almost up to this very moment.'

Then, after everyone had laughed again over this story, Bernardo added:

'A very entertaining source of practical jokes, as well as of jests, is to be found in the pretence that one understands that a man wishes to do something which he most certainly does not. For example, one evening after supper I was walking over the bridge at Lyons and joking with Cesare Beccadello, when we began to seize each other's arms as if we meant to wrestle, at a moment when except for us the bridge seemed to be deserted. However, while we were playing in this way, two Frenchmen appeared on the scene, and when they saw our dispute, asked what was wrong and were stopping to try to separate us, convinced that we were quarrelling in earnest. At this, straight away, I cried out: "Please help me, for at certain phases of the moon this poor gentleman goes out of his mind. And see what's happening now: he's even trying to throw himself off the bridge into the river." Thereupon the two men approached at a run and helped me to take hold of Cesare, grasping him very tightly; and all the while he was telling me that I was mad, as he exerted more force to shake them off, only to have them restrain him all the more. As a result, a crowd gathered to see the tumult, and as Cesare lashed out more and more with his hands and feet (for he was by now getting very angry) so more and more people ran up to see what was happening. And the harder he fought, the more they grew convinced that he wanted to jump into the river, and the more they restrained him. So at length a large number of men carried him bodily into the inn, all dishevelled and without his hat and pale with shame and anger, since whatever he said was of no avail, partly because those Frenchmen did not understand a word and partly because as I led them to the inn I kept lamenting over the misfortune of the poor fellow who was out of his wits.

'Well, as we have seen, there is a great deal to say about practical jokes; but let it suffice to repeat that they arise from the same circumstances as witticisms and pleasantries. So we could give any number of examples from our own day-to-day experiences. Then there are many amusing ones to be found in Boccaccio's stories, such as those played by Bruno and Buffalmacco on their friend Calandrino* and on master Simone, and many other really neat and clever jokes played by women. I have known many amusing

* Boccaccio's Calandrino has already been mentioned. Bruno and Buffalmacco in four of Boccaccio's stories (Eighth Day, Third and Sixth; Ninth Day, Third and Fifth) convince him that he has found a way to make himself invisible; steal his pig; incite Simone to convince him that he is pregnant; and give him a magic scroll to make the girl he fancies fall in love with him.

practical jokers in my time; and among the others whom I recall is a certain Sicilian student I knew at Padua called Ponzio. On one occasion, seeing a peasant with a pair of plump capons he pretended that he wanted to buy them, struck a bargain, and then said that the man should accompany him home since as well as paying him his price he would give him some lunch. So he took the peasant to a certain place where there was a bell-tower standing apart from the church, so that one could walk round it, and a little street which ended directly opposite one of the four sides of the tower. When they arrived, having already thought out what he meant to do, Ponzio said to the peasant: "I have wagered these capons with a friend of mine who says that this tower is at least forty feet around, whereas I say it is not. And just before I ran into you I had bought this string to measure it; so before we go home I would like to settle which of us has won. So saying, he drew the string from his sleeve, gave the peasant one end of it to hold and added: "Now let me hold them" as he took the capons and then, as if he meant to measure the distance, started to walk round the tower with the other end of the string. The peasant was left holding his end of the string at the spot on the other side to where the little street came to an end; and when Ponzio arrived there, he drove a nail into the wall, tied the string to it, and then, very softly, stole away up the street, with the capons in his hand. For quite some time the peasant stood there waiting for him to finish measuring; and at length, after he had cried out a few times: "What's keeping you so long?" he decided to go and see for himself, only to find that it was not Ponzio holding the string but a nail fixed in the wall, which was all the payment he had for his capons. Ponzio played endless practical jokes of this kind. But there have been many other comedians like him, such as Gonnella, Meliolo when he was living, our own Fra Mariano and Fra Serafino who are here now, and many more whom you all know. And, to be sure, this style of humour is laudable in those who have no other occupation; but the practical jokes played by the courtier should, I think, be rather less scurrilous. One must also take care not to let one's practical jokes degenerate into simple fraud (as we see in the case of many wicked men who go about the world using various wiles to make money, and pretending now one thing and now another) or become too ruthless. And in this as in everything else the courtier should above all show respect and reverence for women, especially if there is any question of impugning their honour.'

Then signor Gaspare said: 'Without doubt, Bernardo, you are too partial to women. And why do you want men to show more respect to women than women to men? Isn't our honour perhaps as dear to us as theirs is to them? Do you really think, then, that women should wound men with their jests and japes without any restraint at all, and that men should suffer in silence and thank them for the privilege?'

To this, Bernardo replied: 'I am not saying that in their pleasantries and practical jokes women should not show to men the respect we have already mentioned; but I do say that they may impugn a man's virtue more freely than he may insult theirs. And this is because we ourselves, as men, have made it a rule that a dissolute way of life is not to be thought evil or blameworthy or disgraceful, whereas in women it leads to such complete opprobrium and shame that once a woman has been spoken ill of, whether the accusation be true or false, she is utterly disgraced for ever. Thus since even to mention a woman's honour carries the risk of doing grave harm, I say that we should refrain from this and get at them in some other way; for if our pleasantries and practical jokes are too ruthless, we exceed the bounds that we have already described as suitable for a gentleman.'

After Bernardo had paused a moment at this point, signor Ottaviano Fregoso said with a laugh:

'Signor Gaspare could tell you that this rule you say we have made ourselves is not perhaps as unreasonable as you imagine. For since women are very imperfect creatures, and of little or no dignity compared with men, they are incapable in themselves of performing any virtuous act, and so it was necessary, through shame and fear of disgrace, to place on them a restraint which might foster some good qualities. And it appeared that more necessary than anything else was chastity, so that we could be certain of our own children. In consequence it was essential to bring to bear every kind of skill and art, and all means possible, to make women remain pure, and to allow them to be of little worth in all other things and always to do the opposite of what they should. Therefore as they are allowed to commit all other sins without being blamed, if we try to nettle them with regard to all those defects which, as we said, they are allowed to possess without incongruity, and to which they pay little heed, we shall never inspire laughter: for you have already stated that laughter is inspired by certain things that are incongruous.'

Then the Duchess remarked: 'You speak about women in this fashion, signor Ottaviano, and yet you complain that they do not love you?'

'I do not complain about that,' answered signor Ottaviano. 'On the contrary, I thank them for it, since by not loving me they do not oblige me to love them. Besides I am not giving my own opinion but merely saying that signor Gaspare could use these arguments.'

Then Bernardo said: 'To be sure, it would be a great achievement for women if they could win over to their side two such enemies as you and signor Gaspare.'

'I am not an enemy of theirs,' continued signor Gaspare, 'but you are certainly an enemy of men; for if you still insist that women should not have their honour impugned, you should also impose on them the rule that they should not impugn men with regard to something as shameful in us as unchastity is in women. And why was it not as seemly for Alonso Carrillo to make the retort he did to signora Bobadilla, about his hoping to save his life if she took him for her husband, as it was for her to remark previously that all who knew him thought the King was going to have him hanged? And why was it not as allowable for Ricciardo Minutoli to deceive Filippello's wife and cause her to go to the bathhouse as it was for Beatrice to make her husband Egano get out of bed and be given a beating by Anichino, when she had been sleeping with him for some time? * Or for that other woman to tie a string to her toe and make

* In the Sixth Story of the Fourth Day of the *Decameron*, Boccaccio describes how Minutoli gets Filippello's wife, Catella, to meet and sleep with him in the *bagnio* by pretending that her husband has an assignation there himself. In the Seventh Story of the Seventh Day, Anichino fell in love with

her husband believe she was someone else? For you claim that these practical jokes played by women in Boccaccio are so neat and clever.'

Bernardo smiled at this and replied: 'Gentlemen, since it was my task to discuss only pleasantries, I will not go any further than that, and I think that I have already explained why it does not seem fitting to me to impugn the honour of women either by what we say or what we do, or to impose on them the rule that they should not take advantage of men whenever they are vulnerable. I maintain that with regard to the practical jokes and witticisms that you, signor Gaspare, have cited, what Alonso said to signora Bobadilla, even though it does touch to some extent on the question of chastity, does not displease me, since it is so round about and subtle that it can be interpreted ingenuously, and he could therefore have dissimulated and claimed that he did not mean it in that way at all. However, Alonso did once say something else which, in my opinion, was most unseemly; namely, when the Queen was passing signora Bobadilla's house Alonso noticed that the door was decorated with charcoal drawings of those lecherous animals that are found painted in so many ways about the inns, and going up to the Countess of Castagneto, he said: "See, madam, the heads of the beasts that signora Bobadilla kills every day in the hunt." Now although the metaphor was ingenious and cleverly derived from the way hunters for their glory mount the heads of dead animals on their doors, yet it is scurrilous and shameful; moreover, it was not even meant as a retort, which would be far more seemly as being justified by provocation therefore surely spontaneous. However, to return to the question of the practical jokes played by women, I do not say that they are right to deceive their husbands but I do maintain that some of the deceptions done by women that we read about in Giovanni Boccaccio are very neat and clever, especially the ones you yourself have mentioned. All the same, in my opinion, Ricciardo Minutoli's joke goes too far and is far more wounding than the one

---

Beatrice, took a job as a servant to her husband, Egano, who was tricked by his wife into wandering into the garden dressed in her clothes, while Anichino slipped into his bed.

played by Beatrice, seeing that Minutoli took much more from the wife of Filippello than Beatrice did from her husband; for Ricciardo, by means of a trick, violated the woman and made her do of herself something she had no wish to do, whereas Beatrice tricked her husband in order to do of her own free will something she wished.'

Then signor Gaspare said: 'Beatrice can be excused on no other grounds except those of love, and this should hold good for men just as much as for women.'

'Indeed,' replied Bernardo, 'the emotions of love provide great excuse for every kind of fault. Nevertheless, for myself I consider that any gentleman of worth who is in love ought to be sincere and honest in this, as in everything else; and if the betrayal, even of an enemy, can be properly held to be a base and hateful crime, consider how much worse a crime is the betrayal of someone we love. And I believe that why every tender lover endures so many toils and vigils, exposes himself to so many dangers, sheds so many tears, and tries by so many ways and means to please his love is not principally to win her body but to conquer the fortress of her mind and to break those hard diamonds and melt that cold ice, which are often found in the gentle breasts of women. And this, I believe, is the true and perfect pleasure and the goal aimed at by every noble soul. And certainly, for my part, if I were in love I would rather wish to know for sure that the lady I served returned my love from her heart and had given me her soul, if I had no other satisfaction, than to enjoy her to the full against her will; for in that case I would think myself the possessor of a lifeless body. Therefore those who pursue their desires by means of tricks, that should rather be called treacheries instead, do injury to others, nor, when they possess the body without the will, do they find the satisfaction that ought to be desired in love. I hold the same to be true of those others who in love make use of enchantments, charms, sometimes force, sometimes sleeping potions and other such things. And you must know that gifts greatly diminish the pleasures of love, for they lead one to doubt whether the lady is truly in love or is merely putting on a show for the gains it brings her. This is why the love of a great lady is prized so much, since it seems that its only motive must be genuine and true emotion, nor is it to be believed that a great lady would ever pretend to love her inferior if she did not truly do so.'

'I do not deny,' Gaspare answered, 'that the purpose, the toils and the perils of lovers should have as their principal aim the conquest of a woman's soul rather than her body. But I maintain that these deceptions, which you call treacheries in men and tricks in women, are the best means to the end, since whoever possesses a woman's body also wins her soul. And, if you remember, Filippello's wife, after complaining so much over the way she had been deceived by Ricciardo, realized how much more she savoured the kisses of her lover than those of her husband and, her coldness towards Ricciardo having turned into sweet affection, from that day on she loved him most tenderly. So you see how what it had been impossible to achieve through constant attentions, gifts and so many other affectionate tokens, was in next to no time won by his lying with her. Was it not the case, therefore, that in this instance trickery, or if you wish treachery, proved the sure way to capture the fortress of her soul?'

To this Bernardo replied: 'Your premise is completely false, since if women must always yield their souls to those who possess their bodies, then it would be impossible to find a single one who did not love her husband more than anyone else in the world; and this is far from true. However, like you, Giovanni Boccaccio was a wicked enemy of women.'

Gaspare retorted: 'I am no enemy of theirs. Still, there are very few men of worth who have much respect for women by and large, though occasionally for their own purposes they pretend the contrary.'

'You are doing wrong not only to women,' replied Bernaro,d 'but also to all the men who respect them. However, as I said, for the moment I do not wish to stray from my original subject in order to embark on such a difficult enterprise as the defence of women against so mighty a warrior as you. So I shall end my speech, which has perhaps been far longer than was called for and certainly less entertaining than you expected. And since I see the ladies staying so quiet and bearing the wrongs you do them so patiently, from now on I shall hold for true a part of what signor Ottaviano said, namely, that they do not mind what other evil things are said of them as long as their chastity is not impugned.'

At this, seeing the Duchess making a sign, a large number of the ladies present rose to their feet and, laughing, they all ran towards signor Gaspare as if to rain blows on him and treat him as the Bacchantes* treated Orpheus, saying at the same time: 'Now you shall see whether we care whether evil things are said about us.'

Partly because of the laughter, and partly because all had risen to their feet, it then seemed that the drowsiness that had overtaken some was dispelled from their eyes and minds. And then signor Gaspare began to say:

'There, you see, as they are not in the right they resort to force, wanting to end the discussion just as the Bracceschi would.'†

Then signora Emilia said: 'You will not succeed in your plan, for when you saw that Bernardo was tired from talking so long you began to say so much evil about women in the belief that no one would contradict you: but now we shall appoint a fresh champion who will fight with you so that your crime doesn't go unpunished.'

And turning to the Magnifico Giuliano, who had so far said little, she added:

'You are reputed to be the defender of women's honour; so now it is time for you to demonstrate that you have not earned this title undeservedly. And if in the past you have ever been rewarded for your service, you must now consider that by taking this bitter enemy of ours to task you will put all women so much in your debt that even if they devote themselves utterly to repaying it the debt will last for ever and never be wiped out.'

Then the Magnifico Giuliano replied: 'Madam, it seems to me that you do great honour to your enemy and very little to your

* The Bacchantes were the Thracian women who tore Orpheus to death during one of their Bacchanalian orgies.

† The Italian is *una licenzia braccesca*, literally, 'Braccesque leave'. The phrase is derived from the name of the condottiere Braccio Fortebraccio, whose followers, the Bracceschi, were notorious for their violence.

defender. For, to be sure, so far signor Gaspare has said against women nothing that Bernardo has not answered most competently. And I think that we each and all of us know that it is fitting for the courtier to have the greatest reverence for women, and that no man of discretion and courtesy should ever assail them for lack of chastity, either in jest or in earnest. And so to discuss this obvious truth is almost to cast doubt on what is self-evident. However, I think that signor Ottaviano went a little too far when he said that women are most imperfect creatures and incapable of any virtuous act and of little or no dignity in comparison with men. And then, since trust is often placed in those who have great authority, even if they do not speak the whole truth or speak in jest, signor Gaspare has allowed himself to be led by the words of signor Ottaviano into claiming that wise men have no respect for women; and this is completely false. On the contrary, I have known few men of worth who do not love and pay tribute to women, whose virtue and therefore whose dignity I consider to be not the slightest degree inferior to men's. Nevertheless, if this has to be a matter for dispute, the cause of women would be at a grave disadvantage. For these gentlemen have fashioned a courtier of such excellence and of such inspiring qualities that whoever imagines him so must consider that the merits of women cannot compare. To redress the balance, however, it would first be necessary for someone as clever and eloquent as Count Lodovico and Federico to fashion a Court lady with all the perfections proper to woman, just as they have fashioned the courtier with the perfections proper to a man. And then if the one defending their cause were of merely ordinary eloquence and wit I think that, with the help of the truth, he would show plainly that women have as many virtues as men.'

'Rather,' added signora Emilia, 'far more; and to prove it, consider that virtue is feminine whereas vice is masculine.'*

At this, signor Gaspare laughed before turning to Niccolò Frisio to say:

'What do you think of this, Frisio?'

Frisio replied: 'I feel sorry for the Magnifico who has been taken in by signora Emilia's promises and blandishments and has

* Evident in Italian – *la virtù* and *il vizio* – but not in English.

fallen into the error of saying things that make me blush for him.'

Signora Emilia replied, still smiling: 'You will rather blush for yourself when you see signor Gaspare won over and confessing his own error as well as yours, and begging for the forgiveness we will refuse to give him.'

Then the Duchess said: 'As it is now very late, I should like to postpone everything until tomorrow; and all the more so because I think it sensible to follow the advice of the Magnifico, namely, that before we enter into this dispute we should fashion a Court lady, perfect in everything, just as these gentlemen have fashioned the perfect courtier.'

'Madam,' answered signora Emilia, 'God grant that we do not happen to give this task to some fellow conspirator of signor Gaspare's who might fashion a Court lady knowing only how to cook and spin.'

Then Frisio said: 'But that's exactly her proper business.'

And the Duchess continued: 'I wish to put my trust in the Magnifico who, with the wit and judgement I know he has, will imagine the highest perfection that can be desired in a woman, and also express this in suitable language; and then we shall have something to set against the false slanders of signor Gaspare.'

'Madam,' replied the Magnifico, 'I do not know whether you are well advised to entrust me with an enterprise of such importance that I certainly do not feel equal to it; nor am I like the Count and Federico here, who have fashioned with their eloquence a courtier that never was, nor perhaps ever could be. Yet if it pleases you that I should undertake this task let it at least be on the same conditions as these gentlemen obtained, namely, that anyone may contradict me when he wishes to, and I shall regard this not as contradiction but as help; and perhaps, through the correction of my mistakes, we shall discover the perfection that we are seeking.'

'I trust,' answered the Duchess, 'that what you say will be such that there will be little room for contradiction. So use all your imagination, and fashion for us such a woman that these adversaries of ours will be ashamed to deny that she is equal in worth to the courtier, about whom it will be well for Federico to say no more, since he has already adorned him far too well, and especially as he must now be looked at in comparison with a woman.'

'For me, madam,' Federico then said, 'there is now nothing left to say about the courtier, and what I had thought to say has been driven from my mind because of Bernardo's jokes.'

'If that is so,' added the Duchess, 'let us meet together at an early hour tomorrow so that we may have time to settle both the one matter and the other.'

And then, after she had spoken, all rose to their feet and, after having respectfully taken leave of the Duchess, everyone went to his own room.

THE THIRD BOOK OF THE COURTIER

TO ALFONSO ARIOSTO

We read that Pythagoras in a very subtle and marvellous way discovered what was the size of Hercules' body; and the way he did it was as follows: it was known that the space where the Olympic games were celebrated every five years, in front of the temple of Olympic Jove, near Elis in Achaia, had been measured by Hercules, and that a stadium had been made of six hundred and twenty-five feet, using Hercules' own foot as the standard; the other stadiums which were later established throughout Greece by succeeding generations were also six hundred and twenty-five feet long, though somewhat shorter than the first. So, following that proportion, Pythagoras easily determined how much larger than normal Hercules' foot had been; and thus, having ascertained the size of his foot, he realized that Hercules' body had been as much larger than other men's bodies as, in the same proportion, the first stadium had been to those that followed.[1] Therefore, my dear Alfonso, by the same process of reasoning you can clearly understand from this small part of the whole how greatly superior was Urbino to all the other Courts of Italy, considering the superiority of these games (devised to refresh minds wearied by more demanding activities) to those practised elsewhere. And if the games were such, imagine the quality of the other worthy pursuits, to which we gave ourselves heart and soul; and here I dare to speak in the hope and certainty of being believed, for I am not praising things so ancient that I am at liberty to invent, and I can prove whatever I say by the testimony of many trustworthy men who are still living and have in person seen and experienced the life and customs that at one time flourished in that ducal house. And then, I hold myself bound, as best I can, to bend all my efforts to preserve this bright memory from human forgetfulness and, through my writing, to make it live for posterity. Perhaps in the future, then, there will not be lacking someone to envy our century for this as well; because no one reads of the marvellous deeds of the ancients without forming in his mind a certain higher opinion of those who are written about than the books seem able to express, even though they are truly inspired works. So we wish all those into whose hands this work of ours may come (if indeed it ever proves so worthy of favour as to be seen by noble knights and virtuous ladies) to suppose and believe for certain that the Court of Urbino was far more outstanding and far more adorned with singular men than our writing has been able to convey; and if our eloquence were equal to their high qualities we should need no other testimony to cause those who have not seen it to place complete trust in our words.

Now when the company had come together the following day, at the usual time and place, and all were sitting down in silence, everyone turned to look at Federico and the Magnifico Giuliano and waited to see which of them would begin the discussion. After a moment's silence, therefore, the Duchess said:

'Signor Magnifico, all of us wish to see this lady of yours well adorned; and if you do not show her to us in such a way as to reveal all her beauties, we shall suppose that you are jealous of her.'

'Madam,' replied the Magnifico, 'if I thought her beautiful, I should show her unadorned, and in the condition in which Paris wanted to see the three goddesses; but if these ladies, who well know how, do not assist me to attire her, I fear that not only signor Gaspare and Frisio but all these other gentlemen will be fully entitled to speak ill of her. Therefore, while she still has some reputation for beauty perhaps it would be better to keep her hidden and see what more Federico has to say about the courtier, who without doubt is far more attactive than my lady can be.'

'What I had in mind,' said Federico, 'is not so pertinent to the courtier that it cannot be left aside without loss; indeed, it is a somewhat different subject from what has been discussed so far.'

'Then what is it?' asked the Duchess.

'I had decided,' Federico went on, 'to explain in so far as I could the origins of these companies and orders of chivalry which great princes have founded under various emblems: such as that of St Michael at the royal Court of France, that of the Garter, under the patronage of St George, at the royal Court of England, and the

Golden Fleece at the Court of Burgundy; and how these dignities are bestowed and those who deserve to be are deprived of them; whence they arose, who were their originators, and for what purpose they established them: for these knights are always honoured, even in great courts. As well as discussing the various customs to be found at the Courts of Christian rulers in the matter of serving princes, observing festivals and appearing at public games, I thought also, if there were enough time, to say something on the same lines with regard to the Court of the Grand Turk and more especially the Court of the Sophi, King of Persia. For I have heard from merchants who have stayed a long time in that country that the noblemen there are very valiant and mannerly, and that in their dealings with one another, in serving their ladies and in all their actions they behave with the utmost courtesy and discretion and, on the due occasions, they display in their feats of arms, games and festivals much magnificence, great liberality and elegance. So I have been delighted to learn what fashions they prize most in all these things, what their ceremonies and elegance of dress and arms are like, and in what ways they are different from us or similar, how their ladies amuse themselves, and how modestly they show favour to those who serve them in love. However, it is surely not fitting to begin this discussion now, especially as there are other things to say which are far more to our purpose.'

'On the contrary,' said signor Gaspare, 'both this and many other things are more to the purpose than the portrayal of this Court lady, considering that the same rules as apply to the courtier serve also for her. For she, too, should pay heed to time and place and, insofar as her frailty allows, follow all those other ways that have been so fully discussed in regard to the courtier. And so instead of this it would not perhaps have been wrong to teach some of the particulars of those things that belong to the personal service of the prince, for the courtier ought rightly to understand them and to perform them gracefully; or indeed to speak of the way in which we should conduct our sports, such as riding, handling weapons and wrestling, and to discuss the problems involved in these activities.'

Then with a smile the Duchess remarked: 'Princes do not

employ such an excellent courtier as this for their personal service; and as for recreation and physical strength and agility, we shall leave the task of teaching them to our Pietro Monte, on a more suitable occasion, since now the Magnifico has no other duty than to speak of this lady, whom, I suspect, you have already started to fear and so have wanted to make us stray from the subject.'

Then Frisio answered: 'But surely it would be neither pertinent nor opportune to speak about women, especially as more remains to be said about the courtier, and we ought not to confuse one thing with another.'

'You are greatly in error,' replied Cesare Gonzaga, 'because just as there is no Court, however great, that can possess adornment or splendour or gaiety without the presence of women, and no courtier, no matter how graceful, pleasing or bold, who can ever perform gallant deeds of chivalry unless inspired by the loving and delightful company of women, so any discussion of the courtier must be imperfect unless ladies take part in it and contribute their share of the grace by which courtiership is adorned and perfected.'

At this, signor Ottaviano laughed and said: 'And there you catch a glimpse of the allurement that turns mens' heads.'

Then, turning to the Duchess, the Magnifico continued: 'Madam, since it is your wish, I shall say what I have to, though with great fear that I shall fail to please. Certainly, it would cost me far less effort to fashion a woman worthy to be the queen of the world than a perfect Court lady. For I do not know where to find my model for her, whereas for the queen of the world I would not need to seek far, seeing that it would be enough for me to imagine all the divine attributes of a certain lady and, as I contemplate them, to concentrate on expressing clearly in words what so many see with their eyes; and, if I could do no more, by naming her I should have fulfilled my task.'

Then the Duchess remarked: 'Signor Magnifico, you must keep to the rules. So please follow the order agreed on and fashion the Court lady so that so noble a ruler may have someone to serve her worthily.'

The Magnifico continued: 'Then, madam, to make it clear that your commands can induce me to attempt what I do not even know how to do, I shall describe this excellent lady as I would wish her to be. And when I have fashioned her to my own liking, since I may have no other I shall, like Pygmalion, take her for my own. And although signor Gaspare has stated that the rules laid down for the courtier also serve for the lady, I am of a different opinion; for although they have in common some qualities, which are as necessary to the man as to the woman, there are yet others befitting a woman rather than a man, and others again which befit a man but which a woman should regard as completely foreign to her. I believe this is true as regards the sports we have discussed; but, above all, I hold that a woman should in no way resemble a man as regards her ways, manners, words, gestures and bearing. Thus just as it is very fitting that a man should display a certain robust and sturdy manliness, so it is well for a woman to have a certain soft and delicate tenderness, with an air of feminine sweetness in her every movement, which, in her going and staying and whatsoever she does, always makes her appear a woman, without any resemblance to a man. If this precept be added to the rules that these gentlemen have taught the courtier, then I think that she ought to be able to make use of many of them, and adorn herself with the finest accomplishments, as signor Gaspare says. For I consider that many virtues of the mind are as necessary to a woman as to a man; as it is to be of good family; to shun affectation: to be naturally graceful; to be well mannered, clever and prudent; to be neither proud, envious or evil-tongued, nor vain, contentious or clumsy; to know how to gain and keep the favour of her mistress and of everyone else; to perform well and gracefully the sports suitable for women. It also seems to me that good looks are more important to her than to the courtier, for much is lacking to a woman who lacks beauty. She must also be more circumspect and at greater pains to avoid giving an excuse for someone to speak ill of her; she should not only be beyond reproach but also beyond even suspicion, for a woman lacks a man's resources when it comes to defending herself. And now, seeing that Count Lodovico has explained in great detail what should be the principal occupation of a courtier, namely, to his mind, the profession of arms, it seems right for me to say what I consider ought to be that of the lady at Court. And when I have done this, then I shall believe that most of my task has been carried out.

'Leaving aside, therefore, those virtues of the mind which she must have in common with the courtier, such as prudence, magnanimity, continence and many others besides, and also the qualities that are common to all kinds of women, such as goodness and discretion, the ability to take good care, if she is married, of her husband's belongings and house and children, and the virtues belonging to a good mother, I say that the lady who is at Court should properly have, before all else, a certain pleasing affability whereby she will know how to entertain graciously every kind of man with charming and honest conversation, suited to the time and the place and the rank of the person with whom she is talking. And her serene and modest behaviour, and the candour that ought to inform all her actions, should be accompanied by a quick and vivacious spirit by which she shows her freedom from boorishness; but with such a virtuous manner that she makes herself thought no less chaste, prudent and benign than she is pleasing, witty and discreet. Thus she must observe a certain difficult mean, composed as it were of contrasting qualities, and take care not to stray beyond certain fixed limits. Nor in her desire to be thought chaste and virtuous, should she appear withdrawn or run off if she dislikes the company she finds herself in or thinks the conversation improper. For it might easily be thought that she was pretending to be strait-laced simply to hide something she feared others could find out about her; and in any case, unsociable manners are always deplorable. Nor again, in order to prove herself free and easy, should she talk immodestly or practise a certain unrestrained and excessive familiarity or the kind of behaviour that leads people to suppose of her what is perhaps untrue. If she happens to find herself present at such talk, she should listen to it with a slight blush of shame. Moreover, she should avoid an error into which I have seen many women fall, namely, eagerly talking and listening to someone speaking evil of others. For those women who when they hear of the immodest behaviour of other women grow hot and bothered and pretend it is unbelievable and that to them an unchaste woman is simply a monster, in showing that they think this is such an enormous crime, suggest that they might be committing it themselves. And those who go about continually prying into the love affairs of other women, relating them in such detail and with such pleasure, appear to be envious and anxious that everyone should know how the matter stands lest by mistake the same thing should be imputed to them; and so they laugh in a certain way, with various mannerisms which betray the pleasure they feel. As a result, although men seem ready enough to listen, they nearly always form a bad opinion of them and hold them in very little respect, and they imagine that the mannerisms they affect are meant to lead them on; and then often they do go so far that the women concerned deservedly fall into ill repute, and finally they come to esteem them so little that they do not care to be with them and in fact regard them with distaste. On the other hand, there is no man so profligate and brash that he does not respect those women who are considered to be chaste and virtuous; for in a woman a serious disposition enhanced by virtue and discernment acts as a shield against the insolence and beastliness of arrogant men; and thus we see that a word, a laugh or an act of kindness, however small, coming from an honest woman is more universally appreciated than all the blandishments and caresses of those who without reserve display their lack of shame, and who, if they are not unchaste, with their wanton laughter, loquacity, brashness and scurrilous behaviour of this sort, certainly appear to be.

'And then, since words are idle and childish unless they are concerned with some subject of importance, the lady at Court as well as being able to recognize the rank of the person with whom she is talking should possess a knowledge of many subjects; and when she is speaking she should know how to choose topics suitable for the kind of person she is addressing, and she should be careful about sometimes saying something unwittingly that may give offence. She ought to be on her guard lest she arouse distaste by praising herself indiscreetly or being too tedious. She should not introduce serious subjects into light-hearted conversation, or jests and jokes into a discussion about serious things. She should not be inept in pretending to know what she does not know, but should seek modestly to win credit for knowing what she does, and, as was said, she should always avoid affectation. In this way she will be adorned with good manners; she will take part in the recreations suitable for a woman with supreme grace; and her conversation will be fluent, and extremely reserved, decent and charming. Thus she will be not only loved but also revered by all and perhaps worthy to stand comparison with our courtier as regards qualities both of mind and body.'

Having said this, the Magnifico fell silent and seemed to be sunk in reflection, as if he had finished what he had to say. And then signor Gaspare said:

'You have indeed, signor Magnifico, beautifully adorned this lady and made her of excellent character. Nevertheless, it seems to me that you have been speaking largely in generalities and have mentioned qualities so impressive that I think you were ashamed to spell them out; and, in the way people sometimes hanker after things that are impossible and miraculous, rather than explain them you have simply wished them into existence. So I should like you to explain what kind of recreations are suitable for a lady at Court, and in what way she ought to converse, and what are the many subjects you say it is fitting for her to know about; and also whether you mean that the prudence, magnanimity, purity and so many other qualities you mentioned are to help her merely in managing her home, and her family and children (though this was not to be her chief occupation) or rather in her conversation and in the graceful practice of those various activities. And now for heaven's sake be careful not to set those poor virtues such degraded tasks that they come to feel ashamed!'

The Magnifico laughed and said:

'You still cannot help displaying your ill-will towards women, signor Gaspare. But I was truly convinced that I had said enough, and especially to an audience such as this; for I hardly think there is anyone here who does not know, as far as recreation is concerned, that it is not becoming for women to handle weapons, ride, play the game of tennis, wrestle or take part in other sports that are suitable for men.'

Then the Unico Aretino remarked: 'Among the ancients

women used to wrestle naked with men; but we have lost that excellent practice, along with many others.'

Cesare Gonzaga added: 'And in my time I have seen women play tennis, handle weapons, ride, hunt and take part in nearly all the sports that a knight can enjoy.'

The Magnifico replied: 'Since I may fashion this lady my own way, I do not want her to indulge in these robust and manly exertions, and, moreover, even those that are suited to a woman I should like her to practise very circumspectly and with the gentle delicacy we have said is appropriate to her. For example, when she is dancing I should not wish to see her use movements that are too forceful and energetic, nor, when she is singing or playing a musical instrument, to use those abrupt and frequent *diminuendos* that are ingenious but not beautiful. And I suggest that she should choose instruments suited to her purpose. Imagine what an ungainly sight it would be to have a woman playing drums, fifes, trumpets or other instruments of that sort; and this is simply because their stridency buries and destroys the sweet gentleness which embellishes everything a woman does. So when she is about to dance or make music of any kind, she should first have to be coaxed a little, and should begin with a certain shyness, suggesting the dignified modesty that brazen women cannot understand. She should always dress herself correctly, and wear clothes that do not make her seem vain and frivolous. But since women are permitted to pay more attention to beauty than men, as indeed they should, and since there are various kinds of beauty, this lady of ours ought to be able to judge what kind of garments enhance her grace and are most appropriate for whatever she intends to undertake, and then make her choice. When she knows that her looks are bright and gay, she should enhance them by letting her movements, words and dress incline towards gaiety; and another woman who feels that her nature is gentle and serious should match it in appearance. Likewise she should modify the way she dresses depending on whether she is a little stouter or thinner than normal, or fair or dark, though in as subtle a way as possible; and keeping herself all the while dainty and pretty, she should avoid giving the impression that she is going to great pains.

'Now since signor Gaspare also asks what are the many things a lady at Court should know about, how she ought to converse, and whether her virtues should be such as to contribute to her conversation, I declare that I want her to understand what these gentlemen have said the courtier himself ought to know; and as for the activities we have said are unbecoming to her, I want her at least to have the understanding that people can have of things they do not practise themselves; and this so that she may know how to value and praise the gentlemen concerned in all fairness, according to their merits. And, to repeat in just a few words something of what has already been said, I want this lady to be knowledgeable about literature and painting, to know how to dance and play games, adding a discreet modesty and the ability to give a good impression of herself to the other principles that have been taught the courtier. And so when she is talking or laughing, playing or jesting, no matter what, she will always be most graceful, and she will converse in a suitable manner with whomever she happens to meet, making use of agreeable witticisms and jokes. And although continence, magnanimity, temperance, fortitude of spirit, prudence and the other virtues may not appear to be relevant in her social encounters with others, I want her to be adorned with these as well, not so much for the sake of good company, though they play a part in this too, as to make her truly virtuous, and so that her virtues, shining through everything she does, may make her worthy of honour.'

'I am quite surprised,' said signor Gaspare with a laugh, 'that since you endow women with letters, continence, magnanimity and temperance, you do not want them to govern cities as well, and to make laws and lead armies, while the men stay at home to cook and spin.'

The Magnifico replied, also laughing: 'Perhaps that would not be so bad, either.'

Then he added: 'Do you not know that Plato, who was certainly no great friend of women, put them in charge of the city and gave all the military duties to the men? Don't you think that we might find many women just as capable of governing cities and armies as men? But I have not imposed these duties on them, since

I am fashioning a Court lady and not a queen. I'm fully aware that you would like by implication to repeat the slander that signor Ottaviano made against women yesterday, namely, that they are most imperfect creatures, incapable of any virtuous act, worth very little and quite without dignity compared with men. But truly both you and he would be very much in error if you really thought this.'

Then signor Gaspare said: 'I don't want to repeat things that have been said already; but you are trying hard to make me say something that would hurt the feelings of these ladies, in order to make them my enemies, just as you are seeking to win their favour by deceitful flattery. However, they are so much more sensible than other women that they love the truth, even if it is not all that much to their credit, more than false praises; nor are they aggrieved if anyone maintains that men are of greater dignity, and they will admit that you have made some fantastic claims and attributed to the Court lady ridiculous and impossible qualities and so many virtues that Socrates and Cato and all the philosophers in the world are as nothing in comparison. And to tell the truth I wonder that you haven't been ashamed to go to such exaggerated lengths. For it should have been quite enough for you to make this lady beautiful, discreet, pure and affable, and able to entertain in an innocent manner with dancing, music, games, laughter, witticisms and the other things that are in daily evidence at Court. But to wish to give her an understanding of everything in the world and to attribute to her qualities that have rarely been seen in men, even throughout the centuries, is something one can neither tolerate nor bear listening to. That women are imperfect creatures and therefore of less dignity than men and incapable of practising the virtues practised by men, I would certainly not claim now, for the worthiness of these ladies here would be enough to give me the lie; however, I do say that very learned men have written that since Nature always plans and aims at absolute perfection she would, if possible, constantly bring forth men; and when a woman is born this is a mistake or defect, and contrary to Nature's wishes. This is also the case when someone is born blind, or lame, or with some other defect, as again with trees, when so many fruits fail to ripen. Nevertheless, since the blame for the defects of women must be attributed to

Nature, who has made them what they are, we ought not to despise them or to fail to give them the respect which is their due. But to esteem them to be more than they are seems to me to be manifestly wrong.'

The Magnifico Giuliano waited for signor Gaspare to continue, but seeing that he remained silent he remarked:

'It appears to me that you have advanced a very feeble argument for the imperfection of women. And, although this is not perhaps the right time to go into subtleties, my answer, based both on a reliable authority and on the simple truth, is that the substance of anything whatsoever cannot receive of itself either more or less; thus just as one stone cannot, as far as its essence is concerned, be more perfectly stone than another stone, nor one piece of wood more perfectly wood than another piece, so one man cannot be more perfectly man than another; and so, as far as their formal substance is concerned, the male cannot be more perfect than the female, since both the one and the other are included under the species man, and they differ in their accidents and not their essence.[2] You may then say that man is more perfect than woman if not as regards essence then at least as regards accidents; and to this I reply that these accidents must be the properties either of the body or of the mind. Now if you mean the body, because man is more robust, more quick and agile, and more able to endure toil, I say that this is an argument of very little validity since among men themselves those who possess these qualities more than others are not more highly regarded on that account; and even in warfare, when for the most part the work to be done demands exertion and strength, the strongest are not the most highly esteemed. If you mean the mind, I say that everything men can understand, women can too; and where a man's intellect can penetrate, so along with it can a woman's.'

After pausing for a moment, the Magnifico then added with a laugh:

'Do you not know that this proposition is held in philosophy: namely, that those who are weak in body are able in mind? So there can be no doubt that being weaker in body women are abler in mind and more capable of speculative thought than men.'

Then he continued: 'But apart from this, since you have said that I should argue from their acts as to the perfection of the one and the other, I say that if you will consider the operations of Nature, you will find that she produces women the way they are not by chance but adapted to the necessary end; for although she makes them gentle in body and placid in spirit, and with many other qualities opposite to those of men, yet the attributes of the one and the other tend towards the same beneficial end. For just as their gentle frailty makes women less courageous, so it makes them more cautious; and thus the mother nourishes her children, whereas the father instructs them and with his strength wins outside the home what his wife, no less commendably, conserves with diligence and care. Therefore if you study ancient and modern history (although men have always been very sparing in their praises of women) you will find that women as well as men have constantly given proof of their worth; and also that there have been some women who have waged wars and won glorious victories, governed kingdoms with the greatest prudence and justice, and done all that men have done. As for learning, cannot you recall reading of many women who knew philosophy, of others who have been consummate poets, others who prosecuted, accused and defended before judges with great eloquence? It would take too long to talk of the work they have done with their hands, nor is there any need for me to provide examples of it. So if in essential substance men are no more perfect than women, neither are they as regards accidents; and apart from theory this is quite clear in practice. And so I cannot see how you define this perfection of theirs.

'Now you said that Nature's intention is always to produce the most perfect things, and therefore she would if possible always produce men, and that women are the result of some mistake or defect rather than of intention. But I can only say that I deny this completely. You cannot possibly argue that Nature does not intend to produce the women without whom the human race cannot be preserved, which is something that Nature desires above everything else. For by means of the union of male and female, she produces children, who then return the benefits received in childhood by supporting their parents when they are old; then they renew them when they themselves have children, from whom they expect to receive in their old age what they bestowed on their own parents when they were young. In this way Nature, as if moving in a circle, fills out eternity and confers immortality on mortals. And since woman is as necessary to this process as man, I do not see how it can be that one is more the fruit of mere chance than the other. It is certainly true that Nature always intends to produce the most perfect things, and therefore always intends to produce the species man, though not male rather than female; and indeed, if Nature always produced males this would be imperfection: for just as there results from body and soul a composite nobler than its parts, namely, man himself, so from the union of male and female there results a composite that preserves the human species, and without which its parts would perish. Thus male and female always go naturally together, and one cannot exist without the other. So by very definition we cannot call anything male unless it has its female counterpart, or anything female if it has no male counterpart. And since one sex alone shows imperfection, the ancient theologians attribute both sexes to God. For this reason, Orpheus said that Jove was both male and female; and we read in Holy Scripture that God made male and female in His own likeness; and very often when the poets speak of the gods they confuse the sex.'

Then signor Gaspare said: 'I do not wish us to go into such subtleties because these ladies would not understand them; and though I were to refute you with excellent arguments, they would still think that I was wrong, or pretend to at least; and they would at once give a verdict in their own favour. However, since we have made a beginning, I shall say only that, as you know, it is the opinion of very learned men that man is as the form and woman as the matter, and therefore just as form is more perfect than matter, and indeed it gives it its being, so man is far more perfect than woman. And I recall having once heard that a great philosopher[3] in certain of his *Problems* asks: Why is it that a woman always naturally loves the man to whom she first gave herself in love? And on the contrary, why is it that a man detests the woman who first coupled with him in that way? And in giving his explanation he affirms that this is because in the sexual act the woman is perfected by the man, whereas the man is made imperfect, and that everyone naturally loves what makes him perfect and detests what makes him imperfect. Moreover, another convincing argument for the perfection of man and the imperfection of woman is that without exception every woman wants to be a man, by reason of a certain instinct that teaches her to desire her own perfection.'

The Magnifico Giuliano at once replied:

'The poor creatures do not wish to become men in order to make themselves more perfect but to gain their freedom and shake off the tyranny that men have imposed on them by their one-sided authority. Besides, the analogy you give of matter and form is not always applicable; for woman is not perfected by man in the way that matter is perfected by form. To be sure, matter receives its being from form, and cannot exist without it; and indeed the more material a form is, the more imperfect it is, and it is most perfect when separated from matter. On the other hand, woman does not receive her being from man but rather perfects him just as she is perfected by him, and thus both join together for the purpose of procreation which neither can ensure alone. Moreover, I shall attribute woman's enduring love for the man with whom she has first been, and man's detestation for the first woman he possesses, not to what is alleged by your philosopher in his *Problems* but to the resolution and constancy of women and the inconstancy of men. And for this, there are natural reasons: for because of its hot nature, the male sex possesses the qualities of lightness, movement and inconstancy, whereas from its coldness, the female sex derives its steadfast gravity and calm and is therefore more susceptible.'

At this point, signora Emilia turned to the Magnifico to say:

'In heaven's name, leave all this business of matter and form and male and female for once, and speak in a way that you can be understood. We heard and understood quite well all the evil said about us by signor Ottaviano and signor Gaspare, but now we can't at all understand your way of defending us. So it seems to me that what you are saying is beside the point and merely leaves in everyone's mind the bad impression of us given by these enemies of ours.'

'Do not call us that,' said signor Gaspare, 'for your real enemy is the Magnifico who, by praising women falsely, suggests they cannot be praised honestly.'

Then the Magnifico Giuliano continued: 'Do not doubt, madam, that an answer will be found for everything. But I don't want to abuse men as gratuitously as they have abused women; and if there were anyone here who happened to write these discussions down, I should not wish it to be thought later on, in some place where the concepts of matter and form might be understood, that the arguments and criticisms of signor Gaspare had not been refuted.'

'I don't see,' said signor Gaspare, 'how on this point you can deny that man's natural qualities make him more perfect than woman, since women are cold in temperament and men are hot. For warmth is far nobler and more perfect than cold, since it is active and productive; and, as you know, the heavens shed warmth on the earth rather than coldness, which plays no part in the work of Nature. And so I believe that the coldness of women is the reason why they are cowardly and timid.'

'So you still want to pursue these sophistries,' replied the Magnifico Giuliano, 'though I warn you that you get the worst of it every time. Just listen to this, and you'll understand why. I concede that in itself warmth is more perfect than cold; but this is not therefore the case with things that are mixed and composite, since if it were so the warmer any particular substance was the more perfect it would be, whereas in fact temperate bodies are the most perfect. Let me inform you also that women are cold in temperament only in comparison with men. In themselves, because of their excessive warmth, men are far from temperate; but in themselves women are temperate, or at least more nearly temperate than men, since they possess, in proportion to their natural warmth, a degree of moisture which in men, because of their excessive aridity, soon evaporates without trace. The coldness which women possess also counters and moderates their natural warmth, and brings it far nearer to a temperate condition; whereas in men excessive warmth soon brings their natural heat to the highest point where for lack of sustenance it dies away. And thus since men dry out more than women in the act of procreation they generally do not live so long;

and therefore we can attribute another perfection to women, namely, that enjoying longer life than men they fulfil far better than men the intention of Nature. As for the warmth that is shed on us from the heavens, I have nothing to say, since it has only its name in common with what we are talking about and preserving as it does all things beneath the orb of the moon, both warm and cold, it cannot be opposed to coldness. But the timidity of women, though it betrays a degree of imperfection, has a noble origin in the subtlety and readiness of their senses which convey images very speedily to the mind, because of which they are easily moved by external things. Very often you will find men who have no fear of death or of anything else and yet cannot be called courageous, since they fail to recognize danger and rush headlong without another thought along the path they have chosen. This is the result of a certain obtuse insensitivity; and a fool cannot be called brave. Indeed, true greatness of soul springs from a deliberate choice and free resolve to act in a certain way and to set honour and duty above every possible risk, and from being so stout-hearted even in the face of death, that one's faculties do not fail or falter but perform their functions in speech and thought as if they were completely untroubled. We have seen and heard of great men of this sort, and also of many women, both in recent centuries and in the ancient world, who no less than men have shown greatness of spirit and have performed deeds worthy of infinite praise.'

Then Frisio said: 'These deeds had their beginning when the first woman, through her transgression, led a man to sin against God and left to the human race a heritage of death, travails and sorrows and all the miseries and calamities suffered in the world today.'

The Magnifico retorted: 'If you want to preach a sermon, don't you know that the transgression you mentioned was repaired by a woman who won for us so much more than the other had lost that the fault for which her merits atoned is called a most happy one? But I do not wish to tell you now how inferior are all other human creatures to Our Lady, since this would be to confuse divine things with these foolish discussions of ours; nor do I wish to recount how many women with such marvellous constancy have let themselves be cruelly slain by tyrants for the sake of Christ, or to speak of those who in learned disputation have confounded so many idolators. And if you should say to me that all this was supernatural and owing to the grace of the Holy Spirit, I say that no virtue is more praiseworthy than that which is approved by the testimony of God. And you can discover many more women besides, who are less talked about, especially if you read St Jerome, who celebrated certain women of his time with such marvellous praise that it would suffice for the holiest of men.[4]

'Then think how many other women there have been who are never mentioned at all, because the poor creatures are shut away and do not have the ostentatious pride to seek a reputation for sanctity in the world, as do so many damned hypocrites among the men of today, who forget, or rather despise, the teaching of Christ which lays down that when a man fasts he should anoint his face so that he should not seem to be fasting and which commands that prayers, alms and other good works be performed not on the public square or in the synagogue but in private, so that the left hand may not know what the right is doing. Thus they affirm that the best thing in the world is to set a good example. And so, with bowed heads and downcast eyes, letting it be known that they do not wish to speak with women or eat anything except raw herbs, sweating under their torn habits, they go about deceiving the simple; and they do not hesitate to forge wills, to stir up mortal enmities between husband and wife, and sometimes, to make use of poison, employing sorceries, incantations and every sort of villainy; and then they cite, out of their own head, a certain authority which says: "*Si non caste, tamen caute*",* and by this, they suppose, they can cure every great evil and plausibly convince those who are not cautious that all sins, no matter how grave, are readily pardoned by God, provided they are committed in private and there is no bad example. Thus, under a veil of holiness and in this secret manner, they often devote all their thoughts to corrupting the pure mind of some woman; to sowing hatred between brothers; to controlling governments; to exalting one man at another's expense;

* This means roughly: 'If you can't be chaste be careful.'

to having men beheaded, imprisoned and proscribed; to ministering to the crimes and, as it were, serving as the repositories of the thefts many rulers commit. Others shamelessly delight in appearing dainty and gay, with their bristles well scraped, and wearing fine clothes; and as they pass by they lift their habit to display their neat hose, and bow here and there to show what fine figures of men they are. Others, even when celebrating mass, make use of certain gestures and looks which they think make them graceful and admired. Evil and wicked men, utter strangers not only to religion but to any good way of life! And when they are taken to task for their dissolute conduct, they make light of it all and mock the one who reproves them and they more or less exult in their vices.'

At this signora Emilia remarked: 'You so enjoy talking ill of friars that you have wandered right away from the subject. But you yourself do ill to murmur against men of religion, and you are burdening your conscience for nothing. For if there were not those who pray to God on our behalf, we would suffer even worse scourges than we do.'

Then the Magnifico Giuliano smiled and said:

'How did you guess so easily, madam, that I was talking about friars, since I never mentioned them by name? But truly I should not be accused of murmuring, for I am speaking quite plainly and openly; and I am referring not to the good ones but to the evil and guilty, and even then I haven't said a thousandth part of what I know.'

'Well, say no more about friars,' retorted signora Emilia, 'because I for one consider it a grave sin to listen to you, and so as not to hear I shall go elsewhere.'

'I am quite content to say no more on the subject,' the Magnifico Giuliano continued. 'But, to get back to the praises of women, I maintain that for every admirable man signor Gaspare finds me, I will discover a wife, a daughter or a sister of equal worth and sometimes better; moreover, many women have been the cause of countless benefits to their men, and have often corrected their errors. Now, as we have demonstrated, women are naturally capable of the same virtues as men, and we have often seen the fruits of this. So I do not know why, when I concede simply what they can have, often have had and still have, I should be supposed to be talking about the impossible, as signor Gaspare has alleged. For there have always been in the world and there still are women resembling the Court lady I have fashioned as closely as some men resemble the man fashioned by these gentlemen.'

Then signor Gaspare said: 'I think very little of arguments that run counter to experience. And surely if I were to ask you who were these great women as worthy of praise as the men to whom they were wives, sisters or daughters, or that have been the cause of some good, or have set men's errors to rights, I think you would be rather at a loss.'

'Indeed,' answered the Magnifico Giuliano, 'I would only be at a loss because of the great numbers involved. And if the time were available, I would cite for my purpose the story of Octavia, wife of Mark Antony and sister of Augustus; of Portia, Cato's daughter and wife of Brutus; of Caia Caecilia, wife of Tarquinius Priscus; of Cornelia, Scipio's daughter, and of countless other most remarkable women.[5] And I mean those of foreign nations as well as our own countrywomen: as, for example, Alexandra,[6] wife of Alexander, King of the Jews, who after the death of her husband, when she saw how the people were inflamed with rage and already seizing arms to slay the two children he had left her, in revenge for the way he had cruelly and harshly held them down, at once, such was her spirit, proved able to appease their just wrath and by her prudence win for her children the friendship of those whom their father's long-sustained and innumerable acts of injustice had made bitterly hostile.'

'Tell us at least how she did this,' asked signora Emilia.

'Well,' continued the Magnifico, 'when she saw the grave danger her children were in, she instantly had Alexander's body thrown into the middle of the square; then, having summoned the citizens to her, she said that she knew that their minds were inflamed with just rage against her husband and that the cruel injuries he had done them well deserved it; and so, just as while he was alive she had always striven to make him abandon his wickedness, now he was dead she was prepared to give proof of this and, so far as it was possible, help them to punish him. Therefore, she continued, they should take his body and feed it to dogs, and tear it to pieces in the cruellest ways they could imagine; but she earnestly beseeched them to have compassion on those innocent children, who were not only blameless but could not even have known of the wicked deeds of their father. These words proved so efficacious that the seething anger of the people was at once softened and turned into such a feeling of pity that they not only of one accord chose the children for their rulers but even gave a most honourable burial to the body of the dead man.'

After a moment's pause, the Magnifico added:

'Do you not know that the wife and sisters of Mithridates showed far less fear of death than Mithridates himself? And the wife of Hasdrubal less than Hasdrubal? Do you not know that Harmonia, daughter of Hiero the Syracusan, chose to die in the burning of her native city?'[7]

Then Frisio commented: 'Where there's obstinacy, of course you sometimes find women who will never abandon their purpose: like the one whose husband threw her down a well but she still went on demanding the scissors by motioning with her hands.'

The Magnifico Giuliano laughed and said:

'Obstinacy that produces virtuous acts ought to be called constancy; as in the case of Epicharis, the Roman freedwoman,[8] who, being involved in a great conspiracy against Nero, displayed such constancy that, although racked by the most horrible tortures imaginable, she never betrayed a single one of her accomplices; whereas in the same peril many noble knights and senators weakly accused their brothers and friends and the nearest and dearest they had in the world. And what will you say of that other woman, called Leona,[9] in whose honour the Athenians dedicated before the gate of the citadel a tongueless lioness in bronze, to commemorate the virtue she had shown of steadfast silence? For she, being involved likewise in a conspiracy against the tyrants, was undismayed by the death of two great men, her friends, and though torn by countless most cruel tortures, never betrayed any of the conspirators.'

Then madonna Margherita Gonzaga said: 'I think you are describing these noble deeds of women too briefly; for although these enemies of ours have indeed heard and read about them, they pretend not to know them and would like them to be forgotten. But if you will allow us women to hear them, at least we shall take pride in them.'

The Magnifico Giuliano responded: 'I shall be glad to. So now I wish to tell you about a woman who did something that I think even signor Gaspare will concede is done by very few men.'

And he began: 'In Massilia there was once a custom, believed to have come from Greece, as follows. Namely, they publicly kept a poison concocted of hemlock, and anyone was allowed to drink it who could prove to the Senate that he ought to quit this life because of some personal grief or for some other just reason, in order that whoever had suffered excessive ill fortune or enjoyed unusual prosperity should not continue in the one or lose the other. Well, when Sextus Pompey found himself...'

Here, without waiting for the Magnifico Giuliano to continue, Frisio interrupted:

'This seems to me like the beginning of a very long story.'

The Magnifico Giuliano turned with a smile to madonna Margherita and remarked:

'You see that Frisio won't let me speak. I wanted to tell you the story of a woman who, after she had demonstrated to the Senate that she ought rightfully to die, cheerfully and fearlessly took the poison in the presence of Sextus Pompey, with such constancy of spirit and such thoughtful and loving remembrances of her family that Pompey and all the others who witnessed such wisdom and steadfastness on the part of a woman on the fearsome threshold of death wept not a few tears, and were overcome by wonder.'

At this, signor Gaspare smiled and remarked:

'I, too, recall having read an oration in which an unhappy husband asks permission of the Senate to die and proves that he has just cause, since he cannot endure the continuous aggravation of his wife's chatter and prefers to swallow the poison, which as you say was kept publicly for this purpose, rather than the words of his wife.'

The Magnifico Giuliano answered: 'But how many wretched women there are who would have just cause for asking permission to die on the grounds that they cannot endure, I shall not say the evil words, but the excessively evil deeds of their husbands! For I know several such who in this world suffer the pains that are said to be in hell.'

'Do you not believe,' replied signor Gaspare, 'that there are also many husbands who are so tormented by their wives that every hour they long for death?'

'And what annoyance,' retorted the Magnifico, 'can wives cause their husbands that is as irremediable as that which husbands cause their wives, who are forced to be submissive if not by love then by fear?'

'To be sure,' said signor Gaspare, 'the little good they occasionally do is prompted by fear, seeing that there are few wives in the world who do not conceal in their hearts a hatred of their husbands.'

'On the contrary,' answered the Magnifico, 'and if you remember what you have read, we see in all the histories that wives nearly always love their husbands more than their husbands love them. When did you ever see or read of a husband giving his wife such a proof of love as Camma[10] gave to her husband?'

'I do not know,' replied signor Gaspare, 'either who she was or what proof it was she gave.'

'Nor I,' added Frisio.

The Magnifico continued: 'Well, listen to what I say, and you, madonna Margherita, be sure to remember it.

'This Camma was a most beautiful young woman, adorned with such modesty and such a charming disposition that she was admired for this no less than for her looks. And above all other things and with all her heart she loved her husband, who was called Synattus. Now it happened that another gentleman, who was of a far higher station in life than Synattus and indeed virtually the sole ruler of the city where they lived, fell in love with the young woman; and after having tried for a long time by all ways and means to possess her, but in vain, he persuaded himself that the love she bore her husband was the sole obstacle to his passion, and he had this Synattus killed. But despite his constant solicitations he could never win more for himself than he had before; and then, as his love grew stronger every day, he resolved to marry her, although her social position was far inferior to his. So after Sinoris (as her lover was called) had asked her parents for their consent, they began trying to persuade her to accept him, arguing that her consent would be extremely advantageous and her refusal perilous for her and for them all. After she had demurred for a time, at length she gave her agreement. Then the parents sent word to Sinoris, who was overjoyed beyond words and at once arranged for their wedding to be celebrated. After the two had made their solemn entry for this purpose into the Temple of Diana, Camma called for a certain sweet drink that she had prepared herself. Standing before the statue of Diana and in the presence of Sinoris, she drank half of it; and then with her own hand (this being the usual custom at weddings) she gave the remainder to her spouse, who drained the cup. Seeing her plan succeed, Camma knelt at the foot of Diana's statue and said aloud:

' "O Goddess, thou that knowest what is hidden in my heart, witness how hard it was for me not to take my own life after the death of my dear husband, and with what weariness I have sustained the grief of remaining in this bitter life, which has held for me no advantage or pleasure other than the hope of the revenge which I know has been accomplished. Now, with joy and contentment, I go to seek the sweet company of the spirit whom I have loved in life and in death more than myself. And you, wretched man, who thought to be my husband, give orders that your tomb be prepared for you in place of the marriage bed, for I offer you as a sacrifice to the shade of Synattus."

'Aghast at these words and feeling already the effects of the poison at work, Sinoris sought various remedies, but with no success; and indeed before she died herself Camma enjoyed the good fortune, if such it was, of knowing that Sinoris was dead. After she had learned this, she lay down contentedly on her bed, and with her eyes raised to heaven, calling all the while the name of Synattus, she said: "O darling husband, now that I have given both tears and vengeance as my last offerings for your death, and cannot see what more remains to do for you, I leave this world and a life so cruel without you but once so dear solely because of you. Come to meet me, my lord, and receive this soul as eagerly as it seeks you." And so saying, opening her arms as if to embrace him already, she died. And now, Frisio, tell us what you think of this woman?'

Answered Frisio: 'I think you want to make the ladies weep. But even accepting the truth of your story, I tell you that such women are no longer to be found in the world.'

The Magnifico replied: 'But they are indeed to be found; and to prove it, listen to this. In my time there was a gentleman living in Pisa who was called Tommaso; I do not recall his family, though I often heard them mentioned by my father, who was a great friend of his. This Tommaso, then, was one day making the crossing in a small boat from Pisa to Sicily, going about his business, when he was overtaken by some Moorish galleys which came up so suddenly that those in command of the boat did not see them; and, although the men on board fought back hard, since they were few and the enemy many the small boat and all those in her fell into the hands of the Moors, some wounded and others untouched, as their luck had it, and among them Tommaso who had fought bravely and killed with his own hands a brother of one of the captains of the galleys. As a consequence, angered, as you might imagine, by the loss of his brother, the captain demanded Tommaso for his own prisoner; and beating and torturing him every day he carried him off to Barbary, where he was resolved to keep him a captive for life, in great torment and suffering. After a time all the others, in one way or another, won their freedom, and they returned home to report to his wife, madonna Argentina, and to his children, the hard life and dreadful suffering in which Tommaso lived and would probably continue to live without hope, unless God saved him by a miracle. After his wife and family had been apprised of all this and had tried in various ways to secure his freedom, and when he himself was resigned to death, it came to pass that one of his sons, whose name was Paolo, emboldened and inspired by his anxious love for his father, contemptuous of all possible dangers, resolved either to liberate him or to die himself. He succeeded in doing what he wanted, bringing his father out so secretly that he was in Leghorn before it was realized in Barbary that he had gone. And from Leghorn, Tommaso, now safe, wrote to his wife explaining that he had been freed and where he was and that he hoped to see her the following day. Overwhelmed by the great and unexpected joy of being able to see again so soon the husband she had been convinced she would never meet again, and this through the enterprise and piety of her son, the good and gentle lady, after reading the letter, raised her eyes to heaven, called the name of her husband and then fell lifeless to the ground. Nor, for all the efforts that were made, did it prove possible to restore her soul to her body. This was surely a cruel spectacle, and enough to moderate our human desires and restrain us from longing too vehemently for complete and utter happiness!'

At this, Frisio said with a laugh:

'How do you know that she didn't die from vexation on learning that her husband was on his way home?'

The Magnifico retorted: 'Because the rest of her life was not in keeping. On the contrary, I believe that her soul, not being able to bear waiting to see him through her bodily eyes, moved by desire, fled from her body to where, as she read that letter, her thoughts had already flown.'

Said signor Gaspare: 'It could be that this lady was too much in love, for women always go to harmful extremes in everything; and you see that because she was too much in love she harmed herself, and her husband, and her children, whose rejoicing over his perilous and longed-for liberation she turned into bitterness. So you should not cite her as one of those women who have been the cause of so many blessings.'

The Magnifico answered: 'I cite her as one of those who can bear witness that there are wives who love their husbands; as for those who have brought the world many blessings, I could tell you of an infinite number, and could include those fabled women of the ancient world and those such as Pallas and Ceres who have originated such things that they deserve to be hailed as goddesses. Then I could tell you about the sibyls, through whose mouth God spoke so often, revealing to the world things that were yet to come; and about those who have been the teachers of very great men, such as Aspasia and Diotima, who by her sacrifices delayed for ten years the plague that was to visit Athens. I could tell you of Nicostrata, mother of Evander, who taught letters to the Latins; and of yet another woman who was the teacher of the lyric poet, Pindar; and of Corinna and Sappho, who were such excellent poets.[11] But I do not wish to go so far afield. I can say, however, forgetting the rest, that without doubt women were no less responsible for the greatness of Rome than men.'

'And that,' said signor Gaspare, 'would be well worth hearing.'

'Then listen,' answered the Magnifico. 'After the conquest of Troy, many Trojans who escaped from the devastation fled away, some in one direction, some another. Of these, one band, after being tossed by storms, came to Italy, to the spot where the Tiber enters the sea. After they had landed to search for their necessities, they began to explore the countryside; and then the women, who had remained in the ships, thought up by themselves a practical scheme that would mean the end of their long and perilous wanderings on the sea and win them a new homeland in place of the one they had lost. After they had conferred together, the men still being absent, they burned the ships; and the first woman to put her hand to this work was called Roma. However, they were afraid of the anger of their men, who were now returning, and so they went to meet them; and with a great show of affection, embracing and kissing, some their husbands and others their blood relations, they softened the first impulse of anger; and then they calmly explained the reason for their shrewd decision. Subsequently the Trojan men, partly because they had no choice and partly because they were kindly received by the native inhabitants, were more than pleased with what their women had done, and they settled there with the Latins in the place where Rome was eventually to be. And from this incident arose the ancient Roman custom by which the women kissed their relations whenever they met. So you see the great contribution made by these women to the founding of Rome.

'And the Sabine women made no less a contribution to the expansion of Rome than did the Trojan women to its beginnings. For Romulus, after he had provoked widespread enmity among all his neighbours by carrying off their women, was harassed by attacks on every side. His prowess was such that from these wars he soon emerged triumphant, with the exception of his struggle with the Sabines, which was very bitter since their king, Titus Tatius, was exceptionally able and sagacious. Then after there had been a violent clash between the Romans and the Sabines, with very heavy losses on both sides, and a fresh and cruel conflict seemed imminent, the Sabine women, clothed in black, with their hair hanging loose and torn, weeping and lamenting, with no fear for the weapons already drawn to strike, went between their fathers and husbands, begging them not to stain their hands with the blood of their own in-laws; if they were displeased with the relationship between them, they added, they should turn their weapons against them, the women, since they far preferred to die than to live on as widows, or without fathers and brothers, remembering that their children were begotten of those who had slain their fathers or that they themselves were the daughters of those who had slain their husbands. Weeping and wailing, many of them were carrying in their arms little children who in some cases were already learning to form their words and who seemed to be trying to call out to their grandfathers and demonstrate their affection. And with tears in their eyes as they held the grandchildren out, the women cried:

' "Look at your own blood, which you are seeking so wildly and angrily to shed with your own hands!"

'The piety and wisdom of these women was in this instance so efficacious that not only did the two hostile kings make a pact of indissoluble friendship and alliance but, more wonderful still, the Sabines settled in Rome and the two peoples became one. And this agreement vastly increased the might of Rome, thanks to these shrewd and courageous women, to whom Romulus recorded his gratitude by giving to the thirty wards into which he divided the people the names of Sabine women.'[12]

After a moment's pause, seeing that signor Gaspare was not going to speak, the Magnifico Giuliano added:

'Doesn't it seem to you that these women greatly benefited their menfolk and contributed to the greatness of Rome?'

'Certainly, they deserved great praise,' answered signor Gaspare. 'But if you had seen fit to tell us of the sins of women as well as of their good deeds, you would not have kept silent about the way in which, during the war against Titus Tatius, a woman betrayed Rome and showed the enemy the route they should take to seize the Capitol, where the Romans barely escaped total destruction.'[13]

The Magnifico replied: 'You refer me to a single wicked woman, whereas I have reminded you of any number of good ones; and in addition to those I have mentioned I could quote for my purpose a thousand other instances of the benefits that women have conferred on Rome; and I could tell you why a temple was once built to Venus Armata, and another to Venus Calva, and how the Festival of the Maidens was instituted in honour of Juno, because the slave-girls once delivered Rome from the threats of the enemy. But apart from all these things, did not that noble deed for which Cicero praised himself so highly, namely, the discovery of Catiline's conspiracy, have its beginning chiefly with just a common woman? And because of this it could be said that she was the cause of all the benefits that Cicero boasts of having secured for the Republic of Rome.[14] If I now had the time, I would also doubtless be able to show you that women have also often corrected the errors of men; but I fear my speech is already so long as to prove displeasing; so now that I have performed the task set me by these ladies, to the best of my ability, I propose to give way to someone who may say things more worth hearing than my remarks can be.'

At this, signora Emilia commented:

'Do not rob women of the true praises that are owing to them; and remember that if signor Gaspare and perhaps signor Ottaviano find what you say displeasing we and all these other gentlemen hear you with pleasure.'

The Magnifico was still anxious to have done, but all the ladies began to beg him to continue; and so, with a smile, he added:

'In order not to make Signor Gaspare more my enemy than he is already, I shall just mention briefly a few women whom I recall, leaving out many whom I could tell you of.'

Then he went on as follows: 'When Philip,[15] the son of Demetrius, was investing the city of Chios, during the siege he issued a proclamation that all the slaves who fled the city and joined him should have both their freedom and the wives of their masters. The anger of the women of Chios at this shameful proclamation was so intense that they themselves took to arms and flocked to the walls, where they fought so boldly that before long, to Philip's shame and loss, they succeeded where their men had failed and put him to flight. These same women accomplished a deed no less glorious than this, when they came to Leuconia with their husbands, fathers and brothers, who were going into exile: the Erythraeans, who were there with their allies, waged war against the Chians who, being unable to withstand them, made a pact to leave the city, dressed only in their cloaks and tunics. When the women heard of this shameful agreement, they protested and reproached the men for abandoning their arms and going almost naked among the enemy; and when they were told that the pact was already sealed, they said that in that case the men should leave their clothes and carry their shields and spears, and tell the enemy that this was how they dressed. So, acting on their women's advice, the Chians largely, if not entirely, escaped the shame they deserved. Again, when Cyrus had routed an army of Persians in battle, as they fled in retreat towards the city they encountered their wives outside the gate; and as they approached the women said:

'"Why are you fleeing, you cowards? Do you perhaps want to hide yourselves away inside the women you came out of?"

'When the men heard these and similar remarks, realizing how much less courageous they were than their women, they grew ashamed and made their way back to renew the fight with the enemy, whom this time they routed.'

Having spoken thus far, the Magnifico Giuliano concluded: 'And now, madam, you will allow me to remain silent?'

To this, signor Gaspare replied: 'You will have to remain silent, since you've nothing more to say.'

The Magnifico laughed and retorted: 'You provoke me so much that you run the risk of having to listen all night to the praises of women; and of having to hear of many Spartan women who rejoiced in the glorious deaths of their sons; and of those who disowned or even killed their sons themselves on seeing them act like cowards. And then of how, after the ruin of their country, the Saguntine women took up arms against the forces of Hannibal; and how after Marius had defeated the army of the Germans, their women, unable to win permission to live freely in Rome in the service of the Vestal Virgins, slew both themselves and their little children; and of thousands of others, of whom all the histories of the ancient world are full.'

Signor Gaspare remarked: 'Ah, signor Magnifico, only God knows how those things happened; for those centuries are so remote from us that many lies can be told, and there is no one here who can test their truth.'

The Magnifico answered: 'If you compare the merits of women with those of men in any age whatsoever you will find that they have never been, nor are they now, the slightest bit inferior. For leaving aside all those centuries of long ago, if you come to the time when the Goths ruled in Italy, you will discover that for a long time they had a queen, Amalasontha, who ruled with admirable wisdom; then there was Theodolinda, Queen of the Lombards, of exceptional ability; Theodora, the Greek Empress; and in Italy, among many others, Countess Matilda proved herself a truly exceptional woman, whose praises I will leave to Count Lodovico, since she was of his family.'[16]

'On the contrary,' the Count replied, 'this concerns you, for you know full well that it isn't right for someone to praise his own.'

The Magnifico continued: 'And then, how many famous women do you find in history, belonging to this noble house of Montefeltro! how many belonging to the families of Gonzaga, and Este and Pio! And if we wish to speak of present times, we do not have to go too far afield for our examples, for we have them in this very house. But I will not avail myself of those who are here with us, lest you pretend to grant me simply out of courtesy what you cannot possibly deny. And, to go outside of Italy, remember that in our own time we have seen Queen Anne of France, a very great lady no less as regards virtue than rank, and one whom, if you wish to compare her with King Charles and King Louis, to both of whom she was married, you will find not the slightest bit inferior. Then, consider madonna Margherita, daughter of the Emperor Maximilian, who till now has governed and still governs her state with the greatest prudence and justice.

'But, leaving aside all others, tell me, signor Gaspare, what king or prince has there been in our own time, or even for many years past, in the whole of Christendom to compare with Queen Isabella of Spain?'[17]

Signor Gaspare replied: 'King Ferdinand, her husband.'

'Well,' added the Magnifico, 'that I will not deny. For since the Queen judged him worthy to be her husband, and loved and respected him so much, one cannot say that he does not deserve to be compared with her. Yet I maintain that the fame he acquired because of her was a dowry as valuable as the Kingdom of Castile.'

'I would rather say,' argued signor Gaspare, 'that Queen Isabella was praised for many acts for which King Ferdinand was responsible.'

'Well,' answered the Magnifico, 'unless it's the case that the people of Spain, the lords and commoners, men and women, rich and poor, have all come to an agreement deliberately to lie in her favour, there has been nowhere in the world in our time any more distinguished example of true goodness and religion, of greatness of spirit, of prudence and chaste behaviour, of courtesy and liberality, and, in short, of every virtue, than Queen Isabella; and although her fame is very great and universally known, those who lived with her and were able to witness her actions all affirm that this reputation sprang from her own merits and virtue. And whoever considers what she did, will soon recognize the truth of this. For, leaving aside countless other things that prove what I am saying and could be told were this my purpose, everyone knows that when she came to the throne she found the greater part of Castile held by the grandees; nevertheless, she recovered it all by acting so justly and in such a manner that the very same men who were deprived stayed loyal to her and content to give up what they held. Another notable thing is the great courage and prudence with which she continuously defended her realms against most powerful enemies; and similarly to her only can go the honour of the glorious conquest of the Kingdom of Granada; for in so long and difficult a war against obstinate enemies, who were fighting for their property, their lives, their religion and, as they saw it, for God, she always displayed such great ability in her deliberations and her own person that probably few rulers in our time have dared, I shall not say to imitate but even to be envious of her. Moreover, all those who knew her affirm that her government was so inspired that it seemed necessary for her simply to express her wish, and then with no more fuss everyone did what he should; and even in their own homes and privately, men hardly dared do what might displease her. And to a great extent the cause of this was the superb judgement she displayed in finding and appointing able ministers for the posts in which she meant to use them. Then so well did she marry rigorous standards of justice with the gentle touch of clemency and with generosity that in her day there was not one good man who complained that he was too little rewarded, and not one bad man that he was too harshly punished. Therefore among the people there grew towards her an attitude of the greatest reverence, composed of both fear and love; and this still influences their minds so securely that they appear to believe that she is watching them still from heaven and may well be praising or blaming them from up there; thus those realms are still governed by her fame and by the methods she instituted, in such a way that, although she is no longer living, her authority endures, like a wheel that has been spun vigorously for a long time and then, though no one is turning it any longer, continues to turn for a good space by itself. Consider in addition to this, signor Gaspare, that in our time almost all the great men of Spain and those with any claims to fame were raised up by Queen Isabella; and Gonsalvo Ferrando, the Great Captain, took far greater pride in this than in all his famous victories and all those extraordinary and powerful deeds which have made him both in peace and war so distinguished and illustrious that, unless Fame is without gratitude, she will always publish his immortal glory to the world and testify that in our time we have had few kings or great princes who have not been surpassed by him in magnanimity, knowledge and all other virtues.

'And now, to come back to Italy, I maintain that here too we have no shortage of truly outstanding ladies; for there are two remarkable queens in Naples, where a short time ago there died another, the Queen of Hungary, who as you know was herself outstanding and such as to compare with her husband, the invincible and glorious King Matthias Corvinus. The Duchess Isabella of Aragon, the worthy sister of King Ferdinand of Naples, like gold in the fire, has also shown her virtue and valour amid the storms of Fortune. If you visit Lombardy, you will meet Isabella, Marchioness of Mantua, whose splendid qualities it would be wrong to describe in the restrained terms that impose themselves on anyone wishing to mention her at all. It saddens me, too, that all of you did not know her sister, the Duchess Beatrice of Milan, so that you might never again be surprised at the brilliance of women. Then Eleanora of Aragon, Duchess of Ferrara and the mother of the two ladies I have mentioned, was herself so great that her virtues made evident to everyone both her worthiness as the daughter of a king and her right to far grander possessions than all her ancestors had held. And to mention yet another, how many men do you know who have suffered the bitter blows of Fortune as meekly as Queen Isabella of Naples, who, following the loss of her kingdom, the banishment and death of her husband, King Federico, and of two of her children, and the captivity of her first-born, the Duke of Calabria, still acts as a queen and by the manner in which she bears the trials and tribulations of miserable poverty demonstrates to the whole world that although her fortunes have changed her character has not?[18] There are countless other ladies of rank, and ordinary women too, whom I could mention to you; such as all those women of Pisa[19] whose generous courage and disregard of death, in the defence of their country against the Florentines, have equalled that of the most unconquerable spirits of all time. And for this, some of them have been immortalized by many great poets. I could tell you of certain women who were very talented in letters, in music, in painting and in sculpture. But I do not wish to continue reviewing these examples, which are well known to all of you. It will be enough for you to bring to mind the women you yourselves have known, for then you will recognize without difficulty that for the most part they are not inferior in worth or merit to their fathers, brothers and husbands, and that many of them have been the cause of benefits to men and have often corrected their errors; and if nowadays the world lacks those great queens, such as Tomyris, Queen of Scythia, Artemisia, Zenobia, Semiramis or Cleopatra, who used to subjugate distant lands and erect great buildings, pyramids and cities, neither does it contain men such as Caesar, Alexander, Scipio, Lucullus and those other Roman commanders.'

'Do not say that,' replied Frisio with a laugh, 'for now more than ever there are to be found women like Cleopatra and Semiramis; and if they do not possess such great dominions, power and riches, they certainly do not lack the will to imitate those queens in attending to their pleasures and satisfying their appetites as best they can.'

The Magnifico Giuliano said: 'Frisio, you still want to go too far. But even if there are some Cleopatras to be found still, there are also countless Sardanapaluses,[20] which is far worse.'

'Do not make such comparisons,' added signor Gaspare, 'and don't believe that men are more incontinent than women. Even if they were, it would not be worse, since countless evils arise from the incontinence of women which do not do so from the incontinence of men; and therefore, as was said yesterday, it is wisely made the rule that women are allowed to fail in everything else, and not be blamed, so long as they can devote all their resources to preserving that one virtue of chastity, failing which there would be doubts about one's children and the bond which binds the whole world on account of blood, and of each man's natural love for his own offspring, would be dissolved. So women are more sternly forbidden a dissolute way of life than men, whose bodies do not bear their children for those nine months.'

'Really,' said the Magnifico, 'these arguments of yours are very remarkable, and I do not know why you don't put them down in writing. But tell me why it is not made the rule that men may be condemned for a dissolute way of life as much as women, seeing that if they are naturally of higher worth and virtue, they can all the more easily practise the virtue of continence; and then doubts about one's children would be neither greater nor less. For even if women were unchaste, if the men stayed pure and did not give in to the unchastity of women, they could not produce offspring all on their own. But if you wish to be truthful, you must also recognize that we have granted ourselves the licence by which we want the same sins that are trivial and sometimes even praiseworthy when committed by men to be so damnable in women that they cannot be punished enough, save by a shameful death or at least everlasting infamy. Therefore since this opinion is so widespread, I think it only proper also to punish harshly those who defame women with their lies; and I consider that every noble knight is bound when it is necessary to take up arms in defence of the truth, and especially when he hears a woman falsely accused of being unchaste.'

'And I,' answered signor Gaspare with a smile, 'not only affirm that what you say is indeed the duty of every noble knight but also consider it chivalrous and gentlemanly to conceal the fault which a woman may have committed either through mischance or excessive love; and so you can see that when it is right and proper I am a greater champion of women than you. Indeed, I do not deny that men have arrogated to themselves a certain liberty; and this because they know that it is commonly accepted that a dissolute life does not bring them the infamous reputation that it does to women, who, because of the frailty of their sex, are far more influenced by their passions than men. And if they do sometimes refrain from satisfying their desires, they do so out of shame and not because they lack a very ready will to do so. And so men have instilled in them the fear of infamy as a bridle to preserve their chastity almost by force, and without which, to be honest, they would be little esteemed; for women bring no benefit to the world, save the bearing of children. This is not, however, the case with men, who govern cities and command armies and perform so many other important things: all of which, since you will have it so, I will not dispute women know how to do, but which, quite simply, they do not do. And when men have chanced to be models of continence, then they have surpassed women in this virtue just as in the others, though you do not agree. On this matter, I have no wish to recite for you as many stories and fables as you have done but will merely refer you to the continence of two very great rulers, who were young and flushed with victory, which invariably makes even the mildest men intemperate. First, there is the continence of Alexander the Great, with regard to the very beautiful women of Darius, his defeated enemy; then of Scipio, to whom, when at the age of twenty-four he had taken a city in Spain by force, there was brought a very beautiful and noble young woman, who had been captured among many others. And when Scipio learned that she was the bride of one of the local lords, not only did he refrain from any attempt on her virtue but he also restored her unsullied to her husband, to whom he gave a rich gift besides. I could tell you of Xenocrates who, when a very beautiful woman lay down naked beside him and used all the arts and caresses she knew, and in which she was very skilled, was so continent that she completely failed to arouse his lust, though she spent the whole night trying; or of Pericles who merely on hearing someone praise the beauty of a certain boy too enthusiastically, reproached him harshly; or of many others who have been most continent of their own free will, and not from shame or fear of punishment, by which most of those women who preserve their chastity are influenced; though, to be sure, they do, after all, deserve every praise, just as anyone who falsely impugns their chastity deserves to be severely punished, as you said.'[21]

Then Cesare, who had been silent for some while, remarked:

'Think what signor Gaspare must say when he is criticizing women, if these are the things he says in their praise! But if the Magnifico will allow me to say in his stead a few things concerning how falsely, to my mind, Gaspare has spoken against women, it would be convenient for both of us. For by this means he will obtain a moment's rest and then be able, all the better, to continue describing the qualities of the Court lady; and I shall consider myself greatly privileged to have the chance of sharing with him in the duty of a worthy knight, namely, to defend the truth.'

'Indeed, I beg you to do so,' replied the Magnifico, 'since I was already thinking I had done what I should to the best of my ability, and that this discussion had now gone beyond my purpose.'

Then Cesare added: 'I do not want now to speak of all the benefits the world has derived from women, apart from their child-bearing, because it has already been adequately shown how essential they are not only to our being here at all, but to our well-being once we are. But I do say, signor Gaspare, that if they are, as you allege, more inclined to their desires than men and for all that refrain from satisfying them more than men, which you yourself admit, then the less strength their sex has to resist their natural appetites, the more praiseworthy they are. If you say that they do so out of shame, then it seems to me that you are simply attributing two virtues to them in the place of one; for if shame influences them more than desire and in consequence they abstain from evil acts, I consider that this very shame – which when all is said and done is simply fear of disgrace – is a most rare virtue, and practised by very few men. Moreover, if without bringing men into complete and utter disgrace I could tell how many of them are sunk in shamelessness, which is the vice corresponding to this virtue, I would corrupt the chaste ears that hear me. What is more, these men who so offend God and Nature are already old and make a profession, some of the priesthood, others of philosophy or of sacred law; they govern states with a Catonian severity of countenance that suggests all the integrity in the world; they constantly allege that the female sex is most incontinent. But they themselves regret nothing more than their lack of natural vigour to be able to satisfy the abominable desires still lingering in their minds after Nature has denied them to their bodies; and yet they often devise ways for which potency is not required.

'However, I have no wish to go on. And I shall be satisfied if you grant me that women more than men refrain from living unchastely. Certainly, the only bridle which restrains them is one they put on themselves; and for the truth of this, consider that most of those who are restricted too closely or are beaten by their husbands or fathers, are less chaste than those who enjoy a certain measure of freedom. It is their love of true virtue which is for most women the strongest bridle, along with their anxiety to guard their honour, which many I have known myself hold more dear than their own life. And, if you wish for the truth, each of us has seen the noblest of youths, endowed with discretion, wisdom, talent and good looks, devoting years of their life to the pursuit of love and neglecting nothing by way of attention, gifts, entreaties, tears, in short, doing everything imaginable: and all in vain. Were it not that you would say to me that my qualities have never made me worthy of being loved, I should put myself forward as a witness, as one who more than once came near to death because of a woman's all too severe and unassailable purity.'

Signor Gaspare replied: 'Don't be surprised at that. Women who are begged always refuse to give in to the one who begs them; and those who are not begged do the begging themselves.'

Cesare said: 'I have never come across these men that are begged by women. But I have known very many who, when they realize their efforts have been useless and they have wasted time foolishly, have recourse to that fine way of revenging themselves and claim they have enjoyed in full what they have only imagined; and they think that it is fitting behaviour for a courtier to say wicked things and invent stories, so that slanderous reports are spread among the crowd about some noble lady. People of that sort, who make a vile boast, whether true or not, of having enjoyed some lady's favours, deserve the severest punishment, and even torture; and if this is what they sometimes incur, then no praise is too great for those who have the duty of inflicting it. For if they are telling lies, what could be more wicked than to employ deceit in robbing a respectable woman of something she values more than her life, and solely because of something that ought to win her the highest possible praise? Then, if they are telling the truth, what punishment is harsh enough for a man who repays, with such rank ingratitude, a lady who, won over by false flattery, pretended tears, constant entreaties, lamentation, ruses, trickery and perjuries, has allowed herself to fall too deeply in love, and then has foolishly abandoned herself to the mercies of such a malignant creature? But to answer you further as regards that unheard of continence of Alexander and Scipio, to which you referred, I do not wish to deny that both of them acted in a most praiseworthy manner; nevertheless, so that you may not say that because I am describing things that happened long ago I am repeating fables, I want to give the example of an ordinary woman of our own times who showed far greater continence than either of these great men.

'Let me tell you, then, that I once knew a pretty and charming young girl, whose name I will not reveal in case I furnish matter for scandal to all those idiots who form a bad opinion of a woman as soon as they hear she is in love. This girl, having long been loved by a noble youth of excellent character, began to love him in turn with all her mind and heart; her feelings were quite obvious not only to me, to whom she happily confided everything as if I were, I shall not say her brother, but her dearest sister, but also to all those who saw her in the company of the young man she loved. Loving him as fervently as any loving soul can, she yet for two years remained so reserved that she never once gave him the least sign of her affection, save what she could not conceal; nor would she ever speak to him, or accept his letters or gifts, though not a day went past without her being urged to do both. And how much she desired the youth I well know, since if sometimes she was able to possess secretly anything that had belonged to him, she derived such pleasure from it that it seemed her life-spring and her every good; but for all this time her only concession was to see him and let herself be seen, and occasionally to dance with him, as with others, at holiday times. Since they were so well matched, she and the young man were anxious that their great love for one another should have a happy outcome and that they should become husband and wife. And this was also the hope of all the men and women of their city, with the exception of her cruel father; for he had conceived the perverse and aberrant ambition of marrying her to another and richer man. But the girl's only rebellious act was to shed the most bitter tears. After the ill-fated marriage had taken place, amidst great compassion on the part of the people and to the despair of the unhappy lovers, even that blow of Fortune was not enough to uproot the love that was so deeply embedded in both their hearts; and it continued for the space of three years, though the girl wisely concealed it and sought in every way possible to rid herself of desires which were now hopeless. All the while, she never faltered in her determination to remain chaste; and seeing that there was no honourable way in which she could have the one whom alone she adored, she chose not to wish for him in any way and to follow her practice of refusing to accept either his messages and his gifts, or even his glances. And with that firm resolve, the wretched girl, overcome by the most bitter anguish and wasted by her lingering passion, died after three years, preferring to renounce the joys and satisfaction for which she pined, and finally life itself, rather than her honour. Nor, indeed, did she lack ways and means of satisfying herself in secret, without any risk of disgrace or any other loss; and yet she abstained from what she wanted so much herself and to do which she was constantly urged by the person whom alone in the world she wanted to please. Nor was she motivated by fear or by any consideration other than a pure love of virtue.

'What will you say of another, who nearly every night for six months lay beside her dearest lover; nevertheless, in a garden full of the sweetest fruits, and incited by her own burning desire, as well as by the entreaties and tears of the one she held dearer than life itself, she refrained from tasting them; and though she was taken and held naked in the tight circle of those beloved arms, she never submitted, but preserved the flower of her chastity untouched?

'Now don't you think, signor Gaspare, that these are examples of continence comparable with that of Alexander? For he was burning with love, not for the women of Darius, but for the fame and greatness that spurred him on in the pursuit of glory and let him suffer fatigue and perils for the sake of immortality; and apart from everything else he scorned even his own life in his endeavour to win fame above all other men. So is it to be wondered at that, cherishing such ambitions, he should refrain from taking what he scarcely wanted? For, as he had never seen these women before, it is impossible that he should have come to love them immediately; and indeed he may well have detested them on account of his enemy, Darius. And in this case, his every lustful act towards them would have been outrage and not love. So it is no great wonder that Alexander, who conquered the world as much with magnanimity as with arms, held back from committing such an outrage on those women. The continence of Scipio is also very praiseworthy. Nevertheless, if you consider it carefully, it is not comparable with that shown by those two women; since he, too, abstained from something he did not desire. For he was in a hostile land, new in command and at the beginning of a very important campaign; and he had left the highest expectations of himself in his own country, where he would have to account for his actions to the sternest of judges, who often handed out punishment for even the most trivial blunders and among whom he knew he had enemies; moreover, since the lady concerned was of very noble rank and married to a most noble lord, he also knew that if he did otherwise he would stir up many enemies who might seriously delay and perhaps altogether prevent his triumph. For all these important reasons he abstained from indulging a dangerous whim, and thereby he demonstrated his continence and generous integrity; and this, as we read, won over all those peoples to him and gave him the equivalent of another army with which to conquer by kindness minds that would doubtless never have been conquered by force of arms. Therefore, it was a matter of military strategy rather than simple continence, although even then the report we have of this is not very reliable, since some authoritative writers affirm that he did in fact make love to the girl; whereas there is no doubt at all about what I am telling you.'

'Then,' said Frisio, 'you must have found it in the Gospels.'

'I witnessed it myself,' replied Cesare, 'and so I am far more certain about it than you or anyone else can be that Alcibiades always got up from Socrates' bed like a child leaving the bed of its parents. And indeed it was a strange place and time – in bed and by night – to contemplate that pure beauty which Socrates is said to have loved without any improper desire, especially since he loved the soul's beauty rather than the body's, though in boys and not in grown men, who happen to be wiser. Surely one could find no more fitting example of the continence of men than that of Xenocrates, who, devoted to his studies, in duty bound to his profession (namely, philosophy, which consists in good deeds and not in words), when he was an old man whose natural powers were exhausted, and quite evidently impotent, denied himself a whore who would have been abhorrent to him for that name alone. I would be more inclined to believe he was continent had he shown some sign of being aroused and then held back. Or rather, if he had abstained from what old men desire more than the battles of Venus, namely, wine; and yet to clinch the proof of his senile continence they write that he was full and drowsy with wine. But what in an old man is more alien to continence than drunkenness? And if to abstain from the sport of love at that sluggish and cold time of life is so praiseworthy, how much more praiseworthy it is on the part of those tender young girls, about whom I told you earlier? For the first, maintaining the strictest rule over all her senses, not only denied her eyes their vision but also drove from her heart the thoughts which had long been the sweet sustenance of her life; and the other, passionately in love and finding herself so often alone in the arms of the one whom she adored above all else, fighting against herself and against the one who was dearer to her than herself, overpowered that burning desire that has so often overpowered so many wise men, and still does. Don't you now think, signor Gaspare, that writers should be ashamed of honouring the memory of Xenocrates in this instance, and saying that he was continent? For did we but know, I wager he lay like a corpse all that night till dinner-time the next day, drowned in wine; and no matter how hard that woman shook him his eyes stayed as tightly closed as if he had been drugged.'

Everyone present laughed at this; and signora Emilia, still smiling, remarked:

'Signor Gaspare, if you will think a little harder, I am sure you will remember some other splendid example of continence just like that.'

Cesare replied: 'Don't you consider, madam, that what he cited in regard to Pericles is a splendid example of continence? I only wonder that he didn't also quote the continence and the splendid remark attributed to a certain man who told a woman who had demanded too high a price for the night that he didn't buy repentance so dear?'

With everyone laughing still, Cesare, after a moment's pause, then added:

'Signor Gaspare, do forgive me for speaking the truth; for in short these are the examples of supernatural continence that men have written about themselves, while accusing women – who give countless proofs of continence every day – of being incontinent.

For surely, if you think hard, there is no fortress so unassailable or so well defended that if it were attacked with a thousandth part of the engines and ambushes used to overwhelm a woman's constancy, it would not surrender at the first assault. How many men raised up and enriched by princes, and held in great esteem, being in command of fortresses or strongholds on which their ruler's state and life and every good depended, have, without any shame or worry about being called traitors and moved by avarice, perfidiously surrendered them to those they should not? Would to God there were less of their kind to be found today, so that we might not find it far more difficult to find someone who has done what he should in such instances than to name those who have failed! Do we not see so many going about every day killing men in the forests and scouring the seas in order to rob? How many prelates sell what belongs to the Church of God! How many lawyers forge wills! How many perjure themselves, or give false testimony for the sake of gain! How many doctors poison the sick for that same reason! And again, how many do the most cowardly things from fear of death! And yet a frail and tender girl often resists the most formidable and harsh assaults; for there have been many who have chosen death rather than lose their chastity.'

'I don't think,' said signor Gaspare, 'that we find girls of that sort in the world nowadays.'

Cesare answered: 'I will not now cite the women of the ancient world, but I will insist on this, that many women could be and are found who in such cases are not afraid to die. And now I call to mind that when Capua was sacked by the French, which was not so long ago that you cannot remember it very well, a beautiful young lady was taken from her house, where she had been seized by a band of Gascons, and when she reached the river that flows through Capua she pretended that she wanted to tie her shoe, so that the man who was holding her let her go for a moment; and thereupon she threw herself into the river. What will you say of the young country girl who not so long ago, at Gazzuolo near Mantua, after she had gone with her sister to reap in the fields, was overcome by thirst and went into a house for a drink of water? For the master of the house, a young man, seeing that she was very beautiful and all by herself, put his arms round her and first with kind words and then with threats sought to make her do his pleasure; and after she had resisted more and more stubbornly, at length with many blows he overpowered her by force. So all dishevelled and in tears she returned to the field where her sister was, but for all her sister's urging she would never say what wrong had been done to her in that house; however, all the while, as they were walking home, she grew gradually more subdued and began to speak quite calmly, and she asked her sister to do certain things for her. Then when they came to the Oglio, the river that flows past Gazzuolo, drawing a little apart from her sister, who neither knew nor imagined what she meant to do, she suddenly threw herself in. Crying and grieving, her sister followed as best she could along the bank of the river, which was carrying her swiftly downstream, and each time that the poor girl came to the surface she threw her a rope that she had brought with her for binding the sheaves; and although more than once the rope touched her hands, for she was still near the edge, the girl's constancy and resolution were such that she always refused it and pushed it away; and so rejecting every aid that might have saved her life, very soon she met her death. Neither was she prompted by nobility of birth or fear of a crueller death still, nor by shame, but simply by grief for her lost virginity. So now from this you can realize how many unknown women there must be who perform truly memorable acts; for it was only the other day, so to speak, that this girl gave such a convincing proof of virtue; and yet no one speaks of her or even knows her name. Moreover, had it not been for the death at that time of the Duchess's uncle, the Bishop of Mantua, the bank of the Oglio, at the spot where she threw herself in, would now be graced with a most beautiful monument, in memory of a glorious soul which deserved all the more resplendent fame after death for having inhabited the body of just an ordinary girl when alive.'

Then, after he had paused for a moment, Cesare added:

'A similar affair took place in Rome in my day: namely, there was a beautiful and noble Roman girl who was pursued for a long time by someone who showed a deep love for her but who would never reward him with as much as a glance, let alone anything else.

As a result, by bribery her suitor corrupted one of her maids who, in order to get more money by doing what he wanted, persuaded her mistress, on some minor feast-day, to visit the church of San Sebastiano; and having told the lover everything and informed him what he should do, she led the girl to one of those dark caves which nearly all the visitors to San Sebastiano usually go to see. Meanwhile, the young man had secretly hidden himself there, and when he found himself alone with the girl he loved so much he began to implore her in every way, as gently as he could, to take pity on him and let her former coolness turn to love. But when he saw that all his entreaties were useless, he started to use threats; and then, seeing that this was hopeless too, he began to beat her roughly. He was utterly determined to get what he wanted, and by force if in no other way, and he even asked the help of the evil woman who had brought the girl there; but for all their efforts, she still obstinately refused him; and although her strength was failing, she kept protesting and struggling to defend herself. At length therefore, partly out of anger that he could not get what he wanted, and partly from fear lest perhaps her relations might come to hear of what had happened and make him pay the penalty, that wicked man, with the help of the maid, who shared his fears, suffocated the poor girl and left her there. The man took to flight and managed to escape; the maid, blinded by the crime, did not think to run off and soon gave herself away. So she was arrested, and confessed everything and was punished as she deserved. Then the body of that steadfast and noble girl was borne from the cave with the greatest honour; and then, wearing a laurel wreath on her head, she was taken for burial to Rome, accompanied by a great crowd of men and women, among whom there was no one who returned home without tears in his eyes. So that rare and noble soul was universally mourned and praised by all the people.

'However, to speak about women you have known yourselves, do you not recall having heard how signora Felice della Rovere, on her way to Savona, feared that some sails that were sighted might be Pope Alexander's ships in pursuit, and therefore calmly and deliberately made ready to throw herself into the sea if they should draw near and if there were no chance of escape? And it can scarcely be thought that she did this thoughtlessly, for you know as well as anyone that her singular beauty was matched by her intelligence and prudence.

'And now I must say a word about our Duchess, who has lived with her husband for fifteen years like a widow, and who has not only steadfastly refused ever to tell this to anyone in the world but, after being urged by her own people to escape from this widowhood, chose rather to suffer exile, poverty and all kinds of hardship than to accept what seemed to everyone else a great favour and indulgence of Fortune.'

Cesare was continuing to talk in this fashion, but the Duchess interrupted by saying:

'Speak about something else and say no more about this subject, for you have a great deal to say about other things.'

And Cesare added: 'Well, I know that you will not deny me this, signor Gaspare, nor you, Frisio.'

'No indeed,' replied Frisio. 'But one swallow doesn't make a summer.'

Then Cesare went on: 'It is true that few women provide such examples as these; yet those who resist the assaults of love are truly admirable, and those who are sometimes overcome deserve all our compassion. For surely the inducements of lovers, the tricks they employ, the snares they spread, are so many and so unending that it is a great marvel if a tender young girl manages to escape them. Hardly a day or an hour passes but that the girl being pursued is urged by her lover with money and gifts and all those things that can be thought to give her pleasure. At no time can she even go to her window without seeing her obstinate lover pass by, with a silent tongue but eloquent eyes, with a downcast and languid expression, breathing passionate sighs and, often as not, shedding copious tears. If ever she leaves her home to go to church or elsewhere, he is always there to meet her, and at every street corner he accosts her, with his mournful passion depicted in his eyes as if he expects to expire there and then. And this is not to mention all the dressing up, the inventions, mottoes, devices, festivals, dances, games, masquerades, jousts and tournaments, all of which she knows are for her benefit! And then, she cannot wake up at night without hearing music, or at least the sighs and laments of that restless soul wandering around the house. Again, if she should happen to want to speak with one of her maids, the girl has already been bribed to produce a little gift, a sonnet or something of that sort, and hand it to her on behalf of her suitor; and seizing her opportunity she goes on to declare how the poor man is consumed by love, how he would sacrifice his life to serve her, that his motives are entirely honourable and that he wishes only to speak with her. All possible difficulties are met with the help of duplicate keys, rope-ladders and sleep-potions; the affair is made to seem really nothing to worry about; examples are given of many other women who do far worse: and in short, the path is made so smooth that all she need trouble to do is to say: "I agree." And if the poor girl still resists, yet more inducements are offered, and countless other ways are found to break through the remaining obstacles by repeated assaults. There are also many who, when they see that their blandishments are of little use, turn to threats and say that they will lie about them to their husbands. Others bargain brazenly for what they want with fathers or husbands, who, for money or for favours, compel their own daughters or wives to surrender themselves against their will. Others seek to rob women of the free will given them by God by means of incantations and sorceries; and some astonishing things happen as a result. But I couldn't begin, in a thousand years, to list the endless tricks men devise to make women do what they want. Indeed, apart from what every man discovers for himself, there has been no lack of clever writers to compose books in which they have applied their talents to teaching the ways in which women can be seduced. So how can our simple doves remain safe with so many snares around, all baited so sweetly to entice them? Is it so strange, therefore, that a woman should eventually be persuaded to love a handsome, noble and well-mannered young man, who for many years has demonstrated to her his love and adoration, who risks his life a thousand times a day just to serve her, and thinks only of her pleasure, and who wears down her resistance just as water after a time wears away the hardest stone? Is it strange that conquered by this passion she yields to him what you allege, because of the weakness of her sex, she naturally desires far more than he? Is her lapse so grave that the poor creature, who has been snared by so many enticements, doesn't at least deserve the mercy that is often shown even to murderers, thieves, assassins and traitors? Would you consider the sin so heinous that because some woman or another falls all women must be regarded as despicable and the female sex as impure, regardless of the fact that many of them never yield, and are as adamant against the endless temptations of love and as firm in their profound constancy as the rocks against the waves of the sea?'

After Cesare had fallen silent, signor Gaspare started to reply, but he was interrupted by signor Ottaviano, who said with a smile: 'For God's sake, grant him the victory, for I know you will gain little from this; indeed, I think you will make not only all these ladies your enemies but most of the men as well.'

Signor Gaspare laughed and said: 'On the contrary, the women have every reason to thank me; because if I had not contradicted the Magnifico and Cesare, we would not have heard all that they had to say in their praise.'

'What the Magnifico and I had to say in praise of women,' remarked Cesare, 'and much else besides, was very well known: so it was all superfluous. Who does not realize that without women we can get no pleasure or satisfaction out of life, which but for them would lack charm and be more uncouth and savage than that of wild beasts? Who does not realize that it is only women who rid our hearts of all vile and base thoughts, anxieties, miseries and the wretched ill humours that often accompany them? And if we really consider the truth, we shall also recognize that in our understanding of great issues far from distracting us they awaken our minds, and in warfare they make men fearless and bold beyond measure. Certainly, once the flame of love is burning in a man's heart, cowardice can never possess it. For a lover always wishes to make himself as lovable as possible, and he always fears lest some disgrace befall him which can make him less esteemed by the woman whose esteem he craves; neither does he flinch from risking his life a thousand times a day in order to deserve her love. Indeed, if anyone were to recruit an army of lovers, to fight before the eyes of the women they love, it would conquer the entire world, unless, of course, it were opposed by an army of the same sort. And you may rest assured that Troy held out for ten years against the Greeks for no other reason than that a few lovers, before they went to fight, armed themselves in the presence of their women; and often the women helped them put on their armour, and when they left spoke some words that inflamed them and made them more than men. Then, in battle, they were aware that their women were watching them from the walls and the towers; and so they believed that they would win praise from them for every bold stroke and every proof of courage, and this to them was the greatest reward possible. There are many who consider that women were chiefly responsible for the victory of King Ferdinand and Queen Isabella of Spain against the King of Granada; for on most occasions when the Spanish army marched to confront the enemy, it was accompanied by Queen Isabella and all her maids of honour, and in its ranks there were many noble knights who were in love, and who, before they came in sight of the enemy, would always go along conversing with their ladies; and then each one would take his leave and, before his lady's eyes, go to challenge the enemy with the proud courage that sprang from love and the ambition to let the women see that they were served by men of valour. Thus very often a handful of Spanish noblemen proved able to put to flight and kill a great host of Moors, thanks to their gracious and much-loved women. So I do not understand, signor Gaspare, what perverse judgement has persuaded you to censure women.

'Do you not see that all those charming recreations which please everyone so much can be attributed solely to the influence of women? Who is there who studies how to dance gracefully for any other reason but to give pleasure to the ladies? Who studies to compose verses, at least in the vernacular, if not to express the emotions aroused by women? Consider how many noble poems we would be deprived of, both Latin and Greek, if our poets had thought little of women. Leaving all the others aside, would it not be a grievous loss if Francesco Petrarch, who wrote about his loves in this language of ours in such an inspired way, had turned his mind only to exercises in Latin, which he would have done if love for madonna Laura[22] had not sometimes distracted him? I will not name the distinguished men of talent alive today (and some of them present here) who create something noble every day, and yet find their subject-matter solely in the beauty and virtue of women. Notice how Solomon, when he wanted to write mystically of very exalted and divine things, in order to veil them gracefully imagines an ardent and amorous dialogue[23] between a lover and his lady, since he thought it was impossible to find in this world any more suitable and exact analogy for divine things than a man's love for a woman; and in this way he wished to give us some inkling of the divine reality that through learning and through grace he had come to know better than others. So it was unnecessary, signor Gaspare, to dispute about this, or at least to do so at such length; but in denying the truth you have prevented us hearing a thousand other beautiful and important things concerning the perfection of the Court lady.'

Signor Gaspare replied: 'I don't believe there is anything more to say to you. But if you think that the Magnifico has not sufficiently adorned her with good qualities, the fault has not been his but with the one who decided that there would not be more virtues in the world; for he has given her all there are.'

At this, the Duchess laughed and said: 'But now you will see that the Magnifico will find some more all the same.'

The Magnifico replied: 'Truly, madam, I think that I have said enough, and for myself I am well content with this lady of mine; and if these gentlemen do not want her the way she is made, they may leave her to me.'

Everyone fell silent; and then Federico said:

'Signor Magnifico, to encourage you to say more, I would like to ask you a question about what you wanted as the main occupation of the Court lady, namely, I wish to know how she should behave with respect to one particular that I think most important. For although the excellent accomplishments with which you endow her include wit, understanding, judgement, sagacity, modesty and so many other qualities, with which she ought in reason to be able to converse with anyone and on any subject, I yet consider that she needs most of all to be knowledgeable about what belongs to discussions on love. To win the favours of women, every gentleman and knight makes good use of the noble recreations, fine clothes and elegant manners we were talking about; and so he very rightly chooses his words for the same purpose, not only when he is moved by passion but also, very often, in order to honour the women with whom he is speaking. For he considers that if he declares his love, this demonstrates that she is worthy of it and that she is so beautiful and talented that everyone must want to serve her. So I should like to know the right way for a lady to converse in this instance, and what kind of replies she should give both to someone who loves her sincerely and to another who is deceiving her; and if she should pretend not to understand, or should respond to his declaration, or refuse; and how she should behave in general.'

'Well first of all,' said signor Magnifico, 'it would be necessary to teach her to distinguish between those who are pretending and those who love her sincerely. Then, as for responding or not, I think she must make up her own mind and not be influenced by anyone else's wishes.'

Federico added: 'In that case teach her what are the surest and safest signs by which she can distinguish true love from false, and what proof should be enough to persuade her of her lover's sincerity.'

The Magnifico answered with a smile: 'I don't know the answer, because nowadays men are so cunning that they are always making false demonstrations of love, and sometimes they are quite ready to cry when they really want to burst out laughing. So they should surely be sent to Isola Ferma under the true lovers' arch.[24] However, it is only right and proper that I should place this lady of ours under my special protection, seeing that she is my creation, and so to save her from falling into the errors I have seen so many women make I have to say that she should not be too easily persuaded that she is loved; nor again should she be like some who not only fail to pretend not to understand someone who speaks to them of love, even when he does so with great reserve, but at the first word that is spoken accept all the praises that are offered them or else refuse them in a certain way that is more an invitation than a refusal. Thus the manner in which I should like my Court lady to behave in romantic conversation is for her always to refuse to believe that the man talking amorously to her really loves her. And if he proves to be presumptuous, as so many are, and addresses her with little respect, she will answer him in such a way that he will clearly understand he is giving annoyance; if, however, he proves to be discreet, using modest phrases and hinting delicately at his love for her, in the suave way that I imagine the courtier fashioned by these gentlemen would adopt, then she will pretend not to understand and will take the words to mean something else, trying all the time very modestly, and with the wit and prudence we have already said she should have, to change the subject. Then if what is said is such that she cannot pretend not to understand, she will treat the whole affair as a joke, pretending to believe that the words are meant to flatter her rather than declare what is true, disclaiming her own merits, and attributing the praises she hears to courtesy. In this way she will win a reputation for discretion and she will be more secure against deceit. And in my opinion this is the way the Court lady should behave when the conversation is romantic.'

Then Federico remarked: 'Signor Magnifico, the way you talk suggests that all those who talk about love are bound to be telling lies and trying to deceive the women they are addressing. And if this were the case, then I would agree that your instructions are sound. But if the gentleman concerned is sincerely in love and is experiencing the passion that can sometimes be so terrible, will you not pause to consider what mortal anguish and distress you are causing him in wanting the lady never to believe anything he says? Are all his supplications and tears and other demonstrations of love to count for nothing at all? Take care, signor Magnifico, that we do not reach the conclusion that in addition to the instinctive cruelty to which so many of these ladies are prone you are teaching them more.'

'I have not been speaking about a man who is in love,' replied the Magnifico, 'but about one who is indulging in amorous conversation, where the first rule is that he must never lack for words. But just as true lovers have ardent hearts, so they have still tongues and their speech is full of hesitation and sudden silences; so perhaps it would not be untrue to conclude that the man who loves a lot, says only a little. All the same, I do not think it is possible to give a hard-and-fast rule, because of the many different ways in which men behave; nor could I add anything else except that the lady should always be extremely cautious and always bear in mind that men can display their affection with far less risk than women.'

Then signor Gaspare said with a laugh: 'Signor Magnifico, don't you want this admirable lady of yours to fall in love herself, at least when she knows that she is loved? For if the courtier's love is not returned, then we can hardly think that he will go on loving; and in this case the lady would be robbed of many advantages, and above all of the service and reverence with which lovers honour and almost worship the virtues of their beloved.'

'I do not wish to give any advice in this matter,' answered the Magnifico, 'but I do maintain that love, in the sense you are talking about it now, is suitable only to women who are not married, for when this love cannot end in marriage, the woman is always bound to suffer the pain and remorse caused by illicit things and runs the risk of staining the reputation for chastity that is so important to her.'

At this, Federico laughed and replied: 'This opinion of yours, signor Magnifico, seems to me very austere, and I imagine you must have learned it from some preacher, of the sort that reproach women for falling in love with ordinary laymen, so that they can keep the best things to themselves. Indeed, I think you are imposing excessively hard rules on married women, for there are many to be found whose husbands hate them for no reason at all and do them great injury, sometimes by loving other women, and sometimes by subjecting them to all the annoyances they can think of; and then again, some women are forced by their fathers to marry old men who are in poor health and filthy and disgusting, and who make their lives one long misery. And if these women were allowed to get a divorce from those with whom they are so badly matched, then perhaps it would be improper for them to love someone other than their husband; but sometimes through bad fortune or incompatibility of temperament or some other cause it happens that in the marriage bed, which ought to be a haven of concord and love, cursed and devilish dissension plants its evil seed to produce anger, suspicion and the sharp thorns of hatred which torture those unhappy souls, cruelly bound together till death by an indissoluble bond. And when this happens, why do you not want the woman to be allowed to seek some refuge from her torment and to give to others what her husband not only despises but detests? I certainly maintain that those whose husbands are suited and who are loved by them should not injure them; but if women in other circumstances do not respond to those who love them they are doing an injury to themselves.'

'No,' replied the Magnifico, 'they are injuring themselves when they love someone other than their husband. And yet, since very often it is not within our power to decide not to love, if the Court lady should be unfortunate enough to happen to fall in love with someone else because of her husband's hate or another's passion, I want her to concede her lover nothing save her heart; nor should she ever give him any positive sign of what she feels, either in words or gestures or anything else that can make him certain of it.'

Then, with a smile, Roberto da Bari said: 'I appeal against this judgement of yours, signor Magnifico, and I think I shall have many supporters. But since you want to teach this prudishness, so to speak, to married women, do you want unmarried women to be equally cruel and discourteous, and not allow them to give in to their lovers, at least in something?'

'If my Court lady is to be unmarried,' replied the Magnifico, 'then if she is to fall in love I want her to love someone whom she can marry, and in this case I should not blame her for giving some sign of her love, in regard to which I wish to teach her a general rule in just a word or two, so that she may remember it easily enough: namely, that she should demonstrate what she feels to her lover in all ways except those which can raise in his mind the hope of obtaining from her something dishonourable. And in this matter it is necessary to be very careful, since it is an error into which many women fall, as they usually desire above everything else to be beautiful. And, then, since they think it proves they are beautiful if they have a great many lovers, they devote all their energies to acquiring as many as possible. In this way they often behave immoderately, abandon the restrained modesty that so becomes them, and indulge in certain provocative glances, indecent words and utterly shameless acts, thinking that thereby they draw attention to themselves more easily and that this kind of behaviour makes them loved. But this is not so, for the responses they evoke are prompted not by love but by a lust that is hopeful of being satisfied. Thus I want my Court lady not to appear to offer herself to whoever wants her in these dishonourable ways nor to strive as hard as she can to captivate the eyes and affections of anyone who looks at her but through her merits and virtuous behaviour, her charm and her grace, to arouse in the beholder the true love that is earned by what is lovable and the respect that dashes the hopes of those with dishonourable intentions. Anyone, therefore, who is loved by such a woman must be content with the slightest sign and must value more a single affectionate glance from her than the complete capitulation of someone else. And to a lady of this character I should not know how to add anything, save that she should be loved by a man as excellent as the courtier fashioned by these gentlemen, and that she should love him in turn, so that both may attain absolute perfection.'

Having spoken in this way, the Magnifico then fell silent. And signor Gaspare remarked with a smile:

'Now you cannot complain that the signor Magnifico has not formed a truly excellent Court lady; and from now on, if any such lady be discovered, I declare that she deserves to be regarded as the equal of the courtier.'

Signora Emilia retorted: 'I will guarantee to discover her, if you will find the courtier.'

Roberto added: 'Certainly, no one can deny that the lady fashioned by signor Magnifico is most perfect. Nevertheless, with regard to those last qualities pertaining to love, I still think he has made her a little too hard, especially in wanting her, in her words, gestures and behaviour, to rob her lover of all hope and do all she can to plunge him into despair. For as everyone knows no men desire what is hopeless. Admittedly, there have been some women, proud perhaps of their worth and beauty, who have immediately told their suitors that they need not imagine they would ever get from them what they wanted. And yet subsequently they have been a little more gracious in their reception and the way they look, and thus their kindly behaviour has tended to modify their haughty words. But if this lady drives away all hope by her acts and looks and behaviour, then I think that if he is wise our courtier will never love her, and so she will lack the perfection of having someone who does.'

To this, the Magnifico answered: 'I do not want this lady of mine to drive away hope altogether, but only when it comes to things that are dishonourable; and if the courtier is as courteous and modest as these gentlemen have made him, then he will not even desire such things, let alone hope for them. For if the courtier's love for her is prompted by the beauty, good way of life, talent, virtue, discernment and other commendable qualities with which we have endowed her, then his intention is bound to be virtuous too. Again, if the means by which the courtier is to win her favour are to be nobility, distinction in arms, letters and music, and gentleness and grace in speech and conversation, then the object of his love is bound to be of the same quality as the means through which it is attained. And then just as there exist various kinds of beauty so there exist various desires in men; and so many of them, when they chance to see a woman as grave and beautiful as the one we have described, whether she is passing by, or jesting or joking, or doing what you will, are completely abashed and hardly dare try to serve her because of the respect aroused in all who look at her by the grace which informs her every act. Their hopes aroused, they prefer to turn to those charming and provocative women, who are so frail and tender and whose words, acts and looks express a certain languid emotion that seems likely to turn easily into love. Others, to avoid disappointment, prefer to love the kind of woman who is so free in her eyes, words and movements as to do the first thing that comes to mind, acting with a certain revealing *naïveté*. And then there are those who believe that true achievement lies in overcoming difficulties and that the sweetest triumph is to capture what others think is impregnable; and these bold spirits readily fall in love with the beauties of those women whose eyes, words and ways suggest unusual severity, so as to prove that they are capable of overcoming all obstacles and forcing even rebellious and wilful women to love them. Men who are as self-confident as this, and therefore certain that they cannot be deceived, are also ready to love certain women whose beauty seems cunningly contrived to conceal all the wiles imaginable, or others whose beauty is accompanied by a scornful manner of few words and few smiles and an air of disdain for anyone who looks at them or serves them. And then there are other men who consent to love only those women whose countenance, speech and every movement bring together graciousness, courtesy, discernment and virtue, as if to form a single and exquisite flower. So if my Court lady fails to win the love of those whose intentions are impure, this does not mean that she will lack for lovers; for she will find many who are inspired both by her merits and their own worthiness, which will assure them that they deserve her affection.'

Roberto was continuing to argue, but the Duchess ruled that he was in the wrong and gave her approval to what the Magnifico had said; and then she added:

'We have no reason to complain of the Magnifico, since it is quite clear that the lady he has fashioned for us can bear comparison with the courtier and even has the advantage of him. For he has taught her how to love, and this is something these gentlemen have failed to do for their courtier.'

At this, the Unico Aretino remarked: 'It is certainly right to teach ladies how to love, because I've rarely encountered one who does know how to do so. And their beauty is nearly always accompanied by cruelty and ingratitude towards those who serve them most faithfully and whose nobility, gentleness and virtue deserve to be rewarded. Very often, too, they abandon themselves to the most stupid and worthless rascals, who despise rather than love them. So to help them avoid these gross errors perhaps it would have been as well to teach them first how to choose a man worthy of their love and only then how to love him. But this isn't necessary in the case of men, who know the answer only too well for themselves. I can vouch for this myself, for I was never taught to love but by the divine beauty and inspired manners of a lady whom I had no choice but to adore, and I had no need at all of any instruction or teacher. I believe this holds good for all those who are truly in love; and so it would be more suitable to teach the courtier how to make himself loved than how to love.'

'Well, do tell us about this,' said signora Emilia.

'It seems to me,' continued the Unico, 'to be only reasonable that men should win favour from their ladies by serving them and pleasing them; but what they consider serving and pleasing to consist in must, I think, be taught by the ladies themselves, since they often want such strange things that no man can think what they are, and indeed they often don't know themselves. So it would be very fitting, madam, if since you are a woman and ought to know what pleases women, you undertake the task yourself and put everyone in your debt.'

'But you enjoy such universal favour with women,' replied signora Emilia, 'that you must surely know all the ways in which their favour can be won. So it's fitting that you should teach them to others.'

'Madam,' replied the Unico, 'I could give a lover no more useful advice than that he should ensure that you have no influence on the lady whose favour he seeks; for such good qualities as everyone once thought were mine, together with the sincerest love that ever existed, have not had as much power to make me loved as you have had to make me hated.'

'Signor Unico,' replied Emilia, 'God keep me from thinking, much less doing, anything to make you hated. For not only would this be wrong, but I would be thought very silly if I attempted the impossible in that way. But since you urge me to say something about what is pleasing to women I shall do so; and if what I say displeases you, then you have only yourself to blame. I consider, then, that if a man is to be loved he must himself love and be lovable; and these two things are enough for him to win the favour of women. And to answer your accusation, I declare that everyone knows and sees that you are most lovable; but I am very doubtful as to whether you love as sincerely as you claim, and perhaps the others are too. For by being too lovable you have made yourself loved by many women. But when great rivers divide into several channels they dwindle to small streams; and in the same way when love is given to more than one object it loses much of its force. However, your own constant lamenting and accusations of ingratitude against the women you have served, which do not ring true, considering your great merits, are really designed as a kind of concealment to hide the favours, the joys and the pleasures you have known in love, and to reassure those women who love you and have abandoned themselves to you that you won't give them away. So they too are content that you should openly make a pretence of loving other women in order to conceal your genuine love for them. And so if the women you pretend to love now are not as credulous as you would wish, this is because your technique is beginning to be understood, and not because I cause you to be hated.'

Then the Unico remarked: 'I've no wish to go on disproving what you say, since as far as I can see I am as fated to be disbelieved when I speak the truth as you are to be believed when you tell lies.'

'But admit,' replied signora Emilia, 'that you do not love in the way you say. For if you did, you would desire only to please your lover and to wish only what she wishes, since this is the law of love. But the way you complain of her so much suggests deceit, as I said before, or indeed proves that your wishes are not the same as hers.'

'On the contrary,' said the Unico, 'I certainly wish whatever she wishes, and this proves that I love her; but I complain because she doesn't wish what I wish, and this, according to the rule you quoted, suggests that she doesn't love me.'

Then signora Emilia replied: 'But a man who begins to love must also begin to please the woman he loves and to be ruled by her in accommodating his every wish to hers. And he must ensure that his desires are all subordinate to hers and that his soul is the slave of hers, or indeed, if possible, that it is transformed into hers; and he should see this as being the greatest happiness he could want. For this is the way of those who are truly in love.'

'The greatest happiness for me,' said the Unico, 'would be precisely if a single will governed both her soul and mine.'

'Then you must bring this about,' replied signora Emilia.

At this point, Bernardo interrupted to say:

'Certainly a man who is truly in love without any prompting by others devotes all his thoughts to serving and pleasing the woman he loves. But sometimes his devotion goes unrecognized, and so I think that as well as loving and serving he must demonstrate his love so clearly in some other way that the woman he loves cannot conceal that she knows she is loved; though he should do this so modestly as to avoid any suggestion of disrespect. And so, madam, since you were saying that a lover's soul should be the slave of the woman he loves, I implore you to teach us this secret too, as it seems to me extremely important.'

At this, Cesare smiled and remarked: 'If the lover is so modest that he is ashamed to declare his love, let him write it in a letter.'

'On the contrary,' said signora Emilia, 'if he is discreet as he ought to be, before he makes any declaration he should make sure that he won't offend her.'

Then signor Gaspare said: 'Well, all women like to be begged for their love, even though they mean to refuse what is asked of them.'

At this, the Magnifico Giuliano remarked: 'You are very much mistaken, and I would advise the courtier never to adopt this strategy, unless he is certain that he won't be repulsed.'

'Then what course should he follow?' asked signor Gaspare.

'Well, if he wants to speak or write,' continued the Magnifico, 'he should do so with such modesty and care that to start with his words seem wholly tentative and even ambiguous and affect her in such a way that she may legitimately pretend, if she wishes to avoid embarrassment, not to understand what is meant. Thus if he finds difficulties in the way, he can withdraw easily and pretend to have spoken or written with some other purpose in view, in order to enjoy safely those endearments and kindnesses that women often grant to those who seem to accept them as a mark of friendship but retract as soon as they perceive that they are interpreted as a demonstration of love. Hence those men who are too hasty and make their advances too presumptuously, with a kind of stubborn impetuosity, often lose these favours, and with good reason. For a true lady always considers she is being insulted when someone shows a lack of respect by seeking to gain her love before he has served her.

'Therefore in my view when the courtier wishes to declare his love he should do so by his actions rather than by speech, for a man's feelings are sometimes more clearly revealed by a sigh, a gesture of respect or a certain shyness than by volumes of words. And next he should use his eyes to carry faithfully the message written in his heart, because they often communicate hidden feelings more effectively than anything else, including the tongue and the written word. In doing this, they not only reveal the lover's thoughts but often arouse affection in the heart of the one he loves. For the vital spirits that dart from his eyes originate near the heart, and thus when they penetrate the eyes of the woman he loves like an arrow speeding to its target they go straight to her heart, as if to their true abode; and there they mingle with those other vital spirits and with the very subtle kind of blood which these contain, and in this way they infect the blood near to the heart to which they have come, warming it and making it like themselves and ready to receive the impression of the image they carry with them. In this way, journeying back and forth from the eyes to the heart, and bringing back the tinder and steel of beauty and grace, with the breath of desire these messengers kindle the fire which never dies, since it is fed on constant hope. So one can truly say that eyes are the guides of love, especially if they are graceful and soft, and blue in colour or a limpid and shining black, full of gaiety and laughter and in their gaze gracious and penetrating, like some so profound that one seems to see down to the heart itself. Thus we find that a woman's eyes wait like soldiers in ambush while her body, if it is beautiful and well proportioned, attracts and draws close to itself anyone who sees it from afar; and then as soon as he is near by the eyes dart forth and bewitch him like sorcerers, especially when they send their rays into the eyes of the beloved person just as his are doing the same; for then the vital spirits[25] meet each other and in that sweet encounter each takes on the qualities of the other, as we find in the case of a diseased eye which, by staring hard at a healthy eye, gives it the disease from which it is suffering. So it seems to me that this is the way in which our courtier can, in great part, make his love known. It is true that unless they are carefully governed, the eyes frequently reveal amorous desires to someone whom one would wish to keep in ignorance, because they make deep passion almost visible and thus betray it to others than the one whom it concerns. So a man who has not lost the bridle of reason will govern himself cautiously, paying attention to time and place, and, when necessary, he will abstain from gazing too intently, however hungrily he desires to do so: for there is no joy in love that is known to all.'

Then Count Lodovico replied: 'But sometimes it does no harm for it to be public knowledge, for in this case people often conclude that it does not seek the object every lover desires, seeing that little care is taken to hide it and there is no concern whether it is known or not. So, by not denying it, a man gains a certain freedom that enables him to speak openly with the one he loves and enjoy her company without arousing suspicion. This is not the case with those who try to keep their love secret, since it seems that they hope for and are about to attain some great reward that they do not want others to discover. And I have also seen a woman fall passionately in love with someone for whom to begin with she felt not the slightest affection, and this only from hearing that many persons believed the two were in love with each other; and this, I think, was because she took what everyone thought as sufficient proof that the man concerned was worthy of her love, and it almost seemed that what was common opinion served to bring from her lover messages that were truer and more credible than his own letters or words, or any go-between, could have communicated. Thus if something is generally known and talked about, far from doing harm this may prove advantageous.'

To this, the Magnifico answered: 'Love affairs that are fostered by common talk carry the risk that the man concerned will be pointed out in public; and therefore he who wants to travel this road with caution must pretend to be far less inflamed than he is and must content himself with what he considers too little and dissemble his desires, jealousies, sufferings and joys, often wearing a smile when his heart is breaking, and pretending to be prodigal with what he longs to hoard. But these things are so difficult as to be well nigh impossible. So if he wants to take my advice, I would urge our courtier to keep his love secret.'

'In that case,' said Bernardo, 'this is something to teach the courtier. Certainly, I think it is of no little importance. For, as well as the signs that men sometimes make so secretly and surreptitiously that the one whom they wish to do so reads in their face and eyes what is written in their hearts, I have sometimes heard between two lovers a long and open conversation of love, which those present failed to understand at all clearly or to realize was at all amorous. And this was because of the discretion and wariness of the lovers, for without showing any displeasure at being overheard they whispered the only words that mattered and spoke aloud those that could be interpreted in various other ways.'

'It would be an endless task,' said Federico, 'to discuss in detail such provisions for secrecy. Therefore I would prefer it if we were to talk for a moment about what the lover should do in order to retain his lady's favour, which seems to me something far more necessary.'

The Magnifico replied: 'Well, I consider that a lover can retain his lady's favour by the same means that he employs to win it; and what is essential is to please the woman he loves and avoid offending her. So it would be difficult to lay down any hard-and-fast rule; for there are endless ways in which a man who lacks a fine sense of discretion can make mistakes which seem trivial but which nevertheless give grave offence. This happens most of all to those who are driven by passion; as in the case of some who, whenever they have occasion to speak to the woman they love, lament and complain so bitterly and often seek such impossible things that their importunity makes them tiresome. Others, when they are excited by jealousy, are so carried away by grief that they heedlessly rush into making accusations against the man they suspect (sometimes when he is quite blameless) and even against the woman herself; and they insist that she should not speak to him or even look in his direction; and often this behaviour not only offends the woman they love but causes her to love their rival. And this is because when a lover shows he is afraid that his lady may leave him for someone else, his fear also betrays the fact that he knows he is inferior in merit and worth; and this attitude causes her to love the other man, and all the more when she sees evil accusations being made against him, even if they are true, simply to put him out of favour.'

At this, Cesare said with a smile: 'I confess that I haven't the sense to be able to refrain from speaking ill of any rival of mine, unless you can teach me a better way of causing his downfall.'

The Magnifico laughed and replied: 'The proverb says that when your enemy is in the water up to his waist, you should extend him your hand and pull him out of danger; but when he is up to his chin, then put your foot on his head and drown him quickly. And there are some who act this way towards their rivals: when they see no certain way of bringing about their downfall, they go about dissimulating and even pretend to be their friends rather than otherwise; then if the occasion is such that they know they are in a position to bring about their sure and sudden downfall, by speaking ill of them whether it is true or not, they embrace it eagerly and employ all the tricks and treachery they know. But since I should never like our courtier to practise deceit, I would have him deprive his rival of his lady's favour by no other method than loving her and serving her, and being virtuous, discreet and modest; in short, by being worthier of her than his rival and by being sufficiently wary, cautious and prudent to save himself from certain clumsy follies into which so many ignorant men fall in their various ways. For I have known some use nothing but Poliphilian[26] words when writing or speaking to women and employ such ingenious rhetoric that the women lose all their self-confidence and imagine they must be extremely ignorant, and it seems an eternity till they can end the conversation and get rid of the man concerned. Others indulge in fantastic boasting. Others often say things that redound to their own harm and discredit, like some, who always make me laugh, who profess to be in love and will say in the presence of women: "I've never yet found a woman who loves me...." And they fail to realize that the women listening immediately conclude that the only reason for this must be that they deserve neither love nor even the air they breathe, and they dismiss them as of no account and not to be loved for all the gold in the world. For after all, they think, if they were to love such men they would be inferior to all other women, who haven't loved them. Other men, in order to stir up hatred against a rival, are so foolish that in the presence of women they will say: "So and so is the luckiest man in the world, for though, to be sure, he isn't handsome or sensible or brave, and he can't say or do more than other men, yet all the women love and run after him." But in revealing their envy of the man's good fortune, although he isn't lovable on account of his looks or his deeds, they encourage the belief that there must be some secret reason for his success with so many women; and as a result, the women who hear him spoken of in this way are encouraged to love him still more.'

Count Lodovico then remarked with a smile: 'I promise you that our sensible courtier will never act so stupidly to gain a woman's favour.'

Cesare Gonzaga replied: 'Nor so stupidly as a gentleman I remember, of some repute, whom to spare men's blushes I don't wish to mention by name.'

'Well, at least tell us what he did,' said the Duchess.

Then Cesare continued: 'He was loved by a very great lady, and at her request he came secretly to the town where she was. After he had seen her and enjoyed her company for as long as she would let him in the time, he sighed and wept bitterly, to show the anguish he was suffering at having to leave her, and he begged her never to forget him; and then he added that she should pay for his lodging at the inn, since it was she who had sent for him and he thought it only right, therefore, that he shouldn't be involved in any expense over the journey.'

At this, all the ladies began to laugh and to say that the man concerned hardly deserved the name of gentleman; and many of the men felt as ashamed as he should have been, had he ever had the sense to recognize such disgraceful behaviour for what it was.

Then signor Gaspare turned to Cesare and remarked: 'You would have done better for the honour of women not to have told this story than to have refrained from giving his name to spare the men. For you can imagine what a fine judge was that great lady, to love such an idiotic beast. And perhaps, too, she chose this man as the most discreet out of all the many others who served her, and whom she rejected in favour of someone who wasn't fit to lick their boots.'

Count Lodovico laughed and replied: 'Who knows if he wasn't perfect in other things and behaved badly only when it was a question of paying the bill? However, men often do stupid things when they are head over heels in love; and if you were to be honest, you'd admit that you have perhaps often made mistakes yourself.'

Cesare replied with a smile: 'Good heavens, please spare us from revealing our own errors!'

'But we must reveal them,' added signor Gaspare, 'so that we know how to correct them.' And then he added:

'And now, signor Magnifico, as the courtier has learnt how to gain and keep his lady's favour, and how to deprive his rival of it, you should teach him how to keep his love affairs secret.'

The Magnifico replied: 'I think I have said quite enough. So choose someone else to speak about this.'

Then Bernardo and all the others began to insist that he should continue, and the Magnifico laughed and added:

'You want to tempt me; you are all only too well instructed in love. However, if you want to know still more, go and read your Ovid.'[27]

'But how can I rely on his advice in love,' said Bernardo, 'since he recommends as a good thing that a man should pretend to be drunk in the presence of his beloved? What a fine way of winning her favour that is! And then he suggests that if one is at a banquet a splendid way of letting one's lady know one loves her is to dip a finger in the wine and write it on the table.'

The Magnifico replied with a smile: 'Well, in those days there was nothing wrong with that.'

'Well,' said Bernardo, 'if such sordid behaviour was not displeasing to the men of that time one must believe that the way they served their ladies was far less refined than ours. However, let us not stray from our first purpose, which was how to keep our love affairs secret.'

Then the Magnifico began: 'In my view, to keep a love affair secret one must avoid the things that cause it to become known;

and although there are many of them, one of them stands out, namely, the desire to be too secretive, and not to trust anyone. For every lover wants to let his beloved know what he is suffering; but if he has to rely on himself he has to make many more and stronger demonstrations than if assisted by some loyal and loving friend. Then the demonstrations of affection made by the lover himself arouse far more suspicion than those made through intermediaries; and since people are naturally inquisitive, as soon as some stranger begins to suspect something he at once works diligently to find out the truth, and when he has discovered it he doesn't scruple to tell the world; on the contrary, quite often he is delighted to do so. This is not the case with a friend; indeed, a friend not only helps the lover with sympathy and advice but often repairs the errors into which he stumbles, always ensures secrecy and looks after many things that the lover cannot. Moreover, it is a welcome relief for the lover to be able to unburden himself by telling his sorrows to a faithful friend, just as it augments his joy when he can share it with someone else.'

Then signor Gaspare remarked: 'There is something else which is far more important in bringing a love affair to light.'

'And what is that?' asked the Magnifico.

'The vain ambition of women, along with their folly and cruelty,' added signor Gaspare. 'As you yourself have said, they strive as hard as they can to win a great number of lovers, and if they could they would burn them all to ashes, only to bring them back from death to die a second time. Even if they are in love themselves, they enjoy the torments of their lover, because they consider that grief, affliction and the constant wish for death are the most convincing proofs that they are loved in turn, that their beauty can make men miserable as well as happy, and that they can give them life or death as they please. So they feed on this kind of satisfaction, for which they are so greedy that in order not to go without it they neither give their lovers what they want nor make them utterly despair. Rather, in order to keep them in a continual state of anxiety and desire, they adopt a certain haughty and disdainful attitude, and mingle threats with promises, and they like their slightest word or look or gesture to be received with rapture.

Then they wish to be thought modest and chaste, not only by their lovers but also by everyone else, and so they make sure that their harsh and discourteous ways are well known to all, so that everyone may think that as they treat worthy men so badly they must treat those who are unworthy of love still worse. And then, convinced that this strategy has made their good name secure, they very often lie every night with the commonest of men, whom they hardly know; and so in this way simply in order to enjoy the misfortunes and endless laments of some noble gentleman, whom they love, they deny themselves pleasures that they might be excused for enjoying. And so they are the reason why, in utter despair, the wretched lover makes known to all what ought to be carefully and painstakingly concealed. There are some other women who, if they can trick a number of men into believing they are loved by them, will then stir up jealousies among them by showing favour and affection to one in the presence of another; and if they see that the one they most love has grown confident because of the signs he has been given, they often make use of ambiguous remarks and counterfeit anger to raise doubts in his mind; and then they break his heart by pretending that they do not care for him and want to give themselves completely to someone else. And this provokes hatred and enmity, endless scandal and plain disaster, because in such cases a lover is bound to give vent to the anguish he feels, even though this brings the woman concerned into shame and disrepute. Still other women, not content solely with tormenting men through jealousy, after their lover has given every proof of his love and faithful devotion, and they have responded with some affectionate demonstration of their own disposition, for no reason at all, and when this is least expected, grow aloof and suggest they believe that this ardour has cooled; and so pretending to fear they are not really loved, they make it plain that they want nothing more to do with him. So then, because of these setbacks, the wretched fellow has to start again at the beginning, and demonstrate his attachment as if he were only just starting to serve her. So every day he has to walk about her neighbourhood, and when the lady leaves home he must follow her to church or wherever she goes, and never turn his eyes anywhere else. Then he has to experience tears and sighs and fits of ill humour all over again, and, when he does have the chance to speak with her, entreaties and blasphemies, moods of despair and all the ragings to which unhappy lovers are reduced by those wild beasts who are more bloodthirsty even than tigers.

'These piteous displays are all too evident and well known, and often more by others than by the lovers who are responsible for them; and so in this way within the space of a few days they are so much observed that a step cannot be taken nor the least sign given without its being noted by a thousand eyes. The result is that long before they come to taste the joys of love, everyone supposes and concludes that they have done so; for when a woman sees that her lover is near to death, and that overwhelmed by the cruelty and torments inflicted on him he is utterly determined to abandon the affair, then she begins to show that she loves him with all her heart, to grant him all his wishes and to give herself to him; and this is because, now his ardent longings have abated, the fruits of love are less sweet to him and she is less constrained to do everything to the contrary. And then, since their love is known to all, the consequences that flow from it are now also well known; and so the woman is dishonoured and the lover finds he has wasted time and effort and worried his life away without gaining any pleasure or advantage. For he attains his desires not when they would have been so gratifying as to make him supremely happy but when he cares little or nothing about them, because his heart has been so mortified by his bitter sufferings that he has no feeling left to appreciate the joys and pleasures he is offered.'

At this, signor Ottaviano said with a laugh: 'You held your peace for a while and refrained from criticizing women; and now you have dealt with them so sharply that it seems as if you were resting to regain your strength, like those who draw back to make a more powerful assault. But truly you are in the wrong, and now you should be more conciliatory.'

Signora Emilia laughed and turned to the Duchess to say: 'Just see, madam, how our enemies are beginning to disagree and quarrel among themselves.'

'Don't call me that,' said signor Ottaviano, 'because I am not your enemy. And this dispute has greatly displeased me, not because I am sorry to see the women gain a victory but because it has tempted signor Gaspare to slander them more than he should, and the Magnifico and Cesare to praise them perhaps rather more than their due. Moreover, because of the time taken by this discussion we have missed hearing the many other splendid things still to be said with regard to the courtier.'

'There!' exclaimed signora Emilia. 'You are still an enemy of ours. That is why the discussion we have had displeases you and you would not have wished us to fashion so excellent a lady. And this is not because there was anything to add with regard to the courtier, seeing that these gentlemen have already said as much as they knew, and neither you nor anyone else, I think, could add to it, but because you begrudge women their good name.'

'It really is true,' retorted signor Ottaviano, 'that in addition to what has been said already I should like to hear much more about the courtier. Still, since everyone is happy with him as he is, I am also satisfied with him; nor would I change anything about him, except perhaps to make him rather more friendly to women than signor Gaspare is, though perhaps not to the extent that some of these gentlemen are.'

Then the Duchess remarked: 'By all means let us see if you have the talent to endow the courtier with greater perfection than these gentlemen have given him. So be good enough to say what is in your mind, or otherwise we shall suppose that you too do not know how to add anything to what has been said, and that you have merely wanted to detract from the praises of the Court lady, when it seemed to you that she was the equal of the courtier, whom you wish to be thought, therefore, capable of far more perfection than these gentlemen have given him.'

Signor Ottaviano laughed and replied: 'The way women have been praised and blamed beyond their deserts has so occupied the minds and ears of all of us that there is no room left for anything else. In any case, I think the hour is now very late.'

'Then,' said the Duchess, 'we shall have more time if we wait till tomorrow. And in the meantime the memory of the exaggerated praise and blame which you say have been given to women from both sides will have disappeared from the minds of these gentlemen, and therefore they will be better attuned to the truths you are going to tell them.'

And so saying, the Duchess rose to her feet, dismissed everyone with great courtesy and withdrew to her bedroom. And everyone went off to sleep.

THE FOURTH BOOK OF THE COURTIER

TO ALFONSO ARIOSTO

As I prepare to record the discussions held on the fourth evening, following those described in the preceding books, there is one bitter thought among my reflections that assails me with its reminder of human wretchedness and hopelessness and of how when we are midway in our course, or even nearing the end, Fortune frustrates our weak and feeble plans, sometimes wrecking them even before we sight harbour. For I recall that not long after these discussions took place, untimely death deprived our household of three of its finest gentlemen, while they were still in the prime of life and hopeful of honour. Of these, the first was signor Gaspare Pallavicino who, after he had been ravaged by sickness and more than once brought to death's door, though for a time his resilience kept body and soul together, in his early manhood came to the end of his life: a truly great loss, not only for our Court and all his friends and relations but also for his native land and the whole of Lombardy. Then, not long afterwards, Cesare Gonzaga died; and his death left sad and bitter memories with all those who knew him. For as Nature so rarely produces men of his quality, it seemed outrageous that she should have deprived us of him so soon; because it is undeniable that Cesare was taken away from us just when he was beginning to fulfil his early promise and to win for his outstanding qualities the respect they deserved. By many admirable deeds he had given full proof of his worth, which was brilliantly demonstrated not only in his noble birth but also in his gifts as a writer and a soldier and in so many other commendable ways. His goodness, talent, courage and knowledge were such that there was nothing so great that it might not have been expected of him. A little later, and Roberto da Bari also met his death, to the great sorrow of the whole Court; for everyone rightly grieved over the death of a handsome young man of pleasing manner and faultless behaviour, whose unusually attractive disposition was matched by his robust and manly appearance.

Had these men lived they would, I believe, have achieved such distinction as to demonstrate plainly to all who knew them how praiseworthy was the Court of Urbino and how adorned it was with noble gentlemen, as indeed have nearly all those who were formed there. Indeed, from the Trojan horse there did not come forth so many lords and captains as from this Court have come men of outstanding merit, held in universal esteem. For, as you know, Federico Fregoso was made Archbishop of Salerno; Count Lodovico, Bishop of Bayeux; signor Ottaviano, Doge of Genoa; Bernardo Bibbiena, Cardinal of Santa Maria in Portico; Pietro Bembo, secretary to Pope Leo. The Magnifico rose to the dukedom of Nemours and to his present eminence. Signor Francesco Maria della Rovere, Prefect of Rome, was made also Duke of Urbino; although the della Rovere Court where he was brought up deserves praise not so much for that as for having produced so rare, outstanding and talented a ruler as the kind he now shows himself to be. And I believe that no small reason for this was the noble company he kept at Urbino, where every day he always saw and heard behaviour above reproach. But it seems to me that the cause, whether it is through chance or the favour of the stars, that has for so long given outstanding rulers to Urbino still endures and produces the same results; and it is to be hoped that good fortune should so continue to foster these brilliant achievements that, far from failing, the happiness of the Court and of the state will rather increase swiftly from day to day. Of these, we have already been given many splendid indications, the chief of which I consider to be the fact that heaven has graciously sent us such a lady as Eleanora Gonzaga,[1] the new Duchess. For if ever there were joined together in a single person understanding, grace, beauty, intelligence, refinement, humanity and every other gracious quality, they are in her; and these qualities are so linked that they form a whole that sustains and informs her every act. So let us continue with our discussions of the courtier, in the hope that in the future there will be no lack of those who find in the present Court of Urbino models of virtue and talent as distinguished and honourable as we are now finding in the past.

It happened then, as signor Gaspare Pallavicino used to tell, that the day following the discussions contained in the preceding Book, little was seen of signor Ottaviano; because of this, many concluded that he had retired in order to avoid distraction and give serious thought to what he had to say. So when the company gathered at the usual time in the presence of the Duchess, a search had to be made for him, and he appeared on the scene only after some lapse of time; and so in the meanwhile many of the lords and ladies of the Court began to dance and to amuse themselves in various other ways, believing that for that evening the discussion about the courtier would not continue. In fact, all of them were occupied in one way or another when signor Ottaviano arrived, though he was no longer expected. Seeing that Cesare Gonzaga and signor Gaspare were dancing, after he had greeted the Duchess, signor Ottaviano then said with a smile:

'I was fully expecting to hear signor Gaspare speak ill of women this evening; but now I see he is dancing with one, I suppose he has made his peace with all of them. And I'm delighted that our dispute, or I had better say discussion, about the courtier has ended in this way.'

'It has not ended yet,' replied the Duchess, 'because I am not as great an enemy of men as you are of women; and so I do not want the courtier to be cheated of the honour due to him or of the adornments you yourself promised him yesterday evening.'

So saying, she ordered everyone, when the dance was finished, to sit down in the usual order, and this was done. Then when all were ready and attentive, signor Ottaviano said:

'Since the wish I expressed for the courtier to possess many other good qualities has been translated into a promise that I will say what they are, I am agreeable to do so, with the idea not of saying all that could be said on the subject but only enough to remove from your mind what was alleged against me last evening, namely, that I spoke as I did more to detract from the praises of the Court lady, by having it believed that other qualities can be attributed to the courtier and so, by this trickery, making him superior to her, than because it was the truth. So now, to fit what I have to say into the time available, which is less than we usually have when beginning our discussions, I shall be brief.

'To continue the arguments of these gentlemen, which I wholly confirm and approve, I maintain that among the things we call good there are some that are always good simply in themselves, such as temperance, fortitude, health and all the virtues that foster peace of mind; and there are others that are good in various respects and depending on the end to which they are directed, such as laws, liberality, riches and so forth. I consider, therefore, that the perfect courtier, as Count Lodovico and Federico have described him, can indeed be good and praiseworthy, not, however, simply in himself but in regard to the end to which he is directed. For, to be sure, if the only fruit produced by the courtier's noble birth, gracefulness, charm and skills were just himself, I should not consider it right for a man to put into acquiring the perfection of courtiership all the study and effort that are certainly necessary. On the contrary, I should claim that many of the skills that have been attributed to him, such as dancing, entertaining, singing and playing games, were vain and frivolous, and in a man of rank deserving of censure rather than praise. For these elegances of dress, devices, mottoes and other such things that belong to the world of women and romance often, despite what many may think, serve simply to make men effeminate, to corrupt the young and to lead them into dissolute ways. And the consequences are that the name of Italy is brought into disgrace and there are few who have the courage I shall not say to die, but even to take a risk. And certainly there are countless other things which would be of far greater benefit in both peace and war, given the same amount of study and effort, than this kind of sterile courtiership. But if the activities of the courtier are directed as they should be to the virtuous end I have in mind, then I for one am quite convinced not only that they are neither harmful nor vain but that they are most advantageous and deserving of infinite praise.

'In my opinion, therefore, the end of the perfect courtier (which we have so far left untouched) is, by means of the accomplishments attributed to him by these gentlemen, so to win for himself the mind and favour of the prince he serves that he can and always will tell him the truth about all he needs to know, without fear or risk of displeasing him. And, if he knows that his prince is of a mind to do something unworthy, he should be in a position to dare to oppose him, and make courteous use of the favour his good qualities have won to remove every evil intention and persuade him to return to the path of virtue. Thus if the courtier is endowed with the goodness these gentlemen have attributed to him, as well as being quick-witted and charming, prudent and scholarly and so forth, he will always have the skill to make his prince realize the honour and advantages that accrue to him and his family from justice, liberality, magnanimity, gentleness and all the other virtues befitting a ruler, and on the other hand, the infamy and loss that result from practising the vices opposed to these virtues. Therefore I consider that just as music, festivities, games and other agreeable accomplishments are, so to speak, the flower of courtiership, so its real fruit is to encourage and help his prince to be virtuous and to deter him from evil. Then we must consider that the merit of good deeds consists in two principal things: to choose a truly virtuous end for our intentions, and to know how to find convenient and suitable means for its attainment. And so it necessarily follows that a man who strives to ensure that his prince is not deceived by anyone, does not listen to flatterers or slanderers or liars, and distinguishes between good and evil, loving the one and detesting the other, aims at the best end of all.

'It seems to me also that the accomplishments these gentlemen have attributed to the courtier can be a good means of attaining the end I have in mind; and this is because of the many faults we see in our present-day rulers the greatest are ignorance and conceit. And the root of these two evils is nothing other than falsehood, which is a vice rightly detestable to God and man and more harmful to princes than any other. For princes lack most of all what they must have in the fullest measure, namely, someone to tell them the truth and remind them of what is right. For those who are hostile to the prince are not prompted by affection to perform these offices; on the contrary, they prefer to have him live wickedly and never correct his faults. And then again, they dare not criticize the prince openly for fear of being punished. Meanwhile, among the prince's friends there are few who have free access to him, and these few are wary of reproaching him for his faults as freely as they reproach ordinary people, and often in order to win grace and favour they think only of suggesting things that are agreeable and diverting, even though they may be dishonourable and wicked. In this way, from being friends they become flatterers, and to benefit from their intimacy they always speak and act in order to gratify, and they mostly proceed by telling lies that foster ignorance in the prince's mind not only of the world around but of himself. And this can be said to be the greatest and most disastrous falsehood of all, for an ignorant mind deceives itself and lies to itself.

'The result of this is that apart from never hearing the truth of anything, princes become drunk with the power they wield, and abandoned to pleasure-seeking and amusements they become so corrupted in mind that (seeing themselves always obeyed and almost adored, with so much reverence and praise and never a hint of censure or contradiction) they pass from ignorance to extreme conceit. In consequence, they never accept anyone else's advice or opinion; and, believing that it is very easy to know how to rule and that successful government requires no art or training other than brute force, they devote all their mind and attention to maintaining the power they have and they believe that true happiness consists in being able to do what one wants. Therefore there are some princes who hate reason and justice because they think these would act as a bridle to their desires, reduce them to servitude, and if followed, rob them of the pleasures and satisfactions of their rule; and they suppose that their power would be neither perfect nor complete if they were constrained to obey the call of duty and honour, since they believe that no one who obeys is a true ruler. Therefore following on these beginnings, and letting themselves be carried away by self-conceit, they grow arrogant, and with imperious countenance and stern ways, with sumptuous dress, gold and gems, and rarely letting themselves be seen in public, they think to gain authority among men and to be regarded as gods. But these princes, to my mind, are like the giant figures that were made in Rome last year on the day of the festival in Piazza d'Agone[2] and which outwardly looked like great men and horses in a triumph but inside were stuffed with rags and straw. However, princes of this sort are worse still. For the giant figures were held upright by their own great weight, whereas, since they are badly balanced within and out of proportion in relation to their base, the downfall of these rulers is caused by their own weight, and from one error they fall into countless others. For their ignorance and their false belief that they can do no wrong, and that their power springs from their own wisdom, prompt them to use all and every means, just or not, to usurp states whenever they have the chance.

'But if they decided to know and follow what they ought to do, then they would strive to rule in quite other ways than they do now; for they would realize how outrageous and pernicious it is when subjects, who must be governed, are wiser than the rulers who must govern them. You will agree that there is no harm in not knowing how to play music, or dance, or ride; nevertheless, a man who is not a musician is ashamed and does not dare to sing in the presence of others, or dance if he doesn't know how, or ride if he cannot sit his horse well. Yet ignorance of how to govern peoples gives rise to so many evils, so much death, destruction, burning and ruination, that it may be said to be the deadliest plague of all; and despite that some rulers who know absolutely nothing about government are not ashamed to set about the task of governing before the eyes not of a small group of men but rather of the entire world, seeing that they are so exalted in rank that all eyes are turned towards them and hence not only their great but even their slightest defects are always observed. Thus it is recorded that Cimon[3] was censured for loving wine, Scipio for loving sleep and Lucullus for loving banquets. But would to God that the princes of our own time accompanied their sins with as many virtues as did these rulers of the ancient world, who, if they went wrong in some things, yet did not ignore the counsels and teachings of anyone who seemed capable of correcting their mistakes; on the contrary, they took meticulous care in ordering their lives on the pattern of exceptional men: as did Epaminondas on that of Lysias the Pythagorean, Agesilaus on that of Xenophon, Scipio on that of Panaetius and so on without number.[4] But if some of our rulers were to be confronted by a strict philosopher, or indeed anyone at all who openly and candidly might wish to show them the awesome face of true virtue, teach them a good way of life and how a good prince should conduct himself, I am sure that as soon as he appeared they would loathe him as if he were a serpent or mock at him as if he were dirt.

'I maintain, therefore, that since nowadays rulers are so corrupted by evil living, by ignorance and by false conceit, and it is so difficult to give them an insight into the truth and lead them to virtue, and since men seek to win their favour through lies and flattery and other wicked means, the courtier easily can and should seek to gain the goodwill of his prince by means of the noble qualities given to him by Count Lodovico and Federico. Through these, he should so win over the mind of his prince that he may go to him freely whenever he wishes to discuss any subject without hindrance. And, if he is as has been described, he will succeed in this purpose without great effort and thus he will always be able to reveal the true facts on any subject very promptly. Moreover, he will gradually be able to instil virtue into his mind, to teach him continence, fortitude, justice and temperance, and enable him to relish the sweet fruit which lies under the slight bitterness first tasted by one who is struggling against his vices, which are always as harmful, offensive and notorious as the virtues are beneficial, agreeable and universally praised. And he will be able to incite his prince to virtue by the example of those famous captains and other outstanding men of whom it was customary in the ancient world to make statues of bronze and marble, and sometimes of gold, and to erect them in public places, both to honour the great and to inspire others to work to achieve the same glory through worthy emulation.

'In this way, the courtier will be able to lead his prince along the stern path of virtue, adorning it, however, with shady fronds and strewing it with gay flowers to lessen the tedium of an arduous journey for one whose endurance is slight; and so now with music, now with arms and horses, at other times with verse or with conversations about love, and with all the means these gentlemen have suggested, he will be able to keep the prince continually absorbed in innocent pleasures, while also, as I have said, always accompanying these beguilements with emphasis on some virtuous habit, and in that way practising a healthy deception like a shrewd doctor who often spreads some sweet liquid on the rim of a cup when he wants a frail and sickly child to take a bitter medicine. Thus, under the cloak of pleasure, no matter what the time, or place, or pursuit, the courtier will always achieve his objective, and for this he will deserve far greater praise and reward than for any other good work he could possibly do. For there is nothing so advantageous to mankind as a good prince, and nothing so harmful as an evil one; and it follows that no matter how cruel and atrocious, no punishment can be enough for those courtiers who turn gentle and charming manners and noble qualities to evil ends, and by these means seek to ingratiate themselves with their prince in order to corrupt him and make him stray from the path of virtue into vice. For of these it can be said that they contaminate with deadly poison not a single cup used by one person but the public fountain at which everyone must drink.'

Signor Ottaviano fell silent, as if he were unwilling to add to what he had said. But then signor Gaspare remarked:

'It does not seem to me, signor Ottaviano, that this goodness of mind and the continence and other virtues in which you wish the courtier to instruct his lord can be learned; rather, I think that the men who possess them have been given them by Nature and by God. This must be so, since you will find that there is no one in the world so wicked and ill-disposed, or so intemperate and unjust, as to confess that he is such when he is asked; on the contrary, everyone, no matter how evil, likes to be thought just, continent and good; and this would not be the case if these virtues could be learned, for it is no disgrace not to know what one hasn't studied but certainly shameful to lack what Nature should have bestowed. Thus everyone tries hard to conceal his natural defects of mind or body, as we see in the case of the blind, the lame, the crippled and all those who are maimed or ugly. For although these defects can be imputed to Nature, yet no one likes to think he has them, since then it seems that Nature herself has caused them deliberately as a seal and token of wickedness. My opinion in this is also confirmed by the story told of Epimetheus,[5] who knew so little how to distribute the gifts of Nature among men that he left them far less well endowed than all other creatures; and so Prometheus stole from Minerva and Vulcan the ingenuity and knowledge by which men gain their livelihood. But they still lacked knowledge of the civic virtues and the moral law, because this was guarded in Jove's fortress of Olympus by most alert guardians, by whom Prometheus was so greatly intimidated that he dared not go near them. So Jove, taking pity on the wretchedness of mankind (which because of its lack of civic virtue was defenceless against the attacks of wild beasts) sent Mercury down to earth bearing justice and self-respect to adorn their cities and unite the citizens. And he decided that these should not be distributed in the same way as the other gifts of mankind, where only one man among many needs to be skilled (as in the case of medicine) but should be instilled into every single person. And under the law he ordained all those who were unjust and shameless should be exterminated and put to death as public menaces. So you see then, signor Ottaviano, that these virtues are granted to men by God, and cannot be learned since they come from Nature.'

Then signor Ottaviano replied with a smile:

'So you would have it, Signor Gaspare, that men are so unhappy and perverse in their judgement that they have applied themselves to discovering ways in which to tame the natures of wild beasts, bears, wolves and lions, and by the same skills can teach a pretty bird to fly where they choose it to go and return of its own will from the woods and its natural freedom to cages and captivity, and yet no matter how hard they apply themselves they cannot and will not discover ways by which to benefit themselves and improve their minds by diligence and study? In my opinion this would be as if our doctors were to study with all diligence to acquire solely the skill to heal sore nails and baby-rash and neglect treating fevers, pleurisy and other serious diseases; and as we all realize that would be quite preposterous. I consider, therefore, that the moral virtues do not come to us entirely from Nature, because nothing can ever grow accustomed to what is naturally its opposite, as we see in the case of a stone which, if it were thrown up in the air ten thousand times would still never grow accustomed to flying upwards of itself. So if the virtues were as natural to us as weight is to a stone, we would never become accustomed to vice. Nor are the vices natural to us in this way, for then we could never be virtuous; and it would be too wicked and foolish to punish men for defects that proceed from Nature through no fault of our own. This would be an error on the part of the laws, which do not inflict punishment on wrongdoers for what they have done in the past (for what is done cannot be undone) but have regard for the future, so that the one who has erred may err no more, nor cause others to do so through his bad example. So we see that the laws accept that the virtues can be learned, and this is certainly true; for we are born capable of acquiring virtues, and similarly vices, and therefore we become habituated to the one or the other through the behaviour we adopt, first of all practising the virtues or the vices, and then becoming virtuous or vicious. But the opposite is the case with qualities that are given us by Nature, which we first of all have the potentiality to practise, and then we actually practise, as in the case of the senses. For first we have the capacity to see and hear and touch and then we do see and hear and touch; although many of these faculties too are enhanced by education. For this reason, good masters not only teach children their letters but also polite manners and correct bearing in eating, drinking, speaking and walking.

'Therefore, as with other arts and skills so also with the virtues, it is necessary to have a master who by his teaching and precepts stirs and awakens the moral virtues whose seed is enclosed and buried in our souls and who, like a good farmer, cultivates and clears the way for them by removing the thorns and tares of our appetites which often so darken and choke our minds as not to let them flower or produce those splendid fruits which alone we should wish to see born in the human heart. Thus in this way justice and self-respect, which you say Jove sent on earth to all men, are natural in each one of us. But just as however robust it is a man's body may fail when seeking to accomplish some task, so, although the potentiality for these virtues is rooted within our souls, it often fails to develop unless helped by education. For if it is to pass to actuality and to its full realization, it cannot, as I said, rely on Nature alone but needs the assistance of skilful practice and reason to purify and enlighten the soul by removing from it the dark veil of ignorance, which is the cause of most human errors, since if good and evil were easily recognized and understood everyone would always choose good and eschew evil. Thus virtue may be defined more or less as prudence and the knowledge of how to choose what is good, and vice as a kind of imprudence and ignorance, which leads us into making false judgements. This is because men never choose evil deliberately but are deceived by a certain semblance of good.'

Then signor Gaspare replied: 'Yet there are many who fully understand that they are doing evil, and still do it; and this is because, like thieves and murderers, they are more conscious of the pleasures of the moment than of the punishment they fear in the future.'

Signor Ottaviano remarked: 'True pleasure is always good, and true suffering always evil; therefore these men deceive themselves when they take false pleasures for true and true suffering for false. And so their false pleasures often earn them genuine pain. It follows that the art that teaches us to distinguish the true from the false can certainly be learned; and the virtue which enables us to choose what is genuinely good and not what wrongly appears to be so may be called true knowledge, which is more advantageous in life than any other kind, because it rids us of the ignorance which, as I said, is the cause of all the evils there are.'

At this, Pietro Bembo said: 'I do not understand, signor Ottaviano, why signor Gaspare should have to concede that all evils spring from ignorance and that there are few who realize what they are doing when they sin and do not at all deceive themselves regarding true pleasure or suffering. It is certain that even men who are incontinent form their judgement reasonably and logically, and are fully aware of the evil and sinful nature of what they desire. So they use their reason to oppose and resist their desires, and this causes the battle of pleasure and pain against judgement. Then eventually the desires prove too strong for reason, which abandons the struggle, like a ship which for a time resists the storm but finally, battered by the overwhelming fury of the winds, with anchor and rigging smashed, lets herself be driven by the tempest, unresponsive either to helm or compass. So the incontinent commit their follies with a certain hesitant remorse, as if despite themselves. And this they would not do if they did not know that what they were doing was evil; on the contrary, without any resistance from reason they would abandon themselves utterly to their desires, and in this case would not be incontinent but simply intemperate. And this is far worse, since reason plays a part in incontinence, which is therefore a less serious vice; just as continence is an imperfect virtue, since it is influenced by the emotions. In consequence, it seems to me that one cannot ascribe the follies of the incontinent to ignorance or say that they are merely deceiving themselves without sinning, when they know full well what they are doing.'

'Well,' answered signor Ottaviano, 'your argument sounds very fine. Nevertheless, I don't think that it is really valid. For although the incontinent sin in that hesitant manner, and their reason does struggle with their desires, and they realize what evil is, yet they lack full knowledge and do not understand evil as well as they need to. Possessing only a vague notion rather than any certain knowledge of evil, they allow their reason to be overcome by emotion. But if they enjoyed true knowledge there is no doubt that they would not fall into error. For reason is always overcome by desire because of ignorance, and true knowledge can never be defeated by the emotions, which originate in the body rather than the soul. And if the emotions are properly governed and controlled by reason, then they become virtuous, and if otherwise, then vicious. However, reason is so potent that it always makes the senses obey it, insinuating itself by marvellous ways and means, provided what it ought to possess is not seized by ignorance. In this manner, though a man's faculties, nerves and bones do not possess reason, when the mind begins to stir within us it is as if thought were shaking the bridle and spurring our faculties on, so that all the parts of the body prepare themselves: the feet to run, the hands to grasp or to do what the mind suggests. This is shown by what often happens when someone unknowingly eats food that tastes delicious but is really foul and disgusting; for when he finds out what it was, his mind is revolted and dismayed, and then the body responds so quickly to his judgement that he has to vomit.'

Signor Ottaviano was going on to say more, but he was then interrupted by the Magnifico Giuliano who remarked:

'If I have heard aright, you said that continence is not a perfect virtue because it is influenced by the emotions. Yet it seems to me that when there is conflict in our minds between reason and desire, the virtue which fights and gives the victory to reason ought to be considered more perfect than that which conquers when no lust or emotion opposes it. For in the latter case the person concerned does not refrain from evil out of virtue but because he has no wish to do it.'

Then signor Ottaviano said: 'Who would you think the more admirable: a commander who runs the risk of open confrontation with the enemy, and yet conquers him, or one who uses his skill and knowledge to sap the enemy's strength and render him powerless and so conquers without risk or bloodshed?'

The Magnifico replied: 'The one who conquers by less dangerous means is certainly the more praiseworthy, provided that his inevitable victory is not brought about by the enemy's ineptitude.'

'You have judged aright,' said signor Ottaviano. 'And so I tell you that continence can be compared to a commander who fights manfully and who, when the enemy is strong and powerful, conquers all the same, though not without great difficulty and risk. But unruffled temperance is like the commander who conquers and rules without opposition; and when it has not only subdued but totally extinguished the fires of lust in the mind which possesses it, like a good ruler in time of civil war, temperance destroys all seditious enemies within and hands over to reason the sceptre of absolute power. Thus this virtue does no violence to the soul, but gently infuses it with a powerful persuasion that turns it to honest ways, renders it calm and full of repose, in all things even and well-tempered, and informed in all respects with a certain harmony that adorns it with serene and unshakeable tranquillity; and so in all things it is ready to respond completely to reason and to follow wherever reason may lead with the utmost docility, like a young lamb that runs and walks alongside its mother, stops when she does, and moves only in response to her. This virtue of temperance, therefore, is wholly perfect and especially appropriate for men who rule, for it gives rise to many other virtues.'

Then Cesare Gonzaga remarked: 'Well, I don't know what virtues appropriate for a ruler can spring from temperance, if temperance, as you say, removes all the emotions from one's mind. This might be fitting in a hermit or a monk; but I can hardly think that it is becoming for a prince, who is magnanimous, liberal and valiant in arms, whatever the provocation, never to display anger or hatred or indeed kindliness or scorn or lust or any emotion at all. For how could he otherwise exert any authority either over his people or his troops?'

Signor Ottaviano replied: 'I did not say that temperance completely removes and uproots the emotions from a man's soul, nor would it be well for it to do so, since there are good elements even in the emotions. But what it does do is to make what is perverse and opposed to right conduct in the emotions responsive to reason. So it is not right, in order to remove conflicts, to extirpate the emotions altogether; for this would be like trying to suppress drunkenness by legislating against the use of wine, or forbidding anyone to run since when they do so men sometimes fall over. You are well aware that when someone is breaking in a horse he does not stop it from running or jumping but ensures that it does so at the right time and at the command of the rider. So when they are moderated by temperance the emotions are conducive to virtue, just as wrath strengthens fortitude, hatred against wicked men strengthens justice, and the other emotions strengthen other kinds of virtue. And if they were killed altogether, this would leave the reason weak and languid, so that it would be ineffectual, like the captain of a ship that is becalmed after the winds have dropped. So do not be so surprised, Cesare, if I said that temperance is the cause of many other virtues; for when a man's soul is attuned to this harmony, reason makes it readily receptive to true fortitude, which in turn makes it intrepid and unassailable, and immune to human suffering. And this is just as true of justice, the pure friend of modesty and goodness, and the queen of all the virtues, because justice teaches us to do what should be done and to eschew what is wrong. Thus justice is wholly perfect, since the other virtues perform their work through her, and she benefits both the just man and others as well. And without justice, as it is said, Jove himself could not govern his kingdom well. These virtues are also followed by magnanimity, which enhances them all, though it cannot exist alone since anyone lacking other virtues cannot be magnanimous. And then for their guide, the virtues have prudence, which consists in a certain quality of judgement in making the right decisions. The other links in this happy chain of virtues are liberality, munificence, the desire for honour, gentleness, charm, affability and many other qualities there is not the time to name. But if our courtier behaves as we have suggested he will discover these flourishing in the soul of his prince, and every day will see blossoming there more delightful flowers and fruits than there are in all the lovely gardens on earth. He himself will know great contentment, when he reminds himself that he gave his prince not what fools give, namely, gifts such as gold and silver, vases and garments (of which the prince has too many already and the giver only too few) but what is doubtless the greatest and rarest of all human virtues: the manner and method of good government. This alone would be enough to make men happy and restore to earth the golden age which is said to have existed once, when Saturn ruled.'

After signor Ottaviano had paused for a moment as if to rest, signor Gaspare said:

'What you do think, signor Ottaviano, is the happier form of government and the more likely to restore the golden age that you mentioned: the single rule of a good prince, or the government of a good republic?'

Signor Ottaviano replied: 'I should always prefer the rule of a good prince, since this kind of dominion is more in accord with Nature and (if it is permissible to compare such small things with the infinite) more similar to that of God, who governs the universe by Himself alone. But leaving this aside, you notice that in all human creations, such as armies, armadas, buildings and so forth, the whole is referred to one man who governs as he wishes; similarly, in our bodies all the members perform and carry out their functions according to the decisions taken by the mind. Moreover, it seems fitting that people should be ruled in this way by one head, as are many of the animals, to whom Nature teaches this obedience as a most salutary thing. Notice how deer, like cranes and many other birds, when they migrate always choose a single leader to follow and obey; and the bees, almost as if they could reason, obey their royal leader as respectfully as the most law-abiding people on earth. And all this goes to prove conclusively that government by a prince is more in accord with Nature than that of a republic.'

At this, Pietro Bembo remarked: 'But it seems to me that, since God has given us the supreme gift of freedom, it is wrong that it should be taken from us or that one man's share should be greater than another's. Yet this is what happens when there is government by princes, who for the most part keep their subjects under the strictest surveillance, whereas in well-constituted republics this freedom is always conserved. Moreover, in judgements and deliberations, it more often happens that the opinion of a single man is false than that of many; for, because of anger or indignation or lust, a single man is more prone to lose his equanimity than a multitude, which is like a vast expanse of water and therefore less subject to contamination than a small quantity. I must add that I am not convinced that the examples you give from the animal world are applicable: for the deer and the cranes and all the others do not always prefer to follow and obey a single leader. On the contrary, they change and vary their behaviour, giving full authority now to one from among them and now to another; and in this way they are organized more in the style of a republic than of a monarchy. Indeed this can be called freedom among true equals, when those who sometimes command, sometimes obey as well. Likewise, the example of the bees does not seem relevant to me, for their royal leader is not of the same species; and therefore whoever wished to give men a truly worthy lord would have to choose him from another species, endowed with a nature superior to ours, if they are reasonably bound to obey him, like the herd which obeys not an animal of its own but a herdsman who is human and therefore of a superior species. Because of what I have said, signor Ottaviano, I think that a republic is a more desirable form of government than a monarchy.'

'In contradiction,' answered signor Ottaviano, 'I will deploy just one argument, namely, that there are only three forms of sound government: monarchy, the rule of the good (in the ancient world called the *optimates*) and government by the citizens. And the degenerate and lawless forms taken by these systems when they are ruined and corrupted are, in place of monarchy, tyranny, in place of the best, government by a few powerful men, and in place of the citizens, government by the common people, which wrecks the constitution and surrenders complete power to the control of the multitude. Of these three bad forms of government, there is no doubt that tyranny is the worst, as could be proved by many arguments; and so it follows that of the three good forms of government, monarchy is best, being the opposite of the worst. (For as you know, contrary causes produce contrary effects.) Now, in regard to what you said concerning freedom, I reply that it should not be said that true freedom consists in living as one wishes but rather in living under good laws. Nor is it any less natural and useful and necessary to obey than to command; and some things are born and devised and ordained by Nature to obey, just as others are to command. It is true that there are two ways of exercising rule: one is arbitrary and violent, like that of masters over their slaves, or the way the soul commands the body; the other way is milder and gentler, like that of good princes ruling their citizens through the laws, or the way reason commands our desires. Both of these ways are useful, for the body is naturally so constituted as to obey the soul, and likewise man's desires to obey his reason. There are also many men concerned solely with physical activities, and these differ from men versed in the things of the mind as much as the soul differs from the body. As rational creatures, however, they share in reason to the extent of being able to recognize it; but they do not possess it themselves or profit from it. These, then, are essentially slaves, and it is more advantageous for them to obey than to command.'

Then signor Gaspare said: 'Then in what way are men to be ruled who are judicious and intelligent in the way you said, and not essentially slaves?'

Replied signor Ottaviano: 'By the gentle government of a constitutional monarch. And it is advisable sometimes to let men of this kind take part in the local administration of government as far as their capabilities allow, so that they themselves may also be able to command and to govern those who are less wise than they, though in such a way that the authority of the ruler remains supreme. Then, since you have claimed that a single person is corrupted more easily than many, I also claim that it is easier to find one good and wise man than to find many who are such. And it is to be supposed that a monarch of noble stock can be good and wise, inclined towards virtuous things by his natural instincts and by the example of his illustrious forbears, and trained to excellence in his conduct. And even if he is not of a species superior to ours (as you said with regard to the bees), being assisted by the instructions and teachings and skill of the courtier, whom these gentlemen have made so prudent and good, he will be very just, continent, temperate, strong and wise, full of liberality, munificence, religion and clemency; in short, he will earn glory and favour among men and God, through whose grace he will acquire that heroic virtue that will raise him above human limitations, and be capable of being regarded as a demigod rather than a mortal man. For God rejoices in and protects, not those princes who wish to imitate Him by displaying their great power and making themselves adored by men, but those who, apart from the power they wield, strive also to resemble Him in goodness and wisdom, by means of which they strive successfully to work as His good servants and distribute for the benefit of mankind the benefits and gifts He has given them. Thus just as in the heavens the sun, the moon and the stars exhibit to the world, as if in a mirror, a certain likeness of God, so on earth a far truer image of God is provided by those good rulers who love and reverence Him and display to their people the resplendent light of His justice accompanied by a semblance of the divine reason and intellect. With men such as these, God shares His righteousness, fairness, justice and goodness with other indefinable blessings, which are a far clearer proof of divinity than the light of the sun or the perpetual motion of the heavens and the various courses of the stars.

'Thus, men have been entrusted by God to the protection of their rulers, who should therefore take diligent care to render Him a good account of them, like good stewards to their master, to love them and to regard their every blessing or misfortune as their own, and to strive for their happiness above all else. So the prince must not only be good but make others good as well, like the set-square used by architects that is true and straight itself and also makes true and straight everything to which it is applied. And it is convincing proof that the ruler is good when his people are good, because the way the prince lives acts as a model and guide for the citizens, and the way he behaves necessarily governs the behaviour of all the others. Nor is it fitting for an ignorant man to teach, or a lawless man to order the affairs of others, or one who falls to help raise others up. So if the prince is to perform these duties well, he must put every care and effort into acquiring knowledge; then he must establish within himself and never once deviate from the rule of reason, inscribed not on paper or metal but graven on his very soul, so that it will be not only familiar to him but inherent in his nature and he will live with it as part of himself. In this way, day in and day out, in every place and time, it may admonish and speak to him within his mind, ridding him of the disturbances experienced by those intemperate souls which because they are afflicted on the one hand by, as it were, the stupor of ignorance, and on the other, by the turmoil caused by their blind and perverse desires, are shaken by a frenzy that leaves them no peace, like the strange nightmares that sometimes come in sleep.

'Moreover, the greater the power that evil enjoys, the more harm it is able to do; and when the ruler can do whatever he wants, then there is a great danger that he will not want what he should. So Bias[6] was right to say that the test is how a man performs in office. For just as a cracked vase cannot be detected so long as it is empty but at once shows where it is flawed when filled with water, so corrupt and depraved souls rarely reveal their defects except when they are filled with authority. For then they prove unable to sustain the heavy weight of power, and so they collapse and spill forth on every side their cupidity, pride, rage, insolence and all the tyrannical urges they have within themselves. Without restraint they persecute those who are good and wise, and exalt the wicked; in their cities they do not tolerate friendships or societies or common interests among the citizens; instead they foster spies, informers and murderers, to create terror and turn men into cowards; and they sow dissension in order to keep men disunited and weak. These methods cause the wretched people endless loss and ruin, and often enough ensure the cruel death of the tyrant himself or at least cause him to live in a state of perpetual fear. For whereas good rulers fear not for themselves but for their people, tyrants go in fear of the very people they rule. And so the more people they rule, and the more power they possess, the more they live in fear and the more enemies they have. Consider how frightened and uneasy was Clearchus,[7] the tyrant of Pontus, whenever he went to the public square or the theatre, or to some banquet or other public place; for, so it is recorded, he used to sleep shut up in a chest. Or remember that other tyrant, Aristodemus the Argive, who turned his own bed into a kind of prison; for in his palace he had a little room suspended in mid-air, and so high that it could be reached only by a ladder; and here he slept with his mistress, whose mother used to take the steps away at night and put them back in the morning. In all things, the life of a good prince should be the contrary to this, free and safe, as dear to the citizens as their own lives, and so arranged as to be both active and contemplative, insofar as is convenient for the welfare of his people.'

Signor Gaspare then asked: 'And which of these two, signor Ottaviano, do you think is the more fitting for a ruler?'

Signor Ottaviano replied with a smile: 'Perhaps you are thinking that I am persuaded that I am myself that outstanding courtier who must understand so many things and make use of them for the commendable purpose I have described. But remember that these gentlemen have created him with many accomplishments that I lack. So let us first try to discover him, since I defer to him as regards both this subject and all the other matters that concern a good ruler.'

Said signor Gaspare: 'I think that if you lack any of the accomplishments attributed to the courtier, they are music and dancing and such things of little importance rather than those which concern the education of the ruler and this aspect of courtiership.'

To this, signor Ottaviano replied: 'They are none of them of little importance, all those things that help the courtier gain the favour of his prince, which he must do, as we have said, before he may venture to teach him the virtue of true knowledge; and this I think I have demonstrated can be learned and is as beneficial as ignorance (from which all faults stem, and especially the sin of false conceit) is harmful. However, I am sure I have now said enough, and perhaps more than I promised.'

Then the Duchess replied: 'The more you exceed your promise, so much the more we shall be indebted to you for your courtesy. So I hope you will be happy to say what you think in answer to signor Gaspare's question, and, please, to tell us also everything you would teach your prince if he needed instruction and assuming you had completely won his favour and could therefore speak your mind freely.'

Signor Ottaviano smiled and said: 'If I had the favour of some of the rulers I know, and were to speak my mind freely, I imagine I would soon lose it again. However, since you wish me to answer this question of signor Gaspare's as well, in my opinion princes should lead both kinds of life, though especially the contemplative since for them there are two aspects to this. The first entails clear insight and judgement; the other, issuing lawful commands in the proper manner, concerning things that are reasonable and within their authority, and having these carried out at appropriate times and places by those who have cause to obey. Of this Duke Federico was speaking when he said that the man who knows how to command is always obeyed. Giving commands, then, is the chief duty of a ruler, who very often, however, also has to be present and see them being carried out himself, and in certain circumstances sometimes has to perform himself. All these are concerned with action; but the active life should be designed to lead to the contemplative life, just as war is meant to lead to peace, and toil to rest.

'So it is also the duty of the good ruler to give his people the enduring laws and ordinances that will enable them to live safe and dignified lives in peace and quiet and enjoy in a worthy manner the tranquillity for which they actively strive. For there have always been many republics and principalities which have enjoyed continual prosperity and greatness during times of war only to fall into decay and lose their greatness and splendour, as soon as they achieve peace, as iron grows rusty in disuse. And the sole cause of this is their not having been properly taught how to live at peace or learned how to make use of the fruits of leisure. It is wrong to be always at war and not to seek to attain peace as the objective; although, to be sure, some rulers suppose that their principal aim must be to subjugate their neighbours, and in consequence they incite their people to become bellicose and aggressive in rapine, murder and so forth, and they encourage this with rewards, and call it virtue. For example, it was once the custom among the Scythians not to allow anyone who had not slain an enemy to drink from the cup that was passed round at their solemn feasts. In other parts of the world it was the custom to erect around a tomb as many obelisks as the man buried there had killed enemies. These and similar things were done to make men warlike, simply in order to subjugate others. But this was never feasible, seeing that the process could go on for ever, short of the conquest of the whole world, and was in conflict with reason as propounded by the natural law, which requires us not to want for others what we should not wish for ourselves. Therefore rulers should make their people warlike not for lust of conquest but in order to ensure the defence of themselves and their subjects against anyone endeavouring to enslave or injure them in any way, or to expel tyrants and give good government to those who are abused or to enslave those whose nature is such as to qualify them for slavery, with the purpose of governing them fairly and bringing them peace, tranquillity and leisure. Moreover, to this end all the laws and ordinances of justice should be directed, by punishing the wicked not out of vindictiveness but so as to change their ways and prevent them disturbing the peace of others. Indeed, it is outrageous and deplorable that in war, which is intrinsically evil, men should be valorous and wise, whereas in peace and quiet, which is good, they are so ignorant and inept that they do not know how to enjoy their blessings. So just as during times of war people should apply themselves to the practical virtues that are necessary to attain the objective of war, namely peace, so in peace, to attain the corresponding objective of tranquillity they should apply themselves to the moral virtues to which the practical virtues lead. In this way, the prince's subjects will be good, and he will be far busier praising and rewarding than punishing. And his rule will be very happy both for his subjects and himself: not imperious, like that of a master over his slaves, but sweet and calm, like that of a good father over a good son.'

Then signor Gaspare remarked: 'I would be glad to learn what are these practical virtues that are necessary in war and the moral virtues needed during times of peace.'

Signor Ottaviano replied: 'All virtues are good and beneficial, simply because of their good effects. But especially useful in times of war is the virtue of fortitude, since it frees the soul of emotions and takes away not merely fear but even the awareness of danger; other useful qualities are steadfastness, long-suffering patience and a spirit that is resolute and unperturbed by all the blows of Fortune. It is right, too, that in war, and indeed at any other time, men should possess all the virtues that are conducive to moral excellence, such as justice, continence and temperance. But these are far more important during times of peace and quiet, because often when men are enjoying ease and prosperity, and Fortune is smiling on them, they become unjust, intemperate and easily corrupted by pleasures. So in such circumstances men are in great need of these virtues, seeing that a life of ease is very apt to encourage bad ways and habits. For this reason it used to be proverbial in the ancient world that slaves should never be allowed to take their ease; and it is believed that the pyramids of Egypt were built in order to keep the people occupied, because everyone benefits from the practice of hard work. There are many other virtues which are all most beneficial; but let what I have said so far be enough for the time being. For if I knew how to teach my prince and instruct him in all the virtuous ways we have outlined already, having done so I would think nothing more was needed for me to have achieved well enough the purposes of the good courtier.'

Then signor Gaspare said: 'Signor Ottaviano, you have gone out of your way to praise good education and have indicated that you think it is the principal means for attaining virtue and goodness. So I would like to know whether the instruction which the courtier must give his prince should be conveyed casually during the ordinary conduct of affairs, so as to accustom him to acting in the right way without his being aware of it, or should be conveyed at the outset by formal argument about the nature of good and evil, and explanations, before the prince proceeds any farther, as to what is the right path to follow and what he must avoid. In short, should the prince be encouraged and confirmed in a virtuous way of life through argument and theory, or through practice?'

'You are involving me in too long a discussion,' answered signor Ottaviano. 'However, so that you don't think I want to avoid answering your questions, let me say that just as we are divided into soul and body, so the soul is divided into two parts, one of which contains our reason and the other our instinct. And then just as in generation the body precedes the soul, so the irrational part of the soul precedes the rational; and this we see clearly in the case of children in whom anger and desire are evident almost as soon as they are born, whereas reason appears only with the passing of time. So we must take care for the body before the soul, and for the instincts before the reason, though this is in the first case for the sake of the soul and in the second for the sake of the reason. For just as intellectual virtue is perfected by teaching, so moral virtue is perfected by practice. First, therefore, the prince should learn through practice, which will make it possible for him to govern the instincts that are not yet susceptible to reason and through this commendable discipline direct them towards a worthy end. Then they should be moulded by the intellect, which sheds light at a later stage but enables all the virtues to be perfected in one whose soul has been strengthened through good habits which, in my opinion, are fundamental.'

Then signor Gaspare commented: 'Before you go any further, I would like to know what attention should be paid to the body, because you did say that we should care for the body before the soul.'

Signor Ottaviano replied with a smile: 'Ask those you see here who nourish their bodies so well and look so fat and well; for mine, as you see, is not too well cared for. However, one could also talk about this at some length, as about the proper time for marrying, so that the children are neither too near nor too far from their fathers' age, and about the games and education necessary from the time of birth onwards so that they grow up handsome, healthy and strong.'

Signor Gaspare answered: 'In my opinion, what women would most like so that their children should grow up handsome and attractive would be to have them in common in the fashion that Plato urges in his *Republic*.'[8]

Then Signora Emilia said with a laugh: 'It's against the rules for you to begin criticizing women again.'

'But I mean to praise them highly,' replied signor Gaspare, 'by saying that they are in favour of a custom approved by such a great man.'

Cesare added with a laugh: 'Let us see whether this custom may be included among signor Ottaviano's teachings (for I do not know whether he has yet stated all of them) and if the prince should make it a law.'

'Well,' answered signor Ottaviano, 'the few I have stated would doubtless be enough to make the prince as good as those we find nowadays can be, though if one wished to go into details there would be far more to say.'

Then the Duchess added: 'Since words cost nothing, do please tell us all that comes to your mind in the matter of instructing your prince.'

Signor Ottaviano replied: 'Madam, I would teach him many other things, if only I knew them. And one of them would be that from among his subjects he should choose several of the noblest and wisest gentlemen, whom he should always consult, and that he should give them free leave and authority to tell him their opinion on any subject without hesitation; and he should so behave towards them that everyone would realize he wanted to know the truth about everything and detested lies. Apart from this council of nobles, I would advise him to choose from among the people others of lower rank to constitute a popular council and confer with the nobles concerning the affairs of the city, whether public or private. And in this way the prince, as the head, and the nobles and people, as the members, would form a single united body, the government of which would depend chiefly on the prince, yet would also include the others. And then this state would have the constitution of all three good forms of government, namely, monarchy, rule by the best and rule by the people.

'Next, I should show him that of all the responsibilities that fall to a prince, the most important is justice. And to maintain this, there should be appointed to hold office men of wisdom and probity, who must be good as well as judicious, for otherwise their sagacity is merely cunning; indeed, when goodness is lacking, the skill and subtlety of the prosecutors means simply the ruin and destruction of law and justice, and then the blame for all their errors must fall on the one who has placed them in office. I should inform the prince that it is justice which inspires the reverence for God which is due to Him from all, and especially from rulers who should love Him above all else and direct all their actions to Him as being their true end. And, as Xenophon said, they should always honour and love Him, though especially when they are prospering so that they may all the more confidently pray for His mercy in times of adversity.[9] For it is impossible to govern either oneself or others well without the help of God, who to the good sometimes sends good fortune as His minister, to protect them against grave dangers, and sometimes adverse fortune to prevent their being so lulled by prosperity that they forget Him or human prudence, which often offsets ill fortune as a good player remedies bad throws of the dice by the way he places the board. Nor would I fail to remind the prince that he should be truly religious, but not superstitious or given to the folly of spells and fortune-telling; for if he combines true religion and reverence for God with human prudence he will also enjoy good fortune and the protection of God, always disposed to increase his prosperity in times of peace or war.

'Next, I should tell him that he should love his country and his people, and not rule too oppressively, lest this should make him hateful to them; for this encourages sedition, conspiracy and a thousand other evils. Nor yet too tolerantly, lest he should become despised; and this encourages a dissolute and licentious life on the part of his subjects, rapine, theft, murder and disrespect for the laws, and often the total destruction and ruin of cities and kingdoms. Next, that he should love those near to him, according to their rank, observing in some things, such as justice and liberty, a strict equality; and in other things a reasonable inequality, as in being generous, in rewarding, in distributing honours and dignities, according to the differences in their merits, which should always be less rather than greater than the rewards they receive. In this way he would be not merely loved but almost adored by his subjects; nor to protect his life would he need to trust himself to foreigners, since for their own sake his own people would guard it with their own, and everyone would readily obey the laws, seeing that the prince obeyed them himself and was, as it were, their custodian and incorruptible executor. In this respect, he should command such confidence that, even if sometimes it were necessary to go against them in some manner, everyone would understand that he did it to good purpose, and his wishes would command the same respect and reverence as the laws themselves. In consequence, the minds of the citizens would be so tempered that the good would not seek to have more than they needed, and the bad could not do so. For very often excesssive riches are the cause of great calamities; as in poor Italy, which has been and still is the helpless prey of foreign troops, on account both of bad government and of its abundant wealth. So it would be advisable for most of the citizens to be neither very rich nor very poor, since those who are too rich often become proud and reckless, and the poor cowardly and dishonest. But those of moderate wealth neither seek to ensnare others nor risk being ensnared themselves; being the majority, they are also more powerful; and therefore neither the poor nor the rich can conspire against the prince or stir up sedition. So to avoid this evil, it is very salutary to keep everyone in a middle way of life.

'I would maintain, therefore, that the prince should adopt these and various other appropriate policies so that his subjects should not begin to hanker after new things or a change in government, which they invariably do either in the hope of some gain or indeed honour, or from fear of loss or shame. This restlessness is inspired sometimes by a desperate hatred and anger aroused by the injuries and insults they suffer because of the greed, insolence and cruelty, or the lust, of those who are over them; sometimes by the contempt that is fostered by the neglect, cowardice and worthlessness of princes. These two errors should be avoided by winning the love and allegiance of the people; and this is done by favouring and rewarding the good and by prudently, and sometimes severely, preventing the evil and seditious from growing powerful, something which is easier to do beforehand than it is to crush them once they are strong. I should say that to prevent the people falling into such errors the best way is not to allow them to adopt evil practices, and especially those which become established gradually; for these are the hidden plagues which destroy cities before they can be remedied or even detected. I should advise the prince to endeavour by these policies to keep his subjects tranquil and to ensure that they enjoy spiritual and physical well-being and constant prosperity, the last, however, being promoted for the sake of the former, since unlike bodily well-being and good fortune, spiritual riches are more advantageous the greater and more copious they are. Then if his subjects are good and worthy, and properly directed towards the goal of happiness, the prince will be a very great lord; for it is a great and true dominion in which the subjects are good, properly governed and well ordered.'

At this, signor Gaspare remarked: 'If all the prince's subjects were good, then I think he would be only a petty lord, seeing that the good never number more than a few.'

Signor Ottaviano answered: 'If some Circe were to turn all the subjects of the King of France into wild beasts, would you not consider that he would then be only a petty lord, even ruling over so many thousands of creatures? And on the other hand, if all the flocks pastured on these mountains of ours were to turn into wise men and valorous knights, wouldn't you consider that the herdsmen in charge of them, and by whom they were obeyed, had become great lords? So you see that it is not the number of their subjects but their worth that makes princes great.'

The Duchess and signora Emilia, and all the others, had for a good space of time been listening very attentively to what signor

Ottaviano was saying. But then, after he had paused for a while, as if he had finished, Cesare Gonzaga began:

'To be sure, signor Ottaviano, no one can deny that your precepts are very good and useful. Nevertheless, if you fashioned your prince with their help, I would believe you deserved the name of good schoolmaster rather than good courtier, and he would be a good governor rather than a great ruler. Of course, I am not arguing that the prince is not concerned with ensuring that his subjects are well governed with justice and good customs. Nevertheless, it seems to me that it is enough that they should choose good ministers to take charge of such things, and that their true function is far more important. So if I felt I was the excellent courtier whom these gentlemen have created, and enjoyed the favour of my prince, certainly I would never lead him to do anything blameworthy, but to achieve the noble end that you describe, and which I agree should be the fruit of the courtier's deeds and labours, I should seek first to implant in his soul a certain greatness, along with a regal splendour, a readiness of spirit and an unconquerable valour in arms that should make him so loved and respected by all that chiefly for this would he be famous and renowned in the world. I should also say that his greatness must be accompanied by a certain friendly gentleness, a gracious and amiable humanity and an accomplished manner of discreetly favouring both his subjects and strangers, in varying degree according to their merit; although he must always pay heed to the majesty that befits his rank and never allow his authority to be diminished in the slightest by lowering himself too far or, still less, excite hatred by too unbending a severity. He should be a prince of great splendour and generosity, giving freely to everyone because, as we say, God is the treasurer of generous rulers. He should hold magnificent banquets, festivals, games and public shows, and keep a great many fine horses for use in peace or war, as well as falcons, hounds and all the other things that pertain to the pleasures of great lords and their subjects: after the manner of signor Federico Gonzaga, Marquess of Mantua, in our own day, who in this regard seems more like King of Italy than the ruler of a city.[10] I would also seek to persuade him to erect great buildings, both to do him honour in his lifetime and to be memorials after his death: as did Duke Federico in building this noble palace, and as

Pope Julius is now doing in constructing the church of St Peter's and the street leading from the Palace to his terrace of the Belvedere and many other edifices, and as did also the ancient Romans, of which we see so many remains at Rome, at Naples, at Pozzuoli, at Baia, at Cività Vecchia, at Porto and in so many places, outside Italy as well, giving wonderful testimony to the great stature of those inspired men. The same was done by Alexander the Great who, not content with the fame he had deservedly won from having conquered the world by arms, built Alexandria in Egypt, Bucephalia in India and yet other cities in other countries. And Alexander also thought of reducing Mount Athos to the form of a man, and of building a most spacious city in the left hand, and in the right a vast basin where all the rivers that rise there were to gather before overflowing into the sea. This was a truly noble inspiration, and indeed worthy of Alexander the Great.[11] These are the kind of activities, signor Ottaviano, that I think fitting for a true and noble prince and likely to win him glory in peace or war. They are more suitable than attending to all and every detail of government, and being concerned to fight merely to subjugate and conquer those who deserve to be subjugated, or promoting the interests of his subjects or depriving of political power those who govern badly. For if the Romans, Alexander, Hannibal and all the rest had been concerned with these matters, they would never have attained the height of glory that they did.'

To this, signor Ottaviano replied with a smile:

'Those who were not concerned with such matters would have done better to have been so; although if you reflect on it you will find many who were, and especially those first rulers of the ancient world, Theseus and Hercules. And you must not suppose that Procrustes and Sciron, Cacus, Diomed, Antaeus and Geryon, against whom these magnanimous heroes endlessly waged war to the death, were other than cruel and impious tyrants.[12] So for his having freed the world from such unbearable monsters (as these tyrants must be called) temples and sacrifices were made to Hercules and divine honours paid to him. For the extirpation of tyrants is a service so beneficial to the world that he who performs it deserves a far greater reward than is appropriate for mortals. Now, of those you have named, doesn't it seem to you that Alexander's victories brought advantages to those whom he conquered, since he taught so many good customs to those he overcame that they changed from wild beasts into men? He built so many fine cities in lands that had been sparsely populated, introduced them to a civilized way of life, and, as it were, so united Asia and Europe by the ties of friendship and holy laws that those he conquered were happier than others. For he taught marriage to some, and to others agriculture or religion; he taught others not to kill their parents but to support them in their old age, others to abstain from copulating with their mothers, and a thousand other things that could be cited as evidence of the benefits his victories brought to the world.

'However, leaving aside the ancient world, what more noble, glorious and beneficial enterprise would there be than for Christians to devote their strength to subjugating the infidels? Would not this war be as advantageous for the conquered as for the conquerers, were it to prove successful and cause so many thousands to turn from the false sect of Mohammed to the true light of Christianity? Remember that after he had been banished from his own country and received by the King of Persia and favoured and honoured with innumerable, costly gifts, Themistocles said to his family: "My friends, if we had not been ruined when we were, then we would indeed have been ruined...."[13]

'The Turks and the Moors would rightly be able to say the same, were they conquered by the Christians, for they would find salvation through their defeat. And I trust that we may yet see this happy state of affairs come to pass, if God allows Monseigneur d'Angoulême (who shows such promise as was stated by the signor Magnifico a few evenings ago) to live to wear the crown of France, and that of England the lord Henry,[14] Prince of Wales, who is now growing up in all virtue under his great father, like a tender shoot beneath the shade of a noble and fruitful tree, to renew it when the time comes with far greater beauty and fruitfulness. For, as our Castiglione writes from England, promising to tell us much more on his return, it seems that in this prince Nature has wished to show her power by bringing together in a single body enough virtues for a host of men.'

Then Bernardo Bibbiena remarked: 'Very great promise is also shown by Don Carlos,[15] Prince of Spain, who although he is not yet ten years old displays already such intelligence and such convincing signs of goodness, prudence, modesty, magnanimity and every kind of virtue that if, as many think, he is to be the Emperor of Christendom it is to be believed that he must eclipse the name of many ancient emperors and equal the fame of the most famous men who have ever lived.'

Signor Ottaviano added: 'Thus I believe that these inspired princes have been sent to us by God and have been made by Him to resemble each other in youth, in military prowess, in state, in physical beauty and constitution so that they may also join together in this worthy intention. And if there must ever be any envy or emulation among them, let it be in the wish each one shows to be the first, the most fervent and the most determined in so glorious an enterprise. However, let us now leave this matter and return to our subject. I maintain therefore, Cesare, that the things you wish the prince should do are most important and commendable; but you must realize that if he does not know what I have said he should, and has not formed his mind in that manner and directed it to the path of virtue, he will scarcely understand how to be magnanimous, generous, just, courageous and prudent, or to have any of the other qualities expected of him. Nor would I wish him to have these qualities for any reason other than the capacity to apply them: for just as those who build are not all good architects, so those who give are not all generous. This is because virtue never injures anyone, and yet there are many who rob in order to give, and are generous with the belongings of others. Some give to whom they shouldn't, and leave in wretchedness and misfortune those to whom they are indebted. Others give with a certain ill grace and almost disdain, so that it is plain they are doing so against their will. Others not only do not conceal what they are doing but summon witnesses and more or less proclaim their generosity in public. Others foolishly empty the fountain of their generosity at one go, with the result that there is nothing left.

'Therefore in this as in other things one must know and govern oneself with the prudence that should accompany all the virtues, which, being the happy mean, are midway between the two extremes, which are the vices. And so a man who lacks knowledge easily falls into vice. For just as it is difficult to find the middle or mean point of a circle, so it is difficult to find the point of virtue set midway between two extremes, one vicious because of excess, the other because of insufficiency; and we tend now to the one, now to the other of these extremes. This we see from the pleasure or displeasures aroused within us, for the one extreme causes us to do what we shouldn't, and the other to neglect doing what we should. However, pleasure is by far the more dangerous, since it only too easily persuades and corrupts our judgement. Yet since it is so difficult to know how far one is from the mean, we should readily withdraw, little by little, away from the extreme to which we know we usually tend, like a man straightening a crooked timber. For by this method we draw near to virtue which, as I have said, consists in the happy mean. And this is the reason that we make mistakes in many ways, but perform our proper office and duty in only one way; like archers who have only one way of hitting the target but many ways of missing. For example, very often, in his anxiety to be considerate and affable, a prince will do countless things that are far from appropriate to his rank and lower himself so much that he comes to be despised. Another, to make his dignity and majesty more authoritative, will become harsh and intolerant; and another, in order to be thought eloquent, will adopt all kinds of mannerisms, indulge in circumlocutions and affected phrases, and study his own speech so carefully that he bores everyone stiff.

'So, Cesare, do not call just a detail anything that can in any way improve a ruler, however trivial it may seem. And don't think that I take it as blame when you say that my precepts would make a good governor rather than a good prince; for there could be no greater nor more relevant praise than to call a prince a good governor. So if it were for me to educate him, I should wish him to pay attention not only to the subjects we have mentioned but also to lesser things still; and to understand as far as possible every single question that affects his people, and never to believe or trust any of his ministers so much as to hand over to him alone the bridle and control of all government. For there is no one who is capable in everything, and far more harm is caused when rulers are too trusting than when they are distrustful, which, indeed, is not only sometimes harmless but often brings considerable advantages. Yet in this matter the prince must possess good judgement, and discern who is worthy of credence and who not. I would like him to take care to understand and be critical of his ministers' actions; to clear away and cut short any disputes among his subjects; to act among them as a peacemaker and bind them together by marriage-ties; to make his city united and peaceful in friendship, as if in one family, populous, not poor, tranquil, full of good craftsmen; to favour the merchants and also help them financially; to practise a generous and worthy hospitality towards strangers and priests; and to curb all excesses. For often seemingly unimportant mistakes made in these matters cause the downfall of states. It is right, therefore, that the prince should place a limit on the magnificence of private buildings and banquets, on the size of dowries, on luxury and on ostentation in jewellery and dress, which is simply an addition to human folly; for not only do women often dissipate the wealth and substance of their husbands because of their ambitions and jealousies, but also sometimes in return for some little jewel or trinket they will sell their honour to anyone who wants to buy it.'

At this, Bernardo Bibbiena laughed and said:

'Signor Ottaviano, you are joining forces with signor Gaspare and Frisio.'

Laughing also, signor Ottaviano replied: 'That dispute is finished, and I do not wish to renew it. So I shall say nothing more about women, and return to my prince.'

Frisio put in: 'You may leave him without any worry now, and rest content that he is as you have created him. For without doubt it would be easier to find a lady with the qualities specified by the Magnifico than a prince with those specified by you. So I am afraid that he is like Plato's republic, and that we shall never see the like of him, except perhaps in heaven.'

Signor Ottaviano replied: 'We can still hope for things that are possible, however difficult they may be. So perhaps we shall yet see him on earth in our own times; for although heaven is so reluctant to produce excellent princes that scarcely one has been seen over many centuries, such good fortune may well come our way.'

Then Count Lodovico added: 'I am myself quite hopeful of this; for apart from those three great princes whom we have named, of whom we may expect what has been said to befit the finest example of perfect ruler, there are to be found in Italy today several princes' sons who, although they may not be destined to such great power, may perhaps make up for this by their prowess; and the one among them all whose disposition seems best and who shows the greatest promise seems, in my opinion, to be signor Federico Gonzaga,[16] the eldest son of the Marquess of Mantua and the nephew of our gracious Duchess. For in addition to the fine manners and discretion he shows at so tender an age, those who have charge of him tell wonderful things about his talent, his thirst for honour, his magnanimity, courtesy, generosity and love of justice. So from these good beginnings one cannot but expect the finest results.'

Then Frisio said: 'Now say no more. We shall pray God that we see your hope fulfilled.'

And then signor Magnifico turned to the Duchess with an air of having finished all he had to say and remarked:

'There, madam, you have all that I can think to say concerning the end at which the courtier should aim; and if in this matter I haven't given complete satisfaction, at least it will be enough to have demonstrated that he is capable of further perfections beyond those given to him by these gentlemen, who might, I think, have left out this and whatever else I could say, not because they did not know it better than I but in order to save themselves trouble. So now I shall allow them to continue, if they have anything more to add.'

Then the Duchess said: 'Not only is it now so late that soon it will be time to stop for this evening, but also I do not think it fitting that we should mingle any other discussion with your remarks, in which you have gathered together so many varied and beautiful things that it can be said, as far as the purpose of courtiership is concerned, not only that you are the perfect courtier whom we are seeking and capable of educating your prince correctly, but also that, if Fortune smiles on you in future, you ought to prove a most excellent prince as well, and this would be of great advantage to your country.'

Signor Ottaviano smiled and replied: 'Perhaps, madam, if I were to attain such rank, then I would be like so many others, who know better how to speak than to act.'

Then, after a hubbub of conversation, during which some contradicted and others praised what had been said, it was pointed out that it was not yet time for sleep, and the Magnifico Giuliano said with a smile:

'Madam, I am so great an enemy to deception that I am bound to contradict signor Ottaviano who for having, as I fear, secretly conspired against women with signor Gaspare, has fallen into two errors which, in my opinion, are very serious. First, in order to give this courtier precedence over the Court lady and make him pass beyond what she can achieve, he has set him above even the prince, and this is quite wrong. Secondly, he has given him objectives that are always difficult and sometimes impossible for him to attain and such that if he did so he ought not to be called a courtier.'

'I do not understand,' said signora Emilia, 'how it is so difficult or impossible for the courtier to attain these objectives, or in what way signor Ottaviano has set him above the prince.'

'Do not grant him these things,' added signor Ottaviano, 'for I have not set the courtier above the prince and, as far as the end of courtiership is concerned, I do not think I have fallen into any error.'

The Magnifico Giuliano said: 'Signor Ottaviano, you cannot maintain that the cause which produces an effect with certain characteristics may never have more of those characteristics than its effect. So it follows that the courtier, whose instruction is to make the prince so excellent, must be more excellent than the prince himself. Likewise, he would also be of greater dignity than the prince, and this is quite wrong. Then, regarding the end at which the courtier should aim, what you have said is valid when the prince is about the same age as the courtier (though even so there are difficulties) because where there is little difference in age it is reasonable to expect that there should be little difference in knowledge. But if the prince is old and the courtier young, it is natural that the former should be more knowledgeable. If this is not always the case it does happen sometimes; and then the objective you have set the courtier is impossible. On the other hand, if the prince is young and the courtier old, it will be difficult for the courtier to influence him by means of those accomplishments you have attributed to him; for it goes without saying that sports such as jousting are for the young and of no use to the old, and that at that time of life music, dancing, merrymaking, games and love affairs are simply ridiculous; and it seems to me that these would be most unsuitable activities for one who is to mould the life and behaviour of the prince, who ought to be a man of considerable dignity and authority, mature in years and experience, and, if possible, a good philosopher, a good commander and knowing almost all there is to know. Therefore, the man who instructs the prince should not, I think, have the name of courtier but deserves a greater and more honoured name. So you must forgive me, signor Ottaviano, if I have pointed out this mistake of yours, because it seems to me that I am obliged to do so for the honour of my Court lady, whom you wish to be of less dignity than this courtier of yours, and this I will not allow.'

Signor Ottaviano smiled and said: 'Signor Magnifico, it would be more in her praise to lift her up to the same level as the courtier than it is to lower the courtier to hers. For surely she would also be allowed to instruct her mistress and to aspire with her to the same end of courtiership as I have said the courtier should aim at with his prince. But you are more concerned to criticize the courtier than to praise the Court lady; so I must be allowed to continue to take his part. In answer to your objections, therefore, I say that I did not maintain that the courtier's instruction should be the sole cause of what the prince is to be; for if the prince were not naturally inclined and suited to his role, all the courtier's care and teaching would be useless, just as would be all the endeavours of a good farmer if he set out with the finest seed to sow and cultivate the barren sand of the sea, because the latter is naturally sterile. But when to good seed in a fertile soil and to a temperate climate and seasonable rains, there is added also the diligence of man's cultivation, almost everywhere a rich harvest results. The farmer is not by himself responsible for the harvest, but without him all the other things would be of little or no use. Thus there are many princes who would be good if their minds were properly cultivated, and it is of these I am speaking and not of those who are like barren soil and by nature so alien to good conduct that they can never be taught to follow the right path.

'And since, as we have said already, our character is formed by our actions and virtue is expressed through what we do, it is neither impossible nor surprising that the courtier should introduce the prince to many virtues, such as justice, generosity and magnanimity, which his own greatness will then enable him to practice easily until they become habitual to him. This the courtier himself cannot do, since he lacks the necessary means; and thus the prince can become more virtuous than the courtier, although he has been instructed in the virtues by him. Moreover, you well know that the whetstone is used to sharpen iron, though it cuts nothing itself; so it seems to me that although the courtier teaches the prince it cannot be said to follow that he is of greater dignity than the prince. As for your saying that the end at which the courtier aims is difficult and sometimes impossible, and that when the courtier does achieve it he should not be called a courtier but deserves a greater name still, I do not deny the problem, for it is no less difficult to find such an understanding courtier than it is to attain the end we have stated. But I am convinced that there is no impossibility, even in the example you have cited. For if the courtier is so young that he does not know what we said he should know, then we have no need to speak of him, seeing that he is not the kind of courtier we have in mind; and indeed it is impossible for one who has to know so many things to be very young. Then again, if the prince is so wise and good in himself that he has no need of precepts or advice from anyone else (though everyone knows how unusual this is) it would be enough if the courtier were such that he could make the prince virtuous were he called upon to do so. And then in what he does he will be able to fulfil his other function of not allowing his prince to be deceived, of ensuring that he always has the truth about everything, and of standing in the path of flatterers and slanderers and all those who might scheme to corrupt the soul of the prince through shameful pleasures. In this way the courtier will largely attain his end, even though he will not realize it completely. And it would be unreasonable to criticize him because of this, since he is acting from a good motive. After all, if an excellent doctor happened to live in a place where everyone was in the best of health, we could hardly accuse him of failing to fulfil his function simply because he wasn't curing the sick. And just as the aim of a doctor should be to make men healthy, so the aim of the courtier is to make his prince virtuous. For both of them it is enough to have the capacity to achieve their ends, even if circumstances are such that they are not called upon to do so in practice.[17] Then if the courtier should be so old that it is unbecoming to him to indulge in music, merrymaking, games, arms and similar recreations, even so one cannot say that it is impossible for him to win his prince's favour in this way. For even if he is too old to take part in these things himself, he can still understand them; and, given that he has practised them when young, seeing that years and experience bring with them so much more knowledge of everything, age does not prevent his having a more perfect judgement, and a more perfect understanding of how to teach them to his prince. So in this way, although the courtier who has grown old does not practise the accomplishments we have ascribed to him, he will still attain his aim of giving good instruction to his prince.

'Then if you do not wish to give him the name of courtier, that does not offend me. For Nature has not set such limits on human dignities that a man may not ascend from one to another. Thus common soldiers often become captains; private persons, kings; priests, popes; and pupils, masters. And when they achieve the dignity, they acquire the name along with it. So we can perhaps say that the courtier's final aim is to become his prince's instructor. And yet I do not know who would refuse the name of perfect courtier, which in my opinion is worthy of the highest praise. And it seems to me that just as Homer created two most excellent men as models of human life, namely for deeds, Achilles, and for suffering and endurance, Ulysses, so he also wished to create a perfect courtier, who was Phoenix.[18] For after describing his love affairs and other things that happened to him in his youth, he says that Phoenix was sent to Achilles by his father Peleus to be his companion and to teach him how to speak and behave; and this is precisely the purpose we have attributed to our courtier. Nor do I think that Aristotle and Plato would have scorned the name of perfect courtier, because it is perfectly clear that they themselves carried out the functions of courtiership to the same end, the former with Alexander the Great and the latter with the Kings of Sicily.[19] And as the duty of a good courtier is to know the character and inclinations of his prince and according to the needs and opportunities these present skilfully win his favour, as we have said, by ways that are certain of success, and then introduce him to virtue, so Aristotle knew so well the character of Alexander and encouraged it so skilfully that Alexander loved and honoured him more than a father. And among many other demonstrations of his affection for Aristotle, Alexander ordered the rebuilding of his native city of Stagira, which had been destroyed. For his part, besides directing Alexander to the noble objective of wishing to make the whole world into one single country, in which men would live as one people, in friendship and peace among themselves under one government and one law shining equally on all like the light of the sun, Aristotle educated him so well in the natural sciences and in virtue that he became extremely wise, brave and continent, and a true moral philosopher in deeds as well as words. It is indeed impossible to imagine a nobler philosophy than the one by which he lived. For it brought civilization to peoples as savage as those of Bactria, Caucasia, India and Scythia, giving them knowledge of marriage and agriculture and teaching them to honour their parents and refrain from rapine, murder and other evil customs; it led to the building of so many magnificent cities in distant lands; and so, through the laws it imposed, men without number were led from a brutish to a human way of life. And the author of these deeds of Alexander was no other than Aristotle, employing the method of a good courtier. This was something that Callisthenes[20] did not know how to do, even though Aristotle showed him. For he wished to be a pure philosopher and an austere minister of the naked truth, unalloyed by courtiership, and so he lost his life and instead of helping Alexander won him nothing but infamy. The same method of courtiership was used by Plato to educate Dion of Syracuse. And subsequently when Plato found the tyrant Dionysius to be like a book full of lies and errors, and so in need of complete erasure rather than any change or correction, he decided that it would be useless to use the method of courtiership in this instance, because Dionysius was so soaked in tyrannical habits that there was no remedy for it. This example should be followed by our courtier too, if he happens to find himself in the service of a prince whose nature is so degraded that he is completely sapped by evil, like consumptives by their disease. In such a case he should withdraw his allegiance in order to escape blame for the misdeeds of his master and not experience the anguish felt by all good men who serve the wicked.'

After signor Ottaviano had fallen silent at this point, signor Gaspare said:

'I certainly did not expect to see our courtier honoured so highly; but since Aristotle and Plato are his companions, I think that no one from now on ought to despise the name. All the same, I'm not yet certain that I believe that Aristotle and Plato ever danced or made music at any time during their lives, or performed any acts of chivalry.'

Signor Ottaviano replied: 'It is hardly permissible to imagine that there was anything these two inspired men did not know, and so we may well believe that they practised what belongs to courtiership; for when they come to write about the subject they do so in such a way that those who are the greatest experts in what they are discussing can see that they understand the very pith and essence of it. So it is wrong to say that for the prince's courtier or instructor (as you wish to call him) who aims at the excellent end we have described, the accomplishments ascribed to him by these gentlemen are inappropriate, even though he may be an austere philosopher of the most saintly life; for these accomplishments are not inconsistent with goodness, discretion, wisdom or merit at any age or in any circumstances of time and place.'

Then signor Gaspare continued: 'I remember that when these gentlemen were discussing the accomplishments of the courtier yesterday evening they wished him to be in love. However, when we sum up what has been said so far we could come to the conclusion that the courtier who must introduce the prince to virtue through his own merits and authority must of necessity be an elderly man, for only rarely does wisdom not wait upon age, and especially as regards what we learn from experience. So I do not see how if he is advanced in years it is fitting for the courtier to be in love, seeing that, as has already been said this evening, in old men love is futile and what women take for agreeable courtesies, pleasantries and elegance in the young are in the old inept and ridiculous follies which will cause some women to detest and everyone to deride whoever indulges in them. So if this Aristotle of yours, as an elderly courtier, were to be in love and to do the things that young lovers do (like some we have seen in our own times) I fear he would forget to instruct his prince and doubtless the children would make fun of him behind his back and the ladies would hardly derive any pleasure from him other than to mock him.'

Then signor Ottaviano answered: 'As all the other qualities attributed to the courtier are suitable to him, even when he is old, I don't think it right to deprive him of the happiness of being in love.'

'On the contrary,' retorted signor Gaspare, 'to deprive him of it adds another perfection to him and enables him to live happily, free of all calamity and misery.'

Then Pietro Bembo added: 'Do you not remember, signor Gaspare, that although he is untutored in love in the game he suggested the other evening signor Ottaviano evidently knew that there are some lovers who regard as pleasurable all the storms of indignation, the outbursts of temper, the wars and the torments that they experience with their ladies? And he asked to be taught the cause of this pleasure. Therefore if our courtier were to be inflamed with the kind of love that is agreeable and without bitterness, even if elderly he would not experience any misery or suffering. And then again as a wise man, which we suppose him to be, he would not deceive himself in thinking that everything suitable for a young man to do was likewise suitable in his case. If in love, he would doubtless love in a way that would not only bring him no blame but earn him great praise and complete happiness, free of all vexation, which rarely if ever happens with younger men. And so he would not neglect to instruct his prince nor would he do anything to cause children to make fun of him.'

Then the Duchess remarked: 'I am glad, Pietro, that you have had to make little effort in our discussion this evening, because now we can have all the more confidence in giving you the task of speaking, and of teaching us about this kind of love which is so felicitous that it brings with it neither blame nor displeasure; for doubtless it would be one of the most useful and important of the endowments yet attributed to the courtier. So please, I beg you, tell us all you know about it.'

Pietro smiled and replied: 'Madam, I wouldn't wish my having said that it is permissible for old men to love to cause these ladies to suppose that I am old myself. So please give this task to someone else.'

The Duchess replied: 'You should not run away from being reputed old in wisdom, even if you are young in years. So please go on, and don't make any more excuses.'

Then Pietro Bembo answered: 'Truly, madam, if I do have to talk on this subject I shall have to go for advice to my Lavinello's friend, the hermit.[21]

At this, as if annoyed, signora Emilia exclaimed:

'Pietro, no one among us is more disobedient than you. So it would be only right if the Duchess were to punish you.'

Pietro, who was still smiling, answered:

'Don't be annoyed with me, madam, for pity's sake. For I shall tell you what you want.'

'Then please do so,' replied signora Emilia.

Thereupon, Pietro Bembo remained quiet for a little while. Then, having composed himself for a moment as if to speak of important things, he began as follows:

'Gentlemen, to show that old men can love not only blamelessly but sometimes more happily than the young, it will be necessary for me to enter upon a little discourse in order to make it clear what love is and what is the nature of the happiness that lovers experience. So I beg you to listen attentively, because I hope to make you realize that there is no man to whom it is unbecoming to be in love, even though he should be fifteen or twenty years older than signor Morello.'

After there was some laughter at this, Pietro Bembo continued: 'I say, therefore, that as defined by the philosophers of the ancient world Love is simply a certain longing to possess beauty; and since this longing can only be for things that are known already, knowledge must always of necessity precede desire, which by its nature wishes for what is good, but of itself is blind and so cannot perceive what is good. So Nature has ruled that every appetitive faculty, or desire, be accompanied by a cognitive faculty or power of understanding. Now in the human soul there are three faculties by which we understand or perceive things: namely, the senses, rational thought and intellect. Thus the senses desire things through sensual appetite or the kind of appetite which we share with the animals; reason desires things through rational choice, which is, strictly speaking, proper to man; and intellect, which links man to the angels, desires things through pure will. It follows that the sensual appetite desires only those things that are perceptible by the senses, whereas man's will finds its satisfaction in the contemplation of spiritual things that can be apprehended by intellect. And then man, who is rational by his very nature and is placed between the two extremes of brute matter and pure spirit, can choose to follow the senses or to aspire to the intellect, and so can direct his appetites or desires now in the one direction, now in the other. In either of these two ways, therefore, he can long for beauty, which is the quality possessed by all natural or artificial things that are composed in the good proportion and due measure that befit their nature.[22]

'However, I shall speak of the kind of beauty I now have in mind, which is that seen in the human body and especially the face and which prompts the ardent desire we call love; and we shall argue that this beauty is an influx of the divine goodness which, like the light of the sun, is shed over all created things but especially displays itself in all its beauty when it discovers and informs a countenance which is well proportioned and composed of a certain joyous harmony of various colours enhanced by light and shadow and by symmetry and clear definition. This goodness adorns and illumines with wonderful splendour and grace the object in which it shines, like a sunbeam striking a lovely vase of polished gold set with precious gems. And thus it attracts to itself the gaze of others, and entering through their eyes it impresses itself upon the human soul, which it stirs and delights with its charm, inflaming it with passion and desire. Thus the mind is seized by desire for the beauty which it recognizes as good, and, if it allows itself to be guided by what its senses tell it, it falls into the gravest errors and judges that the body is the chief cause of the beauty which it enshrines, and so to enjoy that beauty it must necessarily achieve with it as intimate a union as possible. But this is untrue; and anyone who thinks to enjoy that beauty by possessing the body is deceiving himself and is moved not by true knowledge, arrived at by rational choice, but by a false opinion derived from the desire of the senses. So the pleasure that follows is also necessarily false and deceptive. Consequently, all those lovers who satisfy their impure desires with the women they love meet with one of two evils: either as soon as they achieve the end they desire they experience satiety and distaste and even begin to hate what they love, as if their desire repented of its error and recognized the way it had been deceived by the false judgement of the senses, which had made it believe that evil was good; or else they are still troubled by the same avidity and desire, since they have not in fact attained the end they were seeking. Admittedly, confused by their short-sighted view of things, they imagine that they are experiencing pleasure, just as sometimes a sick man dreams that he is drinking from a clear fountain. Nevertheless, they enjoy neither rest nor satisfaction, and these are precisely what they would enjoy as the natural consequences of desiring and then possessing what is good. On the contrary, deceived by the resemblance they see, they soon experience unbridled desire once more and in the same agitation as before they again find themselves with a raging and unquenchable thirst for what they hope to possess utterly. Lovers of this kind, therefore, are always most unhappy; for either they never attain their desires, and this causes them great misery, or if they do attain them they find themselves in terrible distress, and their wretchedness is even greater. For both at the beginning and during the course of this love of theirs they never know other than anguish, torment, sorrow, exertion and distress; and so lovers, it is supposed, must always be characterized by paleness and dejection, continuous sighings and weepings, mournfulness and lamentations, silences and the desire for death.

'We see, therefore, that the senses are the chief cause of this desolation of the spirit; and they are at their full strength in youth, when they are stimulated by the urges of the flesh which sap a man's powers of reason in exact proportion to their own vigour and so easily persuade the soul to yield to desire. For since it is sunk in an earthly prison and deprived of spiritual contemplation, the soul cannot of itself clearly perceive the truth when it is carrying out its duties of governing the body. So in order to understand things properly it must appeal to the senses for its first notions. In consequence it believes whatever they tell it and respects and trusts them, especially when they are so vigorous that they almost compel it; and because the senses are deceptive they fill the soul with errors and mistaken ideas. As a result, young men are invariably absorbed by this sensual kind of love and wholly rebellious against reason, and so they make themselves unworthy of enjoying the blessings and advantages that love gives to its true devotees; and the only pleasures they experience in love are the same as those enjoyed by unreasoning animals, though the distress they suffer is far more terrible than theirs. Therefore on this premise, which I insist is the absolute truth, I argue that lovers who are more mature in age experience the contrary; for in their case the soul is no longer so weighed down by the body and their natural ardour has begun to cool, and so if they are inflamed by beauty and their desire for it is guided by rational choice, they are not deceived and they possess completely the beauty they love. Consequently its possession brings them nothing but good, since beauty is goodness and so the true love of beauty is good and holy and always benefits those in whose souls the bridle of reason restrains the iniquity of the senses; and this is something the old can do far more easily than the young.

'So it is not unreasonable to argue also that the old can love blamelessly and more happily than the young, accepting that by old we do not mean those who are senile or whose bodily organs have grown so feeble that the soul cannot perform its operations through them, but men whose intellectual powers are still in their prime. I must also add this: namely, that in my opinion although sensual love is bad at every age, yet in the young it may be excused and perhaps in some sense even permitted. For although it brings them afflictions, dangers, exertions and all the unhappiness we have mentioned, yet there are many who perform worthy acts in order to win the favour of the women whom they love, and though these acts are not directed to a good end they are good in themselves. And so from all that bitterness they extract a little sweetness, and the adversities they endure finally teach them the error of their ways. So just as I think those young people who subdue their desires and love in a rational manner are truly heroic, I excuse those who allow themselves to be overcome by the sensual love to which human weakness inclines them, provided that they then display gentleness, courtesy, worthiness and all the other qualities these gentlemen mentioned, and that when they are no longer young they abandon it completely and leave sensual desire behind them, as the lowest rung of the ladder by which we can ascend to true love. But no blame is too severe for those who when they are old still allow the fires of passion to burn in their cold hearts and make strong reason obey their feeble senses; for they deserve the endless shame of being numbered like idiots among the animals which lack reason, because the thoughts and ways of sensual love are wholly unbecoming to men of mature years.'

Bembo then paused for a moment, as if to rest; and as everyone remained silent, signor Morello da Ortona said:

'But if there were to be found an old man more able-bodied, more vigorous and more handsome than many youths, why would you not wish that he should be allowed to love in their way?'

The Duchess laughed at this and remarked:

'If love is such an unhappy experience for the young, why, signor Morello, do you want old men as well to suffer the same unhappiness? But if you were old, as these gentlemen say, you would not plot such evil against old men.'

Signor Morello replied: 'It seems to me that the one who is

plotting evil against old men is Pietro Bembo, because he wishes them to love in a way that I, for one, cannot understand. And I also think that to possess the beauty he praises so much without the body is a fantasy.'

'Do you believe, signor Morello,' asked Count Lodovico, 'that beauty is always as good as Pietro Bembo says?'

'I certainly do not,' answered signor Morello. 'On the contrary, I remember having seen many beautiful women who were evil, cruel and spiteful; and this seems to me to be nearly always the case, since beauty makes them proud, and pride makes them cruel.'

Count Lodovico replied with a smile: 'Doubtless they seem cruel to you because they do not grant you what you want. But let Pietro Bembo teach you how old men ought to desire beauty, and what they should seek from women, and with what they ought to be satisfied; and provided you keep within these limits you will discover that they are neither proud nor cruel, and they will also grant you what you want.'

Signor Morello showed his irritation at this, and he retorted:

'I don't want to learn what doesn't concern me. Let someone teach you the way in which this beauty ought to be desired by young men who are not so able-bodied or vigorous as the old.'

Then Federico, in order to calm signor Morello and to change the subject, interrupted before Count Lodovico could reply and said:

'Perhaps signor Morello is not altogether wrong in saying that beauty is not always good, for often woman's beauty causes the world endless evil, enmity, war, death and destruction, as was shown very clearly, for example, by the downfall of Troy. And for the most part beautiful women are either proud and cruel or else, as has been said, unchaste; though this last signor Morello would not consider a fault. There are also many wicked men who are endowed with good looks, and it seems that Nature has made them so in order that they may be better able to deceive, and that their agreeable appearance is the bait concealing the hook.'

Then Pietro Bembo stated: 'Do not believe that beauty is not always good.'

Here, in order to return to the original subject, Count Lodovico broke in and remarked:

'Since signor Morello is not interested in learning what concerns him so deeply, teach it to me, and show me how old men may win the happiness of love; for I shall not worry if I cause myself to be considered old, provided I profit by it.'

Pietro Bembo said with a smile: 'First I wish to correct the error made by these gentlemen, and then I shall satisfy you as well.'

Then he continued as follows:

'Gentlemen, beauty is a sacred thing, and I should not wish any of us to act like profane and sacrilegious men in speaking ill of it and thereby incurring the wrath of God. So as a warning for signor Morello and Federico, lest they are punished in the way most suitable for those who despise beauty, and lose their sight like Stesichorus,[23] I say that beauty springs from God and is like a circle, the centre of which is goodness. And so just as one cannot have a circle without a centre, so one cannot have beauty without goodness. In consequence, only rarely does an evil soul dwell in a beautiful body, and so outward beauty is a true sign of inner goodness. This loveliness, indeed, is impressed upon the body in varying degrees as a token by which the soul can be recognized for what it is, just as with trees the beauty of the blossom testifies to the goodness of the fruit. The same is true of the human body, as we know from the way physiognomists often establish a man's character and sometimes even his thoughts from his countenance. Moreover, even in animals the qualities of the soul as far as possible impress themselves upon the body and can be perceived from their physical appearance. Consider how clearly we can perceive anger, ferocity and pride in the face of the lion, the horse and the eagle; and a pure and simple innocence in lambs and doves; evil guile in foxes and wolves, and so with nearly all the animals.

'Therefore for the most part the ugly are also evil, and the beautiful good. And it can be said that beauty is the pleasant, gay, charming and desirable face of the good, and that ugliness is the dark, disagreeable, unpleasant and sorry face of evil. And no matter what things you study, you will always find that those which are good and useful are also graced with beauty. Consider the structure of this great fabric of the universe, which was created by God for the health and preservation of all His creatures. The bowl of heaven, adorned with so many celestial lamps, and the earth in the centre, surrounded by the elements and sustained by its own weight; the sun, illuminating all things as it revolves, in winter approaching the lowest sign, and then by degrees ascending to the other side; the moon, which derives its light from the sun, in accord with whether the sun is approaching or drawing away; and the five other stars which separately travel the same course: these all influence each other so profoundly through the coherence of the natural order that if they changed in the slightest they could no longer exist together and the universe would crumble. Moreover, they have such beauty and loveliness that the human mind cannot conceive anything more graceful. Consider next the structure of man, who may be called a little universe in himself. We see that every part of his body is in the natural order of things made by design and not by chance and that his form as a whole is so beautiful that it is difficult to decide whether it is utility or grace that is given more to the human face and body by its various parts, such as the eyes, nose, mouth, ears, arms and breast. The same can be said of all the animals. Consider the feathers of birds and the leaves and branches of trees, which are given by Nature to preserve their being, and yet which are also of the greatest loveliness. Now let us leave Nature and come to human art. What is so necessary for a ship as the prow, the sides, the mainyards, the mast, the sails, the helm, the oars, the anchor and the rigging? Yet all these things are so attractive that anyone looking at them must conclude they exist as much for pleasure as for use. Columns and architraves support lofty galleries and palaces, but they are no less pleasing to the eye than they are useful to the building. When men first began to build they included the middle ridge in their churches and houses not to embellish their buildings but to allow the water to flow off without trouble on either side; nevertheless, attractiveness of appearance soon became as important as usefulness, so that if a church were to be built in a land which never knew rain or hail, it would seem to lack both dignity and beauty if left without the ridge of a roof.

'Thus to call anything beautiful, even the world itself, constitutes the highest praise. It is praised when we say such things as: beautiful sky, beautiful earth, beautiful sea, beautiful rivers, beautiful countryside, beautiful woods, trees and gardens; or beautiful cities, churches, houses and armies. In short, this gracious and sacred beauty is the supreme adornment of everything; and it can be said that in some manner the good and the beautiful are identical, especially in the human body. And the proximate cause of physical beauty is, in my opinion, the beauty of the soul which since it shares in true supernatural beauty makes whatever it touches resplendent and lovely, especially if the body it inhabits is not of such base material that the soul cannot impress on it its own quality. Therefore beauty is the true trophy of the soul's victory, when with her heavenly power she rules over material nature and with her light dispels the darkness of the body. We must not say, therefore, that beauty makes women proud or cruel, though this may seem to be the case to signor Morello; neither should we impute to beautiful women those enmities, deaths and destructions which are caused by the unrestrained desires of men. To be sure, I shall not deny that we can also find in the world beautiful women who are unchaste. But it is all the same not their beauty which makes them so; on the contrary, because of the bond between beauty and goodness, their beauty turns them away from impurity and leads them to the path of virtuous conduct. But sometimes evil training, the continual urgings of their lovers, gifts, poverty, hope, deceits, fear and a thousand other causes can defeat the steadfastness even of good and beautiful women; and for this and other reasons handsome men can also become wicked.'

Then Cesare remarked: 'If what signor Gaspare alleged yesterday is true, then there is no doubt that women who are beautiful are more chaste than those who are ugly.'

'And what did I allege?' asked signor Gaspare.

'If I remember correctly,' replied Cesare, 'you said that women who are wooed always refuse to satisfy their suitor, and that those who are not, do the wooing themselves. And it is certain that the beautiful are always more wooed and pursued in love than the ugly; therefore the beautiful always refuse, and so they are more chaste than those ugly women who, as they have no suitors, do the wooing themselves.'

Bembo smiled and said: 'There can be no answer to this argument.'

Then he added: 'It also often happens that, like the other senses, our sight can be deceived and can judge to be beautiful a face that is not so at all. For example some women occasionally display in their eyes and looks a certain enticing and suggestive immodesty which is called beauty by many who find these traits pleasing because they promise them the chance of gaining what they desire. But in truth this is simply meretricious impudence, and unworthy of so honoured and sacred a name.'

Pietro Bembo then fell silent, but he was urged to say more about this kind of love and about the true way in which beauty should be enjoyed; and at length he said:

'I think I have shown clearly enough that old men can be happier in love than the young; and this was my premise. So it is not for me to add any more.'

Count Lodovico replied: 'You have demonstrated the unhappiness of the young better than the happiness of the old, whom you have not yet taught what path to follow in love but merely instructed to let themselves be guided by reason. And many people consider that it is impossible to reconcile love with reason.'

Bembo was still determined to say no more, but the Duchess begged that he should do so, and therefore he continued:

'It would be too unfortunate for humanity if our soul, in which such ardent desire can so easily arise, were forced to find nourishment only in what it has in common with the animals and could not direct its desire to its nobler element. So, as this is your wish, I will not refuse to discuss this noble theme. And since I know that I am unworthy to speak of Love's sacred mysteries, I pray him so to inspire my thoughts and words that I can teach this excellent courtier of ours how to love in a manner beyond the capacity of the vulgar crowd. And because I have since boyhood dedicated my life to him, may my words now conform to this intention and redound to his credit. I maintain, then, that since in youth human nature is so inclined to the senses, while the courtier is young he may be allowed to love in a sensual manner; but if in more mature years he should be inflamed with this amorous desire, he must proceed with circumspection and take care not to deceive himself or let himself experience the distress which in young men deserves compassion rather than blame but in old men blame rather than compassion.

'Therefore when he sets eyes on some beautiful and attractive woman, with charming ways and gentle manner, and being skilled in love recognizes that his spirit responds to hers, as soon as he notices that his eyes fasten on her image and carry it to his heart and his soul begins to take pleasure in contemplating her and feels an influx that gradually arouses and warms it, and those vivacious spirits shining from her eyes constantly add fresh fuel to the fire, then he should at the very beginning procure a swift remedy and alert his reason in order to defend with its help the fortress of his heart, and so close the passes to the senses and to desire that they cannot enter either by force or deception. If the flame is extinguished, so is the danger. But if it perseveres or grows, then in the knowledge that he has been captured the courtier should determine to eschew all the ugliness of vulgar passion and guided by reason set forth on the path of divine love. Then first he must reflect that the body in which beauty shines is not the source from which it springs, and on the contrary that beauty, being incorporeal and, as we have said, a ray of the supernatural, loses much of its nobility when fused with base and corruptible matter: for the more perfect it is, the less matter it contains, and it is most perfect when completely separated from matter. He must also reflect that just as a man cannot hear with his palate or smell with his ears, beauty can in no way be enjoyed nor can the desire it arouses in our souls be satisfied through the sense of touch but solely through what has beauty for its true object, namely, the faculty of sight. So he should ignore the blind judgement of these senses and enjoy with his eyes the radiance, the grace, the loving ardour, the smiles, the mannerisms and all the other agreeable adornments of the woman he loves. Similarly, let him use his hearing to enjoy the sweetness of her voice, the modulation of her words and, if she is a musician, the music she plays. In this way, through the channels of these two faculties, which have little to do with corporeal things and are servants of reason, he will nourish his soul on the most delightful food and will not allow desire for the body to arouse in him any appetite that is at all impure. Next, with the greatest reverence the lover should honour, please and obey his lady, cherish her even more than himself, put her convenience and pleasure before his own, and love the beauty of her soul no less than that of her body. He should, therefore, be at pains to keep her from going astray and by his wise precepts and admonishments always seek to make her modest, temperate and truly chaste; and he must ensure that her thoughts are always pure and unsullied by any trace of evil. And thus, by sowing virtue in the garden of her lovely soul, he will gather the fruits of faultless behaviour and experience exquisite pleasure from their taste. And this will be the true engendering and expression of beauty in beauty, which some say is the purpose of love. In this manner, our courtier will be most pleasing to his lady, and she will always be submissive, charming and affable and as anxious to please him as she is to be loved by him; and the desires of both will be very pure and harmonious, and consequently they will be perfectly happy.'

Then signor Morello remarked: 'In reality, this engendering of beauty in beauty must mean the begetting of a beautiful child in a beautiful woman; and it would seem to me a far clearer sign that she loved her lover if she pleased him in this than if she treated him merely with the affability you mention.'

Bembo laughed and replied: 'You mustn't go beyond the bounds, signor Morello; nor indeed does a woman grant just a token of affection when she gives her lover her beauty, which is precious to her, and along the paths into her soul, namely, sight and hearing, sends the glances of her eyes, the image of her face, her voice and her words, which penetrate her lover's heart and convey the proof of her love.'

Signor Morello then said: 'Glances and words can be false witnesses, and often are. So anyone who has no better pledge of love is in my opinion most uncertain; and truly I was expecting you to make this lady of yours a little more courteous and generous towards the courtier than the Magnifico made his. However, I think both of you are acting in the same way as those judges who pronounce sentence against their own people in order to seem wise.'

'I am perfectly willing,' Bembo continued, 'for this lady to be far more courteous to my elderly courtier than signor Magnifico's lady is to the young courtier. And this is with good reason, for my courtier will wish only for seemly things, all of which she may therefore concede to him quite innocently. But the Magnifico's lady, who is not so certain of the young courtier's modesty, should concede him only what is seemly and deny him what is not. Therefore my courtier, who obtains all he asks for, is happier than the other, who is granted some of his requests but refused others. And to help you understand even better that rational love is happier than sensual love, I say that sometimes the same things should be denied in sensual love and granted in rational love, because in the former context they are unseemly, and in the latter, seemly. Thus to please her gracious lover, besides granting him pleasant smiles, intimate and secret conversations, and the liberty to joke and jest and touch hands, the lady may very reasonably and innocently go so far as to grant a kiss, which in sensual love, according to the Magnifico's rules, is not permitted. For as a kiss is a union of body and soul, there is a risk that the sensual lover may incline more to the body than the soul; but the rational lover knows that although the mouth is part of the body nevertheless it provides a channel for words, which are the interpreters of the soul, and for the human breath or spirit. Consequently, the rational lover delights when he joins his mouth to that of the lady he loves in a kiss, not in order to arouse in himself any unseemly desire but because he feels that this bond opens the way for their souls which, attracted by their mutual desire, each pour themselves into the other's body in turn and so mingle that each of them possesses two souls, and it is as if a single spirit composed of the two governs their two bodies. So the kiss may be called a spiritual rather than physical union because it exerts such power over the soul that it draws it to itself and separates it from the body. For this reason, all chaste lovers desire a kiss as a union of souls; and thus when inspired to love Plato[24] said that in kissing the soul comes to the lips in order to leave the body. And because the separation of the soul from things that are perceptible to the senses and its complete union with spiritual things can be signified by the kiss, in his inspired book of the *Song of Songs* Solomon says: "let him kiss me with the kiss of his mouth", in order to express the wish that his soul be transported by divine love to the contemplation of celestial beauty and by its intimate union with this beauty might forsake the body.'[25]

All were listening very attentively to what Bembo was saying; and then, after a moment's pause, he added:

'Since you have made me begin to teach the courtier who is no longer young about love that is truly happy, I want to lead him a little further still. For to stop at this point is very dangerous because, as we have said several times already, the soul is strongly inclined towards the senses; and although reason may choose well in its operation and recognize that beauty does not arise from the body, and therefore act as a check to impure desires, yet the constant contemplation of physical beauty often perverts true judgement. And even if no other evil resulted from this, absence from the person one loves causes much suffering. This is because when beauty is physically present, its influx into the lover's soul brings him intense pleasure, and by warming his heart it arouses and melts certain hidden and congealed powers which the warmth of love nourishes and causes to flow and well up round his heart and send through his eyes those spirits or most subtle vapours, composed of the purest and brightest part of the blood, to receive the image of her beauty and embellish it with a thousand varied adornments. In consequence, the soul is filled with wonder and delight; it is frightened and yet it rejoices; as if dazed, it experiences along with its pleasure the fear and reverence invariably inspired by sacred things, and it believes it has entered into its Paradise.

'Therefore the lover who is intent only on physical beauty loses all this good and happiness as soon as the women he loves by her absence leaves his eyes deprived of their splendour and, consequently, his soul widowed of its good. For, since her beauty is far away, there is no influx of affection to warm his heart as it did when she was there, and so the openings of his body become arid and dry; yet the memory of her beauty still stirs the powers of his soul a little, so that they seek to pour those spirits forth. Although their paths are blocked and there is no exit for them, they still strive to depart, and thus tormented and enclosed they begin to prick the soul and cause it to suffer bitterly, as children do when the teeth begin to grow through their tender gums. This causes the tears, the sighs, the anguish and the torments of lovers, because the soul is in constant pain and turmoil and almost raging in fury until its cherished beauty appears once more; and then suddenly it is calmed and breathes again, and wholly absorbed it draws strength from the delicious food before it and wishes never to part from such a ravishing vision. Therefore, to escape the torment caused by absence and to enjoy beauty without suffering, with the help of reason the courtier should turn his desire completely away from the body to beauty alone. He should contemplate beauty as far as he is able in its own simplicity and purity, create it in his imagination as an abstraction distinct from any material form, and thus make it lovely and dear to his soul, and enjoy it there always, day and night and in every time and place, without fear of ever losing it; and he will always remember that the body is something altogether distinct from beauty, whose perfection it diminishes rather than enhances. In this way the courtier of ours who is no longer young will put himself out of reach of the anguish and distress invariably experienced by the young in the form of jealousy, suspicion, disdain, anger, despair and a certain tempestuous fury that occasionally leads them so much astray that some not only beat the women they love but take their own lives. He will do no injury to the husband, father, brothers or family of the lady he loves; he will cause her no shame; he will not be forced sometimes to drag his eyes away and curb his tongue for fear of revealing his desires to others; or to endure suffering when they part or during her absence. For he will always carry the treasure that is so precious to him safe in his heart; and by the power of his imagination he will also make her beauty far more lovely than it is in reality.

'However, among all these blessings the lover will find one that is far greater still, if he will determine to make use of this love as a step by which to climb to another that is far more sublime; and this will be possible if he continually reflects how narrowly he is confined by always limiting himself to the contemplation of a single body. And so in order to escape from this confinement, he will gradually add so many adornments to his idea of beauty that, by uniting all possible forms of beauty in his mind, he will form a universal concept and so reduce all the many varieties to the unity of that single beauty which sheds itself over human nature as a whole. And thus he will come to contemplate not the particular beauty of a single woman but the universal beauty which adorns all human bodies: and then, dazzled by this greater light, he will not concern himself with the lesser; burning with a more perfect flame, he will feel little esteem for what he formerly prized so greatly. Now this stage of love, although so noble that few attain it, still cannot be called perfect. For the human imagination is a corporeal faculty and acquires knowledge only through the data supplied to it by the senses, and so it is not wholly purged of the darkness of material things. Thus although it may consider this universal beauty in the abstract and simply in itself, yet it perceives it not at all clearly nor within a certain ambiguity because of the affinities that the images it forms have with the body itself; and so those who reach this stage of love are like fledglings which on their feeble wings can lift themselves a little in flight but dare not stray far from the nest or trust themselves to the winds and the open sky.

'Therefore when our courtier has arrived at this stage, even though he can be called most happy in comparison with those lovers who are still sunk in the miseries of sensual love, I wish him not to be satisfied but to move boldly onwards along the sublime path of love and follow his guide towards the goal of true happiness. So instead of directing his thoughts to the outward world, as those must do who wish to consider bodily beauty, let him turn within himself to contemplate what he sees with the eyes of the mind, which begin to be penetrating and clear-sighted once those of the body have lost the flower of their delight; and in this manner, having shed all evil, purged by the study of true philosophy, directed towards the life of the spirit, and practised in the things of the intellect, the soul turns to contemplate its own substance, and as if awakened from deepest sleep it opens the eyes which all men possess but few use and perceives in itself a ray of that light which is the true image of the angelic beauty that has been transmitted to it, and of which in turn it transmits a faint impression to the body. Thus, when it has become blind to earthly things, the soul opens its eyes wide to those of heaven; and sometimes when the faculties of the body are totally absorbed by assiduous contemplation, or bound to sleep, no longer hindered by their influence the soul tastes a certain hidden savour of the true angelic beauty, and ravished by the loveliness of that light it begins to burn and to pursue the beauty it sees so avidly that it seems almost drunk and beside itself in its desire to unite with it. For the soul then believes that it has discovered the traces of God, in the contemplation of which it seeks its final repose and bliss. And so, consumed in this most joyous flame, it ascends to its noblest part, which is the intellect; and there, no more overshadowed by the dark night of earthly things, it glimpses the divine beauty itself. Even so, it does not yet enjoy this perfectly, since it contemplates it only in its own particular intellect, which cannot comprehend universal beauty in all its immensity. And so, not even satisfied with bestowing this blessing, love gives the soul greater happiness still. For just as from the particular beauty of a single body it guides the soul to the universal beauty of all bodies, so, in the last stage of perfection, it guides the soul from the particular intellect to the universal intellect. And from there, aflame with the sacred fire of true divine love, the soul flies to unite itself with the angelic nature, and it not only abandons the senses but no longer has need of reason itself. For, transformed into an angel, it understands all intelligible things and without any veil or cloud it gazes on the wide sea of pure divine beauty, which it receives into itself to enjoy the supreme happiness the senses cannot comprehend.

'The kinds of beauty which every day we see in corruptible bodies with these clouded eyes of ours (and which even so are only dreams and faint shadows) appear to be so lovely and graceful that they often kindle in us a most ardent fire and cause such delight that we count no happiness the equal of what we sometimes feel because of a single glance we may receive from the eyes of the woman we love, so what happy wonder, what blessed awe must we think is that which possesses the soul when it attains the vision of divine beauty! What sweet flame, what ravishing fire must we believe that to be which springs from the source of supreme and true beauty, the fountain of all other beauty which never increases or diminishes! Always beautiful; most simple of itself and equally in all its parts; like only to itself and sharing in nothing other than itself; it is yet so beautiful that all other beautiful things derive their beauty from it. And this is the beauty indistinguishable from the highest good, which by its light calls and draws all things to it and which not only gives intellect to intellectual beings, reason to rational beings and the senses and the desire for life to sensual beings, but also transmits to the very plants and rocks, as an imprint of itself, motion and the instinct of their own particular nature. This love, therefore, is as greater and happier than the others as the cause that produces it is greater. And thus, just as material fire refines gold, so this most sacred fire consumes and destroys everything that is mortal in our souls and quickens and beautifies the celestial part which previously, because of the senses, was dead and buried. This is the pyre on which the poets write that Hercules was burned on the summit of Mount Oeta and through whose fire he became divine and immortal after death; this is the burning bush of Moses, the parted tongues of fire, the fiery chariot of Elias, which doubles the grace and happiness of those souls worthy to see it, when it leaves the earth below and flies towards heaven. So let us direct all the thoughts and powers of our soul towards this most sacred light which shows us the path that leads to heaven; and following after it and divesting ourselves of the human passions in which we were clothed when we fell, let us ascend by the ladder whose lowest rung bears the image of sensual beauty to the sublime mansion where dwells the celestial, adorable and true beauty which lies hidden in the secret recesses of the Almighty where profane eyes may not see it. And here we shall find a most happy end to our desires, true rest from our labours, a sure remedy for our miseries, a wholesome medicine for our infirmities, a most safe harbour from the raging storms of the temptestuous sea of this life.

'O most sacred Love, what tongue is there that can praise you worthily? Full of beauty, goodness and wisdom, you flow from the union of beauty, goodness and divine wisdom, there you dwell, and through it you return to it perpetually. Graciously binding the universe together, midway between celestial and earthy things, by your benign disposition you direct the heavenly powers in their government of the lower, and turning the minds of men to their source, you unite them with it. You unite the elements in harmony, inspire Nature to produce, and move all that is born to the perpetuation of life. You join together the things that are separate, give perfection to the imperfect, likeness to the unlike, friendship to the hostile, fruit to the earth, tranquillity to the sea, its life-giving light to the sky. You are the father of true pleasures, of all blessings, of peace, of gentleness and of good will; the enemy of rough savagery and vileness; the beginning and the end of every good. And since you delight to inhabit the flower of beautiful bodies and beautiful souls, and there sometimes consent to reveal a little of yourself to those worthy to see you, I believe that you now dwell here among us. Consent then, O Lord, to hear our prayers, pour yourself into our hearts, and with the radiance of your most sacred fire illumine our darkness and like a trusted guide show us the right path through this blind maze. Correct the falsity of our senses, and after our long delirium give us the true substance of goodness. Quicken our intellects with the incense of spirituality and make us so attuned to the celestial harmony that there is no longer room within us for any discord of passion. Inebriate our souls at the inexhaustible fountain of contentment that always delights and never satiates and that gives a taste of true blessedness to whoever drinks from its living and limpid waters. With the rays of your light cleanse our eyes of their misty ignorance, so that they may no longer prize mortal beauty but know that the things which they first thought to see are not, and that those they did not see truly are. Accept the sacrifice of our souls; and burn them in the living flame that consumes all earthly dross, so that wholly freed from the body they may unite with divine beauty in a sweet and perpetual bond and that we, liberated from our own selves, like true lovers can be transformed into the object of our love and soar above the earth to join the feast of the angels, where, with ambrosia and immortal nectar for our food, we may at last die a most happy death in life, as did those ancient Fathers whose souls, by the searing power of contemplation, you ravished from their bodies to unite with God.'

Having spoken in that way with such vehemence that he seemed transported out of himself, Bembo then remained silent and still, looking towards heaven, as if dazed. And then signora Emilia, who together with all the others had listened to all he had to say with the utmost attention, plucked the hem of his robe and said:

'Take care, Pietro, that with these thoughts of yours you too do not cause your soul to leave your body.'

'Madam,' answered Pietro, 'that would not be the first miracle that love has worked in me.'

Then the Duchess and all the others began once again to insist that Bembo should continue his discourse; and everyone almost seemed to feel in his mind a spark of the divine love that had inspired Bembo himself. They were all anxious to hear more, but he then added:

'Gentlemen, I have said all that was dictated to me on the spur of the moment by the holy frenzy of love. And now that its inspiration seems to have failed, I would not know what to say; and I think that love does not wish its secrets to be revealed any further, or that the courtier should pass beyond the stage I have been graciously permitted to show him; and so perhaps I may speak no further about this subject.'

'Truly,' said the Duchess, 'if the courtier who is no longer young is such that he is able to follow the path you have shown him he should rightly be content with such great happiness and feel no envy of the young.'

Then Cesare Gonzaga remarked: 'The road that leads to happiness seems to me so steep that I hardly think anyone can travel it.'

And then signor Gaspare added: 'I think to travel this road would be difficult for men, but impossible for women.'

Signora Emilia laughed and said:

'Signor Gaspare, if you return to giving us so many insults, I promise you will not be forgiven again.'

Signor Gaspare replied: 'It is no insult to you to say that the souls of women are not as purged of the passions as those of men or as versed in contemplation as Pietro has said those which are to taste divine love must be. Thus do we not read that any woman has ever received this grace, but we do read of many men who have, such as Plato, Socrates, Plotinus[26] and many others; and similarly many of our holy Fathers, such as St Francis, upon whom an ardent messenger of love impressed the most holy seal of the five wounds[27]. And only the power of love could transport the Apostle St Paul to the vision of those secrets of which no man is allowed to speak, or show St Stephen the heavens opening.'[28]

Then the Magnifico Giuliano replied:

'But women would not be surpassed by men in the slightest as far as this is concerned: for Socrates himself confessed that all the mysteries of love that he knew had been revealed to him by a woman, the famous Diotima,[29] and the angel who pierced St Francis with the fire of love has also made several women of our own time worthy of the same seal. You should also remember that many sins were forgiven St Mary Magdalene because she loved much and that she, perhaps in no less a state of grace than St Paul, was many times rapt to the third heaven by angelic love,[30] and remember many others who, as I told at greater length yesterday, for the love of Christ's name have cared nothing for their own life, nor have they feared tortures or any manner of death, however horrible and cruel. And these were not old, as Pietro wishes his courtier to be, but tender and delicate girls, of the age at which he says sensual love should be allowed to men.'

Signor Gaspare was preparing to reply; but then the Duchess said:

'Let Pietro Bembo be the judge of this, and let us abide by his decision as to whether or not women are as capable of divine love as men. But, as the argument between you could last too long, it would be as well to postpone it until tomorrow.'

'Rather, till this evening,' said Cesare Gonzaga.

'Why this evening?' asked the Duchess.

Cesare replied: 'Because it is already day'; and he showed her the light that was beginning to come in through the clefts of the windows. Then they all rose to their feet, greatly astonished, because it did not seem that the discussion had lasted longer than usual, but as they had started far later and taken greater pleasure in it, those gentlemen had been so absorbed that they had not noticed the way time was passing; nor did anyone feel at all tired: and this often happens when the accustomed time of sleep is spent in wakefulness. So when the windows on the side of the palace that faces the lofty peak of Mount Catria had been opened, they saw that dawn had already come to the east, with the beauty and colour of a rose, and all the stars had been scattered, save only the lovely mistress of heaven, Venus, who guards the confines of night and day. From there, there seemed to come a delicate breeze, filling the air with biting cold, and among the murmuring woods on nearby hills wakening the birds into joyous song. Then all, having taken their respectful leave of the Duchess, went to their rooms, without torches, for the light of day was sufficient; and, as they were about to leave the room, the Prefect turned to the Duchess and said:

'Madam, to settle the argument between signor Gaspare and the Magnifico, we shall come with our judge this evening earlier than we did yesterday.'

Signora Emilia replied: 'On condition that if signor Gaspare should want to criticize women and slander them in his usual manner he shall give his bond to stand trial, for I arraign him as a fugitive from justice.'

NOTES

DEDICATORY LETTER AND FIRST BOOK

1. (p. 35) Theophrastus (date of birth uncertain, died 287 B.C.) was a Greek philosopher, the favourite pupil of Aristotle. The anecdote is based on a story in Cicero's *Brutus* xlvi, 172.

2. (p. 44) These 'emblems' (*imprese*) worn on clothing or armour were very popular in Court society during the sixteenth century. They consisted of a picture and motto, usually in Latin.

3. (p. 47) Fra Mariano – for this Court buffoon, and for Fra Serafino, see the List of Characters.

4. (p. 48) The letter S worn by the Duchess was probably one of the emblems already mentioned, in this case a golden cipher. It has been suggested that the S may have stood for scorpion.

5. (p. 58) Berto – mentioned later for his clowning abilities – was another buffoon in the service of the papal Court.

6. (p. 66) Galleazzo Sanseverino was a mercenary who married into the family of Lodovico Sforza, Duke of Milan, after whose defeat by the French he entered the service of King Louis XII.

7. (p. 69) Apelles, a contemporary of Alexander the Great, was the most famous painter of ancient Greece. He 'discovered' Protogenes and convinced the latter's fellow-citizens of his merits by paying well over the odds for his work.

8. (p. 73) Francesco Petrarch (1304–74) and Giovanni Boccaccio (1313–75) provided the two great Tuscan models, in verse and prose respectively, for writers in the vernacular determined to apply strictly the humanist canon of imitation.

9. (p. 76) Evander was the mythical son of Hermes (by a nymph) supposed to have founded a town on the Tiber, before the Trojan War, subsequently incorporated into Rome.

Turnus was the legendary king of an Italian tribe at the time of the arrival in Italy of Aeneas, by whom he was slain.

The Salii were Roman priests of patrician rank, responsible for guarding the holy shields, fallen from Heaven. Their hymns in praise of the gods were supposed to have become unintelligible.

Marcus Antonius (143–87 B.C.) and Licinius Crassus (140–91 B.C.) were the most notable orators of early Rome and were the chief speakers in Cicero's dialogue, *De Oratore*.

Quintus Hortensius Hortalus (114–50 B.C.) florid in speech and fastidious in dress, was the most respected Roman orator until outshone by Cicero himself.

Marcus Porcius Cato (234–149 B.C.) was an author, soldier and moral reformer, responsible for the demand: *Delenda est Carthago.*

Quintus Ennius (239–169 B.C.) was a Roman subject of Greek birth, a teacher and epic poet.

T. Maccius Plautus (*c.* 254–184 B.C.) was Rome's greatest comic dramatist.

Sergius Sulpicius Galba earned qualified praise from Cicero for his oratory; was consul in 144 B.C.

10. (p. 81) Hesiod was one of the earliest Greek poets after Homer, flourishing about the eighth century B.C.

11. (p. 82) Bidon was a greatly admired chorister in the service of Pope Leo X.

Marchetto Cara was another singer, and composer, who served the Gonzaga rulers of Mantua and also visited the Court at Urbino.

12. (p. 82) Isocrates (436–338 B.C.) was an Attic orator, very successful financially, chiefly as a teacher.

Lysias (458–378 B.C.) was another, noted for the elegance of the speeches he wrote for others.

Aeschines (389–314 B.C.) flourished as a public speaker (after failing as an actor) in rivalry with Demosthenes.

Caius Papirius Carbo was a Roman consul in 120 B.C., a distinguished orator whose murky political career ended in suicide.

Caius Laelius Sapiens was consul in 140 B.C.; his intimate friendship with Scipio Africanus the younger was immortalized in Cicero's treatise *De Amicitia* (*On Friendship*).

Scipio Africanus the younger (*c.* 185–129 B.C.) inherited the name Africanus by adoption from Hannibal's conqueror, Scipio Africanus Major, and lived up to it by capturing Carthage in the 3rd Punic War.

Publius Suplius Sulpicius Rufus (124–88 B.C.) was a distinguished orator who met a violent death during the civil war between Marius and Sulla.

Caius Aurelius Cotta, consul in 75 B.C., was introduced as one of the speakers in Cicero's *De Oratore.*

Caius Sempronius Gracchus was a popular reformer, twice elected tribune of the plebs (123 and 122 B.C.), intrigued against by the Roman senate and killed, at his own request, by his slave.

13. (p. 83) Politian (1454–94) (Angelo Poliziano) was a classical scholar, tutor to the sons of Lorenzo de' Medici, and a charming and important poet.

Lorenzo de' Medici (1448–92) was effective ruler of Florence, scholar, patron and poet, and the father of the Giuliano de' Medici who takes part in the conversations of *The Courtier*.

Francesco Diacceto (1466–1522) was a writer and philosopher, influenced by the ideas of Ficino, whose own influence is discernible in the neo-Platonic passages on love in the Fourth Book of *The Courtier*.

14. (p. 85) Demosthenes' rejoinder to Aeschines is reported in Cicero's *Orator* viii, 26–7: Demosthenes said the fortunes of Greece didn't depend on his using this word or that, or extending his hand in this direction or that.

15. (p. 87) The 39th Ode of Catullus (*c.* 87–47 B.C.), *In Egnatium*, begins 'Egnatius, because he has white teeth, smiles wherever he goes. . . .' And nothing, Catullus adds, is more pointless than a pointless laugh.

16. (p. 88) Monseigneur d'Angoulême (1494–1547), son of the Valois Charles d'Angoulême, succeeded to the French throne as Francis I in 1515.

17. (p. 89) These references are drawn from Plutarch's *Lives*, Cicero's *Tusculan Disputations* and the *Life of Hannibal* by Cornelius Nepos.

Lucius Licinius Lucullus and Lucius Cornelius Sulla were Roman generals (consuls in 74 B.C. and 78 B.C. respectively).

18. (p. 91) Aristippus flourished about 370 B.C. and founded the Cyrenaic school of philosophy which took its name from his birthplace Cyrene in Africa. Diogenes Laertius in his *Lives of the Philosophers* says that when Aristippus was asked what he had chiefly learned from philosophy he replied: 'The ability to meet all men with confidence.'

19. (p. 94) Grasso (Fatty) was the nickname of a courtier and soldier in the service of the Medici, well-known in Florence and in Court circles in Rome and Urbino.

20. (p. 95) Lycurgus (probably ninth century B.C.) was the great legislator of Sparta reputed to have been responsible for all its laws and constitution.

Epaminondas (fourth century B.C.) was the famous Theban general who destroyed Spartan supremacy by his victory at Leuctra in 371 B.C.

Themistocles (*c.* 514–449 B.C.) was one of the greatest of Athenian generals and statesmen, responsible for the defeat of the Persians at Salamis in 480 B.C.

Achilles, of course, was the hero of the *Iliad* who was educated by Chiron the Centaur, half-man and half-horse.

21. (p. 100) The anecdote about Protogenes and Metrodorus comes from Pliny's *Natural History.*

Demetrius I of Macedon was the son of Antigonus, King of Asia, one of the generals of Alexander the Great. He besieged Rhodes with gigantic machines in 305 B.C., when he won the name of Poliorcetes or Besieger.

Metrodorus is recorded in Pliny as a painter and philosopher.

Lucius Aemilius Paulus was a Roman consul (181 and 168 B.C.) and general.

22. (p. 102) Zeuxis flourished as a painter in 424–380 B.C. and was noted for his naturalistic effects. His most famous picture, referred to here, was of Helen of Troy.

23. (p. 104) In their volume of the Pelican *History of Music* (Volume 2: *Renaissance and Baroque*, Penguin Books 1963) Alec Robertson and Denis Stevens remark:

'The fifteenth century was the great age of the dance. The *basse dance* reached the French and Burgundian courts from Spain some time before 1445. It was second in favour only to the morris, which had the added attraction of fancy dress. Dances proved an agreeable ending to a festal evening, but they were also a symbolic act in the ritual of courtly love. . . .' After noting that in Italy the *bassadanza* was 'a particular balletic creation of an individual master, a spatial exercise in the true Renaissance manner', Robertson and Stevens add: 'All sorts of characteristic and national dances became the rage towards the end of the fifteenth century; the *tedesca*, the *branle*, the *schiavo*, round dances, the *zingaresca*, Spanish, Polish, Turkish and Neopolitan dances, and latterly the *pavane* are amongst those recorded. . . .'

SECOND BOOK

1. (p. 108) What Themistocles said is recorded in Cicero's *De Oratore* lxxiv, II. A learned man came to him and offered to teach him the art of good memory; when Themistocles asked what use it was, he was told it would enable him to remember everything. Themistocles answered that it would be better if he were taught how to forget what he wanted to.

2. (p. 109) Duke Filippo Maria Visconti (1391–1447) was the last Visconti ruler of Milan, a despot with modest literary interests, fearfully suspicious and superstitious.

Duke Borso d'Este (1413–71), ruler of Ferrara, was a patron of the arts and literature greatly admired by contemporary humanists.

Niccolò Piccinino (1380–1444) was a *condottiere*, with a reputation for wit, who served Duke Federico of Urbino.

3. (p. 118) The *brando* was a dance of Spanish origin. In a sixteenth-century description quoted by Cian 'all the men dance with all the ladies, leave their partners and kiss the lady they join, dance away and then kiss their partners when they join them again.'

4. (p. 121) Minerva (the Roman name for Athena) is said to have thrown the flute away when she saw in a spring the effect it had on her face. Alcibiades 'refused to learn the flute, which he regarded as an ignoble accomplishment and quite unsuitable for a free citizen. He argued that . . . once a man starts blowing into a flute, his own friends can scarcely recognize his features.' (Plutarch's *Rise and Fall of Athens: Nine Greek Lives*, translated by Ian Scott-Kilvert, Penguin Classics.)

5. (p. 128) A quotation from *Luke* xiv, 8–10.

6. (p. 132) Titus Manlius Torquatus was a Roman consul (in 347, 344 and 340 B.C.) whose son disobeyed a command not to engage in single combat with the enemy and was, in consequence, executed before the troops on his father's orders. The story is referred to in Plutarch's *Lives*.

7. (p. 133) Publius Licinius Crassus Mucianus was Roman consul in 131 B.C., when he fought in Asia Minor against Aristonicus of Pergamus. The story comes from the *Epitomes* of Livy's History.

8. (p. 137) In Greek legend, Orestes (the son of Agamemnon and Clytaemnestra) after the murder of his father fled to Phocis, where he formed a close friendship with Pylades, the son of King Strophius. The reference may have been suggested to Castiglione by a passage in Plutarch's *On having Many Friends*.

Theseus, the legendary hero of Attica, struck up his great friendship with Pirithous (King of the Lapiths in Thessaly) after the latter had stolen his cattle. Subsequently, they fought the centaurs together.

9. (p. 145) Jacopo Sannazaro (*c.* 1455–1530) was a Neapolitan poet (much admired by Castiglione) who wrote both in Latin and Tuscan and is best known for his *Arcadia*.

Josquin des Près (*c.* 1450–1521) was one of the great composers of the early Renaissance who served a number of rulers including Lorenzo de' Medici, and whose music today 'does not seem strange or remote, but makes essentially the same appeal as Byrd, Bach, or even . . . Wagner.' (Pelican *History of Music: Renaissance and Baroque* p. 15.)

10. (p. 148) Nicoletto was the fifteenth-century philosopher Paolo Nicola Vernia, who studied and then taught at Padua, whose bishop very forcefully persuaded him to change his ideas from Averroism to Thomism.

11. (p. 149) This painter is undoubtedly Leonardo da Vinci. In his *Life* of Leonardo, Giorgio Vasari remarks that on his death-bed Leonardo said he had offended God and mankind by not working at his art as he should have.

12. (p. 154) Cardinal Galeotto della Rovere was the favourite nephew of Pope Julius II, a generous patron of the arts and very popular.

13. (p. 155) Democritus (*c.* 460–361 B.C.) was a Greek philosopher, noted for his cheerful frame of mind, his wealth and his formulation of the 'atomic theory'.

The reference here is from Cicero's *De Oratore.*

14. (p. 163) The *Bucentaur* or *Bucintoro* was the name of the galley used for important ceremonies in the Republic of Venice including the wedding of the sea mentioned here. The last *Bucintoro* was demolished in 1824. The name survives in a Venetian rowing club.

15. (p. 168) Girolamo Donato (1457–1511) was a Venetian diplomat and scholar.

16. (p. 171) Sadoleto (1477–1547), a philosopher and Latinist and secretary to Pope Leo X, who was made a cardinal by Pope Paul III.

17. (p. 172) Camillo Porcaro or Porzio was a Roman aristocrat and scholar, created Bishop of Teramo by Pope Leo X, brother of the Antonio mentioned on page 170.

Marc'Antonio Colonna fled from the Borgias in 1502 and spent the rest of his life fighting in the Italian wars.

18. (p. 173) The Great Captain (already mentioned) was Gonzalo de Cordoba (1443–1515), a commander of great adaptive genius who played a part in the conquest of Granada, from 1494 fought successfully in Italy against the French, and was made Constable and Viceroy of Naples. Subsequently he fell into disfavour with King Ferdinand and was recalled to Spain.

19. (p. 174) Giovanni Gonzaga (1474–1523) was a soldier and diplomat, the third son of the Marquess Federico of Mantua (1442–84) and uncle of Marquess Federico Gonzaga whose service Castiglione entered in 1516.

20. (p. 177) Niccolò Leonico Tomeo (1452–1531) was born in Venice of an Albanian father, taught and wrote about (Aristotelean) philosophy at Padua, was a poet, an art collector and a wit.

21. (p. 179) In 1502 Cesare Borgia carried out a campaign on behalf of Pope Alexander VI for the conquest of Camerino and Urbino. Duke Guidobaldo retired from Urbino to the fortress of San Leo, about eighteen miles distant, and then fled first to Mantua and subsequently to Venice.

22. (p. 181) Alonso Carrillo has been identified as the nephew of an Archbishop of Toledo.

Signora Bobadilla was probably Beatriz de Bobadilla, Marchioness of Moya, a close friend of Queen Isabella of Spain.

23. (p. 183) Rafaello de' Pazzi (1471–1512) was a Florentine exile who fought for Cesare Borgia and Pope Julius II, and died fighting against the French in the battle of Ravenna.

The Prior of Messina has been identified as a Spanish soldier, don Pietro de Cuna, who was also killed at Ravenna.

Paolo Tolosa was a contractor for supplies to the Imperial armies.

24. (p. 183) The advice given by Giannotto de' Pazzi (possibly a Florentine, Giovanni de' Pazzi who lived 1476–1523) was, literally; 'Take the words and deeds of the Cardinal of Pavia.' The cardinal (also referred to earlier) was Francesco Alidosi, a descendant of the rulers of Imola, who was patronized by Pope Julius II. He was made a cardinal in 1505 and Archbishop of Bologna in 1510. A violent and persecuting prelate, he was driven out of Bologna in 1511 and murdered by Francesco Maria della Rovere, Duke Guidobaldo's nephew and successor, in the same year.

25. (p. 184) Peralta, Aldana and Molart are identified by Cian as three captains (the first and third Spanish, the second French) who fought with foreign armies in Italy.

Molart taunted Peralta for being a *marrano*, a fairly common term of abuse at the time, and referring originally to Spanish Jews or Moors forcibly converted but remaining at heart unbelievers.

26. (p. 185) 'My monsignor' being Cardinal Giovanni de' Medici, the future Pope Leo X, to whom Bibbiena was secretary.

THIRD BOOK

1. (p. 207) The anecdote is taken from the *Noctes Atticae* – extracts from Greek and Latin writers – of the Latin grammarian Aulus Gellius.

2. (p. 218) The subtleties discussed by Giuliano de' Medici were based on scholastic philosophy, whose terminology is used fairly loosely in various parts of *The Courtier*. In this passage the key words are 'essence' – or that which answers the question, what a thing is – and 'accidents' – which modify what a thing is. The usual distinction is between 'substance' and 'accidents'.

3. (p. 220) The 'great philosopher' is Aristotle.

4. (p. 224) St Jerome, one of the early Fathers of the Christian Church, in his *De viris illustribus*.

5. (p. 226) Octavia was abandoned by Mark Antony for Cleopatra.

Portia, who killed herself after the death of Brutus, the assassin of Julius Caesar, is said to have wounded herself after learning of the assassination plot in order to demonstrate her courage and ability to keep a secret.

Caia Caecilia Tanaquil appears in Roman legend as the wife of one of the early kings of Rome, whose rise to power she assisted through her virtues, ambition and powers of divination.

Cornelia was the daughter of P. Scipio Africanus the elder, the devoted mother of the two Roman tribunes, Tiberius and Caius Gracchus, and reputedly a distinguished literary stylist.

6. (p. 226) Alexandra was the wife of Alexander Jannaeus, King of the Jews in 104–78 B.C.

7. (p. 227) In the *Life* of Lucullus, Plutarch describes how after his defeat by the Romans, Mithridates VI, King of Pontus, gave orders for his wives and sisters to be put to death, to save them from outrage.

Hasdrubal was the Carthaginian general who, during the third Punic War after the siege and capture of Carthage by the Romans, in 146 B.C., threw himself on the mercy of the victors, whereas his prouder wife threw herself into the flames of a burning temple.

8. (p. 227) In the *Annals* Tacitus describes how Epicharis, involved in a plot against Nero (in A.D. 65) throttled herself with her breast-band when on the way to be tortured a second time.

9. (p. 227) Leona or Leaena was an Athenian *hetaera* mentioned in Pausanias' *Itinerary of Greece*, involved in the assassination of the brother of the Greek tyrant Hippias in 514 B.C. and tortured to death. She bit her tongue out, rather than betray the assassins.

10. (p. 229) The story of Camma is derived from Plutarch's *De Mulierum Virtutibus* (*On The Virtues of Women*).

11. (p. 233) Pallas Athene was one of the chief divinities of ancient Greece, the daughter of Zeus and Metis.

Ceres or Demeter was the sister of Zeus, and the daughter of Cronos and Rhea.

The sibyls were the prophetical women of the classical world.

Aspasia, one of the most famous of the Greek *hetaerae*, became the mistress of Pericles.

Diotima was the fictitious woman of Mantinea introduced by Socrates in the *Symposium*.

Nicostrata or Carmenta (mentioned in Plutarch and Livy) was the mother of Evander, legendary founder of Pallantium on the Tiber which later became part of Rome.

Pindar, the greatest lyric poet of ancient Greece, is supposed to have been taught by Myrtis, of Anthedon in Boeotia.

Corinna was another poetess, also from Boeotia, and a contemporary of Pindar, flourishing *c.* 500 B.C.

Sappho lived about 600 B.C., was enthusiastically admired for her lyric poetry, fragments of which survive, and established a women's literary society at Mytilene.

12. (p. 234) The story of how the Trojans settled in Italy is derived from Plutarch's *On the Virtues of Women*; that of the Sabine women from Livy's *History of Rome*.

13. (p. 235) The young girl who betrayed the Romans to Tatius, King of the Sabines, is said by Livy to have been crushed to death by their shields (*History of Rome*, Book I).

14. (p. 235) A temple was built to Venus Armata (the Armed Venus) by the Spartans (according to the fourth-century Christian writer, Lactanius); the Romans built two temples to Venus Calva (the Bald Venus) one explanation of the name being that it was to commemorate the occasion when Roman women cut off their hair to make bow-strings during a siege by the Gauls. The story of how the slave-girls saved Rome from the Latins (by taking the place of free-born girls demanded as hostages and then disarming their hosts) is told in Plutarch's *Life of Camillus*.

Catiline's conspiracy took place during the consulship of Cicero in 63 B.C. The woman who is supposed to have informed Cicero was called Fulvia.

15. (p. 235) Philip reigned over Macedonia from 220–198 B.C., and twice warred against the Romans. The story is again derived from Plutarch's *On the Virtues of Women*, as is the account of the bravery of the Persian women.

16. (p. 237) Amalasontha was the daughter of Theodoric the Great, King of the Ostrogoths, who ruled Italy for about thirty years till his death in 526. She is said to have been strangled by her second husband on the instigation of Theodora, wife of Justinian the Great, who was jealous of her intellectual accomplishments.

Theodolinda, the daughter of Duke Garibald of Bavaria, was married first to Autharis, King of the Lombards, then to Duke Agilulph, Duke of Turin; she was famous for her piety and learning, and corresponded with Pope Gregory I.

The Theodora referred to is probably the wife of Theopilus, Emperor of Constantinople from 829–42, who was canonized by the Greek Church.

Countess Matilda (1046–1115) was the daughter of Duke Boniface of Tuscany and Beatrice of Lorraine, renowned for her culture, religious zeal and austere life.

17. (p. 238) Anne of Brittany (1476–1514) was the daughter of Duke Francis II of Brittany, which was joined to France through her marriages to Charles VIII and Louis XII.

Margaret of Austria (1480–1530) after being rejected by Charles VIII (while Dauphin) in favour of Anne, married first Juan of Castile and then Duke Filiberto of Savoy. After she was widowed again, in 1507 her father entrusted her with the government of the Low Countries and the education of her nephew, the future Emperor Charles V.

Isabella the Catholic (1451–1504) married Ferdinand (1452–1516) in 1469. This accomplished the union of the Crowns of Aragon and Castile, a major step towards the unification of Spain under the Emperor Charles V. The Arab kingdom of Granada was conquered in 1492.

18. (p. 240) The two 'remarkable queens' were probably Joanna III of Aragon, the widow of Ferdinand (Ferrante) of Naples, and her daughter, Joanna IV, the widow of Ferdinand II of Naples (Ferrantino).

Matthias Corvinus (1443–90) was proclaimed King of Hungary in 1458 and married Beatrix of Aragon (who failed to give him the heir he needed) in 1476. She returned to Naples in 1501, and died shortly after the conversations recalled in *The Courtier* took place.

The Duchess Isabella of Aragon (1470–1524) was the daughter of Alfonso II of Naples. In 1489 she had married Gian Galeazzo Sforza, to find that he was increasingly deprived of authority by the regent, Lodovico il Moro. Gian Galeazzo died in 1494, and the following year, her family were driven from Naples by the French.

Isabella d'Este (1474–1539) was the daughter of Duke Ercole I of Ferrara. Her sister Beatrice married Lodovico Sforza; she married Francesco Gonzaga, who succeeded as ruler of Mantua in 1484. She was, therefore, a friend of Castiglione's who corresponded with her and gave her a presentation copy of *The Courtier* in 1528.

Eleanora of Aragon (1450–93) was the daughter of Ferrante I of Naples and the elder sister of Beatrix, mentioned above. In 1473 she married Duke Ercole I of Ferrara; her two daughters, as we are told, were Isabella d'Este and Beatrice.

Isabella of Naples was a daughter of the Prince of Altamura, and the wife of Federico, who became King of Naples in 1496 and at whose expense King Louis XII of France and Ferdinand of Spain made their treaty for the partition of Naples in 1500.

19. (p. 240) In 1499, the Florentines sent an army under the mercenary captain, Paolo Vitelli, to attack Pisa, during the siege of which

the women acted with conspicuous bravery – according to Francesco Guicciardini (the diplomat and historian who was a near contemporary of Castiglione), helping throw up new fortifications and urging their men to die rather than submit.

20. (p. 241) Sardanapalus was one of the great kings of Assyria, who reigned for about forty years from 668 B.C., conquered (and lost) Egypt, and was a notable patron of Assyrian literature. He had a perhaps undeserved reputation for voluptuousness.

21. (p. 243) Alexander the Great finally defeated Darius, the last King of Persia, in 331 B.C. His restraint towards the king's women was highly commended by Plutarch.

The tact shown by Scipio Africanus Major when commanding the Roman armies in Spain in 210 B.C. (at the age of twenty-four) is described by Valerius Maximus (an assiduous compiler of anecdotes who lived during the reign of Tiberius) in his *De Factis Dictisque Memorabilibus* (*Memorable Sayings and Deeds*).

Valerius Maximus also supplied the material for the story of the notable self-control of Xenocrates, philosopher, friend of Plato and Socrates, who lived 396–314 B.C.

The account of just rebuke given by Pericles (the great fifth-century Athenian statesman and general) comes from Cicero's *De Officiis* XI, where he says to the poet Sophocles: 'Hush, Sophocles, a general should keep not only his hands but his eyes under control.' (Loeb translation.)

22. (p. 256) Laura, whom Petrarch first saw in 1327 was very probably Laura de Noves, wife of Hugues de Sade. Petrarch's love for her provided the constant theme for his lyric poetry, collected together to form the great *Canzoniere*.

23. (p. 257) Solomon's 'amorous dialogue' was, of course, the *Song of Songs* (or *Canticle of Canticles*).

24. (p. 258) Isola Ferma is referred to in the Spanish romance *Amadis of Gaul* as containing a garden at whose entrance is an arch supporting the statue of a man holding a trumpet which is blown sweetly at the approach of true lovers but with a dreadful sound to repel the false.

25. (p. 268) The idea of the vital spirits – *spiriti vitali* or *vivi spiriti* – was inherited by the Renaissance as a medical concept from the Middle Ages to be blended with the neo-Platonism in vogue in art and philosophical theory from the end of the fifteenth century. The concept expounded by Castiglione is to be found in similar form in the writings of neo-Platonists such as Marsilio Ficino (1433–99), in the *Candelaio* of Giordano Bruno (1548–1600) and in the poetry of Petrarch, Michelangelo and Donne.

26. (p. 271) Francesco Colonna's *Hypnerotomachia Poliphili* was a curious romance story (first published in 1499) whose vocabulary was a bizarre mixture of Italian and neologisms derived from Latin stems. In an Elizabethan translation the effect is conveyed by the adjectives 'flamigerous' for maids, 'remigiall' for bones, 'cavernate' for eyes and 'wrympled' for foreheads. (Quoted by E. H. Wilkins in *A History of Italian Literature*, Harvard 1954.)

27. (p. 273) Namely, Ovid's *Ars Amatoria*.

FOURTH BOOK

1. (p. 282) Eleanora Gonzaga (*c.* 1492–1543), the eldest daughter of Francesco Gonzaga and Isabella d'Este, married Francesco Maria della Rovere, nephew of Pope Julius II, in 1509.

2. (p. 286) Piazza d'Agone (today's Piazza Navona) on the site of the Circus Agonalis, the ancient stadium of Domitian. Before and after Castiglione's time it was used for jousts and open-air sports.

3. (p. 287) Cimon (died 449 B.C.) was the great Athenian commander who won several notable victories against the Persians. Plutarch recorded that he 'earned a bad name for disorderly behaviour, heavy drinking, and in general for taking after his grandfather . . .'. (*The Rise and Fall of Athens*, Penguin Classics.)

4. (p. 287) These examples are based on comments by Cicero and Plutarch. Lysias was a sixth-century philosopher and follower of Pythagoras, who fled from Italy to Thebes when the Pythagoreans were persecuted.

Agesilaus was King of Sparta from 398 to 361 B.C., an outstanding commander and a friend of the historian Xenophon (born *c.* 444 B.C.) who fought with him against the Persians and the Athenians and who wrote his life.

Panaetius was a Stoic philospher from Rhodes who settled in Rome where he became friendly with Scipio Africanus the younger. It was Panaetius whom Cicero was following in *De Officiis*.

5. (p. 289) The story of Epimetheus is taken from Plato's *Protagoras*. Epimetheus (afterthought) and Prometheus (forethought) were sons of the Titan Iapetus and Clymene, daughter of the god Oceanus.

6. (p. 300) Bias, who lived *c.* 550 B.C., was one of the Seven Sages of Greece, quoted quite often by Plutarch in the *Moralia*.

7. (p. 301) Clearchus was tyrant of Heraclea (now Eregli) on the Black Sea in the fourth century B.C. The story of how he and Aristodemus (any one of several possible ancient tyrants) slept was told by Plutarch in the *Moralia*.

8. (p. 306) In Book Five of *The Republic* it is suggested that men and women Guardians 'should be forbidden by law to live together in separate households, and that wives should be held in common by all; similarly, children should be held in common, and no parent should know his child . . .'. (H. D. P. Lee's translation, Penguin Classics 1955.)

9. (p. 307) In Xenophon's *Cyropaedia* – the story of Cyrus, founder of the Persian monarchy – these sentiments are expressed by Cyrus.

10. (p. 310) Cian notes that although this praise for Federico Gonzaga may have been excessive, together with Isabella d'Este he ensured that at the end of the fifteenth and beginning of the sixteenth century the Mantuan Court was a great centre of artistic and cultural life.

11. (p. 311) These enterprises of Alexander the Great echo the words of Plutarch, who says that Bucephalia was named after Alexander's favourite horse and that though he liked the idea of a city on Mount Athos he rejected it on learning that it would have to depend on imports.

12. (p. 311) Procrustes (or the 'stretcher') was the notorious robber of Greek legend who used to tie his victims to a bed and either stretch or lop them to fit. He was killed by Theseus, anxiously emulating the heroic deeds of Hercules.

Sciron was another great robber, who liked to make travellers wash his feet on the Scironian rock, and to kick them into the sea while they were doing so. He, too, was killed by Theseus.

Cacus was the giant son of Vulcan who stole Hercules' cattle, cunningly dragging them into his cave by their tails to confuse their tracks. However, he was betrayed by their bellowing and killed by Hercules.

Diomedes, son of Ares, or Mars, was also slain by Hercules because of his habit of feeding his horses on human flesh.

Antaeus was the giant who remained invincible so long as he kept in contact with his own mother, earth. Hercules, therefore, held him up in the air and crushed him to death there.

Geryon was a triple monster of Hesperia (Spain) whose cattle were stolen by Hercules as one of the twelve labours imposed on him by Eurystheus.

13. (p. 312) This anecdote about Themistocles is told by Plutarch in several versions. In the *Lives* he is made to remark to his children when a magnificent banquet was set before him: "My children, we should have been ruined now, if we had not been ruined just when we were!" (*The Rise and Fall of Athens*, Penguin Classics.)

14. (p. 312) This 'lord Henry' was the future Henry VIII. The reference to Castiglione's being in England maintains the fiction that he had not yet returned from his mission to accept the investiture of the Order of the Garter for Guidobaldo, and to bring suitable gifts to Henry VII. Castiglione, knighted by Guidobaldo before he left, landed in Dover in October 1506, was received, as 'Sir Balthasar Castileon' by Sir Thomas Brandon, and lodged in London with Paulus de Cygeles, the Pope's Vice-Collector. At Windsor on 9 November as 'proxie' he went through the ceremony of installation, and on his return to London was presented to the Prince of Wales. At the end of February he was back in Urbino.

15. (p. 313) Don Carlos (1500–58) was the future Emperor Charles V, ruler of Spain, the Netherlands, Naples, Sicily and Austria.

16. (p. 316) Federico Gonzaga (1500–40), first Duke of Mantua, succeeded his father, Francesco, in 1519. In his *Autobiography*, Benvenuto Cellini records making for him, on the recommendation of the painter Giulio Romano, a 'reliquary for the blood of Christ'.

17. (p. 320) This is a paraphrase of an ugly sentence which makes use of the Aristotelean distinction between Potentiality and Actuality and reads literally: '... and to both the one and the other it suffices to have this intrinsic end in potency, even when the failure to realize it extrinsically in act arises from the subject to which the end is directed'.

18. (p. 320) Phoenix was the son of Amyntor. In Book IX of the *Iliad* he describes how he ran away from home and was adopted by Peleus, King of Phthia, who put him in charge of Achilles' upbringing, even to cutting up his meat.

19. (p. 321) Aristotle was invited by Philip of Macedonia to educate his son, Alexander, in 342 B.C.

Plato, during his journeyings after the death of Socrates (399 B.C.), is supposed to have known Dionysius, the tyrant of Syracuse, but to have earned his displeasure and been sold by him into slavery. After he had set up school in Athens he was invited back by Dion (a relation of Dionysius) to help make a better man of the tyrant's son, Dionysius the younger.

20. (p. 321) Callisthenes, who was one of Aristotle's pupils, accompanied Alexander the Great to Asia but fell into disfavour for being too outspoken.

21. (p. 324) In Bembo's prose work, the *Asolani* (published 1505) in the third book Lavinello is instructed by a hermit about the nature of Platonic love.

22. (p. 325) The word 'intellect' in English fails to convey the significance of *intelletto* for Renaissance thinkers and poets. Possibly

'intuition' comes nearer, in the Latin sense of 'intellect' as a perception or perceiving, and also reflecting the scholastic concept of angelic intelligence as a kind of understanding gained from data given directly by God, i.e. not through the senses.

In *De Officiis*, Cicero distinguishes between the two essential activities or forces of the soul: appetite, which 'impels a man this way or that' and reason 'which teaches and explains what should be done and what should be left undone'. But the content of this magnificent concluding speech of Bembo's is essentially a blend of Christian and Platonic concepts and imagery, derived from Plato and from the works of Renaissance neo-Platonists such as Ficino and Bembo himself.

23. (p. 330) Stesichorus of Sicily was a Greek poet of the seventh century B.C. who was supposed to have been struck blind after composing an attack on Helen of Troy.

24. (p. 336) The person whom Bembo calls, literally, the 'divinely enamoured Plato' may or may not have been the great philosopher.

25. (p. 337) At the beginning of the *Song of Songs*: 'Let him kiss me with the kiss of his mouth: for thy breasts are better than wine,/ Smelling sweet of the best ointments.' (Douai version.)

26. (p. 343) Plotinus (*c.* A.D. 203–62) was the founder of the Neo-Platonic system, to whose mystical and theological doctrine, rather than to Plato himself, the humanists turned in reaction against the scepticism and aridity of late medieval philosophers.

27. (p. 344) St Francis of Assisi (1181–1226) was the first great saint to receive the *stigmata* (in 1224), the miraculous wounds of Christ on hands, feet and side.

28. (p. 344) The references are to 2 Corinthians xii, 2–4: '... that he was caught up into paradise and heard secret words which it is not granted to man to utter'; and to the Acts of the Apostles vii, 55: '... And he said: Behold, I see the heavens opened and the Son of man standing on the right hand of God.' (Douai.)

29. (p. 344) Diotima, as already noted, was the fictitious woman of Mantinea introduced by Socrates in the *Symposium* to describe the ascent of the soul from the world of the senses to the eternal world: 'from one instance of physical beauty to two and from two to all, then from physical beauty to the beauty of knowledge, until from knowledge of various kinds one arrives at the supreme knowledge whose sole object is that absolute beauty. ...' (Plato: *The Symposium*, translated by W. Hamilton, Penguin Classics.)

30. (p. 344) A pious tradition about St Mary Magdalene ('Many sins are forgiven her, because she has loved much' – Luke vii, 47) is that she was uplifted by angels during prayer.

INDEX

Note. The names of the people taking part in the conversations, occurring continually throughout the text, have not been included in this index and the reader is referred to the biographical notes on pages 23–9. *Italic* entries refer to the numbered notes in the text.